MW00462699

THE FAREWELL DISCOURSES

ADRIENNE VON SPEYR

THE FAREWELL DISCOURSES

Meditations on John 13–17

TRANSLATED BY E. A. NELSON

IGNATIUS PRESS   SAN FRANCISCO

Title of the German original:
Die Abschiedsreden
Betrachtungen über Johannes 13–17
©1948 Johannes Verlag, Einsiedeln

Cover by Victoria Hoke Lane

ISBN 0-89870-111-2
Library of Congress Catalogue Number 86-80790
Printed in the United States of America

CONTENTS

FOREWORD

The truth of revelation can be expressed in many ways. There is the more abstract, conceptual language of scientific theology, which has created a certain web of concepts for the mysteries of Trinity, Incarnation, grace, Church and sacraments—concepts that aim above all at the clarity and correctness of human thought and have therefore become the indispensable basis for all study of Holy Scripture and Tradition, for all proclamation and preaching. But this does not mean that this scientific language of the theologians is necessarily the most fruitful one for prayerful contemplation of the divine mysteries. The abstractions, for example, that theologians differentiate in the mystery of the Trinity—being, Person, relation, property, opposition, appropriation, notion, mission, circumincession—all this, both with regard to the laity and in itself, may not be the most direct way to make clear to the Christian the life of love between the Father and the Son in the Holy Spirit. These concepts are by all means correctly formed, and also indispensable in guarding against false interpretations, and yet they are not the direct language of Christ when he speaks of the Father and the Holy Spirit. For the simple, prayerful contemplation of the Christian who is untrained in theology, a simpler mode of expression that stays nearer the language of Christ is to be recommended. True, this language can be in danger of speaking often all too naively and all too humanly about divine things, but if it is led and informed by the proper Christian love and the mind of the Church, it can afford a glimpse into the mysteries of God to many who would otherwise have been deprived of it.

Perhaps this book of meditation on the Farewell Discourses could also be accused here and there of a mode of expression concerning God and the relations between the Divine Persons that comes all too close to human modes of imagining. But let us not forget that all the words of the Lord, indeed all of Holy Scripture, speak to us humans "anthropomorphically", that is, "in human form". If we were to separate God from all imaginings and words related to creaturely limitation, with its living development and growth, transformation and decay, we would be left with a rigid, dead image of God. In the end we could say almost nothing about God except what he is not. But that is not the meaning or the tone of the new revelation from the Father. The Son wants only to afford us a concept of what the Father is—what he is for him, the Son, and what he is for us. He wants to bring the Father humanly closer to us, even at the risk of our making ourselves a human image of God. Christ's love for the Father, which he gives to us in grace, will be powerful enough—especially if we devote and consecrate ourselves to this love with all our heart and soul—to carry us again and again over and beyond our limited imaginings into the openness and infinity of the ever-greater God. Any comparisons or images that lead us closer to God, that give us a more living, more correct, warmer idea of infinite love, have fulfilled their purpose. In this sense the meditations in this book should be read and understood: as an exercise in understanding God's love.

— *Hans Urs von Balthasar*

INTRODUCTION

The Lord has come to the end of his earthly work: he has preached, worked miracles, instituted sacraments and sketched the outlines of the Church. His life's work appears to lack only the crown: the Passion, through which he will breathe soul into the images he has formed: redemption from sin, the Holy Spirit, interior understanding of all the divine mysteries and the divine power of growth. But between his nearly completed earthly life and work and his future work within the Church and souls, he sees a chasm so great that it threatens to rend his work of redemption in two. His visible work seems to him all too earthly, too much bound to human concepts and imaginings to be able to offer enough starting points to those who are later to receive the divine Spirit, so that they can understand the inner mysteries of God. And his future work in the grace of the sacraments seems to him so hidden, so supernatural, that he is afraid of being too remote from mankind's daily life to make himself understood by them. The chasm that separates the two parts of his mission is in the Passion: the ever-deepening separation from the Father, up to complete forsakenness on the Cross. The further the Lord penetrates into the world of the approaching Passion, and the more the darkness of the coming separation engulfs him, the more unavoidable, immense and final does the night that receives him appear to him. Viewed from this night, his human nature also begins to see his past work in its limitations: how little he has achieved! How weak is the understanding of the Father's world that he has been able to awaken in a few souls! How meager was the harvest of his life, how ineffectual in comparison to what he had intended before his incarnation: to bring the whole world redeemed back to the Father! How little he can entrust to these few men he will leave alone in a few hours to endure the night of the Cross, in the confusion of their stranded understanding, in the collapse of their plans and dreams, in the bankruptcy of their life's hopes! He himself wants to taste, in his humanity, this anxiety about his work; he wants to measure this work with his own human powers and not make the task lighter by using his divinity, the whole sweep of his omniscience or the power of his omnipotence. He wants to feel the whole burden of redemption and of the Church on his human shoulders. And out of this sentiment he wants to fill to the brim the last moments that remain to him in the circle of those who are his own. He wants to do everything humanly possible to round off his work, yes, and more: he wants to attempt to shape this conclusion in such a way that at the same time it will form a bridge over the chasm of separation of the Passion. He wants to demonstrate clearly and indisputably—not to himself but to the Father and the disciples—the unity between his visible and invisible works. In this his last hour, he wants to let his whole earthly work, which even before was concerned with nothing other than the heavenly Kingdom and the Father, open up in a last explosion into the dimensions of the beyond; to surpass his own human words and deeds once more in such a way that the divine becomes as though immediately transparent in them. On the other hand, he wants to clarify, as if in anticipation, the future invisible reality of his remaining and working in the Church, in these words and deeds of transition—actions that are of such divine evidence that all future divine life in the Church will simply appear to be a development of them.

Thus he fills his farewell hour with something twofold, with a concluding deed and a concluding word; both are the crowning of his earthly work and the anticipation of his future, hidden existence. Both, in transition, already breathe the Spirit of the transfigured Lord in the Eucharist. The deed itself is, again, a double one—foot-washing and meal—whereby the foot-washing is related to the meal as confession is to Eucharist, on the one hand, and as the visible symbol is to the invisible, true content, on the other. And both are possible only through anticipation of the Passion, of whose course and fruits the Lord disposes in advance. The place to which he goes for the foot-washing is the place of suffering, the deed he accomplishes is the forgiveness of sin, and the gifts of flesh and blood that are given and poured out expressly refer to his coming bloody sacrifice on the Cross.

Living from the same anticipation, the Farewell Discourses are connected to the two deeds, the foot-washing and the meal. On the one hand, they are an exuberant summary of all that the Lord gave to his own in the course of his years of teaching. But they are more. They are like the spiritual side of the Eucharist: the divine word's condition of being given out and poured forth. While the Synoptic Gospels present us more with the sacramental aspect of the eucharistic mode of being, John lets us take a look into its spiritual aspect. The Farewell Discourses are the Eucharist expressed in word. After all, the Lord is the word of God, given to the world by the Father. And when this word has been broken and given to the utmost for mankind, when everything in it has been distributed and poured out, it sounds like the Farewell Discourses sound. Whoever hears them and accepts them in loving faith hears more than a lesson about God such as a man could present it, but he also hears more than a lesson about the Father as the incarnate Son in visible flesh preached it. He hears the content of the Eucharist and thus the Lord's ecclesial situation, in which he lets the very last of his love flow from himself: water and blood from the wound in his side, the wound mankind struck in his body, his spirit, his divine love.

But the Lord remains conscious that it is the hour of parting. Therefore he makes this hour a concluding, enduring memorial of his earthly life. For the dizzily high tower of his teachings he lays a firm, plain foundation, completely grounded in human daily life: a meal is held. Later in the Church, too, his spiritual presence and effectiveness will always be traceable back to this simple deed, which makes him present and is connected to the act in the room of the Last Supper: "Do this in memory of me." In marriage the whole variously interwoven destiny of the partners and all the transformations of their love are traced back again and again to the day of their wedding, to the simple consent, the simple ceremony, which encompasses and holds everything and confirms everything in its truth. And every later consent of love is like a re-presentation of the first and definitive consent, anchoring it deeper in life and soul. In like manner, the Lord sets the deed like a simple and unshakable foundation, in order to interpret it afterward, letting the richness of its being become visible in word. His bearing is as firm and unshakable as his deed; he teaches and consoles and puts anyone wavering or doubting back on his feet. And yet he himself is overcome by the sorrow of parting, and more: deeply troubled by the shadows of the approaching night and separation from God and man. Even earlier, at

Lazarus' grave and afterward in the Temple, these pre-Passion shadows had darkened his soul. They also breathe through his Farewell Discourses. He consoles his own and his Father out of his own desolation [de-solation]; he radiates his light out of his own night. But this night does not darken the light streaming from him. On the contrary, he lets night stream over his soul only in order to give all the light in it to the Father and to mankind. In this transition he is already the grain of wheat that dies and brings forth fruit a hundredfold; he already exercises his power of giving his life, in order to receive it again later from those to whom he has given it—the Father and mankind—in the form of his eucharistic love. In these Discourses his whole being is self-giving, and therefore prayer. Thus, the Farewell Discourses necessarily flow into the High Priestly Prayer, in which he definitively assumes his place as mediator: one with the Father, and one with the Church and with us.

THE FOOT-WASHING

13:1. *It was before the feast of Easter. As Jesus knew that his hour was come to go out of this world to the Father, and loving his own who were in the world, he loved them to the end.*

The hour of return to the Father is near. The Lord is thinking, however, not of that, but of accomplishing the highest and most definitive act possible in the time remaining to him on earth, of realizing the uttermost love. He knows that he comes from love and is going to love, and that he himself is love. This love he wants to give to his own, just as he possesses it: wholly and prodigally. In everything he does, he desires only to love. This love does not permit him to turn his thoughts away from the coming Passion. For he is conscious that the coming agony, and everything unbearable that will now come upon him, will be a source of love for mankind. He cannot withdraw from suffering, because for him that would mean withdrawing love from the men he loves. Rather, he will prove this love to them to its uttermost end, to the Cross, and also all along the way to it, as long as he is still free to give. He does not think now about his return to the Father, for that would mean consolation. He wants, not to be consoled, but to squander his love. He gives his whole attention to those whom he loves here—to his own who are in the world. And yet the love with which he loves them is not a different kind of love from his love for the Father. It is for the Father's sake that he loves mankind so much. There are not two loves: therefore he does not experience one as a comfort and the other as comfortless. He does not want this dichotomy; if he were to seek consolation from the Father, mankind would have to appear to him as comfortless. He seeks no consolation for himself; it is his consolation to love the Father in wholly doing his will and loving mankind. In this he does not turn away from the Father, for in his extravagant giving to mankind he is wholly occupied with the Father's will.

And yet in this action he consoles the Father as well; he makes it easier for the Father to turn away from him afterward. He prepares his own forsakenness by seeking the Father now wholly in love for mankind. He does not skip over his suffering in spirit, for if he were to look now beyond the Cross, at the glorification, he would speak, superficially as it were, about suffering, and bracket it mentally. That is not what he wants; in the freedom of love, he wants to give his whole attention to suffering. He wants neither to turn away from suffering and let himself be distracted nor to let himself be so imprisoned by it that he would no longer see his essential purpose: love for mankind. By loving he prepares himself for suffering, and in this he does the Father's will and is thus with the Father and so consoles the Father above and beyond the coming Passion.

He wants to love his own in the world *to the end* (*telos*). In this word lies, first of all, the fulfilment of a promise. He himself, as the word that was in the beginning, was this promise: a promise of love, which is now being translated from word into deed. Further, this word implies that he will walk his path to its final end. Everything along this path, up to his last breath, will be love, and particularly the last thing: no longer to know that he loves. But this *end* likewise implies the abolition of every finite limitation. For he is going to the uttermost of love, which, as such, is already the uttermost, and yet always has room for a course of events, a history, a development. Never has love come up against a barrier; rather, everything uttermost is a new beginning for love. Where the Lord has given his uttermost, he goes beyond the condition of love that gives into the condition of love that is given.

Much in the Lord's mission is incomprehensible: that he has mercy on mankind and yet seems to make excessive demands of it, that he deigns to have disciples and followers and much else in his life. But every riddle is transcended, every boundary exploded, by the incomprehensibility of the Lord's love. Today it is as much a puzzle as then. And what is least comprehensible is this course of love unto the end, this torrent of love, this elemental catastrophe of love. A great deal in this *end* is played out between Father and Son alone and is no longer, like the earlier things, accessible to us. The whole Gospel empties into this inexplicable *end*, into this apotheosis of love. The mystery in the love between Father and Son that now prevails is somehow similar to the mystery of parenthood. Children live in the sphere of this parental love, but they do not see all of it; they do not participate in everything belonging to the intimacy of parental love. Perhaps they know there are things to which they have no access, although nothing of parental love is denied them through these things. For they live from and in this love of the parents for each other, and not only from the love of the father for the child and of the mother for the child. Thus we, too, live like children in the mystery between Father and Son, without really knowing this mystery. But we are ignorant of it, not because it is withheld from us, but because we are not yet ripe to understand it. Later, as adults, the children will have an inkling of their parents' mysteries, and we too will grow in the knowledge of God's love.

But the intimacy between Father and Son is as free as it is great. It does not require any mutual assurance or repeated affirmation. Parents must occasionally renounce their intimacy in order to devote themselves more, or entirely, to their children; they do not feel this as infidelity but as something that was always included in their love and freely accepted in their marriage bond. In like manner, the Son now turns wholly to mankind, not to be unfaithful to the Father, but in the freedom the Father's love guarantees him.

13:2. *A meal was held, during which the devil had already put it into the heart of Judas Iscariot, the son of Simon, to betray him.*

Right beside the uttermost love of the Lord stands the uttermost malice of the devil. But this nearness is fully concealed. Nobody looking at those gathered around the table would have thought that in one of those present dwelt the incarnate God, and in another the incarnate devil. And yet both sit at the same table: the Lord, all love, and Judas, possessed by his evil intention. And while Judas is in complete unrest, because he suspects the Lord's love but cannot see it all and knows himself to be totally exposed to him, the Lord radiates perfect calm. He knows Judas' intention. But his thoughts do not revolve around Judas and the devil, although they are so obtrusively and unmistakably near him; his thoughts go beyond, to dwell on the hour that is now coming, on the work of love that he wants to perform, on the promise to the Father that he wants to fulfill.

The Lord's love is so strong that the devil can do nothing against it.

But the weak love of the other disciples who sit at the same table will participate in Judas' betrayal, although the disciples do not know it now. Where there is Christian love, Satan is not far away, because he makes his best catches where true love becomes weak, where it cools off, where it imperceptibly lets itself be falsified into something that still bears the name of love but is the opposite of love—self-seeking enjoyment. The devil's presence at the table forces Christian love to be on guard even in the harmless joys willed by God and to take on the inner form of renunciation. If Christians no longer knew that they really had to fight against the devil, their Christianity would slip into a superficial optimism in which a light-headed enthusiasm would replace the earnestness of love. Love and renunciation are an earnest unity. Love desires to do everything in its power. When it renounces, it does so not in a pathetic or tragic mood or for the sake of the joy that lies in the act of renunciation. Rather it attempts, as far as it can, to purify itself and prepare itself for the Lord's arrival. Lent, for example, signals the Christian's earnest engagement in the Lord's coming Passion. The Christian wants neither to watch passively, leaving the whole burden to the Lord, nor simply to wait until the Lord himself imposes a renunciation on him. He goes, so to speak, to meet the Lord, by attempting through deeds to demonstrate his gratitude and his readiness to endure. He knows very well that it is no more than a poor attempt, but he also knows that his action, as a token, will be taken into account through the Lord's grace. Just as the Lord should be able to see in the way in which we celebrate our human feasts that we are ready to celebrate his divine feasts with him, so should he also be able to recognize in the quality of our renunciation that we are also ready to go with him through the mysteries of his Passion.

13:3–5. *Knowing that the Father had given everything into his hands, and that he had come from God and was returning to God, Jesus rose from table, put off his clothing, took a linen towel and put it around his waist. Then he poured water into a basin and began to wash his disciples' feet and dry them with the towel around his waist.*

Knowing that the Father has given everything into his hands, knowing that he comes from the Father and returns to him, he now wants only to gather incentive to suffer to the utmost. He knows what awaits him and how he will be delivered up to suffering. In spite of this, he sees this deliverance as *his* way from the Father to the Father, given to him by the Father. Uttermost powerlessness is given into his power. His submitting to all this is *his* affair. It is the affair resolved on in the love between the Father and the Son, which he may now make his own. For he must take possession of this suffering, and not only thoroughly taste it; he must have and possess it as his own by letting it possess him. He holds it so firmly that none of this suffering escapes him. None of it will be only half-suffered. Here the Father must do the Son's will, since he has given suffering, like everything else, into the Son's hands.

The Lord is thinking about love. Therefore he now sees his leaving and his returning, for love consists in this movement. In everything he does he looks to the ideal, the best possibility of love. So too in the foot-washing, which now follows. In this too there is a distancing and a coming near, a stepping down and a being raised, a setting himself apart from the disciples and a new binding himself to them. The Lord's humility in his self-abasement will be so great that the disciples will find it difficult to accept; just as the Father himself finds it difficult, as it were, to endure the Son's abasement, which is implicit in his Incarnation and his Passion. He could have achieved everything at less cost by showing his ministering love for the disciples in another way, thus acquiring the work of salvation more quickly from the Father. That he goes so far as to come before the disciples as a servant and before the Father as a human being is part of the inventiveness of his supreme love.

He rises from table. The meal at which they are now gathered together is not *yet* the Eucharist as instituted sacrament. But it is its beginning: a gathering of the disciples in the Lord, in order to take a communal meal with the Lord, each according to his need. The Lord is among them like an equal among equals. Until now, his outward attitude has not differed from that of the disciples in any respect. But now he stands up and separates himself from the others, as on that other occasion when he sat on the foal of an ass. Both anticipate his being raised up on the Cross. Now he begins to perform a series of deeds, all of which he does voluntarily and all of which will involuntarily show up again in his Passion. It is an action that presages the Passion.

The common element in these individual acts lies in the fact that the

17

Lord separates and humbles himself in order to purify men. On the one hand, this work points ahead to the Passion, and on the other hand, it points to the sacraments to be instituted: to the Eucharist and to its preparation, the sacrament of penance. The Eucharist is the completion, the goal, so to speak, of the foot-washing, and confession parallels its preliminaries.

In the foot-washing the Lord humbles himself not only to the level of the disciples, but lower, beneath them. He must place himself beneath them in order to be able to purify them. A misunderstanding might be possible if he places himself among them as one among equals. The disciples might perhaps feel better, but they would not understand his humiliation and would therefore not be able to be purified. They cannot confess their guilt to an equal, for he would be no different from them. If the Lord wants to remove all disgrace from mankind, he must place himself in a position in which one need not look up to him, but can look down to him. Only when the love that towers over mankind appears in its lower mirror image of humility will purification in the form of confession be possible. And only when this purification is accomplished through the Lord's humiliation is mankind capable of accepting him as its equal. It is, then, a work done solely out of love and for the sake of love. The Lord does not think: I must wash the feet of these men if they are to be worthy to sit at table with me. Rather, it is much more: What a pitiful state they are in; if they notice how impure they still are, they will be unhappy; I must wash them! The work that he does is not simply a preliminary humiliation or merely a means to a later exaltation. Rather the whole, the purification as well as the state of being pure, is one indivisible work of love, which humbles itself and is therein exalted, which annihilates itself and is therein glorified. In this lower position that he adopts, he courts us, earnestly and urgently, and not just in passing. So low does he place himself that none of the lofty or the lowly can feel themselves passed by. The Lord in his humility will always stand lower than any other human being.

The work begins with his setting himself apart. He stands up. He must withdraw and distance himself from them. In order to complete this work of greatest intimacy, he must approach them from a distance. Then he *puts off his clothes,* for he wants to expose himself that he might catch the dirt and take it on himself. He wants no mediation between himself and sin; he wants to endure it naked. He wants to receive directly whatever is worst in us, whatever humiliates him more. In this undressing, the whole realism of his action becomes clear. It is not only a sublime symbol. The disciples really have dirty feet—they had simply not noticed it. Every individual, when the Lord comes to him, thinks perhaps to himself: If I had known that the Lord was going to do that, I would have washed beforehand. But they did not know, nor did he announce it, for he *wants* to take on and bear their dirtiness. Nor could they remove it themselves. Without him, they could not repent of their sins, for if this penitence were merely human, it would be nothing (it would be an ambition to be more than one is). But if it is the Lord's gift, it is the fruit of his humiliation. In any case, he bears the burden. We should take note of this realism; it is not the business of religion to paint over and explain away the harsh and unappetizing aspects of life. Rather, we should see how earnestly the Lord concerns himself with them, how he, so to speak, "wallows in them". And from this we should learn to find him in the midst of these sullied realities of life, a thing far removed from letting ourselves be hindered by them in our life with God. The Lord does not simply generously overlook the distress of human life. He looks it in the face without illusions. He is a match for misery in all its forms: hunger, sickness, death, filth and corruption. If he were simply to overlook all this, then the longer we were in his company and the better acquainted we became with his purity, the more embarrassed these things would make us feel in his presence. He must be the one to take them away in order to reestablish equality.

He washes sin away with the *water* of his grace. Repentance itself belongs to this water; it too is grace, a part of the washing agent. He pours this water *into a basin,* that is, into a form. He gives his grace (which, like water, of itself can only flow and spread out) a particular sacramental shape. It is given a visible outline. One can contemplate grace in this form; in this container of grace it has a "water level". No one can heedlessly pass by this form of grace into which the Lord has poured it. Nobody can take the content without the form.

Now the Lord has indeed *put a linen towel around his waist,* but it is not said that he used this towel for washing. Rather, he uses it first for drying. The Lord attends to the washing himself. He not only washes, he washes with himself. He himself is the instrument of washing. He is so low and humiliated that he is not only the active element that washes, but also the passive element used for washing. He is this completely servile, taken-for-granted instrument, which is not spared and is wrung out along with the dirt it contains. However humiliating confession may be, the Lord humiliates himself even more. And the penance lies not least in having to let the Lord have his way in this work.

Not until the washing is over does the Lord use the towel, with which he girded himself and which belongs to the Lord's body, to the priest. By virtue of his ordination and his virginity, the priest stands wholly in the service of the Lord and of his body. His vocation also implies the tender mystery of his being chosen as protection and covering for the Lord. Perhaps this was even the unavowed reason that moved him to enter the Lord's service: he wanted to cover him, he wanted, so to speak, to give him the opportunity of sparing himself, at his cost. But because the Lord found protection through his priest, he for his part guarantees him his divine protection; and thus the priest, who offered himself to strengthen the Lord's work, first found his strength in the Lord.

Thus the priest is the towel that the Lord has put around his waist and used for drying. The priest does not wash, for the washing is the Lord's deed. He removes sin as already repented, that is, at the moment in which the Lord has already washed and rectified it. Hence it is no longer dangerous or contagious for the priest. He belongs to the Lord and is proof against sin. In requiring the priest to hear confession, the Lord does not humiliate him or force him into any impure occupation. What is impure about it has already been taken over by the Lord. Those who come to the confessional are already the beloved of God, children of the Father and brothers of the Lord, who in repentance already have an idea of love. He imparts it to them completely in the absolution, and he arranges that nothing of the purification process remains. He reintegrates the purified ones into the community by taking the sign of confession away from them. No one can notice in a person who has just left the confessional that he is still "wet", just freshly purified.

Confession consists primarily in being washed by the Lord, and only secondarily in confessing sin. This primary element is so much first that on the Cross it will become the only one: the simple, one-sided removal of the whole horror of sin. Not until afterward will the Lord give the command: Confess your sins. Furthermore, the Lord requires confession in such a way that the secrecy of the confessional is preserved at the same time. He does not demand a public, detailed confession of sins from his disciples. It is enough that each one knows: I must be purified by the Lord. The disciples know nothing about each other except that each had dirty feet, which the Lord had to cleanse. No one pays attention to the feet of the others; it is enough that the Lord has seen his shame and removed it. It does not even occur to anyone to look at the others' feet. Confession should not be public in the Church. The only thing public about it is that each person knows that everyone else needs confession, too. The Lord guards the secret of the confessional with exacting care. No one, then, can resist confession. All must accept it. Nobody puts on airs. One is simply next in line and must confess. The foot-washing, finally, is like the penitential act in the Mass; all confess their very great guilt, but all to the Lord alone. And this, again, is similar to Purgatory, in which the last, definitive confession of guilt is made before admittance to the heavenly banquet.

The foot-washing is the immediate preparation for the institution of the Eucharist. Between confession and Communion there is this immediate transition. Confession is not an end in itself; it is a purification for a particular goal. Once purified, one no longer looks at one's feet, but only at the Lord with whom one is sitting at table. Thus, the foot-washing flows into the Eucharist; indeed it is implicit in it, for the Lord's humiliation to the deepest depths is the very soul of the Eucharist. The sacraments are not only side by side but at the same time within each other, and their indivisibility is proven by the Lord's deeds.

13:6. *Thus he came to Simon Peter. He said to him: Lord, are you going to wash my feet?*

Peter, the first to be washed, feels most especially disconcerted. In his love for the Lord, he wants to know that a distance is kept between them. He does not know what he will later become. He knows only that his life will be one of service to the Lord. For the Lord, however, Peter embodies what he already is and what he will be. And the words he speaks are words of the Lord's grace. Without understanding or grasping it, Peter already speaks the language of hierarchy. He feels the Lord's present humiliation very strongly; he sees how he is condescending to the lowliest ministries—he to whom Peter looks up in respectful love. This overpowers Peter more than anything else. He senses exactly the distance separating him from the Lord. He feels the distance between the Church and the Lord. The Church, after all, is simply the community, and the community is to serve the Lord. He knows very well that the Lord is the summit of the Church, and he feels he cannot approve of the Lord's reversing this order. That is what is hierarchical about Peter: his desired distance from the Lord. In grace, the Lord lets him say more than he is aware of himself. He himself is referring to his personal relationship with the Lord, but his office is already speaking from within him. This is how it always is in the Church, and that is what is catholic about her: everything personal transcends itself. The personal contains something more than personal. It is at the same time ritual, liturgical and official in the broadest sense. It is inserted into a transcendent framework.

Peter's word is a word meant as love. Peter would not be so astonished if one of the others washed his feet. He knows that others are better and cleverer than he; he knows that John, not he, is the disciple of love. Peter is humble, but it is not that his humility cannot bear the Lord's greater humility. Rather, he does not feel pure enough to be touched by the Lord, who is so pure that Peter does not want anything impure to come into contact with him.

13:7. *Jesus answered him: What I am doing, you do not yet understand; afterward you will understand it.*

The Lord does not explain his behavior; on the contrary, he says that for the moment it is not understandable. Not until later will everything become clear. Peter is thereby challenged not to persist in this matter. He should remain where he is, surrender where he cannot understand. It should suffice for him to know that this is what the Lord wants. So it is here, and so it will be again and again in the Church. What the Lord indicates always surpasses what man anticipates, and he should allow himself to be surpassed by it. He should call a halt at a certain point where what is greater, purer and hence more incomprehensible in the

Lord begins. He should accept everything, submit, let it be done to him, by placing himself only at the Lord's disposal. He should stop desiring to be the subject himself, should let the Lord be the subject and entrust himself to him as object. Or let the Lord be the subject of his own subject. He should do this with the unshakable certitude that everything required by the Lord is right, but that nothing in us can explain the Lord's workings before he wills it, before he gives understanding. He is the sole judge of when the time for this has come. His judgment can begin here below or, equally well, only in the beyond. Because it has to do with a new sacrament here, he promises understanding in this world to Peter, representative of the Church. But other deeds of the Lord can remain mysterious even to the Church. Much in the destiny of individuals will always remain unclear and will be illuminated only in the world beyond. Every path leading a man more personally to the Lord holds many mysteries and obscurities, which are only illuminated later, along the way or at the goal. Not only his surroundings, but also the person affected, must wait. He has met the Lord; this unique, tremendous fact is clear, but certainly not what will follow from this meeting. That will reveal itself only by stages.

Basically, we never understand the Lord's actions while they are being done. He lets stone jars be filled with water; he prepares a paste out of spittle and dirt; he has the stone rolled away from the grave. All of these very simple actions always have an entirely different meaning and content from what we imagine and assume. For although the Lord's actions are outwardly similar to ours, they always have a wholly unexpected meaning. They are, so to speak, explosive. They have a geometrical progression where we expect an arithmetical one; they have divine meaning where we see only a human one. They are deeds of the *Lord,* for it is he who institutes the sacraments. Here he speaks expressly of *his* deeds and does not say that the Father works them in him. They are his deeds as Redeemer, and these we do not comprehend.

Man is to let the Lord's deeds happen without desiring to comprehend, just as Mary, in her assent to the angel, let everything happen without coveting an overall view. As she then bore the Son within her, she most truly bore the principle of everything explosive and transcendent. She gave her assent to him who is always greater. But she received this assent from God in the form of her love for the Son, and together with the Son's assent she gives it back to God. Her Yes is more than she herself is: it transcends her, coming from God and leading to God. She already loves the Son in the moment in which she first expects him and carries him within her, without knowing him. She knows him, within her, to be coming from God, and in saying yes she gives him back to God again: she agrees with his Yes to God. Expecting the Son, she already has that heightened openness that is finally crowned by the always-more of the Son's self-giving, whereby the Mother, too, is always giving us the Son. He will have traits that come from his Mother; he will have his Mother's humility. Here at the foot-washing he has it and knows, too, that as man he has it from her.

Mary desires that God's will be done. Peter, on the other hand, does not want it to be done. Both speak out of humility, and we cannot say that Peter's humility is false or hypocritical. Mary knows that she is to become the instrument of an overflowing grace, which will take shape from her, and that her own role in this regard is a wholly diminishing one. Thus she speaks as woman. Peter is, first of all, a man. His surrender is not immediate. He is also animated by the sense of hierarchy and of distance from the Son. The invitation to motherhood lies, so to speak, in the direction of Mary's humility; she needs only to adapt and surrender herself to it. The invitation to the foot-washing, on the other hand, appears upside down to Peter. To be able to accept it, he must first completely relearn everything. Mary says yes because she humbles herself; Peter says no because the Lord is humbling himself. The Mother sees that she will be able to respond because she is looking to the Child; Peter has before him the Man, whose complete response shows him the inadequacy of his own response.

13:8. *Peter said to him: You shall never wash my feet. Jesus answered him: If I do not wash you, you have no part in me.*

Peter now speaks an open No. Before, it was astonishment; now it is rejection. He says no, even though the Lord tells him that he will understand later. He cannot free himself from the thought that there must be some mistake. He knows very well that the Lord is wholly pure, and that he himself is a sinner. And he certainly has a much higher respect for the Lord's opinion than for his own. But this obvious distance is just what intensifies his rejection. The gentleness with which the Lord met his first objection only strengthens his feeling of distance. But now that he says a forceful No, the Lord answers with a categorical Yes. *If I do not wash you, you have no part in me.* If Peter does not submit, he can expect nothing more from the Lord, have nothing more in common with him. For him it is a matter of being or nonbeing. He must let himself be washed; for himself and for the Church, he must affirm this humiliation of the Lord. Where the Lord decides, he may raise no objection, however well meant. Peter's agreement is necessary. When the Lord blots out sin, when he lays the foundation walls of the future sacrament of penance in this form of the foot-washing, he does it within the Church he founded, within the office entrusted to Peter. Thus, this deed no longer belongs exclusively to the Lord; Peter has the right of codisposal over it. It is not as though Peter were asked for his opinion and voice, for Peter obviously understands nothing of what is happening here. But the Lord forces him to accept this purification, to put up with it, and this acceptance is the categorically imposed condition of any further communion between Peter and him. Unconditional obedience is required precisely of him who embodies the authority of the Church. Now that Peter realizes that the Lord's humiliation and service to him are inseparable, he is overcome by this relation. He sees that redemption requires contact between purity and sin; he sees his own sin and the Lord's humility in a new light and is filled with the true humility that desires to give itself completely—for true humility and true self-giving are one. For the humble person, the only important thing in himself is what belongs to God and to others— belongs, because he owes it to them, and therefore places it again at their disposal. Because it belongs to them, it is valuable to him, and most valuable when he can give it back to them, so that they use everything that is usable in him. Thus, humility fulfilled is one with self-giving.

13:9. Simon Peter said to him: Then, Lord, not only my feet, but also my hands and my head.

Now Peter demands to be washed completely. To some extent, he would like to place himself even more at the Lord's disposal than the Lord requires. He is struck with the love revealed in the Master's humility.

In the light of this love he is convinced that he is a complete sinner, all of whose members participate in sin. And he thinks that the Lord, who washes his feet in order to accept him, will accept him all the more, the more thoroughly he is cleansed.

Peter has grasped only a part of the Lord's intention, but he acts as if he could see the whole situation. On his own behalf, however, Peter cannot be his office. Here he must leave the office to the Lord; he does not have the gift of discernment in his own regard. He is to submit to the simple rule of the Lord, just as later penitents in confession will have to submit to the Church's office. They will have to confess their sins in the way appointed by the Church, not as it suits themselves. In confession, too, there is an order established by the Church, and the penitent must submit to it. In the end, one confesses those things that the Church has specified in her norms for confession. Peter has not yet grasped this. He has understood that when the Lord prescribes something, there can only be submission. But he has not yet understood what the Lord wants—a very particular, ordered washing: washing in line with his service and the Church's service, washing in preparation for what awaits the Lord. The standard lies with the Lord. Peter's readiness certainly is touching, but confession is designed not only to move and edify the Christian people but also to enable the Christian to place himself more at the Lord's disposal. It is not a subjective outpouring or an institution for working off personal guilt feelings or a means to self-knowledge and self-reflection, but an objective purification by the Lord, for the purpose of a deeper union with his mission in Communion.

Peter, then, should hold to the Lord's command. He should let only his feet be washed and not his hands or his head. One might think that now, as the disciples are seated at table, the feet would be hidden, not to be taken account of, and that the hands and head would be much more important. But in this purification, which is certainly a communal act, the point is not the edification of one's neighbor. The damage done to one's neighbor is not the standard of confession, nor is the public character of sin the focal point but rather what the Lord sees, what he wishes to cleanse. Just as the cleansing itself, in all its circumstances, is determined by the Lord, so also is the member to be cleansed.

The cleansing of the feet implies that what is seen at this moment by the Lord as being really dirty should be purified, even if it be the same thing at each confession. It is the feet that are dirty again each time. One should not want to confess something different "for the sake of variety". Or to show hands and face, in order perhaps to spare the Lord the coarser work. It is an effort to wash another's feet, but the Lord desires this effort; in requesting the feet, he takes on the coarsest job, and he wants to take it on again and again. We are to be aware that we need it again, that we need it most just where it costs him the greatest effort. It might occur to someone to wash himself beforehand, in order to spare the Lord the work. He could bend over backward to avoid sin at all costs just to prove to the Lord that he is already clean and needs no confession. But even if someone could manage that, he would still have to be freed from the much worse filth of self-righteousness. He would have avoided sin out of pride and not out of love for the Lord. So each person should offer his feet, for the Lord himself decides what he wants to wash, and here ecclesial office follows him. They determine where the crux of the sin lies. They also determine what the Lord washes and what the person himself must wash. The apostles should wash their own hands. Certain things do not belong in confession. The confessor can tell the penitent not to mention certain things in confession in the future (so that more attention will be given to the real sin or so that the sinner will be less concerned with himself). It can also happen that someone has not even thought about his feet, that the Lord or the priest must first show and reveal to him where the center of his sin lies. For often enough a person's chief fault is hidden from him, and the priest, by virtue of his office, can reveal it to him. Finally, there is a certain limit in confessing with which the penitent must be satisfied. There are things that one may overlook and forget in confession and need not repeat if they were forgotten in an earlier confession. They are, or were, already included in one's general disposition. But there are also things that, if forgotten, one would have to repeat, because here the Lord requires confession of the details.

13:10. *Jesus said: Whoever has bathed needs only to wash his feet, for he is entirely clean. You too are clean, but not all.*

When the Lord and the Church say that purification is already accomplished, the individual has claim only to a limited confession. The disciples were purified for the first time when they came to the Lord, offering and surrendering to him themselves and everything belonging to them. At that time the sacrament of penance had not been instituted. But as soon as the sacrament exists, it applies in the way the Lord has instituted it. It is a personal act of the Lord, who determines what is to occur. It is not an act left to the arbitrariness of the faithful, not a psychological confession, not a public communal confession, not a confession for edification, not a mutual foot-washing by the apostles. Rather, it remains a precisely determined sacrament. Now, the individual Christian is washed for the first time in baptism. Because of this washing, he afterward has the right and the duty to go to confession, and he should and may accuse himself only of those sins committed since his last cleansing. He should not anxiously refer to things that happened earlier. Whoever lives in grace should confess and renounce whatever in him is resisting grace. He should not start nagging and picking again at what, through the Lord's grace, is really clean. He should not let the garment of grace become threadbare from continual washing. Rather, he should thank the Lord for purifying him. Nevertheless, a confession of one's whole life, or a general confession, remains possible. But it should be done only where the Lord and the Church require or recommend it. In no case may it be regarded as an insurance or a supposed strengthening of absolution, but only as a renewed opening of the soul to grace.

You too are clean, but not all. The Lord considers the disciples clean, although he has just set about washing their feet. But they are clean only if they do not resist and only in view of the washing to come. This is already included in the Lord's look and words. Thus the penitent is clean, even before he has confessed his sin to the priest. The will to subsequent confession is included in his repentance, for both, repentance and confession, form a recognizable unity in the Lord's sight. This cleansing is pure grace. The whole work is one of God's perfect love and humiliation. He cannot spare us our own humiliation in this, but he does not rejoice in it. On the contrary, through his own humiliation he wants to make ours as little felt as possible. In every confession, Christians should feel God's humiliation much more ardently than their own.

13:11. *For he knew who was to betray him. That was why he said: You are not all clean.*

The Lord knows his betrayer, but he does not point him out, for outwardly he still belongs to the community, although inwardly he has turned away from the Lord. The Lord does not expel anyone; a person who goes away has excluded himself. Before the community, the Lord does not even give a hint as to who will leave it soon, for the scandal is not yet public. So, too, the Church will not bring scandals to light before the instigators themselves give occasion for it.

The scandal of Judas was one that had to happen, but many another scandal in the Church has no visible cause. Yet the Lord does not spare her such scandal. Is it because the Lord himself took upon himself the scandal of the Cross? Is it because through one person's scandal the other members of the Church are horrified and thus strengthened in their loyalty to the Church? In any case, the offense is tolerated, even if it affects the Church's holy of holies. The Lord endures it in the room at the Last Supper. The Church *must* endure scandal; she may not circumvent or deny it, or act as if it were not there, or distance herself from it. Nor is it said that the Church should immediately and by all means stifle the scandal by eliminating the evil, for perhaps the sinner may still repent. Nor does the Lord cast Judas out—it can be better to let an abscess ripen than to put a knife to it too soon and kill it in its early stages. Not every scandal-rousing book needs to be immediately banned, even if it may not keep the Church's doctrine intact. Perhaps it is better to let people talk first and to clear up misunderstandings by the light of day, and fairly. Many in the Church are sinners, and every sin is a tacit scandal and a heresy. But the Church is held together by love.

The Lord knew his betrayer from the very beginning. Yet he called him into his company of the elect. By this he indicated that it will always be this way in the Church, too. No chosen person can nestle down securely, thinking that he could never betray the Lord. We should build, not on our calling, but on the Lord's grace. Out of the innermost circle of the apostles comes the decisive betrayal. It comes from one to whom the Lord's whole love was offered, but who did not accept it. Many are called in reality, not just apparently, to the priesthood and to the religious life, and in spite of this become betrayers.

THE EUCHARIST

13:12. *Then after he had washed their feet, and put on his clothes and reclined again, he said to them: Do you know what I have done to you?*

After the Lord has clarified everything in his conversation with Peter, he washes the feet of each individual disciple. Once it has happened officially, it continues to happen, and each member of the Church has a turn. The Lord himself will do it for each one.

Then he clothes himself again, resumes his place and begins to speak about what has happened. He speaks of it, not as the naked Lord, but as the reclothed Lord, who again sits at table with the others. The action, then, is concluded, so much so that he wastes no words with anyone— not even with the unclean one—about what has really occurred. He keeps the secret of the confessional. His visible humiliation is over. If he were to sit down at table without his robe, the disciples would be reminded of what has been. But the Lord goes further. He clothes himself as if nothing had happened and sits down to do something new: to explain and institute the Eucharist. The disciples, for their part, are clean and relieved, and their sin no longer hinders them from understanding the Lord's words. Subjectively, each one of them has gone through confession and hence is capable of grasping the ensuing objective, impersonal instruction on the essence of purification, which already belongs to the future sacrament of penance. This natural distancing from the subjective experience creates, on the one hand, a lack of constraint between penitent and confessor; and, on the other hand, it removes from the penitent every kind of subjective enthusiasm over the experience that could perhaps move him to an all-too-rapid repetition of confession. After the whole affair slips into the past, one can undertake an entirely factual and impersonal consideration of the event, which itself is only the transition to new happenings. The disciples are now free for their apostolic task of passing on the grace they have received. They must, therefore, first of all objectively understand of what this grace consists. The Lord does not minimize what has just happened or diminish it through this explanation, and he certainly does not take away its personal beauty. Above all else, he points out that he himself was necessary to it. It was not the deed of just any person, but of the Lord. At this moment, he does not even attribute his action to the Father but claims it for himself, for he is the Lord, and the dispenser of the sacraments.

13:13. *You call me Master and Lord, and you speak rightly, for so I am.*

The Lord is, indeed, ruler of those who acknowledge him and give expression to their acknowledgment through these titles *Master* and *Lord*. Such an acknowledgment means not only recognizing him as Lord and Master but also acknowledging all the consequences of this confession. It means letting ourselves be drawn into everything that the Lord demands of us, placing ourselves unhesitatingly at his disposal. To acknowledge the Lord is to open a door that one may not close again. It is to take a look into the Lord's world, which, however, as soon as we catch sight of it, wants to become our own world. The Lord removes our fear of this acknowledgment, which could stem from our having unconsciously committed ourselves more deeply than we wanted. For his part, he acknowledges this acknowledgment: *You speak rightly, for so I am.* He confirms his own title, with everything it includes in the way of obligations. As soon as a person has begun to seek, and makes the first acknowledgment, he receives this encouragement and affirmation from the Lord. Yet he waits until after the foot-washing to give it. He allows his disciples to call him Master and Lord only when they have acknowledged that they are sinners. It would not do to seek and acknowledge the Lord out of a feeling of one's own perfection, out of the fullness of one's self-complacency. The preliminary step to acknowledging God is always the feeling that one does not suffice of oneself. Whoever acknowledges himself a sinner will be immediately acknowledged by the Lord and thus enabled to acknowledge the Lord. The humbling that the Lord wishes as a prerequisite is made easier by the fact that the Lord has already humbled himself so much more. Nowhere is the Lord's love so evident as in confession.

For so I am. This is said conclusively, as a sign that confession has been instituted by him personally, in a very special fashion, as a way and witness of redemption. Therefore he does not refer to the Father here, but speaks of himself. Because he is speaking and answers for it, no one needs to torture himself with the thought of how his sin looks in the Father's eyes. The Lord answers for it. Thus the confessor embodies not the Father, but the Lord. In this way, confession acquires the character of intimacy with the Son; it is a closed secret between the sinner and his Redeemer. In confession the Lord places himself wholly at the sinner's disposal, enfolding the sinner in his mantle.

In the end, of course, the sacraments lead back to the Father, like everything that the Son has done and instituted. He dispenses them in an attitude of perfect humility and surrender to the Father. Thus it was at the raising of Lazarus, as the Lord in prayer to the Father worked the miracle that foreshadowed confession. So it was at the foot-washing, when he heard confession in an attitude of deepest submission. Thus it will also be on the Cross, where the origin of the sacraments will coincide with the Son's return to the Father. He wants to be the Lord and the personal dispenser of the sacraments only by returning everything to the Father at the same time, for the sacraments themselves are instituted in view of the world's being returned to God. In them the Lord accompanies the redeemed on their way to the Father, in such a way that he repeatedly pardons their sins, preparing them in this temporal redemption for the great redemption in heaven, when he will definitively give them back to the Father.

13:14. *Now if I, the Lord and Master, have washed your feet, you must also wash one another's feet.*

Here for the first time, the Lord makes the immediate transition from his deed to his commandment. For the first time, the Lord's commandment is heard: the commandment of love, as participation in the Lord's deed. Only after the participation itself has been instituted can the Lord pronounce this commandment. Until now one could see only the Lord's love for the Father and the world and, to some extent, our love for the Lord. But now, in being granted participation in confession and in the Eucharist, this love of ours for the Lord can bind itself to the Lord's love. Now, by participation in this love, our narrow, personal love can let itself be expanded to the dimensions of his love, which is limitless and all-embracing in every respect. The Lord suffers for each individual person and carries each one within himself in suffering. Through this love of his, embracing everyone, we all become brothers; because he lets us participate in his love, we can also love each other as brothers. When we love him, he gives us his love, but his love is love for his brothers.

We receive the Lord's love first of all in the sacrament in which he cleanses us. Thus the first love of neighbor is sacramental and official: it is the love between the priest and the penitent. But because the Lord is present and represented in this completely official relationship, the official dimension immediately passes over into the personal one. Just as the penitent reveals what is within him, so too the absolution contains a squandering of the priest's substance, which is included in the Lord's self-squandering. A dividing boundary between the Lord's love and the priest's surrender is no longer perceptible. If the official participation is one enacted in word, the personal participation is one carried out in life. But in the sacrament both merge. Therefore the forgiveness of sins is always an act of making room for love; on leaving the confessional, a person is more loving than before, more ready to love, not only the Lord, but also his neighbor. But for the priest, too, every confession he hears means an increase of love. He experiences the grace of the Lord, who humbles himself before him so much that he, the Lord, bears the whole burden, while the priest receives the confession in simple love. Thus, love of neighbor is the origin of the sacramental relationship between confessor and penitent, inasmuch as both are united in the one love of the Lord. In the confession of sin, this love allows the one to speak his confession in love, and the other to listen in love. Accordingly, the one listens to the word of redemption in the counsel and absolution, and the other speaks it in love. There is mutual love, then, in this official relationship of confession, for the penitent also gives the priest love. His confession is love offered to the Lord, in which the priest has a share. He receives insight into things that the Lord sees and knows, into mysteries of love. The priest can also be salutarily shaken and humbled through a confession; some saints have even confessed with the secondary intention of converting the priest hearing their confession.

This official form of love of neighbor is accompanied by the purely personal form, that of bearing our neighbor's sins, which we assume in love and—like the Lord at the foot-washing and on the Cross—encounter naked, so that they touch and contact us directly. It is the readiness to

33

help other persons out of love in such a way that our help really acquires the aspect of a washing. It is the attempt to do what the Lord does, irrespective of the particular person concerned. Aware that we are washing someone's feet, we do not desire to know whose feet they are. We only want to recognize the person's feet insofar as is necessary to give help. Here also, only the feet are washed, while everything else is passed over silently in love. We wash these feet that we are holding in our hand, lovingly in the love of the Lord; we do what is necessary and then move on. The whole action is a commission from the Lord, not a personal giving or teaching. Whoever does it will be just as ready to let himself be helped as to help others. It is marked by a mutual simplicity that holds itself out without making a fuss and does not secretly wash its own feet beforehand in order to appear purer before the others.

It is odd that the Lord introduces love of neighbor on the occasion of the foot-washing, this procedure involving dirty feet. But the Lord's commandment, now proclaimed, is a realistic one; there is nothing fanatical about it. What is unclean must be washed, and whatever one has to show must really be shown. Thus love appears in the midst of the filth of this world. Precisely what is most hidden must be shown. The Lord has willed it so.

13:15. *An example I have given you, that you also should do as I have done to you.*

The Lord has given the perfect, shining example of love, which not only consists in the deed of love itself but has its roots in his love for the Father, and therefore points back to the Father's love. In the breadth of this prototype the Lord has included everyone: beloved John and official Peter, betraying Judas and the multitude of those who are strangers to him and have turned away from him. His example is a universal one, for he has performed the foot-washing on each person. So, too, the penitential act at the beginning of the Mass applies to each one—the one who has confessed as well as the one who has not, the loving one and the lukewarm one. After the Lord has given this example, no one can consider himself untouched by or excluded from his act of love. Nobody can be indifferent to it. Each person will either receive love from others or give it to others, whether these others are fellowmen or the Lord.

By virtue of this example of the Lord, we are, first of all, committed to each other, because each one has received directly from the Lord the commission to wash his brothers' feet. Through this commission we are further obliged to let our feet be washed sacramentally by the office he instituted. And, finally, this example obliges us to let ourselves be loved by the Lord precisely in the manner decreed and instituted by him. The first and second points finally merge into the third, into our readiness for the Lord's love; for every *do this* of the Lord goes back to his *I have done it.* This is the origin of a person's whole response of love: his readiness to let himself be led by and taken into the Lord's love. Everything official and everything personal, any individual way, deed and possibility of love are, as such, nothing, if they do not express and represent the Lord's love in the world. Thus, in the end, one who loves does not confess in order to gain an advantage but because confession is an expression of the Lord's love. For the sake of this love, those who truly love the Lord's disciples love one another.

13:16. *Truly, truly I say to you: The slave is not greater than his lord, nor is the one sent greater than he who sent him.*

The disciples are right in regarding the Lord as their Master and Lord. Since they are the servants, they are not greater than he. They are not smaller because of their service, however, but because of their being human, while the Lord is the Son of God. Service, on the other hand, does not lower the one performing it. Although the Lord lowers himself so much that he renders the service of the lowliest slave, he still remains the Lord. When the lowliest servant lets the Lord wash his feet, he does not thereby become Lord but remains the servant. The distribution of offices lies in the superior's hand, in the Lord's hand.

The one sent is not greater than he who sends him. People are sent by the Lord to different tasks. The Son was also sent by God. In assuming his office from God, he did not become greater than God who sent him. He remained the same as he was. Yet he was enriched in assuming the mission. This mission, to which he fully consented, was the fulfilment for which he had waited from all eternity, although it did not make him greater than the Father; in their essential attributes the three Persons in God remain equal. None grows beyond the others. Yet the one who receives a mission grows in the sense of his mission, and the Son fulfills his sonship in his earthly mission too. In the same way, a human being grows in his mission and is fulfilled in it, and only in it, but he never outgrows the one who sent him.

Because men grow with their mission and within it are enabled to correspond to it, the Lord can at the same time construct a hierarchy through this response, in which no servant is greater than the one who appointed him: the ecclesiastical hierarchy with Peter at the top. Here, every person appointed must remember who appointed him. He must remain aware that he can never be greater than, should never presume to want to be greater than and may never tolerate being considered greater than the one who sent him. Rather, he must make every effort to be regarded as one who is under the giver of the commission. This admonition is directed not only against any self-aggrandizement in an ecclesial office, but also, no less, against any official fanfare that would suggest that the office one holds is more important than the Lord. The Lord is love, and no person or office in the Church is more important than this love. A man's task, his mission, is not above the Lord, nor are a commission and its apparent absoluteness ever reasons to disregard the Lord, his love and his commandment of love.

13:17. *If you know these things, you will be blessed if you do them.*
To know means being seized by a truth, for the purpose of reasoning about it and interpreting it, yes, but all the while trusting in the Lord's knowledge, trusting that he is right. It is the readiness to accept everything the way the Lord intends it—that is, a way much greater than one can imagine. To know means to agree with God not only with our understanding, but also with our heart's whole readiness for love, with our whole longing for God. Not only to want to grasp the truth, but to insert ourselves into the truth, letting ourselves be grasped by it. Not only to stand for the truth because we have thought about it, but to throw ourselves into its arms—to love it. Finally, to know means to move on to obedience and discipleship. *If you know these things,* then, means: if you are ready to follow me on an uncharted course, which is mine nevertheless.

If the disciples know these things, they will be *blessed.* They will fulfill the ultimate that can be expected from them: readiness for unending love and for unconditional surrender. In having fulfilled, they themselves are fulfilled: that is blessedness. But this fulfilment should constitute not only a beginning and a start, but a permanent state to the end. That is what the Lord means in saying: *if you do them.* This persevering contains a great promise of the Lord: that of participation in him, as he promised to Peter. The whole verse, then, presents the movement of a person drawn into, and letting himself be drawn into, the Lord's movement: partly walking along himself, then more strongly drawn and in the end simply taken along, despoiled, possessed by the Lord.

13:18. *I do not say this about all of you. I know whom I have chosen. But the Scripture must be fulfilled: He who ate my bread has lifted his heel against me.*

The Lord did not say this of everyone. Therefore, everything that has been said is to be tested once more on the basis of this restriction. Not everyone should let his feet be washed in the spirit of confession, but only those who are chosen for it. Not all should be smaller than their own particular lord, for it is true of many that they are only to be smaller than *the* Lord, not the particular lord set over them. And not all those sent are meant, for some are sent whose sending has no limits, but rather looks—if one ignores for the moment its origin in God—as though one *cannot* say that the one sent is not greater than he who sent him. And not all who fulfill their mission are to be called blessed, because the emphasis of some commissions lies so much in the beyond that here below only desperation is visible, and the whole blessedness of the fulfilled mission will appear only in heaven.

But the Lord at once goes beyond what has been said and gives it a new form, when he continues: *I know whom I have chosen.* He suddenly introduces an essential difference between those chosen and those not chosen. Many are chosen for a particular position in the Church, whether to represent Christ officially or to participate in his life in a manner distinguished by particular signs. They may be chosen for a particular path that clearly bears the Lord's footprints, for some action that points toward him, for a contemplation that, in imitation of his life, receives the burden of tasks and destinies that onlookers cannot completely comprehend. And yet all these differentiations do not pertain to the fulfilment itself, but only to this-worldly, visible-invisible contours that are surpassed by what is only now coming: by the Cross, which brings redemption not for some, but for all.

He who ate my bread has lifted his heel against me. Those who are now eating with the Lord, sharing his bread, do so in the spirit of guests eating at a table at which they are welcome. They do so with a feeling of gratitude. They were hungry, and now they are being sated. Their understanding does not yet reach any further. They do not know that this banquet is an infinitely overflowing grace. They see the relationship between hunger and satiety. And in fact, these two concepts are at the base of every banquet. When the Lord wanted to institute his Eucharist in the form of a meal, he had to take hunger and satiation into consideration. They are very simple concepts, taken from everyday life, to which the Lord, in his self-giving, imparts a new, infinite, spiritual sense. He wants to express his whole relationship to us in these two concepts. Hunger, then, would be everything that we have to bring to him, and satiation, everything that he gives us. In the end, everyone experiences hunger in one way or another, and one cannot say from the outset that the bad experience either more or less hunger than the good. And, likewise, everyone is sated, for his sacrifice exists not only for a few elect individuals, but for all. He says it here himself: even the one who betrays him, that is, the one who will betray him in the future, is included in the company of those who can share or are actually sharing his bread with him. Thus, the hunger of the world and its satiation by the Lord complement each other.

Food is expected to fulfill its purpose of stilling mankind's hunger. This applies also to the Eucharist, except that in its case no limits can be given to satiation. Nor can one say when satiety from one Communion ends and hunger for a new Communion begins, for both are simultaneous. Both hunger and satiety bring the receiver nearer to the Lord. From him stem both desire and its satisfaction. The kind of satiation varies. One person will be sated with less food than another, without having felt less hunger. Something similar can happen at the Lord's meal. But the Eucharist, as related either to hunger or to satiation, is always an expression of a still greater love.

All this is so because *the Scripture must be fulfilled.* It is all determined from the beginning; it was already determined when the Son was still in the Father's bosom. During his earthly life he freely institutes the means of salvation, but all these free acts are already indicated in prophecy. In creating new forms, he fulfills the forms of ancient prophecy. In this fulfilment of the old he lets himself be recognized as Lord. If a person without faith and Tradition were to enter a Catholic church today and see the rites and forms of the liturgy, he would find them incomprehensible, because he would not see through to their inner meaning. In them Christ would be prophesying, as it were, that he will one day reveal himself to him in these forms and fulfill them for him. Thus did the Lord fulfill the forms of the Old Covenant, thereby showing himself to be the Lord of the Old as well as the New Covenant. If he had only fulfilled the Old without creating the New, he would have remained the servant of the Old, not its Lord. But if he had not created the New as the fulfilment of the Old, he again would not have proved himself Lord of the Old. The unity of the two is demonstrated by the theoretical truth of his messiahship as well as by the existential truth of his personal power to fulfill. The fulfilment of the prophecy shows the whole world *that* he is the Messiah; the institution of the sacraments shows the infinity and inexhaustibility of his life, which gives itself personally for each individual. The fulfilment of the Old is not a meager, carefully measured one, but an extravagant overfulfilment. Nor does the Lord fulfill only a few passages of Scripture in order to give the world a merely sufficient proof. Rather, through the institution of the sacraments he fulfills everything, the whole form of the Old Covenant, by overfulfilling it so much that everyone receives from this extravagance: not only the deserving but also those who have lifted their heel against him.

Everyone sits at his table, the pure as well as the impure. And he expects them all. Every gradation is present: from the pure, loving John to the impurest sinner, Judas. It is impossible to see a demarcation line between the worthy and the unworthy. All who come to this table say: *Domine, non sum dignus.* This is not only the confession of personal unworthiness, but just as much the expression of one's belonging to the community of all those who approach the Lord's table. The individual stands in this community simply as one unworthy person among others, without in any way being able to claim a place or status, without wanting to be worthier or unworthier than another. He is simply an unworthy member, one of those who have lifted their heel against the Lord. This does not exclude the fact that each person, in declaring himself unworthy, does what he can and what is expected of him. The disciples too, in offering their feet, confessed their unworthiness, and on the occasion of this confession they were cleansed by the Lord. But they will not declare themselves worthy on the basis of this cleansing. They are still able to fall into worse sins than before. They are still bound to the communal sin of all in the Church, and together enter into the confession of their unworthiness. And no one ever confessed his whole sin, for every confession remains summary and incomplete. The unspoken, unacknowledged remainder is included in this *Domine, non sum dignus.*

13:19. *I tell you this already, before it happens, so that when it happens, you will believe that I am he.*

All those present have already seen enough. They have witnessed miracles, heard the Son telling about his origin and mission and listened to his conversations with his Father. He used everything he said and did to bear witness to himself. Now he uses even the bitterness of betrayal to bring them to faith. Will they believe him when it happens? And who is it who will believe in him then? The one who already believes. Who is it who will not believe? The one who does not yet believe now. The Lord is not looking for new conversions through Judas' betrayal. What the Lord wants is to strengthen the faith of the faithful from all sides, to expand it and bring it to an unbroken fullness. He wants to awaken in them a universal faith that goes through him to the Father but that also contains every human capacity for comprehension, leaves no room for doubt and is so well grounded from every side that no one can say he requires further proofs.

The Lord, in his grounding of faith, has treated each person according to his nature and his need. *One* miracle would have sufficed to ground the faith of all. But he heaps up the proofs. He thereby also shows how varied the paths are that lead to him, not only insofar as he is the fullness of all paths and human capacities — and through this fullness is glorified by humanity as the one who effects everything, bears everything, embraces everything in himself and is everything — but also because he continually opens up a new way for people to imitate him. Each person follows him on a different path, and each receives from him a different commission. His word is so wide and spacious that it spans the life and activity of each individual, at the same time allowing each one his own personality and individuality.

13:20. *Truly, truly I say to you: Whoever receives him whom I send, receives me; and whoever receives me receives him who sent me.*

When someone is sent in the Lord's name and comes by his authority, he must pass on what the Lord has given him, namely, himself. He must, then, let himself be received in such a way that the Lord will be received. For he comes in the full power of the Lord and with his message: he brings the Lord and not himself. This knowledge gives the one sent the security—and impresses on him the necessity—of acting in the name of the Lord whom he represents. The receiver, who knows that the one sent has been commissioned by the Lord, is obliged to receive him as if he were the Lord himself. This is true first of all for those officially representing the Church; in them, the Lord's commission becomes visible. But it is just as true for the life of all the Church's members, for every encounter between people, down to the smallest and most insignificant of the Lord's commissions. No one is without such a mission in the Church; every Christian is sent to those who are to be drawn to the Lord through the Church. This drawing and being drawn to the Lord must take place in the whole fullness and breadth of possibilities offered in the Lord's sendings: from the priest's words, to the example of the laity, to the neediness of the poor person who asks us for a glass of water. They all open us to love, however different their missions may be. Each one is a means by which the Lord draws us to himself, and he draws us to himself in order to send us out to others. And it is good to recognize a mission even in cases where the one sent is not aware of it. The priest who admonishes us is aware of it; the beggar who asks of us is not. Yet both are equally sent by the Lord.

Whoever receives me, receives him who sent me. One can receive the Lord as Martha and Mary received him: as the human friend and master, who then gradually reveals himself as our divine Lord. One can also receive him in the sacramental form of the Eucharist, which the Lord himself has predetermined and to which we must adapt ourselves. Each is a polar form of faith. The Eucharist implies personal reception and gives this reception a Christian setting.

Whoever receives the Lord in one of these forms, receives God. It is not possible to stop at one of these forms, to be content with the Lord's humanity without going further to God. Whether one is Martha or Mary, whether one receives the Lord in the Eucharist or in faith, one always receives something greater than one was prepared to receive or capable of receiving on one's own. No one knows what he receives when he receives the Lord. He cannot imagine the infinitude that visits him, for it will always be God whom he receives, and God will always be the transcendent One. Our mission in life will always be greater than our life itself. This is because he whom we receive and who sends us grows beyond himself into the Father, and through his humanity introduces his divinity, and thus the Father, into us.

This word of the Lord is spoken so much within his mission from the Father that only the mission and the Father are of any consequence; the Son himself appears to be extinguished. In this word he has withdrawn wholly into the Father's world; his entire activity is that of his commission in him. In his very next word, the supplementary side of this condition becomes visible: the passivity of suffering.

13:21. *When Jesus had said this he was shaken in spirit, and he testified and said: Truly, truly I say to you, one of you will betray me.*

The Lord begins to suffer anew, for he must testify that one of the disciples will betray him. But for him this testimony of his betrayal is not a purely intellectual imaging of the future, but a foretaste of coming truth, an anticipation of darkness. The Lord knows no possibility of distancing himself from reality and sealing himself off from it, as it were. He says this just after he has explained that whoever receives him receives the Father. He is just as open to betrayal as to the Father. But now that he is speaking of his betrayal, he is shaken in spirit; he no longer sees his going home to the Father. He sees the Cross until death, but no longer his mission and return to the Father. If he were not in darkness, there would be some human consolation even in knowing of the betrayal; he would be able to see through suffering to glory. But this is prevented by his distress, which leaves him as though robbed of hope. And this happens immediately after he has described perfect faith. Now he is looking only to the Passion, no longer at its flowing into the Father. In this distress he foretells Judas' betrayal. He is looking now only at the sin of this one man, not at the betrayal of all sinners, which he now covers with love.

Sin occasions this new darkening that occurs visibly before the disciples' eyes. All of them—and especially the beloved disciple, John—notice the transformation of the Lord's features, which show all the human signs of deepest agitation and sorrow. This happens so that mankind will be reminded once more of how fully human the Lord's feelings are. The redemption takes place not only between him and the Father in a superhuman world but just as much in the human nature that the disciples have in common with the Lord. The Lord shudders at this communality: one who has the same nature as he is his betrayer. He shudders less at feeling betrayed than at knowing of the sin of a person so near to him.

If he had considered this sin earlier, before the imminent Passion, perhaps it might not have shaken him so profoundly. But now, in the light of the Passion, he sees the direct connection between sin and atonement, our guilt and his suffering. He sees an uninterrupted connection leading from this concrete sin here beside him to his suffering, a line that does not break off before the final forsakenness on the Cross. Something completely unique becomes evident in this situation, namely, how the fire of sin passes over directly into the fire of reparation. And because in the Lord, who is drawn into this connection, sin is wholly lacking since he is wholly pure, this connection shakes him much more than it could move a sinner who bears in himself something that requires atonement. In this unique situation, something of the essence of confession becomes clear: that it, too, is concerned with a cobearing of others' sins. The Lord is completely pure and therefore bears our sins completely. But what he is and does, he allows us to carry out after him, imperfectly and by approximation, as it were. In confession there is the simple confession of our general, limited sins. But in confessing, one also knows that one might have been capable of something else entirely, from which only a special grace has protected us. Others have perhaps not received this special grace, and so the one who has received it is, to some extent, obligated to stand for those others in a special way. That is the beginning of all vicarious suffering and atoning in the Church. Therefore a direct path leads from confession to the Cross. The Lord himself has nothing to confess; he knows only of the coming betrayal and of its connection with his suffering. A human person, however, must always know that he shares in the guilt of that for which he is trying to make reparation. Whenever someone betrays us, we must tell ourselves that through our lack of love we gave him a hand in that betrayal.

Earlier, at the foot-washing, the Lord had still differentiated between the clean and the unclean. But now it is only: *one of you*. This indicates that all have a share in it somehow: "one of his kind". Although he can precisely differentiate between Judas and the others with respect to attitude, intention and basis of sinfulness, he still puts his finger on this kind of solidarity. So he once more declares the necessity of having to suffer together, even in imperfection and sinfulness. In saying this he inserts all those present into the work of coredemption. He does not go alone into suffering, nor is his suffering an affair between him and the Father alone. Rather, he includes them. He not only confides his trouble to them but shows them how they have part in it, as sinners and as lovers, for he expresses his trouble as a lover to lovers. He makes them, who are sinners and lovers both, confidants of his inner suffering. He communicates something of his suffering, so that they can also share in the mystery of its fruitfulness. It is, so to speak, an indirect but by no means a merely apparent participation. It is something like a man's being told about his wife's labor pains, so that he knows of them during her difficult time; for the child, after all, belongs to both of them. The woman informs her husband, not in a spirit of accusation, as if he were guilty of her pain, but in order to let him share in the mystery of love that involves them both. Thus too, the disciples are to be initiated into a mystery of the future, for many a fruit of the Cross can be given only when the giver himself has had a share in the Cross. It would be too late if the disciples were to recognize the Cross and its effect only after the suffering were past. They are to have part in the very begetting of the mystery and trace its whole path. The issue is a personal enlightenment, indeed a consecration: their whole life will be appropriated for this mystery. Thus Catholicism obligates in a wholly different way from a religion that contents itself with the fact and the proclamation of the simple result, the Redemption. The Lord's religion is also universal in demanding the whole life of the Christian, hour by hour, and not just its happy conclusion in a "good death". In everything the Christian does, he must know of the mystery of redemption. The Lord wants to see his life being lived out immediately. For him who can see it, this also implies the immediate obligation to seek the religion of participation as represented by the Catholic Church of Christ.

In these words of the Lord a kind of communion of life becomes visible, in and along with the sacramental Communion that the Lord institutes at this Last Supper. He sees the community of sinners and gives them a share in the community of his life and suffering. This word does not contain the institution of the sacramental community as much as it does the community of saints. This community begins in the distress in which the Lord not only sees a betrayer before him, but sees him as *one of you*. All the disciples have experienced the foot-washing together, all sit together with the Lord and Judas at table and all see the Lord's distress. The character of Judas is stamped as one of the community. It is because of this community character that he attracts the Lord's gaze. And we too would be much less shaken, moved and disturbed by the betrayal if Judas were not one of us, if he did not have everything in common with us. Thus, with this observation, the Lord wants to include us and touch us even more, by giving us a share in his distress—he who stands in the middle between God and mankind, wholly pure and wholly betrayed, sacrificing and yet sacrificed, loving and yet led to the Cross.

13:22. *The disciples looked at one another, having no idea of whom he spoke.*

When the disciples look over one another, they are looking for the betrayer. Each one looks for him in another, and none but Judas thinks that it could be himself. For the others the tangible dimension of their fellowship in sin is not yet present. They do not yet sense that they are in it together and are coresponsible. They still behave pharisaically in the face of their own sin. Each one thinks: Whoever it is, is essentially different from me. They feel as though they are the Lord's friends and do not even know that they share the guilt of his death. They in no way

45

suspect what it means to sit together at the same table with the Lord and his betrayer—what consequences and demands that involves. They see in their sin something wholly personal, closed off and private. They do not yet know that every sin always reaches out into the community as well. And they do not know this at the very moment in which the Lord is about to institute the sacrament of community-in-him. It is high time for the Eucharist to appear and restore true community at last, for they still think that what they have done, their sin, is easily understandable and can be settled between them and God; its essence and its effect are confined to the personal sphere. It has nothing to do with the others, because they are not affected by it. Every person has his own area, his limited, recognizable sin. Therefore they look at each other to find out if one of them bears the mark of this particular sin of betrayal. Yet the Lord's word has already made an end to all that. In indicating Judas, he has also uncovered a community of sin. By revealing the impossibility of a purely private sphere of sin, he has created the prerequisite for the Eucharist. But the apostles notice nothing yet of this transformed situation. Each one considers himself a disciple and witness of faith, not suspecting how weak he is in fidelity.

13:23. *One of his disciples lay on Jesus' breast, the one whom Jesus loved.*

Everything that happens here is full of incomprehensible leaps. Thus it is strange that John mentions something new just now. For in doing this, he places himself in a completely different relationship to the Lord from that of the other disciples. The others are still wholly caught up in themselves, enclosed in their own spheres; now they are gradually becoming disturbed and opened up. Perhaps they will soon begin to grasp something and be led more deeply, through the mystery of the Eucharist, into the world of suffering and love. John, on the contrary, rests on Jesus' breast. He is sheltered there; since he already rests on this breast, he no longer needs to walk the path that the others have to walk. He knows only one thing, and it fills his whole soul: the Lord loves him, and he lets himself be loved by the Lord. That is the single content of his life; that is his office.

It is almost as if John, in this resting on the Lord's breast, no longer even needs expressly to report the institution of the Eucharist. The

Lord's love is so real for him, so substantial and all-embracing, that everything is included in it, even its sacramental sign. John possesses this deepest intimacy with the Lord, being allowed to lean his head on his breast. He embodies love; he is love; he needs basically no other form of love, no expression, no detour—everything is already so fulfilled that it could hardly be intensified. He loves the Lord so much that he leaves the sacramental union with the Lord to the others, without envy. This is a mystery, a mystery of generosity. John's love for the Lord begins even before the Eucharist, whereas the others are truly fired to this love only through the Eucharist. If someone had to give presents to a list of friends whose number was greater by one than the number of gifts, the giver would pass over the person he loves most, because that person would least need this testimony of love. He is already fulfilled and informed by love. As soon as love for the Lord is really there, communion with him is also already present. This does not imply any neglect or omission of sacramental Communion. John too will eat the Lord's bread and drink his chalice, but he possesses the fruits of this meal even before he partakes of it. The hierarchical Church, for which the sacraments were instituted and which is their steward, does not exclude the Church of love, with its immediate contact between loving souls and the Lord.

Why does the Lord permit this uttermost sign of love: resting on his breast? Is it because he himself is a man? Or is it because John is a lover? Both reasons are valid. The Lord is human, and every human being needs tangible love. The Lord will soon renounce every love, will be completely forsaken by every love. So he must receive the most complete love—possible in the most complete purity—in order later to be able to be deprived of it to the core. He allows himself this love, he experiences and savors it, knowing that it will be that much more frightful afterward not to have it anymore. But John, too, may savor his love for the Lord. He too will miss it afterward, but what he has experienced will allow him to find this love again—according to the Lord's commission—in love for his brothers. Through it he has become more capable of loving and of finding the Lord's substance again in others.

But neither the Lord's love nor John's has a purpose at this moment. Although the purposes of love are fulfilled, love rests entirely in itself, is simply loving love, having its own meaning in itself. John symbolizes love, as Peter does office. Both were called at the very beginning. Since then, Peter has been singled out in many respects, but here John is clearly given preference. It shows that such love for the Lord really exists, and that it takes this form. This is made evident to all, without the others feeling set aside. For John embodies the love of all. He is love becoming visible. One sees in him what love is. The Lord condescends to this form of love's expression so that the others will recognize love in it. He does not embrace all of them by turns. He also bestows an office of love. This office is frequently hard to grasp or is evident only to a few, because often it has no external deeds to show. Only love can see and understand it.

Here John is at the same time the first priest, and, as such, an incitement to love. He shows that the priestly office, far from excluding the office of love, rather has love as its center. As long as a priest does not venture to lay his head on the Lord's breast, his love is not yet completely given. What John, the model, does is perfect self-giving in love, resting in love, in a love that is not continually doing and demanding, but ultimately is simply love and rests as love.

John also represents masculine love without the slightest trace of disorder; the love between men who share the same orientation in their work and tasks, looking in the same direction, but then turning at times to each other and resting with each other, beyond office and work. The Lord wants us to seek and see not only restless intensification in love; he wants us to find the fulfilment of love as well. We should allow ourselves this time of fulfilment and not distort the growth and the always-more of Christian life into a kind of athletic achievement. This generosity, which gives itself time and takes a break, is likewise masculine.

13:24. *Simon Peter beckoned to him to ask Jesus whom he meant.*

Characteristically, John is entrusted with this commission by the representative of the official Church. In conversation with the Lord, too, he is always love, and only love may question the Lord. For whoever does not love has no access to the Lord and neither the will nor the commission to question him.

The commission to question extends from what is most personal to what is most objective. One can ask the Lord what one personally does not know or cannot do, things that at first only have sense and meaning for the questioner. But one can also question at another's bidding, finally even at the Lord's bidding, because it is important to the Lord that he be asked. John's question to the Lord will be asked in the name of and at the bidding of the Church. The official Church does not ask on her own, but rather has the question asked. She has particular concerns prayed for; she recommends certain questions and anxieties to the prayer of the faithful. The ones to whom she leaves these things are the lovers. Everything that the Church wants from God always passes through love. Even the most official things—a Council, a definition—are mediated only through love.

The Lord posed a problem: *One of you will betray me.* The Church, the community, cannot be indifferent to this. She must deal with the question. But it will not do for every member of the Church to seek his own solution. The head of the community sums up the Church's question and gives it to the lover, who communicates it. That is his office. He exists in order to accept these commissions. All who really believe have this office, yet it is often more especially represented by a particular group of the faithful—for example, by a convent, in which one has the religious pray for an intention, and within the convent, or in the world perhaps, by a certain person who rests on the Lord's breast and passes on the question. The Church can ask nothing of the Lord except in love, regardless of what the content of the request might be; from the most public to the most private concerns, everything passes through love. Certainly, the more a person belongs to the Church, the more his question will be no longer a private one but an ecclesial question, expressing the Church's interests. The lover's conversation with the Lord cannot be a private conversation, for the lover, through love, will let himself be deprived of his rights more and more in order to become an instrument of the Lord and of the Church. He will increasingly conform his thoughts and concerns to the thoughts and concerns of the Church. The Church will of course leave those who love every freedom to formulate their prayer and their questions according to the impulse of their love. But she turns to the lovers, who lean their head on the Lord's breast, expecting the Church's concerns to be best presented through them.

Peter only *beckons.* He does not even say his request aloud. In the life of the Church, not everything can be expressed in laws and paragraphs and edicts. And prayer, especially, needs a free space. But for John a motion from Peter suffices, for as a lover he possesses the true ecclesial attitude of "feeling with the Church". He understands the gesture and needs no express commission. In this beckoning from one disciple to another, genuine and love-filled freedom within the Church becomes evident. Everyone who senses such a beckoning in the Church must cooperate. When one person in the Church will not pray with her, the whole Church lacks something. Every Christian should also sense the agreeability and wholesomeness of the ecclesial air, this living atmosphere, this quiet, spiritual configuration that is the opposite of a rigid form. All forms of prayer exist not only to be simply prayed in the spirit of the Lord, but also to be used freely and creatively and translated into one's personal life. They are themes on which the praying person may play his variations; they are occasions of love.

13:25. *He then inclined on Jesus' breast and said to him: Lord, who is it?*
True prayer in the Church consists in inclining oneself lovingly to the Lord. The Catholic prays neither standing nor sitting, but, rather, inclined to the Lord. He can do so because he already rests on Jesus' breast. This movement of the apostle is a pure mystery of tenderness. He builds himself a nest in the Lord's heart. He dares to approach and bend over the Lord, because he has true humility, which does not strain away from the Lord, but enters into him: a humility that turns away from itself and loses itself completely in the Lord. To kneel before the Lord, lost in the mystery of his love, is something so radiant, so blinding, that no greater happiness can be conceived. John is in fact overjoyed to be permitted to hand over to the Lord's love a commission of the Church. In this happiness he senses the Lord's greatness on approaching him; he makes himself smaller in order to be nearer to him. In the shadow of his greatness he can pray almost as if extinguished, almost impersonally. He inclines, not because he is such a miserable sinner, but because the Lord is so great and good. He inclines, not in order to lower himself, but so that God will be greater. He has the love that does not reflect, that measures no distances, but simply senses the glory of the Beloved. It is in no way a

simply supernatural happiness that floods him: it captivates him, entirely and simply, in all his senses. Nor is it intoxication, but rather absolutely pure humility, in which the disciple does as he has been commissioned and asks the Church's question. He is not in a luxurious ecstasy in which he no longer knows what is going on around him. He is completely alert to Peter's beckoning, and he wants to obey in love, to fulfill his mission as mediator between the Church and the Lord. In doing so, he forgets himself, is not aware of himself. He is like a child who brings his concerns before an adult without a trace of self-consciousness or claim to personal importance. He need not make any effort in order to be aware of himself, for he lives immediately and naively in love.

Because he does so, the others receive the right to imitate him and share his feelings. They are surprised, certainly, that such intimacy is possible. But because it is possible, it is not closed to them, for love knows no exclusivity; all are invited to take part in its mysteries. This participation occurs in the Eucharist. All the disciples see its essence first in the relationship between the Lord and John; through this look, they themselves are suddenly drawn into love, and in its light they suddenly see the meal they are having as a banquet of the Lord's love.

With John, we experience for the first time a fully immediate conversation with the Lord: from love to love. Here therefore, for the first time, the Lord responds directly to the question posed him. To love's question he gives love's response, a very clear, conclusive response. It is as if, in John's love, the Lord receives the disciples' love for the first time in complete mutuality. That is Eucharist.

13:26. *Jesus answered: He it is, to whom I shall give this morsel when I have dipped it. So he dipped the morsel, took it and gave it to Judas, the son of Simon Iscariot.*

The Lord now openly says who will betray him, and he does it at the moment in which he hands the bread that embodies him to Judas. Thus John's love and Judas' betrayal stand at opposite poles, to the right and left of the one and only self-giving love of the Lord. To this one love, which gives itself, correspond the extremities of human receptivity. A man can receive as lover and as betrayer. Both representatives of these utter extremes are united at the one table of the Lord.

The love that questions is basically unconcerned about the answer. John, to whom the answer is given, is so captivated by love that he passes on the answer meant for all, without holding onto it for himself. He embodies all those whose love is simply in the Lord's hands, who love and suffer with him without troubling themselves anymore about their destiny. Yet it is love that must learn that it is the betrayer who sits at table together with the Lord. The lovers are there to catch the lash of the answer. If they were not lovers, this lash would not be given them. The more they love, the more they will suffer, but their love will always be greater than their suffering.

As the disciple's love inclines over the Lord's love, it asks the Lord to give and say everything he wants to give and say. But the Lord gives the disciple what is most heinous to him, for love always wants to share. So it will receive this hateful thing in love, but perhaps the time will come when it sees only what is heinous and no longer senses love. Then its inclining over the Lord will become dryness, disgust, blindness and suffering—so greatly will it be overwhelmed by the Lord's answer, by the betrayal.

The Lord dips the morsel that he gives to Judas. After this action the morsel looks different than it looked before. The Lord transforms it into something belonging to him, bearing signs of his having taken possession of it. It is the sensible sign of transubstantiation. The actual transubstantiation is not seen: we only believe in it and love it, and we see it only with the eyes of faith and love. But the first transubstantiation had to be expressed in this sensible way. The Eucharist itself is to be considered already instituted. The Synoptic Gospels have described it phase by phase. John, who rests in the very heart of love, who sees only the unity of love, perhaps did not even see its phases individually. He sees everything from within, as it were, where it no longer matters what happened before or after.

The Lord hands the morsel, thus transformed, to Judas. The disciple of love mentions only the Communion of the betrayer. But in this one, who is *one of you,* all are included. All are present at this scene. All are called disciples of the Lord: those who follow him and those who will betray him. The Lord has washed the feet of all and because of this washing has conceded them the right to be present at his meal. All are to be redeemed, and they are not now judged according to their degree of sinfulness. Just as he dies for all, he also institutes the Eucharist for all. Indeed, the Eucharist itself is the beginning of the Passion, which is suffered precisely for sinners, the evil ones and the betrayers. It is for the worst that he will suffer most, and therefore the meal is prepared for them as well. Judas is merely the most extreme case and is therefore particularly mentioned. The cornerstones, as it were, are laid: the Lord's love for John, which is a mutual love, and the Lord's love for Judas, which remains one-sided. The *Lord, I am not worthy* is fully true in Judas and only hinted at in John.

Judas is *the son of Simon Iscariot*. With this characterization he is placed, inserted into the framework of human society. He stands as one of the many in this society and is not conspicuous for being particularly demonic. He is related to all the rest of humanity through both his betrayal and his Communion.

13:27. *And after the morsel, Satan entered into him. Jesus said to him: What you do, do quickly.*

Satan's coming into him—and after his Communion at that—is the consequence of his unworthy reception. But this reception is unworthy because Judas let his feet be washed without giving up his design of betrayal. Betrayal runs rampant in him, while he outwardly appears to surrender. He lets himself be fed by the one whom he firmly intends to betray. His not having faith, and nevertheless acting as though he possessed it, opens the way for Satan. A Communion is a confession of faith; the consummated betrayal consists in someone's receiving the Lord's bread knowing that he wants no part of the Lord. If the person were in the grip of a spiritual struggle or in doubt, everything would be different. But he receives in a state of clear rejection. It would be less evil to reject the Lord by not receiving him. But this is the worst: to reject him in receiving him.

The Lord knew that everything would turn out this way. He does not oppose Satan. Rather, he confirms: *What you do, do quickly.* Now is not the time to fight against Satan, for the Lord knows that suffering is now impending, and he sees the whole action of the battle there. He will fight everything out by himself. He is almost impatient, waiting to be permitted to prove his love to the Father. For Judas, too, he wishes everything to be over soon, so that his sin will not be too drawn out and extended. For himself, he wishes the deed to take place; for Judas, that it take place soon. In spirit he sees him after the deed, and therefore speaks a word of love to him. A person pregnant with the intent and will to commit a sin, steering all his thinking and doing toward this act, is in a worse state than one who has already committed the deed, has it behind him and to whom the possibility of conversion opens. Jesus does not even confront Satan or enter into a discussion of Judas' sin. Neither stands at the center now. Only the beginning of the suffering is important. The battle and the discussion are contained in the suffering itself and do not need Judas. Neither are up for negotiation now. Only his mission of suffering is important. The battle and the discussion, contained in the suffering itself, no longer need to be expressly mentioned. But the Lord's suffering is initiated by the betrayal, which is perpetrated precisely in the hour of his most complete self-giving.

13:28. *None of those at the table understood why he said this to him.*

The other disciples are living as if in a fog. At this point they are not at all capable of understanding what they are experiencing. The events transcend by far their ability to comprehend them. To be sure, each of them already has office, but in such an incipient state that he cannot and does not want to appreciate its implications. Each of them believes to some extent, but to believe fully and to scan the whole world of faith is withheld from him for the present. None of them understands, and none of them even tries to understand. In making special mention of this, John is describing the Christian's perpetual situation before the Lord. It is always the same: the Lord is the focal point of an event that he himself establishes, and to which those who love him are never equal. And this at the most active moment of the Passion: when Satan takes possession of Judas. Christians never know what is going on in the Church at the moment, what the Lord is doing in her, what is really happening. Yet they ought to know or suspect it. John's word contains a genuine and important accusation. We act as if we always knew everything exactly, but we know everything only theoretically. We do not put ourselves at the disposal of what we know and thus have no *experience* of it. Knowledge and experience ought to be one in us. We form a unity out of faith and knowledge on the one hand, and out of faith and love on the other. But between the two there is a gaping chasm. We fail to build a bridge between theory and praxis. We ourselves ought to be this bridge, but we rebel against this. Therefore we never understand, in the end, what we ought to understand, and we fail where we ought to create a unity between the receptive and productive, the contemplative and active dimensions in all the situations and possibilities of our life.

The disciples' noncomprehension is even more serious since they have already asked and received an answer. The answer was absolutely clear, and yet they did not grasp it. They do not want to let themselves be attuned to the Lord's way of thinking. They are always asking questions, but they always misunderstand the answer. On the one hand, they hold themselves up as if they were the measure of things; on the other hand, when the Lord addresses them, they refuse to be taken seriously as this measure. They expect to be maintained by the Lord somehow, but they themselves want to contribute nothing to this maintenance. They want to be courted, but they will not guarantee to make a resolve and accept his courting. They reserve for themselves the right to be distracted as well. Perhaps they would prefer to say nothing at all, but they expect their partner to show all his cards. They resemble those converts who gladly let themselves be taught during instruction and are eager to know everything, but everything remains without obligation; they reserve for themselves the right to withdraw again. They are interested; they have a need for stimulation. But scarcely have they posed a question, when they are already only half-interested in the answer. Again and again they circle around the life of the Church from the outside, but they do not want to be thrown into the center at any price: into the Lord's life and the mystery of the Cross. They relate every mystery to themselves: this one attracts them, it speaks to them; the other "says nothing to them" or repels them. They set up an account of pros and cons according to which they evaluate Christianity, the Church, the Lord.

In this lukewarm distraction, the disciples are at the same time witnesses—of their own question and the Lord's answer, witnesses too of the signs of betrayal. The Lord needs witnesses, who ought to live as such. To live as a witness, however, means to live in self-giving, because the truth to which one bears witness is love. But one cannot love theoretically. In order to witness, one would also have to love and therefore have a part in the event.

13:29. *Some believed, because Judas held the purse, that Jesus had said to him: Buy what we need for the feast; or that he should give something to the poor.*

The disciples give the Lord's answer to Judas a perfectly one-sided, earthly meaning, refusing to believe the unearthly aspects of the event. Maintaining their own standards of measurement, they want to judge everything only from their own narrow, personal viewpoints. They do not want to let themselves be surpassed. They have seen how the Lord clearly answered their question by handing Judas the morsel; they have heard what the Lord added in explanation. But they have not believed, for they did not *want* to understand it. They understand exactly as much as they want to understand; therefore they understand amiss. They understand what is purely human. In the Lord's life there are always human elements; they content themselves with these. For a feast one needs all kinds of things; on this material level they do understand. It is good to give alms; they understand the moral aspect as well. They stop at these two elements.

First of all they think about the feast, and in spite of what the Lord has said to them, and although he has been deeply shaken twice before their eyes, they still see it as an amusement. They fail to hear everything else; they do not want to let the feast be spoiled. Judas cares for the money; he has enough to buy something for the feast—that is what captivates their ' thoughts. They have not the slightest idea that they themselves are committing a kind of betrayal by willfully mishearing everything. The Church needs money, and it is quite correct that one person hold the funds and look after the material needs.

The Lord himself has allotted the material aspect its place in the Church and given it its particular meaning. But it is not right for the disciples, who have just communicated, to have their minds on the feast and money. Because they are distracted in this fashion, they cannot hear what the Lord says to them about Judas. In their eyes Judas only embodies their wealth. They are materially and bodily present, but in spirit they

are not with the Lord. They measure everything according to its corpo-
rality and materiality. They relate everything to this standpoint, even the
Lord's words, and therefore they are incapable of placing themselves at
the standpoint of his words. It is not that they do not love the Lord. But
they leave both their love for what is earthly and their love for the Lord
side by side without any connection. They do not venture the leap from
the first to the second. They do not let the second become the standard of
the first. They are thinking about their property, all the while not
knowing that they are the Lord's property. Money exists to be spent, but
they themselves do not want to be spent like money. They want to
remain as they are, untouched. They see in the money, which already
belongs to the Church, its possibilities of use. But they do not see how
they themselves might be used. To them, the Church is only a material
institution; if money rolls in to her, she will be living. They do not see
that they themselves are the living Church. In materializing the Church,
they dematerialize themselves by regarding themselves as a constant
quantity. It would be wiser to dematerialize money by thinking less
about it, and materialize themselves by being with the Lord with their
entire substance. They do not grasp that they themselves need to be
bought for this feast, which will be a feast of pain: that they themselves
could be a gift for the poor by the living love in which they ought to
embody the Church.

They know money and its stamp very well, but they themselves are
not stamped by the Lord; they are not coins in his hand. Money has a
predetermined value, and they should have the value that the Lord gives
them. But they can get this stamp from the Lord only by receiving him
vitally. A simple material presence does not suffice for this: to receive the
stamp really ineradicably, they would have to let themselves be poured
out like fluid into the Lord's form. They know the whole process of
producing money, up to the finished coin. But they do not want to
know about their own development; they think it would be enough to
offer the raw material, when they ought to make themselves available for
the whole process of transformation. In the very moment of offering
themselves, they draw back. They do not want to take the Lord's
novitiate on themselves.

That is the first mistake the disciples make: they know the physical needs of the Church and her need to celebrate and prepare feasts. Even the Christian must have nourishment, and one needs to decorate and spend in order to celebrate worthily the liturgy and other ecclesial functions. Since the Church is adapted to human life, she too has her everyday fare and her feasts. The disciples understand this from their own personal lives, but they confuse the earthly, material life and the life of the Church that is lived in the Lord. Therefore, too, they make the second mistake. They see money's other possible use: one can give it to the poor. They understand this because they know that they themselves might become needy and would be thankful for help in such a situation. They are completely in sympathy with the organization of mutual support and would like best to become completely absorbed in this charitable activity. Thus they substitute morality and the social question for the word of God.

In this momentous mix-up they misunderstand the whole essence of Christian charity, because they do not consider the one fact that the Lord himself assumes the place of a poor man and a beggar among them. Hence, they cannot recognize the Lord in the poor. They overestimate the material meaning of alms in regarding almsgiving as the essential Christian activity. At any moment in which the most essential event—the Lord's Passion—is taking place, they are not with it; thinking about their own human compassion prevents them from noticing what the Lord is pointing out to them. They are so occupied with the social question and with their own plans for reform that they, the Church's official representatives, miss hearing the Lord's decisive word.

Flight, whether into the material or the moral-social sphere, will always remain the direction of the Church's disobedience. In that direction she fails to hear the Lord's word. Both considerations must be silent as soon as the Lord begins to speak. Certainly the Church wants to hear the Lord's word; she asked for it. But when it sounds, she does not listen, because her interest in Judas' purse is greater than in his betrayal.

13:30. *Judas then received the morsel and went out at once, and it was night.*

At the Lord's word, Judas leaves at once. Now he obeys. Certainly he only apparently obeys the Lord; in reality he is following Satan, who possesses him. In the Church, one can indeed act as if one were obedient, and yet follow the devil. One can even be installed in an ecclesiastical office and not be at all concerned about obedience to the Lord. One can do this in such a way that the Church does not even notice it. The disciples think that all is well with Judas.

And it was night. Not the night of the Lord, but the night of Judas, the night of sin. The night of him who willfully turns away from faith, and thereby opens himself to Satan and every evil deed. It is a night that can be confused with day, that can be called day by the sinner. He is able to evaluate it as such. The Lord's night, on the other hand, can never be taken for day by the one who suffers it: for him it is unequivocally night, while for God it is unequivocally day.

The night of sin can be a multiple one. It can be the night of someone who is seeking the Lord, is on his way to the Lord. He knows that he himself is in the night; he feels his night as a night of sin and wants to step over into day. There is also the night of original sin. The unbaptized person living in it is offered a grace from God—baptism. This will help him to attain to the Lord's light, and perception will follow. In order to attain to this, a way through the night will be pointed out to him: he sees, as it were, lamps and lighted houses, by which he can orient himself. Wholly different is the night of him who is content in it. He is sated; he seeks nothing. Therefore he turns the night into day. He feels comfortable within his world and does not want to be disturbed. His night is reality for him. A believer who staked his whole life on the one work of God appears foolish to him. He regards the believer's hope as something completely fantastic, unreal. He laughs at faith. For him, faith would mean something completely different, new, and he does not want that. He rejects all contact with the light. There is the night of him who has turned away from the light. He has a recollection of the light, and he also knows how the light enlivens all contours, brings out all contrasts. Yet he would rather dwell in the night; he finds it delightful to grope.

This sensation gives his personality a markedly heightened importance. He gets everything by feeling and touching. That gives his sin an unbelievable capacity for development. He knows very well that the light is the only thing that could overcome his sin. But he wants to sin. He weighs and balances: light and grace, darkness and sin. He knows both possibilities—the acceptance and the denial of grace. He is also conscious that he cannot calm himself with the thought that grace will find him even in his perdition. Rather, he knows that it would be up to him to open himself and surrender himself to the light. Then again there is also the other chance, that the Lord will perhaps redeem him because of his suffering. So within his night he builds his own theories about the light. Such a person, who has knowingly turned away, often has great influence on others. He can testify to the light; he can recount how he became acquainted with it all and saw through it. After the light disappointed him, his "life experience" began—that the darkness is richer and more enjoyable than the light. Before, when he was still in the Church and had not yet seen through his error, the light still seemed sublime to him. Today he can look back on all that with a smile. Such a person always stands in the center, for himself and for others. Whoever lives in the light tries to make himself insignificant before the Lord. One who lives in the night seeks to make as much of himself as possible. In the night, a person who has surrendered something of his own in order to let another work is regarded as betrayed and poor, whereas the happy man is the one who succeeds in pushing ahead in life. One can always excuse oneself on the grounds that one is only fulfilling a demand of nature, which strives toward development. What else are the instincts for, if not to be satisfied?

In this night the Lord is not present. It is opposed to the light that is the Lord. Judas goes forth to where this light does not penetrate. He goes out into the distance from God, there to carry out his work against the Lord. He goes out of the light only by closing himself to it: one only needs to shut one's eyes in order to declare that it is night. If he opened his eyes, he would immediately see the light. We should not be afraid of letting ourselves be blinded by the Lord's light, even if it should be so strong as to appear like night to us. The human night is a negation of the light; the divine night is its highest affirmation.

WORDS TO THE DISCIPLES

THE COMMANDMENT OF LOVE

13:31–32. *When he was gone, Jesus said: Now is the Son of Man glorified, and God is glorified in him. If God is glorified in him, God will also glorify him in himself, and he will glorify him at once.*

Judas has disappeared into his night. The Lord, who is the light, remains; and the disciples remain, all touched by this light somehow and not trying to interfere with it. To them the Lord now speaks, and he begins: *Now is the Son of Man glorified.* He speaks of his glorification as of an accomplished fact, although his entire suffering is still before him. But it is so much in process that it can no longer be broken off or canceled. This glorification is inerrantly unfolding toward its consummation—so much so that it already exists as attained reality. The betrayal has happened: with this the Passion began, and thus too glorification. Perhaps the Lord could have said that it was the beginning of the Passion and of glorification, and their development would follow. But he does not say this; rather, he represents the present as something completed, because for him it already belongs to what is consummated. He knows for certain that his suffering will glorify him and that God will be glorified through it. For himself, he equates betrayal and glorification, because he knows that when the betrayal occurs, his mission and commission are fulfilled. Included in the betrayal is that which he promised the Father: to love him more than the world betrays him. In the betrayal, what is finally conclusive from now on becomes actual. Hence he feels himself glorified.

And God is glorified in him, because the whole mission came from God, and God's glorification is its goal, and because the mission is fulfilled in this glorification of God through the Son. The Lord sees the completion of his return to the Father included in Judas' betrayal.

If God is glorified in him, God will also glorify him in himself. Father and Son are glorified in and through one another: the Father in the Son through the Son's obedience in suffering; the Son in the Father through the Son's return to glory. This is the arrangement between Father and Son, and now the Lord puts this pact before the disciples' eyes. Deep

63

within he knows, now too as a human being, that everything between him and the Father is the same today as it was the moment when he parted from the Father to come to earth. The love is the same, and the sacrifice he offered is accepted. He is nearer to the Father than ever. He lingers with the Father now, not because of any particular connection—a mission, a sending—but within the glory that is theirs in common. And this precisely in the moment of betrayal. He is pressed to tell the disciples everything, even though, or even because, they comprehend nothing of it. Perhaps they obscurely sense the betrayal; it is in the air. Maybe they suspect danger. If the Lord spoke of it, they would understand him. But he does not speak of it; he speaks only of his glorification. Possibly they were waiting for the Lord to be indignant over having been betrayed. Instead he calms them by showing them the glorification in the betrayal. By so doing, he explodes everything that mankind expects or can humanly endure; he teaches them to turn what is worst into what is most beautiful. The Lord appears to be delivered up, but more than ever he has everything under control. No human being now has the power to insinuate himself into this glorification with a view to impeding it. Everything is consummated in spite of man—indeed, through man's apparent opposition. Whoever sees or suspects the betrayal may not stop at that; rather, he is *at once* drawn in to the divine mutual glorification of Father and Son. For *he will glorify him at once*. The Church sees or suspects Judas' sin; it could be an object of endless, horrified meditation for her. But the Lord does not let her stop there. He shows at once that nothing can hinder his glorification and diverts all attention from the betrayal to the glorification. The Church should learn to consider it a duty immediately to turn her eyes from all the night of betrayal to the light of God's glory.

13:33. *Little children, only a little while will I still be among you. You will seek me, and as I said to the Jews, "Where I go, you cannot come", so I say it now also to you.*

Ever since John leaned on the Lord's breast, all of them have become his little children. He loves them all as one loves small children. He cannot be angry with them now, not even with their lukewarmness and their incomprehension. He attributes all that to their state of childhood.

He considers them not only as children but as his children, and as little ones. He is ready to take a father's responsibility on himself regarding them, to care for them and, above all, to love them totally. He loves all of them; those who have an office and those who still have none. He loves them with a new, incipient love. The Church is still very young; the apostles have not yet done anything for him. Rather, he loves them with the love of the beginning, with the love that he had in the beginning with God, which he knew from the Father and also received from him in the beginning. For in the beginning was love, and here it takes on the color of human tenderness.

He announces to them that he will soon go away. But he binds them at the same time in the unity of childhood. Because they are all his little children, all of them are bound to each other. Regarding the time in which he will still linger with them, he says nothing except that it is short. That leaves them the possibility of finding in themselves the courage to make use of this short remaining time. He leaves them the hope of being able still to love him and prove their gratitude in this short span. He does not separate them from himself by informing them of the coming separation; on the contrary, he draws them closer and more firmly to himself.

Nor does he want to console them completely about his going. He shows them that they will feel a gap, for they will seek him, they will long for him. By the way he spoke to them he showed them his love. Now he also shows them their love for him by *promising* them that they will seek him. So he binds them still more closely to him: not only as loved ones, but as true lovers who will seek him, the Beloved.

And as I said to the Jews, "Where I go, you cannot come", so I say it now also to you. What he said to the unbelievers, he says now to the believers as well. Thus he establishes the distance that will separate him from mankind as a whole. The place to which he will go will be inaccessible to everyone, in spite of faith. Faith has until now allowed them to follow him, to be where he was. But this faith will not suffice to take them where he is going now. The separation is unavoidable: he can do nothing to avert it, nor can they. The place he is going now is a place he chose in his ultimate love for the Father, and it will be the place in which the Father and Son separate and are able to reunite. It is an innermost place of love between Father and Son. The Lord emphasizes this to the believers and lovers at the moment in which he grounds them, as children, in love.

13:34. *A new commandment I give you, that you love one another. As I have loved you, so should you love one another.*

This commandment is new. It is the Lord's personal commandment, issued at the moment in which he was betrayed, and also at the moment in which he promises that they will seek but not find him. He does not exclude himself from their love through this, but rather gives them the possibility of living in him without seeing him. He creates for them a substitute, as it were. But it is more than a substitute, because this commandment is his gift, because he lives in this gift, because the *one another* of this new love proceeds from the *one another* between Father and Son.

Why should we love one another? First of all, simply because the Son of God once dwelt among us as a man who came in love and who was love. Because that happened once on earth. But further, because the Lord lives in each individual. If we cannot love one another because, being sinners, the sin in the Thou resists us, we can still love one another because the Lord lives in the Thou. For he is in each one whom he loves, and he loves everyone. Through his love he makes a place for himself in each one. In his love, then, we can all love one another. He says this to his disciples whom he loves, to this particular, limited circle. But the circle of his followers expands into limitlessness. Yet love may not become indefinite through this expansion. Expansion should also entail the intensifying of the definite and particular, because the requirement of love applies everywhere in an entirely concrete and immediate way.

The measure of this love is his own: *As I have loved you, you should love one another.* His love for us sprang from his love for the Father. Out of precisely the same love, we should love each other: a wholly pure love, which comes through the Son from the Father; a love having the same characteristics as the Son's love for the Father and that is, therefore, extravagant. The love that the Son receives from the Father and returns to him is a totally burning, giving, poured out, consumed love. The love between the children of Christ should have exactly the same form. Even if this love is wholly chaste, it should not burn the less. Nor should it be less universal than the Lord's love for mankind.

The Lord's love stems from the Father. But he also has a Mother. When this Mother accepted the Son and regarded the Father's will as the substance of her life, she loved God with a love of incredible proportions. This love has passed over to the Son: as a small child he learned to know love in this form. Hence, too, the love that the Lord leaves behind for the disciples is completely saturated with the love between Mother and Son. It is also love for her who is their Mother, the Mother's love for them, the disciples' maternal love for each other, feminine openness and devotion in their love of God and feminine self-giving in their love for each other. In the love with which the Lord commissions them, the divine and the human are inseparably mingled. It is love that is heavenly as well as earthly, masculine as well as feminine, but all in the purity of the Lord and therefore without a touch of selfishness.

This love of the Lord for mankind, which he now gives to them, which he received from the Father and the Mother and which in addition bears his own Sonlike traits, his character as Redeemer, is a gratuitous, selfless, everlasting and absolutely constant, persevering love. It loves the person in whatever situation he may find himself. It is independent of acceptability and unacceptability, of goodness or evil, of beauty or ugliness. So also should our mutual love be. It should always be as it is at the beginning, at its first arising, at its source, and never at a later stage, in some psychological process moving toward a natural end in cooling and indifference. Christian love does not distance itself from its beginning: it always remains at the origin, like the love between Father and Son, and between Son and Mother. Here there is no distance and no difference between giving and taking, no alternation between good and bad days, no moods, no misunderstandings, no estrangements. It is precisely this love that the Lord brings as a gift to his disciples and to all men.

It is a love that is ready to take everything on itself, even the Cross. It is perfect not only in origin, but also in its consequences. It is so strong that in its extravagance it has borne and put up with everything. For love of love, everything is suffered. For love there is only one thing: love. It is so precious to itself that any price must be paid for it, and it pays any price for itself. If the Lord should break off his path of suffering at one of the stages, his love would no longer be infinite, no longer final, absolute. But because love is limitless, no limits can be set to suffering.

It is a love that fully renounces itself and therefore bears everything. It bears the whole sin of the world. The love that the Son knows from the Father is a love that knows only love, is born out of love and returns to love and thus ultimately counts on love. The infinite love of the Son is filled out of the infinite love of the Father and pours back into it again. It is no solitary love, but a love living only in mutuality. In order to be able to establish mutuality on earth, love must first clear away all the hindrances blocking the path, by taking them on itself: it must atone for sin through loneliness, forsakenness, fear, shame and death. For love, this is the way to be able finally to attain mutuality in its relationship to mankind, to give love to mankind in such a way that it reciprocates. The Son comes into the world without experience of sin. He is like the child who puts his hand into the fire: he does not know what the fire of sin is, and he must first become bitterly acquainted with its essence in order to taste what the opposite of love is. In this experience he will learn what doubts are. And he will experience betrayal, something he would never have thought possible. From heaven he had anticipated only the great and ravishing aspects of love; all the small and mean aspects of sin, which attacks his love, he could learn only on earth.

The measure of his love is that it takes everything on itself. It does not calculate; it only gives out extravagantly and bears whatever can be borne in the name of love. Love and suffering know no measure and should have none for mankind. To be sure, mankind will never possess them in their true infinity. Love remains a commandment, but mankind should have this star over it. It should live oriented toward love, into love. It should also let itself be increasingly drawn, through the Lord, into the Lord's love, which has no measure anymore, which spends itself wholly and bears everything.

The Lord issues his commandments without limitations. No one has ever been able to stop along this path and say "enough!" Because the Lord's love and suffering are limitless, every standard of measurement for our love is wrested from us. We can never set up a relation between the measure of his love and his suffering, and what we set about achieving by way of love and suffering. The prototype of love is limitless, and so too the demands on it remain limitless. Because the Lord sets no limits for himself, he also sets none for us. Eternally he has the right to expect *more,* for he himself is eternally *more.* Because he uses a comparison in his commandment: *As I have loved you, you should love one another,* one might be tempted to understand this as a measure, as his measure. But his measure is that he has no measure.

The disciples who hear this commandment are surely very disconcerted and astonished at this demand of the Lord. They would never have dreamed of anything like this. They would have expected that their talents, their manly characteristics and capabilities would be claimed and used. And now the whole content of their lives is to be nothing other than love? This is outrageous; it is scarcely possible. Indeed, it is really a new, hitherto unheard-of commandment.

13:35. *By this all will recognize that you are my disciples, if you have love for one another.*

Even before the Lord's appearance, there were people who loved each other: husband and wife, parents and children, friend and friend, but it was not possible to read a way to the Son in this love. Not every love shows that it bears a relation to the Son. Because he establishes a *new* love, a love without measure and limit that knows only one direction— toward God—his disciples will be able to be differentiated from other lovers by this new criterion and recognized by this characteristic as his disciples. The gratuitousness of their love, which they have received from him and possess, will be the sign that their love is his love and that hence they are his disciples. This will not be apparent primarily because they proclaim that they love the Lord, or because of their deeds that testify to the Lord; but on the basis of their love that they feel *for each other,* it will be evident to whom they belong. This commandment, so distinguished by its limitlessness and its exorbitance that the uninitiated cannot even acknowledge it as a commandment, will suffice to show to everyone, *even* the uninitiated, that they belong to the Lord. In giving this commandment, the Lord opens up an infinite perspective: on the one hand, he gives the disciple his own love with which to love his neighbor unlimitedly; on the other hand, he bestows his limitless love just as directly on this neighbor, so that he may know he is unlimitedly loved by him; and finally, to the third person who observes this, even if he is unbelieving, he gives the possibility of recognizing in this limitlessness that it is the Lord and no mere human being who stands behind this love.

In using the comparison "as", the Lord has taken our love into the measure and mode of his own. We should love, not "as" we ourselves tend to love, but "as" he loves; not for the sake of earthly and external characteristics and advantages: beauty or elegance or cleverness or goodness. Rather, we should regard the beloved thou with the Lord's eyes and love. In this way, he robs our love of a certain limited and earthly mode of loving that lies in the purely human realm, in order to give us his infinite mode in its place. In robbing us of every purely human love, he makes us in our love more incomprehensible to a third person who faces the Lord as a stranger. He will always assume that we love our neighbor for the sake of some characteristic attached to him, and yet he will perceive that that cannot be the final meaning of Christian love. He will at least acknowledge that, in Christian love, earthly values receive an entirely different meaning and place. They are not devalued, but somehow they are drawn into the supratemporal, heavenly realm. They no longer awake and find love as such, but are only something in which an already existing love expresses itself, and of which it remains, in the end, independent. In the Cross everything worldly can burn away without the Lord's love suffering the slightest damage: beauty and spirit, power and even life, everything can disappear without love starting to waver. If temporal goods and values are bestowed, they are used to express love. If they are withdrawn, love makes their withdrawal an occasion for higher and still purer love.

In the end, the "as" implies the impossibility of a differentiation between love for God and love for neighbor. The Lord himself loves and suffers without differentiation between the Father and mankind. He no longer differentiates and cannot even differentiate, for the Father's commission has mankind as its content. So it is with us: we love—and perhaps love while suffering—God and man, undifferentiatedly. The unity of our love and its original source are the Lord's commandment: we never love under our own commission, but always under the Lord's. Only thus are we guaranteed the possibility of loving as he loved.

13:36. *Simon Peter said to him: Lord, where are you going? Jesus answered: Where I am going you cannot follow me now, but later you will follow me.*

Here Peter no longer asks by making a detour via John; he turns directly to the Lord. For slowly his commission is clarifying within him: he knows that he himself must get to know the Lord's path. Therefore he asks about the "where". This question implies no empty curiosity, but a need. It dawns on him that what he embodies must walk the path of the Lord. He surmises more than knows it, but he acts as if he had a kind of foreknowledge of it. When betrayal was the issue, Peter let John ask the question. Here, he himself must take over the whole process of originating and putting the question. He comprehends that it has something to do with him. He knows that neither the Lord nor the Church can stop along the way. What has been set, established and begun is only a beginning that cannot rest on itself: it requires an ongoing path. The two paths—of the Lord and of the Church—will not be without similarity and parallelism. The Church will walk its path as community and institution, but surrounded and illumined by the Lord's path. Therefore Peter must know this path.

The Lord answers: *Where I am going, you cannot follow me now.* Not now, because the Lord goes before the Church. He is not only the Church's signpost, but her leader and pathfinder: he walks the path, preparing and lighting it with his light. When he characterized himself earlier as the light, he did so in reference to all mankind. Here he is the light of the Church. In saying "not now, not yet", he shows the distance between himself and the Church. He is the Lord who goes forward alone, and he needs this distance just as the light needs it in order to illuminate. This does not imply any separation or remoteness, but a leaving of room so that the light can shine. Man should always have the Lord's "always-more" before his eyes, even in the distance of time. There is no assimilation between the Lord and the Church, but only the relationship of following.

But later you will follow me. These words have a double meaning. Peter personally will have a path to walk that is like the Lord's path. This may be a consolation and an encouragement for him at the moment. But just as clearly, the Lord sees in Peter the Church as a whole. He knows how much of his path of suffering she too will have to walk. Without his suffering the Church will not develop, but in developing she will receive the power to suffer. His example is first of all a source of strength, which in turn imparts the possibility of discipleship.

Now, none of the disciples has the power to suffer properly. They have it neither as individuals nor as a community. This power is now very limited in them; it still lies within the limits of their personal character and destiny. It will be expanded and configured to their mission only in following the Lord. But this becomes possible only when the Lord goes before with his example, and the one commissioned to suffer sees in this example how he is to suffer. His suffering can be a superhuman one; as sufferer he can be overtaxed, not only with respect to his feelings, but in reality. Yet he will never be alone on this path of discipleship; the suffering he receives is given him by the Lord out of the treasure of his own Passion. Even incapacity, failure, being completely overtaxed, stem from this treasure. If the disciples were to be overtaxed in this way *now,* while still within their small personal destinies, it would drive them to suicide. For when a human being can do no more, he sets an end. But when they are overburdened *later,* their being overtaxed flows into that of the Lord. They are taken into it. They are caught up in it, lifted up into it. Here there is no end, and no being-let-fall. In the *Now* their power to suffer would be entirely finite and exhausted at once, but in the *Later* it will be infinite, because the boundary of their "no more" is overstepped, not into emptiness, but into the infinity of the Lord's suffering. Here lies the meaning of the strict prohibition of suicide in the Church: no despair of life can be more profound than the Lord's weariness on the Cross. There exists an indissoluble contradiction between faith and suicide.

13:37. *Peter said to him: Lord, why can I not follow you now? I would give my life for you.*

Peter, who senses all this only very unclearly, is becoming impatient. He knows nothing yet about the patience of faith. He has only the impatience of faith, the impatience of one who wants to attain a limited measure of faith, established by himself. But he does not know the patience of one who leaves everything to the Lord in faith. He has noticed that the Lord has often pressed a point: with Martha; with the Jews who were to walk in his light; with Judas, who was to carry out his work quickly. Peter presumes perhaps that to be a Christian and to press forward are the same thing. He does not see that the Lord holds the measure in his hand, and that he can also wait and let others wait.

Besides, Peter recognizes neither his personal limits nor those of the Church. He is somehow *anxious* about the office that has been given to him. He imagines that it must become visible now, and he wants to be able soon to put on a tangible performance. He is shocked at being rejected, for, after all, he wants to *give up* his *life* for the Lord. He does not lie in saying this. He will actually do it. Yet there is something untrue in what he says, because he does not consider what a grace of the Lord it is to be allowed in spite of everything to give up one's life for him. He who is not *now* able to give the Lord his daily life in patience will yet be made worthy to give it to him *later*. Peter is thinking only of physical death, and he still does not see the greater thing: to be allowed to *live* his life for the Lord, to receive it from the Lord day by day, in order to give it back to him just as often. He thinks that this resolve to give up his life is something difficult, but surely something uniquely limited. He does not see that something much more difficult is included in this offer: to give his life to the Lord continually, without interruption. And yet he means well. The truth that he expresses has something at once manly and touching about it. He believes that he wants to give up his life for the Lord, to give the highest he possesses. Only later will he grasp that it is still more to live, dying, for the Lord, in order finally to die for him, living.

13:38. *Jesus responded: Your life you will give for me. Truly, truly I tell you, the cock will not have crowed before you will have denied me three times.*

The Lord's word—*your life you will give for me*—represents both a statement and a question, the fact that Peter will give his life as well as the fact that he does not want to do it. In this second sense, the sentence is an astonished and painful question. Both feelings exist simultaneously in the Lord: acknowledgment of the Christians' path of suffering, and pain at their lighthearted claim that they are able to follow him, when they will still deny him. The second will occur first, and therefore the Lord must first humiliate Peter, and with him the Church. He announced Judas' betrayal only in a very general and veiled manner, not exposing the betrayer. Peter, on the other hand, is exposed without restraint, very openly and dryly, as the denier. It is a prophecy: a small one that refers to Peter and a large one that includes all Christianity.

The Lord, who is love, knows no leniency here. Peter is a "saint" certainly, but that will not hinder him from denying the Lord three times. The Lord does not overlook the mistakes even of his saints. He reveals precisely this sin of Peter's, in front of the whole Church and for the whole Church. To those who want to be with him he will always clearly say where their mistake lies, where their denial occurs. He expiates and covers the sin of mankind, but at the same time he enables them, in his love, to become acquainted with their sin in order to repent and confess it. He creates this possibility of recognizing sin first in Peter, the head of the Church, and thus creates in him the prerequisite for hearing confessions—that of having a grasp of the mistakes of others and of seeing them, in the love of the Lord, as sins. Through Peter he gives this possibility to each one who serves the Church as Peter does. He says it only after he has affirmed to Peter: *Your life you will give for me.* This word contains no scorn, but rather the Lord's gratitude, his love and acknowledgment of Peter and of all Christians and also his pain over their denial.

Every aberration of the Church's members is included here; they live for the Lord and yet deny him. Both of these are truth; both happen. It is no accident that it is Peter who will deny and who will be charged with the sin for which the Lord will have to suffer. For him, for the head of the Church, the Lord will have to atone in a special way. The Church, which is something holy, which is the bride of the Lord, must know about this betrayal and this denial; she must perpetually live in the awareness that she is mentioned very emphatically at the beginning of the Passion.

The cock crows at a certain time. And Peter will deny at a certain time, within this short span. He will do so three times; he will persist in his sin. He will not be able to say, either as an individual or as a disciple of the Lord or as head of the Church, that he denied only accidentally, fleetingly and inadvertently. He will deny, deny again and once more deny. The repetition implies confirmation, insight into it and will to do it. His guilt will be an unmistakable one. It will certainly not be a premeditated sin. But he could think ahead now, so as to avoid it later. He does not think of it now, and therefore he will not think of it later. He is so convinced of being a good disciple that he mishears even the Lord's word, which shows him the pit into which he will fall. He wants to be the stronger one; he wants to affirm *his* claim, bask in *his* devotion and savor *his* love—so much so that, incomprehensibly, he misses the Lord's warning. It is by no means a case of Peter's being unable to act otherwise, just because the Lord had foretold his fall. Not at all! Rather, the Lord merely foresees his disciple's free, unpardonable sin. Never will Christians be able to refer to the Lord's prophecy as an excuse for themselves: the Lord's warning only underlines their guilt.

This situation is very strange: the Lord has administered confession and instituted Communion; he has cleansed Peter and united him with himself, like the others. So Peter is clean. He has the will to walk the path of the Lord; he is already in office, he is already representing the Lord and he has the assurance that he may do so. Yet he still has the denial before him. Although he does not intend to do it, he knows that the Lord has told him he will do it. He should know himself capable of this sin. But he thinks he is incapable of precisely *this* sin that the Lord has shown him. There he stands in this twilight, along with the whole Church: in the fullness of purification by the Lord, he is still, by his own act, the denier. In her infallibility given by the Lord, the Church is again and again, by her own act, the failing one. Certainly it will always be possible to distinguish between office and person. Officially, Peter is infallible; as a person he can make mistakes. But when was the Church ever permitted to conceive her office impersonally? When was she released from the obligation to place her whole person at the disposal of office? And when did the personal not influence the official? When did personal sin not damage office and lame the power of its mission? And all this applies not only to the highest peak of the hierarchy and its particular infallibility, for the whole Church took part in the foot-washing and the Eucharist and was cleansed there from all guilt. Every priest embodies, in his office, the Lord. Omnipresent, from the humble curate up to the Pope, the same requirement applies: to make office and person coincide. Yet in the Lord's word both the question and the promise are inexorably included: *Your life you will give for me.* This is something the Church is to do; she will fail to do it, and yet through the Lord's grace she will be empowered to do it.

WAY, TRUTH, LIFE

14:1. *Let not your heart be troubled. Believe in God and believe in me.*

The Lord turns anew to his disciples, endeavoring to encourage them. They should not let themselves be troubled by what is coming. Still, what is coming will contain much that can trouble them; much that can awaken doubt, fear, disbelief, anxiety and horror in them. It will contain everything that might take them away from the Lord, for it could become too difficult for them to remain with the Lord. But the Lord says: *Let not your heart be troubled.* Let it remain strong and become strong. They will necessarily be terrified, but they must not regard these things as terrible. Even when everything around will be in a state of maximum disturbance and horror, they should preserve supreme peace, which is capable of everything, even of understanding the utter night that surrounds them as a work of God, indeed as his most radiant work.

Therefore he recommends faith to them: *Believe in God and believe in me.* For only in faith will they be able to experience, live through and master what is coming. For this they will need none other than the faith that stems from love—to be specific, faith in God and faith in the Son. He separates the two for the first time. Until now he has always let the current of faith flow from the Father through himself and back to the Father. He mentioned himself only as one element within this single faith in the Father. Now he separates, because the separation is coming, the separation of the Cross. And he would like them to suffer this separation with him. But they should not suffer through it as though they were forsaken, for only *he* is to be forsaken in this space of time between his departure and his return. They, on the other hand, during this time of his forsakenness, should believe in the God whom he described to them: in the Father of the Son, and their Father, in the God of the Covenant whom they know and in the God of love whom he has proclaimed to them. They should believe while he himself will not be able to believe anymore. At the same time they should believe in him, who comes from the Father and is going to the Father and who *has been* their brother. In suffering, he does not want them to believe in him as their present brother, for in suffering he wants, in love, to be separated from them. During this time they should believe in him as the Son of God, how he lived among them, how he left them an example in his life, how he taught them and was one with his teaching. Thus should they see him and thus believe in him. In the separation they should not see him as trinitarian, or as what he will become: the one forsaken by God. Their faith should be completely objectified, for they should not let their hearts be troubled in the separation. He requires of them now an almost intellectual faith, which cannot be shaken by anything. They should be manly enough to stand beside the Cross and only believe; the whole teaching that they draw from this sight of the Cross should serve for nothing else than the strengthening of their faith. From the Cross he will not be able to impart any more teaching to them. Therefore he instructs them now as to how they are to behave then. Now he excludes everything that might be love, compassion, anxiety or doubt. He wants only one thing: to confirm their faith. He instructs them now, because now he is still capable of it; for when he himself will be immersed in the night's overtaxing he will no longer be able to tell them these things.

Not by chance does he mention faith in God first of all. He does not know now how much power will remain to him on the Cross to encourage them and strengthen their faith in him. Therefore he puts the Father first. Even if their faith in him, the Lord, should be shaken, faith in the Father must in any case remain unshakable. Faith in the Father may under no circumstances be drawn into his fall. Even should they notice something of their own darkness and his forsakenness, their faith in the Father may in no case be darkened. Let the Father's greatness remain inviolate in them, whatever may happen between Father and Son; let it remain inviolate even when the Son's own greatness sinks into the night. Thus he now carefully separates faith in God and faith in himself, so that the Father's honor may suffer no damage through his Passion.

14:2. *In the house of my Father there are many dwellings. If that were not so, I would have told you. For I go to prepare a place for you.*

The Father disposes together with the Son over these dwellings in the Father's house. In the final disposal, both are one. It is he who has really sought who will enter. No one will find the dwelling if he did not work for it. Such a man works for it, seeks it, because he wants to be with the Father. Thus he knows the Father, and if he knows him and desires to be with him, he also loves him. For those, then, who love the Father, these dwellings are there—for all who love him, without differentiation. Yet there is not only one dwelling; there are many, because there are many ways that lead to the Father. But none of these ways leads past Christ, for he is the way for each one who strives toward the Father. Through him all lovers attain to the Father. The Old Covenant too has its dwelling there, and pagan people who had no opportunity to get to know Christ.

A dwelling is a place where one settles down to stay. In this world one may not settle down. Here below we find no lasting dwelling place; we feel like aliens and wanderers. The Father rewards this by giving us a dwelling with him. But to find none here below in which we can settle down does not simply mean that we are to live like vagrants, driven here and there. Rather, it means that we are ready to walk the way, in the Lord, that God has ordained for us. The provisional mode of our life is grounded in the constancy of our readiness. Our apparent unprotectedness in this world is grounded in our protectedness in God.

Grace alone, and not merit, decides the dwelling we are to enter. This grace is not that of the Redemption as such, but of the mission and the particular path of life ordained for us in God. Those who belong to the Lord do not need to spend time wondering which dwelling they will come into and how it will look. The Lord's word suffices for them: *I go to prepare a place for you.* These words contain the guarantee that this dwelling is the highest and most beautiful one that the Lord's grace can prepare for them. He speaks this word to his disciples, whom he has endowed with various offices; the dwellings that they will receive will correspond to these offices and missions, to a purpose. Their offices and their missions, which appeared temporary on earth, will in no way be obsolete in the final dwelling. Rather, they themselves will attain their ultimate forms. Every earthly office, every earthly mission issued by God continues to exist in eternity.

If this were not so, I would have told you. If their hope in eternity and the final meaning of their mission were vain, if in the beyond they would not continue to live in their personal characteristics and unique identities, the Lord would have told them. Then he would have had to speak to them very differently. He would have had to undertake a kind of leveling process between them, even in this world. He could have erected no hierarchy in his Church, or differences of mission, of standing, of state of life, for his Church is no temporary work, but the beginning of eternal life. Everything that God differentiates in her is established eternally and definitively in this differentiation. If there were only one single dwelling for everyone with the Father, every earthly differentiation would be something entirely ephemeral and relative, and it would not be distinguished from the differentiations of the ephemeral world. But this is not the case, either regarding the mission and the office that come from God or the character imparted by God in the sacraments. All this will remain in the heavenly Kingdom and will in no way be extinguished or leveled. The heavenly community of saints will show the characteristic differences that distinguished the earthly community of the Church, and in this mutual variety will exist the capacity for the greatest love.

The Lord opens this view of faith into eternity just now, when his concern is to console the disciples, for everything that has been might appear transitory in his suffering. Their faith should be anchored where everything is final: they should believe in God, who will eternally preserve them with all that they are, and they should believe in the Son, who will lead them now to this eternal dwelling.

That is the purpose of his going away. He goes in order to prepare a place for them. Until now he has only said that he is returning to the Father. Now he indicates the purpose and meaning of this path: he wants to *prepare a place* for them. He returns to the Father different than he went forth. He went forth from him alone, but he returns as one who is bringing guests along. And this is true quite apart from the Redemption: he brings along those whom he has met along the way in this world. This had already been arranged between him and the Father. He need not ask the Father first if his new friends are acceptable in the Father's house. He already has the Father's permission to bring along all who bear his seal, all those in whom the Father will recognize the Son. With this seal they enter into the eternal dwelling; indeed, the seal of each individual is itself his dwelling. We come as friends and chosen ones of his Son. We would feel very uncomfortable in the Father's dwellings were we to

arrive there as the persons we are. But we come as the Son wants the
Father to see us. We come adorned with new qualities that the Son in his
grace has given us. They are stamped into us as unambiguous signs and
qualities, but they stem from the Son and are the signs and qualities of
the Son. Everything in heaven corresponds to the condition of grace in
which we come, and in no way to the taste of our earthly being.

But because we come over with much that is still very earthly and not
according to God's taste, there is Purgatory. Here everything that does
not correspond to the Lord's grace must be burned out of us: our
profound readiness to sin, all the painful aftereffects of our earthly, sinful
condition. When the Lord prepares a dwelling for us with the Father, he
also prepares an outer chamber in which we can cleanse ourselves on
entering. Here all egotism must be set aside: the egotism of preoccupa-
tion with one's sins and virtues (for we should be occupied only with
love for God and neighbor), as well as the egotism that sees our neighbor's
faults instead of regarding him in the light of the Lord's love. The
burning out of this double egotism happens through an increasingly
personal, unavoidable realization of the Lord and of his suffering for
each individual sinner. The soul sees itself only in his mirror so long and
so completely that it finally forgets itself in the Lord and his love. The
one being purified does not see his neighbor and his faults at all. He is
wholly occupied with God and with himself. He sees his brother only
after he is so cleansed by the Lord's love that he can regard him with the
Lord's eyes. Now he is able to bear his neighbor, in his different dwelling,
without envy or criticism, to understand the variety of the Lord's ways
and acknowledge their validity in love, to delight in the different construction of the Father's dwellings. In all the dwellings he will see the
Lord, his personal paths, missions, guidance and tasks; and everything
that used to seem strange, foreign and perhaps even unbearable will now
appear meaningful to him in the Lord's love.

14:3. *And then, when I have gone and prepared a place for you, I will come
again and take you to myself, so that where I am, you also may be.*

His going from the world and returning to the world both lie within
his greater path, which goes forth from the Father and returns to the
Father. This going and this return form a part of his mission, which he

received from the Father, which begins with the Father and ends with the Father. The inner, smaller circle, which apparently runs in opposition to the outer circle, begins now with the Passion and will be completed at Easter. In suffering he goes, and in the Resurrection he returns. In this return he takes us to himself, for as soon as we are redeemed we are with him, if we believe in him. He is indeed in heaven after the Resurrection, but even so, he is with and in each person who believes in him and loves him. From now on he is no longer limited to one place; he is free to be in several places at once. He is in heaven, and he is with us in the world. But because he, the unlimited One, is with us who are limited, we too are basically everywhere the Lord is, whether we know it or not.

On leaving, the Lord goes to the Father and returns again. His going is a preliminary one. But this preliminary movement implies at the same time the final state, for suffering lies behind him, never to return. The separation between him and the Father is over for all eternity. Therefore, too, from now on the Father is where he is. They are one again forever, beyond all separation. When the Lord comes again he no longer brings the Father with him primarily in his mission, but rather as one who lives with him and dwells in him. The final unity between the two can no longer be even partially obscured. But the preliminary aspect of his going and returning consists in the fact that his whole mission will be completed only when all will be redeemed from sin and be with the Father. Yet here, too, the final state lies hidden in the preliminary one for us as well; for whoever has been redeemed once is redeemed.

But the purpose of the whole redemption is that we should be where the Lord is, that the judgment of righteousness that once awaited us has become a judgment of love, that the Son has fulfilled what he promised the Father: to bring back to him from the world more love than the abuse he had already received from it. This love that, stemming from the Father, is brought back to him by the Son, contains our love as well. By his grace, our love passes into his own, so that it may be where his own is. He has loved us, he has placed his grace in us and, because of this grace, has discovered something in us that, in grace, he calls our reciprocal love: he binds this something to his love and brings the whole back to the Father. This something of love that he finds in us does not stem from us but is effected by the Holy Spirit. It is the Holy Spirit who wakens our inmost soul and instincts, in order to elicit true love. Through his presence and his working, something awakens in us that was unknown to us, that would never really have been in us without his working. From afar this awakening of love resembles the first stirring of the passions in young lovers, who until now, in their innocence, have known nothing of these passions. Their love receives a different coloring, a different intensity. A new world opens up to them in love. So too, the presence of the Holy Spirit awakens something entirely new in the love between the Lord and mankind. It transforms the whole spiritual landscape. Through him, love becomes mature and living; through him the Lord and the human person are united in a here-and-now love. He works as a catalyst, indefinable in his measure and his way of awakening; one only notices that without him the same reaction would not be possible, that in it he has invisibly effected something mysterious: the unity of love between the Son and mankind, through which man can be where the Lord is.

14:4. *And where I am going, you know the way.*

There is no conjecture on the Lord's part, but knowledge. He has told them often enough; now he expects them to know it precisely: he is going to the Father, and they know just as precisely the paths by which one attains to the Father. For he has told them that no one knows the Father except the Son. They have not seen the Father himself, but they know him through the Son; and through the way of the Son that goes to the Father, they know enough about the Father. They know of the Father that he is the place to which the Son is going. This place is not an empty, unknown one for them. They know that the Father is love; that he preordained the way of the Son in love; that he is attainable on the way of the Son, which is a way of love; and that they must follow in the Son's footsteps in order to come to the Father. They know, then, where the Son is going, and they also know the way. Still they have not seen the Father. They will not see him until they themselves have arrived at where the Son is going now. Then it will be seen that the Father is much greater than they had ever suspected. The narrow image that they now have of the Father will be expanded into an infinite one. The place to which the Son is going will infinitely transcend them. They can certainly prepare for this journey and make many arrangements, but all these are only little hints and obscure premonitions, distant analogies and frail concepts, which will all be surpassed with arrival in the Father. The actual arrival will be related to the image they now have of the Father, just as the sight of a journey's goal that one has never seen before is related to the image that one had of it before the journey. Everything will be completely different then, everything near and real and infinitely bigger and more beautiful than one had thought. They know the way, but the goal itself is the endless openness into which the journey goes.

The Son's "where" is the place of his communion with the Father. He not only goes up to the Father: he returns into the Father, enters into the Father. His humanity enters into the Father's infinite Divinity. His love enters into perfected community without a shadow of mystery, the communion between Father and Son. Their union is so complete that nothing in heaven separates them, for they have everything in common. Their union is the expression of their eternal unity of essence. This communion is the unattainable image of our Communion with the Lord. If we were to give ourselves to him completely, as he gives himself to us, we might receive into ourselves the communion of Father and Son. In this return of the Son, Father and Son enter into each other fully; they know everything, they behold each other completely, they are entirely open to each other and their mutual joy penetrates them both perfectly. They appear to be nothing more than the infinite joy of seeing each other again. When two lovers have yearned for each other for a long time, and the moment finally comes when they meet again, in this moment everything is borne up and overwhelmed by an infinitely transcending, all-enveloping joy. Perhaps what they do and what they have to say to each other is almost unimportant; it stands in no relation to the extent of their love. But it is transfigured through their love, it suffices for them completely and everything appears right to them in the light of their love. In the meeting of Father and Son, beyond all human hesitations and restraints, there will be only the enveloping love of reunion.

The disciples know the way to this joy. It is the way that leads through separation and suffering. They see how the Lord sets about walking this path. But they will truly know it only when they themselves travel it, when they experience this way. Their experience will not be that of the

Son, who walked the path unswervingly. Their walk will be a hesitant one, at best the beginning of a movement in the right direction, an attempt interrupted again and again, only to begin anew just as often. They were already put on this way through baptism: every confession and Communion brings them back to it when they fall. Their path is marked by the sacraments, without it being possible to say that from one reception to the next they have climbed to a higher level or completed a stretch forward. One cannot compare the sacraments even with one another; one cannot say that Communion brings us nearer to the Lord than confession. One can keep to this way in grace, but cannot measure any distances on it. Only one thing is certain: this way does not mean gradually coming step by step nearer, in the sense that a person forty years old would be more perfect and nearer the goal than someone who is twenty. The temporal pace and accumulation are in no way to be understood as a progression, and the sacraments are not to be played off against each other. There is true movement, however, indeed an increase, but this lies entirely in the Lord. For the grace offered will always be much richer than that expected and accepted. In this consists the way and its unceasing movement. What moves is the impatience of love. This impatience for the Lord is always present and may not be put off into the future. It must always be now. No one may immediately look forward from today's Communion to tomorrow's. That would be ingratitude and a kind of spiritual pleasure-seeking, referred not to God but to oneself. Love must live today, even when it expects increase and knows that tomorrow will be greater than today.

The way is known. But it is the way of the Lord's mysteries, and mystery always transcends man. If the mystery did not go beyond him, he would not yearn for it, and there would be no way. Yearning for the mystery is good when it comes from God, when it stems from love and not from man's desire to grow, for what grows on this way is the mystery. If man were to grow, the distance between him and the mystery would always become less, and the mystery would be always becoming less mysterious, losing its divine character. Just because it is always becoming more of a mystery, the way generates an increasing motion and becomes more beautiful. What progresses is the depth of the mystery, and on this preordained way one attains to God.

14:5. *Thomas said to him: We do not know where you are going. How should we know the way?*

Thomas is the devotee of human and comprehensive clarity. He does not know the "where" of the Lord because this place is not in the world that he knows. Grasping and measuring everything only with human senses, he cannot imagine any place not spatially and temporally limited. By his question he is trying to gain certainty. Petty and limited, yet it is also touching. He wants to see everything and stake out boundaries everywhere. The only path he can imagine is one with two gutters and many milestones. Perhaps he understands that the Lord is going somewhere, but not that he is on the way to the Father. He believes that the Lord has a destiny and that the disciples are somehow woven into this destiny, but he cannot picture anything definite. He cannot make the transition between faith and life. On one side he sees a doctrine about God, and on the other side a human destiny, perhaps a disaster. The two fall asunder for him, because he imagines both of them finite and limited. That the Lord's way goes into the infinity of the Father is wholly incomprehensible to him, and so he rightly says he does not know the place.

Therefore he also believes that he does not know the way. For him, a way is something that leads to a very particular goal. One must know this goal if one is to take the right way. One chooses the goal, and then one starts off on the way indicated. Thomas imagines the way to God to be equally goal oriented. He sees the Lord's teachings, his new commandment, the sacraments that he has instituted. All this appears beautiful and valuable to him, but initially only as milestones along a finite way, on which one must ascertain the distances. For him all this has not yet in any way become an inner element of the infinite movement toward the Father. Thomas would perhaps be a zealous priest, but he would do parish work for the sake of the parish, not seeing how everything is only a moment in the life of the Lord himself. He always wants to be certain. He would always like to know and grasp everything. He is like the person who would be happy to know how many years of Purgatory await him: then he would calculate how many indulgences he must gain and add a few more for safety's sake. But he would be forgetting that the Lord inserts all his people into his own Evermore, letting them everywhere partake of the uncreatedness of his grace.

14:6. *Jesus said to him: I am the way, the truth and the life. No one comes to the Father except through me.*

The conversation continues beyond Thomas' question. The Lord does not let himself be discouraged or checked by the disciple's blindness and security craving. On the contrary, the question becomes an occasion for him to reveal his whole secret, as far as that is possible. Of course, basically he is revealing it continually, but mankind does not understand it. The simplest word that the Lord speaks contains such incredible power that, if one were to expose oneself wholly to this power, one would be completely overwhelmed by it in thought and feeling. In two ways we can try to hear the Lord's words: either as our understanding can grasp them, as they are suitable for us, according to our greater or lesser receptivity; or in that we try to comprehend how the Lord said them. In the second case, we do not pit our limited receptivity against his infinite content, but let him be the receptor himself within us. He is the speaker before us and the receptor in us. We understand the infinity of his word only by whatever of himself lives in us. We ought to do this, but we do not; we fail to let him step into this place. We always want to receive and understand him by ourselves. Therefore the Lord does not weary of continuing to speak until perhaps we eventually learn what it means to believe. He says:

I am. He proclaims himself. He says who he is. He presents himself; he places himself in the foreground. Earlier, if he spoke of himself, he did it only in order to point at once to the Father. Now he stops at himself, for now he must show them the way that leads to the Father, and he himself is this way.

I am the way. Not a way, but *the* way. The only way, beside which there is no other. He is at once the way ordained, traveled and ongoing. These three ways are one and cannot be split apart: together they form one, the way that is the Lord. It is, first of all, the way *ordained,* the way planned in heaven, discussed and arranged between Father and Son: the way proceeding from the Father and returning to him. The whole length of this way is methodically thought out: everything that the Son encounters is a conscious encounter, and inasmuch as he is the way indicated, everything that happens to him is itself ordained—his conception, his birth, his growth, his work, his suffering, his death. Everything is outlined even to the least detail, and in his life he fulfills the Father's design. It is impossible for him to be spared anything on the way ordained. In his suffering too, there can be no abbreviations, no reductions. Everything that he experiences he must experience fully, feel fully, savor fully; each experience is filled to the brim. There is no distraction, no dampening, no dimming, no mitigation, for each station of his way must possess the full validity planned in God. Everything that is to be seen from heaven's vantage point must be wholly translated into earthly reality. Nothing is inadequate; everything is integral.

So completely was this way planned in heaven and thought out between Father and Son that the plan included not only the ordaining, but also its full carrying out. It is also ordained that this way as a whole is to be *walked,* and specifically by the Lord himself, who is the prototype and can therefore take everyone else with him on this way. He so completely corresponds to the way ordained by God for mankind that he fully embodies it on earth: he himself is the way, and hence can become so for everyone else. Because he is the perfectly traveled way, every way is a way only through him. He is not a special, closed, private way; rather, as the perfect way, he is the way for everyone. Nevertheless, for everyone it is a grace to be allowed to walk this way. He himself walks his way in love, feeling it a grace to be allowed to walk the way of the Father. For him, as the man who is also God, it is a divine grace to remain true on this way of the Father. This love and grace belong to the essence of his way, and each person who travels it will receive, through it, a share in this love and grace. No one needs anything on this way other than his love and grace. He has, of course, a certain insight on the way: he knows where he comes from and where he is going. But the overview as a whole lies with the way itself, with the Lord. In choosing him as the way, one must also leave to him the overall view of the way. Whoever chooses a way lets himself be guided by this way, entrusts himself to it and decides not to swerve from it. Anyone who has really entrusted himself to the Lord's way is no longer able to deviate from it; he cannot do so any more than the Lord himself could. Just as the Lord walked his own way in the Father's grace and love, and this love prevented him from turning aside from his way, from himself, so too the one who follows him walks the way of the Lord, encased and held in his love.

Finally, since this way is a stretch that one must walk, the Lord is the *ongoing* way, continuously moving on toward the Father. His love for the Father is a love in motion, and the grace of the Father is a grace in motion. In this movement the Lord goes his way, without ever asking if he is tired or not, if he can still go on or not, if he still sees the way or not. He is so completely the way that he simply walks it, in complete trust in the Father. Even when it leads into the darkness, this way is always full of light. No stretch of it is unclear or confused, but everything lies clear to the end in the Father's light. And the Lord who walks his path is himself light. But he too, in order to see the way, needs a light, and this light is the Holy Spirit. In the light of the Holy Spirit he perceives his way step by step. He does not want to see his way in his own light, but only in the light that the Father has given him, the light of the Holy Spirit. In this light too he endures the darkness of suffering. He walks, then, seeing his way, yet not by his own power, but in the light of the Father's love. He wills that we too should be an ongoing way, trusting in God. He walks the way, seeing by the Father's light; we walk it blind, in the Lord, taken along on his way. He takes from us any responsibility of surveying the whole path and desires only that, like him, we too may travel the way in the light of the Father's love, in the Holy Spirit.

I am the truth. The Lord is the truth because he is the Father's witness. He is not simply a true word that the Father speaks: as the word, he is the whole truth of the Father. What he declares about the Father, what the Father testifies in him, is not a single word, a single sentence, a single truth, whose object—what is testified—stands over against it as a different, second thing. Rather the Son, as Word and witness, is at once the reality and the proof of what has been said and testified. He himself is the surety between the witness and what is witnessed, the saying and what is said. He is no empty word, but the eternal, eternally fulfilled Word of the Father; not only his likeness, but his image; not only his promise, but also his fulfilment; in this he is the truth. In this he declares the absolute about himself. Were he only the way, there would still be the possibility of relativization. One could still think of other ways; one could imagine one's own way differently. One could conceive of the Lord's way itself as something changeable and temporary. But now he says of himself the most absolute thing that can be said. He is the full truth, the fullness of truth. Every partial truth encountered in the world exists only if it has a place within his truth and is capable of opening to his truth, of rising to his truth. This evolution of our truth into his truth is the guarantee that our truth has part in his and does not fall out of the eternal truth as a lie. In this openness our truth is measured by his, which is absolute, and accepted and acknowledged as truth. To the extent to which a partial truth is prepared to give itself up and open itself up to the total truth, it will participate in this total truth. Everything that we know in the world and in our life, that we experience, see, think, enjoy and endure, is partial truth, and regarding all of this we can repeatedly question whether it is true. For it often appears to be untrue, full of deception and illusion. It will be true if it has space within the Lord's truth. In our lifetime we will not exhaust or grasp this all-embracing truth of the Lord. Nor does the Lord ask it of us. He only demands that we evaluate the little partial truths that we can survey according to whether or not they have a place within his truth and remain subordinate to him. Every earthly truth that inspires us, or perhaps appears infinitely great to us, so that it completely overfills us, has a right to fulfill us, and we may give ourselves to it, if one condition is fulfilled: if it has a place within the Lord's all-embracing truth.

The Lord gives us this truth as faith, love and hope. They are our participation in the relationship between Father and Son. In this relationship to the Father, the Son is the truth, and in it he is also the prototype of faith. For in it he takes over the whole truth of the Father—not simply theoretically, but by living it, indeed by *being* it. There is not the slightest distance between the acknowledgment of the Father's truth and the living of this truth as the Son's own. In this full certainty between his receiving the Father's truth and living the truth, the Son is the archetype of faith. But precisely in this unity he is already love, for only in love does the cleft between knowledge and life close. It is love that conforms to knowledge in such a way that it becomes life, because love lives wholly in assimilating the truth and life of the beloved. Hope is the principle of the continuity and expansion of this love, the perpetual opening up of the incarnate Son to the Evermore of the Father's truth. Faith, love and hope together form an indivisible unity. Each enhances the other, and none ever weakens the other. In their unity they express life in the truth, indeed, the truth itself.

This truth expands and explodes in all directions. At very first sight, it is an infinite demand that looks and points in all directions simultaneously. We are drawn to respond and subscribe to it in all its aspects at the same time. In the will to correspond to this demand, one begins to love, and in love one is overwhelmed anew by its infinity. But precisely because the Son, in faith, love and hope, is so completely overwhelmed by the Father's truth, he himself becomes the truth: when he sees the Father's infinite life and knows himself poured over into the Infinite by it, he himself receives and becomes the eternal light. The spark that springs everywhere into faith, love and hope, igniting everything and ever blazing up anew, is the Holy Spirit. Thus he is also the witness of this love, its infinite objectivization. In human life, a witness disturbs the intimacy of lovers. In God, on the contrary, he is the infinite sealing of this intimacy. A child can disturb its parents in the intimacy of their love. The Holy Spirit, on the other hand, is the eternal spur to intimacy between Father and Son. A worldly witness disturbs because an incongruity can become evident between the infinite meaning of love and its finite expressions. The Holy Spirit, however, witnesses that the love between Father and Son is limitlessly as well as totally expressed. In this love every fixation is abolished, because the Holy Spirit lets a new promise proceed out of every fulfilment.

I am the life. The Lord names life last. To a certain extent, he lets it take its origin in the way and in the truth. He lets it be born and develop in him and through him. He lets it develop long enough for it to end in God, flow over into God. This life eludes ready and conclusive concepts. It is a life that *lives* and so can never be grasped, because it is always growing and expanding by virtue of its vitality. It is a life not exhausted by the earthly concept of life, and yet has this in common with it, that in its vitality it is perpetually changing. It changes, though, within the life itself and not like physiological life, which comes into being and dies off, leaving other generations behind. The Lord's life knows no such sequence. It is not a series of biological processes, of distinguishable life functions that somehow are dependent on one another. Rather, his life, which comes from God and goes to God, is one single, unified, eternal movement within its two limits: from God and to God. Insofar as its movement is a going out and a return, his life is one with his way. And insofar as this movement is the expression of the life of God himself, his life is one with his truth. His life, then, is limited by its beginning and ending in God, but these limits are not really limits, because beginning and end are one and God is in him: its having no limits is even the chief characteristic of his life. It is so little limited that it has its origin in eternal life and flows into eternal life, and yet is eternal change, change in the Father's love as well as in love for the Father and for us. His love is so rich that it can eternally change, without growing less or being altered. In every circumstance it is entirely itself and proves its vitality in this eternal capacity for transformation. Even, and especially, now, when he sets about to suffer, transforming his love into the feeling of total forsakenness, he shows his love's infinite vitality and capacity for change.

The fact that he issues his commandment of love in the same moment that he describes himself as the *life* means that we, loving each other, must also live each other, live for each other—and specifically within his life, in him. His life is so rich that it has place for each of us. But we would never comprehend that there was such a place for our life in his life, if he did not reveal a particular part of his life to each of us who live for him. This communication of a part of his life does not imply that he had to divide and rend his life in order to communicate it to us, for the bond uniting our life with his is itself living and tolerates no division or fragmenting. He gives to us of his life, while retaining his life in himself; he pours his own life into the life of those who are his. One cannot say that he would be less living if he did not also beget his vitality in us. Still his life bond with us is absolutely necessary for his life. This necessity, though, is not one of poverty but of fullness, not of need but of love. It is not a necessity that we, with our human concepts and arguments, could arrive at and call for, but a necessity of God's love, which is shown to us in faith and love.

The life of the Lord is a life of *truth.* His whole life is based on the truth that he has from the Father, never alienated from this truth for a moment. He fulfills the Father's truth not only in seeing and believing it, but above all by living it. He lives it before the Father, when he is alone with the Father; in the world he also lives it before mankind, in that each section of his life reveals, bit by bit, the Father's truth. In this he often withdraws into the Father, and it might appear as if he were hiding himself for a moment, perhaps to draw new energy, to rest in the Father. Whatever he may do, he will never do anything that is not in the truth or would shut us out of the truth. Even his withdrawal into the Father happens only so that he can take us even more deeply into the Father's truth. This being taken into the Father signifies a deeper inclusion, through the truth, into his *way*. The way is the origin of the proclamation of the truth. For the Lord's truth is not static or quiescent but is always growing; it is always somewhere. It is itself under way: it proceeds from eternal life and flows into eternal life. This eternal life itself is not a standstill, but is eternal *life*. This penetration of way, truth and life occurs in love. Love is always going somewhere, always in the truth, always life. It permeates the intensification from way to truth to life, so that the life of love is the highest. One could mark out the way step by step and show that every part of it is love; one could construct a whole system of truth and show that every part of it is love. But all that would still be a matter of differentiations; in life itself there are no more differentiations, because the Lord's life itself is love, and the two merge fully in each other. His whole life is love, and his whole love is life.

No one comes to the Father except through me. Up to now he has been at pains to show us that we can live in him; now he shows us that we must come to the Father in this life. One can live in the Lord, be in him, accompany him on his living way. But to do this is to go to the Father. He must appear independently before the Father. This independence consists in letting himself be brought to the Father through the Son. This is apparently paradoxical. The Lord has shown that his life is eternal growth and eternal change; now he shows that in this eternal growing and changing a way to the Father is prepared, a way that each person must walk. Each one who comes to the Father can attain to him only on this way. At first one seemed to be wholly protected and enveloped in the Son's life. The way was imagined to be a way within the Son, remaining in the Son. Now it becomes evident that the entire way leads beyond the Son, into something else: into the Father. There is a moment when the covering rips apart and the human person steps out of the Son, before the Father; a moment when the Son gives us over, naked and coverless, to the Father. It is a dangerous moment in which we step out of the Son's protection, no longer covered by him. In this moment, when the Son offers us to the Father, when he himself steps back in order to hold us out to the Father, the Father will see us as we are—certainly, with the grace we have received from the Son that lives in us, but without being covered by him. The Son no longer stands before us, but behind us. If Christ really lives in us in this moment, we need not be afraid before the Father. But if he had lived not in us but only around us, then the Father would see us unaccompanied by the Son. He would see us poorer. Our hope in that moment rests solely on the fact that it is the Son who holds us out to the Father. It is he who presents us. In this moment God must recall more than ever before that it is the Son who brought mankind to him. He may not look so much at those presented as at the one presenting them. He must firmly recall the pact that he made with the Son. When he really takes us in his arms, and the way of the Son flows into the Father for us as well, then it is above all because of God's love for his Son.

The gesture with which the Son offers us to the Father is the same one a mother uses when showing her child. It is a gesture he learned from his Mother. He carries us the way his Mother carried him, with the same naïveté with which his Mother carried him. His Mother knew the weight of what she bore, but she did not withdraw her mother love from him. The Son knows at what price he has purchased the permission to bring us to the Father. But the fact that he is our brother and at the same time the Son of God is so overpoweringly good and great to him that it makes him forget the suffering of the redemption, just as his Mother forgets her pains. He has learned from her motherliness not to desire to see any further than the momentary well-being of the child, to be absorbed in this gesture of giving.

From us he desires that in this moment of giving we should be nothing other than he was in the arms of his Mother: only a child, purely trusting. We are to be only what we are: children of God, returning to the Father through the Son's grace, without any fear of surrender, of death, of love. Everything else that might be done out of anxiety or worry over one's salvation would only be a turning away from the Lord. Anything we would like to do for ourselves would only be done against him. The only thing he demands for us is that we let him give us over to the Father, not so that everything will turn out for the best for us in the end, but simply so that his commandment may be fulfilled: love one another. Here the Lord is only the symbol of the neighbor to whom we should give ourselves, and fulfilling his own commandment, he gives us over to the Father.

THE FATHER IN THE SON

14:7. *If you had known me, you would also have known my Father. From now on you know him and you have seen him.*

The two parts of this verse seem completely to contradict each other. In the same breath the Lord seems to say that the disciples do not know him yet, and that they have known him. But to know the Lord means to know him as he has made himself known: as way, as truth and as life. And this, again, means to know him as the light of one's own existence and as that to which we are most sensitive: as love. Love is like a return route in this knowledge: for love is contained in his commandment, not only as a requirement but as containing his life; and this life is none other than the one that he lived before us as a human person. The disciples know this life and have discovered that it was love. Perhaps someone might lack a sense of light: he might be blind; or of the way: he might be lame; or of life: he may have had no possibilities for development, no longing for life. But no one lacks a sense of love: it is implanted in each person, and each has brought this seed to some development. Some have taken it no further than developing it into self-love; others have made it into a goal—love for a fellow human being who is bound to their own person; still others pass through all the levels up to real love for the Lord. Thus, this seed of love, planted in mankind, is infinitely capable of forming and developing. The Lord uses this seed in order to lead a person to know him. Full surrender to the Lord implies full knowledge of the Lord. Increasing development of the seed of love through all the levels of surrender means increasing development of the knowledge of the Lord.

The human person will be judged according to this knowledge. In the Lord's eyes it replaces the other, theoretical knowledge. He uses this feeling, which each person can know, as a means of access to himself. Along this way, the ego restriction of love can always be expanded and overcome, up to full knowledge of the love of the Lord. He does not build, then, on something spiritual. Rather, he lays the foundation on the living center in us. He makes contact with and appeals to this. We do not possess this living center of ourselves: he himself has embedded it in us. In conjunction with this living seed, we are inwardly enabled to let even what is our own become actual love. When we love the Son, then, this love replaces all further knowledge. We know him. But we cannot love the Son without loving the Father. Every love contains this all-embracing and inclusive character: it must love everything that the beloved loves. The more comprehensive a love becomes—beginning perhaps on the purely sensible level—the more it will also receive knowledge of the spiritual world of the beloved, in order to participate in it, to love the beloved in it and thus gain an expanded capacity for love. Now the spiritual world of the Son is the Father. It would be an insult to the Son if we were to love him without loving the Father. For himself, the Son demands only love; he is content with this and wants to reckon this love to us as knowledge. But for the Father he demands knowledge, because he himself burns in love for the Father to be known.

The Father, too, in order to receive us, is content that we love the Son. He does not demand theoretical knowledge of the Son any more than the Son does. He wants us to distinguish good and evil according to the standard of his love, and that is enough for him. As soon as the Son appears in the world, everything must be measured by the plumb line of God's love. Even the Ten Commandments, which the Father issued in the Old Covenant, have received a new face through the Son's new commandment, and have become dependent on this new commandment. In the Old Covenant one would be judged according to the individual laws. But as soon as the Son's commandment is issued, it is taken into consideration in judging all the others. It also creates new approaches to the old Commandments, making them lighter. Even if the old Commandments are no better kept today than earlier, we have an additional help from the Lord that comes from the knowledge of the new commandment. For instance, someone can break the old Commandment by despising his parents, and he may not succeed for a long time in overcoming this sin. But he knows the new commandment; he knows that the Lord suffered for his parents too and that he is ready to accept them in grace; he himself receives so much love from the Lord that out of this store of love he can supplement his deficiency in filial love. Thus on every side the strict righteousness of the old law is moderated through the newly disclosed love, even where the old law is not, as it ought to be, kept in the full power of the new.

The Father himself condescends to insert and place himself in the Son's new commandment. The Son has not come from himself with this commandment but from the Father, and the Father lets himself be drawn into the world of the Son. The Father himself has willed it so, for Father and Son have sanctioned the new law in the pact of redemption. The Father willed to recognize the Son and his mission everywhere he encountered the new love. The Father knows us, then, by the commandment of love. We, on the other hand, always know the Son by it, for in this love we know him as the one who comes from the Father and goes to the Father. Love is our indicator on this way. If we were to try with our whole soul to grasp the Son in the power of his commandment, his mission from the Father and to the Father could not possibly remain hidden from us. The more his love for us becomes visible, the more strongly we see how the Son strains over and beyond himself into the Father. And his love wants to take us there with him.

In this connection we are like a convert who is not yet able to grasp the truth of the Church in its pure objectivity. Thus he learns to regard it first through the eyes of a Catholic friend. Through his love for this person he learns to treasure and to love what his friend loves. Even when he has later succeeded in understanding and loving the Church wholly independently of his friend, a trace of that first mediation will adhere to his way of seeing. Thus too do we learn to love the Father's world by regarding it through the eyes and the love of the Son. We can never grow beyond this mediation; our access to the Father will always be the Son. When a priest receives a convert into the Church, his mediation is a purely official one, and if his personality played a role in it at first, it can wholly retreat and pale in the convert's later life. With the Lord, on the other hand, when he lays us in the Father's arms, his office and person cannot be separated: he possesses the omnipresence of the Mediator, who is the only way to the Father. Both mediations lead into the Ever-Greater. The priest leads the convert by the hand out of his narrowness into the mystery of the Church, which opens up before the eyes of the new arrival as something vast and ever-deepening. But the Lord leads us by the hand into the mystery of the Father, into the illimitable sea of Divinity opening up before our eyes. This catching sight of and being flooded by God's ocean is the knowledge of the Father. *From now on you know him and have seen him.* From now on means from the moment in which they not only keep the Lord's commandment but grasp that he is way, truth and life; grasp it as they can, imperfectly but in the light of perfection. They know the Father, then, because they see so many ways that lead to him, how many possibilities he has at his command, how rich he is, how many gifts emanate from him, what the Son himself embodies and represents of him. Each time it is only a little presentiment, but each of these presentiments, when realized, becomes a reality that puts their boldest expectations in the shade. By knowing the Lord, we learn to know the Father. But in the end, the essence of knowing the Lord is that everywhere and always one comes up against his being greater, and any image we have of him is far surpassed by his reality. Our senses and our gifts of imagination do not suffice even to hint at what he is. This is the highest knowledge that we can possess of him—to know that he is More. When we know him thus, when we find ourselves surpassed on all sides, when we are so encompassed by his grace that we meet with it everywhere, then we have finally seen the Father in the Son, as we are able to see him—with our human eyes, which at all points are convinced that there is more to see; with our human spirit, which now really knows that there is still infinitely more to comprehend; and finally, with our human love, which we feel as something infinitely poor compared with his love.

14:8. *Philip said to him: Lord, show us the Father, and it suffices us.*

Philip is far behind what the Lord has said. Where the Lord wanted to show him the unlimited, he is seeking an entirely limited meaning. Where there is nothing more to measure, he still wants to apply measuring rods. Where all our concepts fail, he still wants to conceptualize. He demands an image of the Father that would fit in with his human view—a view that would have nothing mysterious about it anymore, but would stand on a level with other views. He thinks that the Father will let himself be put in the category of isolated objects accessible to him.

This is his view, and he wants to see it confirmed. Then he will declare himself perfectly content. He is the archetype of those who let themselves be convinced and satisfied by some argument—a clear image, a simple concept, anything tangible. He thinks this will suffice him. Yet what the Lord has previously said implies the opposite of sufficiency. The Lord desires that we never become sated, never get enough, always discover that there is more; that even if we apply all our senses to his essence, and still more that of the Father, we would despair if we did not know that his grace is the eternal sufficiency. It should suffice us, then, that the Son knows the Father, and that we approach the mystery only in such a way that we possess nothing final and are continually directed to seeking, but to a seeking and striving that are eternally sheltered in his love. What one sees with sensible eyes, one possesses. But one cannot possess the Father and the Son without being fully overwhelmed by them. There is no such thing as a practice exercise toward God. One cannot impress God on oneself bit by bit, in order to learn him by heart like a picture. True knowledge of the Father lies in the continually overflowing love of the entire, incomprehensible God.

14:9. *Jesus said to him: So long a time have I been with you, and you have not known me, Philip? Whoever sees me, sees the Father. How can you say: Show us the Father?*

The Lord calls the time since he met Philip a long one. Just as in the conversation with Martha and at other times, here too he shows a certain impatience. He always wants the whole, immediately. This answer contains a solid disappointment, for he also knows that he will not remain long in this world. People will never again be together with him in the world for as long as these disciples were, yet even this time was not long enough for them to know him. But it is the disciples who are later to proclaim him and make him known on earth, and not only him, but the Father also. Thus Philip's question seems to question everything that has happened in these years of their being together. It is all so shaky, so fragile: they do not understand the essentials, either of his teaching or of his love. Otherwise Philip would not have been able to ask this question.

But the Lord does not withdraw. Untiringly, he repeats the word that he came to proclaim, the word that reveals the Father: *Whoever sees me, sees the Father.* For this world, the Son embodies the Father. The Father himself will not take on a visible form in order to show himself to the world, as did the Son. There will never, then, be two possibilities of seeing God: one through the Father, the other through the Son. Rather, the Son is the revelation of God the Father, and whoever has seen him, seen him as loving faith can see him, has seen the Father. *How can you say: show us the Father?* For the disciple is seeing what the Father wills to show of himself: the Son. He sees the Father in the Son. Previously, the Lord demanded entire openness to the eternal Evermore of the Father. Now on the contrary, he demands a final decision: be content with the Son! But the conclusion that the Lord demands here has nothing in common with the prepared programs the disciples are always demanding of him. It puts an end to the uncertain groping for correct access to the Father and signals the beginning of real movement, the authentic finding-in-seeking and seeking-in-finding. It is the end of egotistical ponderings and the start of handing on what one has. For the more the disciple gives away what he possesses, the more his possessions will increase. One only possesses what one squanders. What one wants for oneself, on the other hand, for the satisfaction of one's knowledge or pleasure, is already dead: it has already run out.

14:10. *Do you not believe that I am in the Father and the Father is in me? The words that I speak to you, I do not speak of myself: the Father who remains in me, does his works.*

The first part of this sentence puts utterly excessive demands on Philip and the disciples. Perhaps they could grasp that the Father is in the Son, that he represents and embodies the Father. But that he is *in* the Father, that he whom they see in their midst on earth, should at the same time be in the Father, in heaven: how could they grasp it? Not just a part of him, perhaps a hidden part, is in the Father, but he himself altogether. That is how the Lord is. When we fail to understand a thing, he does not go back to explain it step by step, but actually moves further ahead. Each time human comprehension is completely at an end and surrenders its arms, the Lord pushes forward in earnest. After all, the Lord wants to mediate not concepts but life, which does not stagnate and involves eternal motion, eternal increase. Man's failure is no occasion for him to scale down his demands, nor is man's success. The Lord measures nothing in the Christian's life according to human success or failure. Failure does not lead to a smaller task, or success to a greater one, but in both cases one is faced with the Evermore. Everything badly done calls for something infinitely better, and if one really has achieved something better, that calls for something much better still. The entire Christian life is one single conspiracy against the system of step-by-step progress. It is not a case of waiting until one learned something thoroughly. Yet nothing is rushed, feverish or chaotic. There is order everywhere—in the Lord's life, in the Church—order to the point of institutional rigidity. But this order exists only to cause everything to flow; it is what makes the inner richness of life possible.

The Son, then, is in the Father. But now, while he lingers on earth, the way he is in the Father is different from that before the Incarnation. The Father commissioned the Son to leave him in order to redeem the world; and the Father not only confirmed this commission, but he has accompanied it, shared in its execution in his fatherly fashion. He lets the Son go.

Metaphorically speaking, it is as if the Son had separated himself from the Father at the Incarnation, and in doing so had bequeathed everything to the Father: all his love for the Father, all his thoughts for the Father, all the divine glory he possesses with the Father and finally the pact they had made with each other. All this remained in the Father, as strong and as living as if the Son were still in him—indeed, almost stronger and more living, because the Father now bears for them both the responsibility for what they have resolved to do. Not that the Son feels relieved of responsibility. On the contrary, he takes over his own more earnestly; precisely because the Father has taken over the divine responsibility for them both, the Son feels more deeply bound not to disappoint the Father in his responsibility, not to let him bear the burden alone, and more than ever bound to carry out his commission as perfectly as possible. It is a mystery of love that when the lover assumes responsibility for both parties in an issue, the beloved feels even more deeply bound. Before the Son's parting, then, the Father had burdened himself with total responsibility. He allowed the Son to go into the world and live out the whole adventure, but he keeps with him the Spirit, the love and essence of the Son. He is somehow grateful that part of the Son remains behind; that it is there, so that his loneliness as Father is not total. One cannot say that his life is lived in simple recollection of the Son. For the separation is only temporal, and the Father, as God, bridges this time much more quickly and easily than the Son, who is human. He is also always aware of the Son's love, just as the Son is aware of the Father's love. Because this love remains in him, the Son lives in him.

The Father must also become used to the fact that he will no longer be the sole judge, but that from now on the Son's love will introduce and determine a new kind of judgment. This new state of affairs for the Father arises in the course of the Son's earthly life, especially during the Passion. The Son's love left behind in the Father helps him to get over this time of the Son's suffering. Looking ahead to the fruit of the Son's suffering, he finds help to survive this time of the Passion. This shows us a side of the Father's love that, carried over into our temporal world, can only be expressed as a building, a trusting, indeed even a "hoping" in the Son.

When people suffer who do not yet believe in and love the Son, since they are not yet Christians, they draw from this "hope" of the Father's. It is consolation in a life without prospects. It is not yet the Son's hope, which he pours into us in love as a fruit of his suffering. It is something completely undifferentiated, through which the searching sufferer is strengthened and supported. Indeed, no one comes to the Son unless the Father draws him. In suffering, such a person has come to know the Father's attitude of "hope" in the Son. The Son's hope itself is not thereby devalued, for what lives in the Father, awakening hope in him and keeping it alive, is precisely the love of the Son. In searching, every seeking person has arrived at the place where the Father holds the Son hidden within himself. He has stumbled on the mystery of the Son in the Father. He is suffering so much that he can no longer help himself, so he looks around for help, for one who will guide him on the right way. And he comes on the Father, who leads him to the Son. The Father has the Son in him, as a friend has within him his friend on whose behalf he knows he can act and to whom he can refer, because, even without asking, he can count on him and build on him.

The words that I speak to you, I do not speak of myself. Here the Lord shows once again that he is one with the Father. He does not speak on his own, not even now in saying this. Because of the Father's indwelling in him, he can never act as if he were alone. He is continually considering the Father: he has him, he follows him, he belongs to him. When he speaks, it is only in agreement with the Father: or even more, at the Father's commission. It is not as though every word had to be agreed to with the Father first. But he is in the Father's mission, which accompanies him and determines everything that he does and says. He speaks the language of the Father, as mankind speaks its original mother tongues. Human beings, not conscious that they bear the words and concepts of their ancestors in their mouths, often give the vessel of language a new, self-determined content. When the Son speaks the language of the Father, however, the content itself belongs to the Father; he speaks the Father's language not only outwardly, according to syntax and vocabulary; every single word that he says is, in content and form, in origin and purpose, a word of his Father. He does not even say what, of himself, he would otherwise say. He has given up speaking his own personal language. So completely has he laid his entire life in the Father's hands that he sees no possibility of saying or doing anything but what is the Father's.

The Father who remains in me does his works. The Father's indwelling in the Son fills out not only a part of his soul or his spirit, but possesses him completely. In the Son there is no boundary line between his possessing the Father and his being possessed by the Father. Both are one. Therefore the Father does his works in the Son. They are so much one that in his own works the Son wants to see nothing but the works of the Father, even though he himself collaborates in these works. He could certainly set boundaries to distinguish what stems from him and what from the Father. But that would run contrary to his essence. As they are, he leaves his works to the Father, acknowledging them as the Father's works and wanting to know nothing about what is his own. He does this so as not to let the Father become lonely. Actually he speaks this word to the disciples, to show them the hidden power of the Father in his works. But he says it somehow more profoundly to the Father, that in the loneliness to come he may rejoice in the Son's work: that it might not be someone else's work, but his, the Father's own work. Here the Son shows himself as the true lover, who does not leave the beloved alone during the forsakenness he knows is coming. He gives him tokens, remembrances, souvenirs. He heaps up before him whatever he possesses, so that when the Father no longer has the Son, he can still console himself with the Son's work, not sorrowfully as with the abandoned work of one who is distant and has disappeared, but with his own work. It is the sort of extravagant love that loves and gives not only for the present, but also reckons with and bridges the coming difficulty in advance. Yes, in the end this love of the Son is so extravagant that it is not even limited to time, but gives timelessly, as long as it has any possibility at all of squandering itself in giving.

14:11. *Believe me, that I am in the Father and the Father is in me. If not, then believe because of the works themselves.*

Within the same self-squandering love, the Lord turns to mankind. He knows that the chief work he is to accomplish in the Father's name and at his commission is the foundation of faith in their hearts. In order to elicit this faith in them, after having spent his entire love on the Father, he squanders his whole love once again on them. What he said before was meant above all as assurance of his love for the Father. Now he wants to give mankind this love of God, which is only to be experienced and grasped in faith. But his turning toward mankind is not a turning away from the Father, not a restriction of his love to something smaller, but on the contrary its further expansion. For previously he squandered his love on God, who is in him and in whom he is; who, then, was already the possesser of this squanderer of love and of this entire squandering. But now it is to be turned to those who do not yet possess it, those who are just acquiring faith. With these he now shares himself, as he distributes himself in the Eucharist without counting, without limit, without measure, giving himself full and undivided to each individual of this countless multitude.

In the end he only points toward his works. He takes what still remains of himself, the works, placing them—insofar as they are the Father's works—wholly in the service of the faith which is to be created. It is as though he wanted to eliminate himself, so that God would no longer see the Son, but only love, in the works; as though he feared that his person would stand in the way of the Father's immediacy to mankind, whereas nothing but God's power ought to be at work in animating mankind's faith through the works. Since the Father's essence is to work on mankind through the Son, the Son makes himself invisible, as it were; he withdraws in order to expose the world even more immediately to the Father's workings. In this way, he answers Philip's request to be shown the Father. He draws the last curtain away from the Father, namely, himself.

14:12. *Truly, truly I tell you: Whoever believes in me will do the works that I do, and he will do greater than these; for I am going to the Father.*
The Lord's words are always so simple that the human person almost fails to hear them. The Lord does what he can to waken attention to them. Therefore he again begins with the double *truly*. He says it twice, so that no one may fail to hear this word. He is in dead earnest to be heard and understood.

What he proclaims to us is this: *Whoever believes in him will do the same works* that he has done, because the Lord will be living in him. And the more vitally he lives in someone, the more this person will become capable of doing the Lord's works. For the power that is attested to in these works is the power of God. It is no finite might, adapted to our creaturely relativity, but an absolute, sovereign might. It is at the same time a might of faith, of trust, of love. The Lord possesses it perfectly, so perfectly that he lets it become living in every work. When we possess this same faith, we can also perform his works as he performs them. We can truly do the same works as he. But we can do so only when we possess faith—that is, *his* faith, which is stronger than anything, stronger than the world and its laws. There is no law of the world, however rigid and brazen it might look, that cannot be surpassed and exploded by the power of faith. To define this power, one would have to say that it knows no limits other than those of God, but God is limitless.

Whoever believes in God can act on his behalf. If he really believes, then he possesses what God possesses. When he first begins to believe, he possesses certain qualities stemming from God. The chief characteristic of these qualities is that they are perpetually exploding, perpetually expanding, to flow into limitlessness. How this limitlessness looks is inexplicable; it is only clear that all previous barriers are transcended; the laws of space and time, of physics, biology and psychology, all fail where the miracle begins.

Whoever believes can do the works of God. But what is even more than doing them is *not* doing them. Not to do them oneself, in order to let God do them; not to do them out of one's own impulse and resolution, but to leave these to God. Compared to what he might have done, the Lord worked very few miracles in his life. In this regard, he restricted himself as much as possible, and in this very restriction lies the work of God. For this holding back is not a simply external limitation or simply ethical moderation. Its origin lies in the Father's invisibility. With the greatest ease, the Lord could have healed every sick person on earth. The truly believing person could also do so. But because they seek only what God wills, desiring to do nothing of themselves, they do God's work by avoiding the miracle rather than working it. In this they resemble the Lord in his holding back. The essential element in working miracles lies in restriction, for God's chief miracle in the world remains the Cross. Anyone who was to darken the brightness of the Cross in the world through the brightness of miracles would no longer be a Christian. Miracles are only intimations of God. They are nothing more than gentle hints and indications; there is something *even greater!* Only in this sign of the Cross can and may miracles occur. Miracles are never perfect, rounded-off deeds, but are always just questions thrown out for those who can hear and see: What is there here to believe? Where does God stand here? What is his grace? What are his demands? They serve to glorify God, but only in order to awaken faith in the neighbor who sees the miracle. The miracles are road signs. They are even less; they are the making visible of a hidden way, a contact—not between the one who as instrument works the miracle and God—but between the one who is to be affected by the miracle and God. They should be gentle, as every touch of God is gentle; they should not tear anything asunder. This means that no consideration at all is given to the believer who works the miracle, but every consideration is due the one who is witness, who should be moved to faith, hope and love.

The Lord promises to believers *even greater* deeds than the ones he accomplished, giving as reason for this his return to the Father. This sounds very mysterious: because the Lord will be with the Father, believers will perform greater works. What is greater about their work will naturally not consist in the greatness of the person who believes and works—although this worker now bears both Father and Son in himself, and specifically Father and Son in unity, because the Son has returned into the unity. Rather, the greater dimension will be that the working of miracles through human beings will be more striking. Now that they are robbed of the Lord's visible presence, they have become much more receptive to miracles. That the Lord worked miracles was almost self-evident to them; it lay in his nature as Son of the Father. But what is one to think and say when a human person like all others, in whom one sees nothing special, suddenly begins to do the works of God? That is much more striking than with the Lord, in a good and a less good sense. In the good sense, the Father and the Son will value the miracles more highly, for both will recognize the one sent by both in the one who performs the Father's works in the name of the Son. Both regard him exceptionally well: the Father praises him because he acts in the Son's name, and the Son praises him because he does the Father's works. Thus both more highly value what has happened. On the other hand, the miracles will also be more striking in a less good sense. Because the indolence and lukewarmness of the non- or only half-believers are always increasing, the entire way of the Son is no longer lived as vitally by Christendom as it was in the beginning. Therefore more striking and sensational miracles are necessary.

14:13–14. *And whatever you will ask in my name, I will do, that the Father may be glorified in the Son. When you ask something of me in my name, I will do it.*

To ask in the Lord's name means to ask in his Spirit. But as mere humans we can neither live nor ask in his Spirit. We can only attempt it over and over, in his grace. To ask in his Spirit means to expect him to bestow his Spirit on our requests, to translate them, to a certain degree, into his sense, so that in the end both the request and its fulfilment originate in his Spirit: the request, in that we step back before him and leave it to him to hear it as he pleases; the fulfilment, insofar as it will follow from this hearing. The fulfilment will only seldom bring us what we expect. It can, of course, correspond with our request, but it can also take a completely different form. Still, it will be the fulfilment of a particular request, for if we have prayed in the name of the Son it will infallibly be granted to us to hear in the name of the Son. But God's answer will always be an infinitely greater one than we could expect on the basis of our request, even when we have apparently received exactly what we asked him for.

The Son fulfills our request, *so that the Father may be glorified in him.* Not only for love of us will the Son fulfill our requests, but above all for love of the Father. Here the life of Father and Son in each other, which the Lord explained to Philip, is more plainly manifest. The Father is in him, he is in the Father; nothing that one of them does (except the Passion) is done alone but always has communal character. Always a deed of mutual love, it is therefore also one of mutual glorification of Father and Son. Everything that the Father does, he does for love of the Son; everything that the Son does, he does for love of the Father. This love is so completely one that the deed also is one single deed. This is what constitutes glorification. It is not as though the deeds of the Father or of the Son were directed toward something extrinsic to their innermost being. Glorification is not a purpose but is intrinsic to love itself. Glorification consists in the deed's being one of mutual love, without any other purpose. The deeds of love that the Father and Son do together are a mutual exchange and testimony of their love, and we receive a share in this flow of love when we ask for it in the Lord's name.

Prayer is a participation in the stream of love between Father and Son. Every prayer, every stammering of the human person, is an attempt at participation in the eternal dialogue between Father and Son. We do not know what is discussed in this dialogue; at best, we sense it from afar. We cannot become involved in this dialogue as though we were equally entitled partners. We can only ask, on the one hand—that is the simplest and most childlike form of prayer—and, on the other hand, listen to and contemplate the eternal dialogue of God in praise and awe. To ask is never forbidden us, if it is done in God's Spirit. But the fulfilment of our request, which is always greater and richer than the request itself, will at the same time open up a way for us to go over from the mere request into contemplation, which loses the character of request and approximates more and more to the dialogue between Father and Son. As the request rises vertically from earth to heaven, the Son receives it in heaven, expanding it into a participation in God's eternal life and thus preparing it for the return from heaven to earth. The prayer of petition has something finite about it: one can assess it somehow. One can never assess contemplation; at the start one does not know the goal of its movement, nor does one see its fruit and effect afterward. In the prayer of petition one expects an answer to a particular question; in contemplation one seeks something one does not even know. A person's own ego must disappear in contemplation. Every real prayer ends in some fashion in contemplation, and contemplation given from above is somehow the transition and accompaniment from one human prayer of petition to another. For one who believes, the fulfilment of a request lies above all in its being accompanied by the Lord, and this is given in contemplation. In petition one attempts to seize something of the veil of mystery, but in contemplation one is covered by it. Certainly we may never go over to contemplation so completely that we would ignore petitioning, for we remain creatures with needs, and even if we wanted to ask nothing for ourselves, there would still be the world and the Church. Nor may we ever forget how great is the grace of contemplation itself, and how much we need to ask for it. Contemplation leads further than petition, but it always leads back to petition.

The actual contemplation of God and of the life of Christ can be accomplished only by the individual for himself alone, in solitude. The prayer of petition, on the other hand, can be a prayer of the community. But there is also a prayer in the community in which petition and contemplation unite: the *Rosary*. Here contemplation is learned in the prayer of petition itself, through contemplation of the life of the Mother of the Lord. Her life was a contemplative life. Her first assent implied a devotion to the will of the Father and the life of the Son, involving full openness to conception, and hence the pure, contemplative attitude. This is not the attitude of motherhood alone, but one that includes the transition to bridehood from the outset because everything in her is already subordinated to the Son's will, to his life and his mission. Precisely this ordering of one's own existence to the mysteries of the Lord's life, the readiness to make these mysteries the meaning of one's life, is the essence of the contemplative attitude. Under the Cross Mary is the Bride, who once was Mother. In her bridehood, then, motherhood lies hidden at the base. Therefore all bridehood with the Lord in the Church is a mystery of fruitfulness and at the same time of contemplation. Mary's life was a service to the Lord's life, and the meaning of her own life is absorbed in this service. That is what is contemplative about her. In her first assent, she takes on herself a life of loneliness for the Son. In this loneliness she leads the contemplative life of Mary of Bethany (the identity of names is certainly no accident); she fulfills the duty of contemplation in the most perfect way. Therefore it is right when Christians learn to contemplate through her, and contemplate her contemplation in the prayer of the Rosary. The way through Mary to Jesus is above all a mystery of contemplation. The Mother is involved wherever the inner, hidden essence of the Son is to be revealed to a person. If Christ lacked this motherly mediation he would be robbed of an entire sphere of possibility for imitation. For the Lord to be able to accomplish his work of redemption, he had to be received by someone who was ready to be his Mother. She sacrificed herself entirely for him in order to make his sacrifice possible. She thus became the Son's way into earthly existence, but for us she becomes the exemplary way to receive the Son. She shows us how to begin to imitate the Lord's life. In that she was the first to be open to God, she can show us her mystery and take us with her on her way. The Son is open to the Father and to mankind because he is God and man at the same time, and thus he can be the mediator. The Mother is open to the Son and to mankind, and so she can be the mediatrix between the Son and us. This mediation occurs in her womanly role of accompanying the Son, in her particular way of sharing the Son's mystery: in contemplation. Her consent does not mean that she is able to assess the mystery of the Son. Even for her the Son remains a mystery infinitely exceeding her grasp. But she is taken into his mystery; she has part in it. She has chosen it once and for all as her mystery; she has irrevocably entered into her Son's world. Even for the Mother the measure of communication, of penetration, of vision, of revelation lies wholly with the Lord. In contemplation, the human person lets God dispose. Dryness and forsakenness are conditions of contemplation that are grounded in its essence. Into this the Mother is increasingly initiated, up to contemplation of the total night of the Son on the Cross, her own total night.

III

14:15. *If you love me, keep my commandments.*

The Lord sets up a criterion by which to gauge love for him: the keeping of his commandments. In order to know whether they love him, he will look back and make his judgment according to whether they kept his commandments. He speaks now of his commandments in the plural, although until now he has issued only one commandment: love one another. But this one commandment includes everything he has shown mankind, the entire fullness of his deeds, so that his commandment can be newly read out of each of his deeds. Every one of his works includes, as its substance and quintessence, the one commandment of love. In every point of his existence perfect unity reigns between what he does and his love for God and for us. Each time there is a perfect mutual inclusion of his way and his deed. Each one of his deeds, then, however varied they may be, is an immediate and total embodiment of his commandment of love; and in the sense that he lets each of his deeds become a commandment, he can speak of a plurality of commandments. Demanding nothing but love, he demands that those who love him walk his path, and that means keeping his commandments.

Or, to say it another way: he expects that if we love him, we will also love one another in our actions. That suffices him completely. He will provide everything else. He makes lovers out of us, for whose ongoing life he ultimately bears responsibility. If we were really lovers, if our love corresponded with his, then nothing more could befall us. All our deficiencies and sins stem simply from the fact that we do not love as we ought. There is a schism in us between the love that is demanded of us and the love we actually give, or also between the love the Lord actually gives us and our willingness to accept it from him. In both cases there is the same deficit. In this consists our sin; this is where it lodges and grows. In both equations, the missing elements coincide. Accordingly, no one can say that the Lord loves him more than he is capable of receiving, and that he is, therefore, not responsible for this lost surplus. Rather, the Lord offers his love in such a way that a person would have to sense it as a whole, if he did not close himself to it. Whoever loves as the Lord might expect him to could ask anything of the Lord because of this love. But the dichotomy within him between his will and the Lord's will must disappear. This dichotomy eclipses the Lord's love as well as his will, thus thwarting his working too.

If you love me, says the Lord, *keep my commandments.* If we do not love him, we need not even venture to approach his commandments. If we love him, nothing remains for us but the attempt to keep them. But if we keep them, we must want the whole. By saying this the Lord deprives us of the one possibility we have, namely, of being mediocre Christians. In the Lord's commandment there is no mention of levels, of progress. It does not stipulate: if you love me a little, then keep my commandments a little. Rather: if you love me at all, keep my commandments. He leaves us no possibility of continuing as we are. The possibility that he opens up to us is not ours at all. But as soon as this possibility of love is put before us, we have no choice: we must declare for it. And since he speaks to us as if we were capable of it, he evidently considers us capable. He simply sees us in terms of human beings who love and therefore act, for in this moment he himself is so human that he believes, acts as if and pretends that he is speaking with people who cannot think otherwise than he. He wants to regard us as people who are assimilated to him and equal to him.

THE FIRST PROMISE OF THE CONSOLER

14:16. *And I will ask the Father, and he will give you another Consoler, that he may be with you always.*

This is no doubt the Son's first request to the Father that is announced as such. He asks for something that is to be understood as the result of his mission: that someone shall remain continually with mankind. He asks the Father for this; he does not demand it. He does not ask now, but will ask in the future, that is, on his return to the Father. The fact that he asks and does not demand is also a consequence of his return to the Father. He returns in the fullness of love, and this fullness of love obliges the Father to fulfill every wish for him, who did everything for love of the Father. But the Son who returns feels himself to be entirely the Son again; he wants to be nothing more than the one who from now on lives once more by God's grace alone. He is like one who left the Father with a mission, and then, without making any claim on the Father, simply returns as pure love, but at the same time with new suggestions. For along the way he has gathered experience in his humanity. He has also discovered that man cannot live without a consoler. He has tasted this himself in the most bitter fashion. Even now, when he has not yet been through utter loneliness, he knows that on earth it is impossible to live without a consoler. In his eyes, to be robbed of the consoler is the utmost of what he will have to go through: it is something completely inhuman. To die in faith is easy, but to die forsaken is terrible. Until now in his earthly life he has always had at his disposal the Father dwelling in him. He sees that men also need something to dwell in them, making them capable of really belonging to him and to the Father, of making more room for them, and that can only be the Holy Spirit. Again it is the Spirit that binds and fuses, creating the unity between God and man.

The Son with his demands would never have prevailed among men if there had not been the Spirit to transform their mind and attitude into that of the Son. The Son might have issued his commandments of love, without men feeling that it concerned them. People might have objected that this commandment did not interest them at all, that very different things, like making discoveries, reading books and practicing politics, were able to engross their spirits. They could have turned away from the commandment of love. But the Spirit transforms them into the attitude of Christ. There is nothing fortuitous about this, for it was the Spirit who had already prepared the place for the Son in the Mother of the Lord. The Mother speaks her consent. She speaks it of herself. But because she speaks it, the Son develops in her through the Holy Spirit. So we, too, must speak our consent at some point; then the Holy Spirit lets the Son grow in us.

The Holy Spirit is always sent by the Father. He never works other than in this sending from the Father, which is the fruit of the Son's request. It is unthinkable that the Spirit should blow somewhere where the Father and Son are not—that he could, for example, convert a person today from paganism to Judaism. He always blows between the Father and Son, between Son and Father, belonging to both.

He caused the Son to grow in the Mother. He came down on the Son himself and has guided him ever since. But now that the Son has lived in the world and exercised an immediate effect on it, now that his mission is heading toward its end, everything could slacken and die. That would happen, too, if everything were not firmly held in the state of immediacy by the Spirit. That this is possible is a consequence and function of the Cross. But it is through the Spirit that the Cross itself does not become a single concluded fact but remains a continual, living presence and yet endures as a perpetual, continuing fact. Both are his working: the eternal factuality and the factual eternity of the Redemption. He is the constant enlivening of the Son; he expands souls according to the mind of the Son. He gives souls the right contours and grades their degree of importance. He takes root in the innermost base of the soul, in its unconscious powers and impulses; he is related to these impulses in a mysterious fashion; he steers them, enlivens them, rules them, directs them to what should be. He watches over the soul's whole unconscious and uses it in God's purpose. That a Christian marriage can be lived so completely in the Lord that even what is instinctual can be used and included rightly and without problems, is entirely a work of the Holy Spirit. But also the spiritual life of the human person, his spiritual and intellectual work, becomes meaningful and fruitful through the Holy Spirit. Without him it would remain dead and dessicated, an idle game; through him it becomes living and useful for God and for humanity. Not for nothing is the Holy Spirit a spirit of knowledge and wisdom and all spiritual gifts. He understands how to make Christian needs out of all the natural and legitimate needs of the human person. He also understands how to form, out of each human situation that threatens to come to a dead end—for instance, out of a childless marriage—something with a new beginning, something meaningful and living in God. Through him everything becomes fruitful, and always in such a way that he begins in the deepest essence of the human person, in the most human part, and turns this outward to God, turning, as it were, what is innermost outward.

Now in the sense that he gives everything finite and senseless in human life a divine and eternal meaning from within, he is the *Consoler*, the Counselor. The very point at which something seems humanly futile is his point of departure. And what could be more futile than the task with which the Lord has entrusted us? He has set us the task of keeping his commandments out of love for him. But he also sees *his* task of asking the Father to send us the Consoler, so that we will not be overpowered by the hopelessness of keeping the commandments, of our entire life in the Lord. He has commanded us to love, and he gives us the Consoler so that we may not despair at the impossibility of this commandment. The Consoler is always there to mediate the living relationship between us and the Lord; to mend it where it appears broken by sin and inconstancy; where it is alive, to render it even more vibrant. Nothing ever lies behind us: everything always remains living future. Through the Spirit there is no more human "why". The cramped existence to which most people are condemned; the constant renunciation of so much in life; the senselessness of *being* in general; the baffling way in which goods and destinies are distributed; the obscurity of a particular fate; the ennui of existence; the irretrievability of the human condition; the desolation of aging; the recognition that nothing will ever be complete; the impossibility of living a destiny different from the one laid on us against our will; the irreversibility of time; the riddles as to why we are lay people and not priests, priests and not lay people, Christian and not heathen; why this person is in the Church and this one not; the unattainability of our inborn impulse toward perfection, toward expansion of our boundaries, toward universal life—all this is resolved at a stroke through the Consoler, the Holy Spirit. It would be unbearable if the choice of the thousand possibilities that life places before us, all of which we would like to choose and might choose, were decided only by an incomprehensible fate; if being the one thing we have to be meant bidding farewell to and renouncing everything else that we could be, want to be, ought to be. The Spirit's consolation is that everything can still be contained in this one-time life. This puny human life can be so rich that God's infinity has room in it. That is the consolation, and it suffices.

But the Spirit not only takes away what is meaningless in our life; he also brings us nearer to the Lord. His creative activity is directed not only away from us, but toward us. He leads us to God, but also God to us. He does this, not in the sense of strengthening our ego, but by giving us the Lord's life. For he is, after all, the Spirit of the Lord, awakening him in us. He is always the one who excites and vitalizes; he is the thrilling one, the very opposite of all ennui, the enemy of all spiritual death. He expands, he liberates, he blows where he will. Yet there is nothing arbitrary about him, for he was sent by the Father at the Son's request. In his sending, then, he is determined wholly by the Father and the Son. He proceeds from this fidelity between Father and Son and therefore also mediates this fidelity. He is never to be separated from the Father and Son and made independent as the Spirit, in a free-floating spirituality that is not the spirituality of the Father and the incarnate Son.

That he may be with you always. It is one of the qualities of the Spirit that, when he has once settled in, he remains always. One cannot separate from him, either voluntarily or involuntarily. As the Mother of the Lord became Mother through him and therefore remains Mother in eternity, and this quality cannot be taken from her, so too each individual Christian is eternally what he is through the Spirit. The mark that the Spirit stamps into a person is ineradicable. It is unthinkable that a human person, for instance Joan of Arc or little Thérèse, who exercised a certain function in this world and had a mission to fulfill in the Spirit, no longer possesses this mission in heaven. A person's mission and singularity can be expanded but not abolished: the function remains. Every particular office on earth will be continued on earth, in and from heaven. So completely does the Holy Spirit permeate the missions and the special orientations of the apostolate that what he makes out of a person remains for always. Therefore, he lives eternally in us too. The Christian's being permeated by the Spirit has its parallels in the character of priestly ordination: now the soul is marked with the ineradicable sign of office, now with the sign of mission. This sign is more or less strong in individual Christians, but it is always present.

14:17. *The Spirit of truth, whom the world cannot comprehend, because it does not see him or know him. You know him, because he remains with you and will be in you.*

For only a very few people is truth something consoling. Unless they happen to possess a particular impulse toward research, or to be fanatically engaged with a particular truth, the truth usually interests very few. What occupies and fills them is practical, instinctual life, the pleasant and useful things they encounter daily. Truth, on the other hand, is only a means to an end for most people. For the most part they prefer to live in illusion rather than in the truth. They find the former beautiful and intoxicating, the latter cold, sobering and pitiless. And yet the Lord sends the Consoler not as the Spirit of love or of hope, of joy or of inspiration, but precisely as the Spirit of truth. Thus he shows us that everything coming from the Father is true in the most basic, original fashion, creates truth and changes our life from a deceptive and illusory one into a true one.

Despite appearances to the contrary, precisely this truth is the most important thing there is to life. It acts with objectivity, free from any deceptive wrappings of subjective life. This naked objectivity affords the only possible access to true life, every beginning of a life developing toward the Father. If a human person is to be able to emerge from his subjective bias and approach God, he must first be led into objective truth, the Being of God, the infallible certainty, indeed demonstrability of his existence, Christ's mission and divinity, the signs of the true Church, the requirements of Christian life and of personal apostolate, prayerful intercourse with God: all this is the fixed framework in which new life can unfold. Earlier it often seemed as if truth were not an elementary necessity, as if love and its involuntary, almost blind movement toward God would suffice. Love even seemed to replace truth. Now the fully original essence of truth becomes evident. Now it is possible for us to realize that there *is* something like a truth of God even before we discern love. It is the Holy Spirit who leads the human person to this inescapable truth, perhaps through a person, a book or any sort of encounter, and through this encounter with the truth, this person's tiny subjective world is suddenly expanded. To enter into the Kingdom of truth, love is certainly necessary. But the basic fact of truth strikes the person with elemental force at first, through the Spirit of truth included in it. Truth has its own life, which already lives somehow in the one who vigilantly seeks the truth. In the subjective search, in the urge for truth, this Spirit of truth that God has imparted to us through his Son, is astir with great energy. Every human person needs to find his place somewhere, to let himself be inserted into some framework that encompasses and includes him, that is greater than his own subjectivity. This can be some form of human society or simply being complemented by the opposite sex. Adam could not live alone on earth; he immediately had to be complemented by Eve, in order to be able to live in the truth. Anyone who attempts to live without society has either not yet understood anything about the meaning of life, or has been so badly disappointed that something in him is shattered. But when a person encounters the opposite sex, when complementarity is offered him, he immediately realizes that he will forever be only a certain part of the whole. The Holy Spirit is there in that moment to console him. For the Spirit also makes partial, fragmentary and particular truth possible, because every individual, through the Spirit, has an eternal mission in the whole, and can place himself, in love, at the disposal of the whole. So in the end it is love, after all, that leads to life in the truth. One can be led into the Church through truth, but only through love does one become a real member of the community.

The world cannot receive him, because it does not see him or know him. The world consists of those who do not belong to Christ, who thus do not know him and therefore do not receive from him the Spirit of truth. There is an indissoluble connection between the Spirit of truth and Christ. For the Spirit comes at the Son's request and leads to the Son. But the world does not want to be led. It is sufficient unto itself; it does not want to be fetched out of its finished forms. It defines its forms and frameworks itself. The basic condition is that they must not overpower or surpass the ego. They must correspond to momentary, personal, surveyable need. Therefore the world can neither receive nor comprehend the Spirit or truth because he lies outside its defined borders. For the world, on the other hand, truth lies within the circle it has drawn around itself. The Spirit does not acknowledge such barriers, for his truth, as objective truth, is also a progressive and infinite truth. It cannot stop at a partial obedience that is not the expression of a total obedience to God. Therefore the only one who receives and sees the Spirit is the one who, together with the Spirit, transcends the world's frameworks and forms. He receives the Spirit because he can only overstep these barriers through the Spirit. And he sees and perceives him in the way that he can be seen: in his explosive effects, which are at the same time fulfilling. In exploding restrictions, the Spirit fulfills something the Christian needs, which he begins to need because of the working of the Spirit in his innermost nature. Knowledge of the Spirit is something that occurs within man's realization that his own limits are not rigid and final. As soon as he is no longer fascinated by himself in a particular question and no longer seeks the solution within himself, but is overwhelmed by some opening into what is Greater and Better beyond himself, he begins to sense the Spirit and, sensing him, to know him. This applies to every way that leads from the world to Christianity, and it applies also within Christianity itself. There is too a closed Christianity, in which everything — prayer, the reception of the sacraments, the points of view one represents — are related to the ego. "It does my soul good to communicate; it feels strengthened by prayer; it is part of my spiritual hygiene to give alms; it suits my physical needs to be a Christian, for this religion is tailored entirely to my needs, my person. Therefore I gladly comply with all its requirements." A person who lives in such a closed Christianity will first be made uneasy by the Spirit, insofar as he still lets himself be touched by him. The Spirit tries to undermine these walls, seeking to make them collapse. He makes the person uneasy just as he unsettles those non-Christians who have at one time come up against the fact that there is something higher. In both cases this uneasiness stems not from the human person, but from God. It comes not from within, but from without. It is not the human person's cleverness that has discovered that there is something greater outside the framework. Rather, this knowledge is always grace, requested by the Son, granted by the Father in the Holy Spirit.

You know him. These very apostles whose response is so meager, who fail so much, know the Spirit because they experience with ever-new uneasiness that the Lord surpasses them. Nor will this change when the Spirit descends on them. Indeed, then, most truly, they will never be able to rest. Anyone who has received the Spirit can no longer have rest and relaxation. Even if he submits to the Spirit and tries to do what is expected of him, he will still be far from feeling at ease in doing so, let alone imagining himself at the goal. Herein lies the knowledge of the Spirit. The truth is certainly something absolute, but at base it is so absolute that no one has ever attained it. Doors keep opening just when we think we have entered the last room. From the truth, which is a midpoint, ways go out in all directions, like rays from a star. But everyone who wants to perceive the truth must remain completely at the center, and yet stride forth in all directions. Even if he specializes in a particular way, through his choice of profession, for example, he is still not allowed to forsake the midpoint of truth and to forget that there are still an infinite number of other rays. And the more someone progresses in perceiving the truth, the more strongly he must be rooted in the center. In no case may he only touch on the center and then move over to settle down on the periphery. All individual action must always arise out of the totality that is the Lord. If one no longer had a vital awareness that the Spirit of truth is the Spirit of the Lord, which is indivisible, and that this Spirit is requested by the Son and given by the Father, then one would quickly slide into the spirit of untruth. If the Spirit of the center no longer vitally penetrates to the uttermost periphery, then the periphery dies and its apparent truth is only a dead skeleton. This applies to every branch of Christian knowledge, including theology. The Spirit of truth is the Spirit of God. He arises from the Son's humility toward the Father, as an expression and result of their mutual love. The whole truth has its origin in this eternal relationship of love. And only the person who corresponds to this origin in love, who thus remains in the Son's love and humility, can receive the Spirit of truth from the Father through him, and in this Spirit perceive the truth. Although truth is rational and objective and even absolute, it can never be fixed in such a way that one might separate it from grace. It remains a gift of grace that is never given once and for all, but is poured out ever anew as a perpetual gift.

This Spirit now *remains with* the apostles, and he *will be in them.* Even now he is remaining with them, and because the Lord still lingers among them, they can still question him about much that the Spirit impels them to know. Later the Spirit will be in them. Then it will go harder with them, for they will be alone with the Spirit in them and will have to begin to converse with him. The Lord has laid the foundation in his teaching, and the Spirit he leaves behind for them will have to suffice to show them the respective concrete application and interpretation of his teaching. This foundation that the Lord has laid is enough. The disquietude caused by the Spirit may not degenerate into an inconstant, anguished, problematical search. The way from the foundation once laid to its interpretation is a sure way, a way from the center to the periphery, on which one need not, and indeed should not, abandon the center itself. Nor is it necessary to get lost among all the ramifications. To analyze everything to the limit would be to fall into a labyrinth without exit. Rather, one needs the courage to break off. In Christian life there is an element of trust, in which one no longer examines where one stands, but simply gives oneself. A certain pushing ahead, a certain untroubled daring are part and parcel of Christian existence.

THE SON IN US

14:18. *I will not leave you behind as orphans; I will come to you.*
If the Lord were not there, his disciples would be orphans. He came, indeed, as their Lord and as their brother. Still, if he were not there, they would be orphans, because of their feeling of forsakenness, and even more because of their perplexity and the doubt and despair that would necessarily be aroused in them. The Lord's influence would gradually weaken in their life. They would, of course, remember the time of his existence and would do much as a response to this memory, which, however, would lose more and more of its immediate urgency. An emptiness, the expression of their orphanhood, would then have arisen in their life, for they would in truth have lost their Father. The Lord not only showed them and taught them the Father; in his dealings with them, he represented him. Having lost him, they would be robbed of the Father. Father and Son are now so much one that the Lord's relationship to mankind can be called fatherly as well as brotherly. Even at the beginning he took a Father's place for them, and the more he reveals to them of the Father, the more fatherly he himself becomes for them. But he will not leave them behind as orphans; rather: *I will come to you*. At Easter, he comes back to them bodily as the Risen One. And he returns to them spiritually in the sending of the Holy Spirit at Pentecost, by affirming that he has now attained to the Father, redeeming his promise. Finally he comes back to them in the Eucharist, in a visibility that corresponds to his Incarnation and at the same time possesses qualities of the Father: limitlessness and omnipresence. This omnipresence is at the same time bound to mankind: they will have to discern where he will rest in the form of the real Presence.

During his human life on earth, he did not shun anyone who wanted to see him. In the future, too, he will never reject the Church and her will to possess him. Thus the return is accomplished: the *Son* himself returns bodily and in the Eucharist, and the *Holy Spirit* comes as the one whom he sends, and by virtue of this return mankind will not be orphans, but possess a *Father*. Hence the entire circle of Christian mystery is completed in this return: after the Resurrection there is no longer any possible separation between the Father, the Son, and the Spirit. Whereas during his earthly life the Lord almost always spoke only of his going forth from the Father and his return to the Father, now on entering his Passion he opens up the mystery between himself and the Father and shows their unity in the Holy Spirit. From this center of love, he now reveals more deeply the meaning of everything he said earlier. Precisely because the separation between the Father and the Son in his humanity will cease after the Resurrection, their unity in the Holy Spirit will become finally visible, and thus too the full form of their Trinity-in-Unity.

14:19. *Yet a short while, and the world will no longer see me. But you see me, for I live, and you also will live.*

Yet a short while the Lord will live among his own: until his death on the Cross. Then the world will no longer see him. The world will not see his life on the Cross, his life of the Passion. It will follow this life outwardly with physical eyes, but not inwardly, with love. It will survey the individual stations of his way of the Cross, perhaps even empathize with his situation, but what is actually happening will remain fully closed to it all the same. It will not know that the peak of suffering lies not in bodily death, but in the final isolation, laden with all the sins of the world, in separation from the Father. This separation, which will last only *a short while,* will have the weight of an eternity for the Lord. On the Cross he will feel lonesome unto death, unto a limitless, eternal death in which every temporal moment and viewpoint will completely disappear. What will be a short while for mankind will be an eternal while for him.

Henceforth he will disappear forever from the eyes of the world. In future he will not be visible for those who do not believe. To the eyes of the world he will submerge like a destiny that has come to an end, like a life that leaves no other tracks behind it except those of memory. The Lord cannot describe the few who still believe in him as "the world".

But you see me, for I live. Those who believe in him will see that he will survive the Cross. He does not say: I will live, but rather: *I live.* And he does not say: you will see me, but rather: *you see me.* For his Cross, his death, his descent into hell, his Resurrection and Ascension; all this is his present life. His death is not an interruption and not an end of his life, but only a form, a new manifestation of his life. Everything that he is and does, is life; even his dying is life. When he gives back his spirit to the Father; when he dies in loneliness, travels to hell, enters into the utmost forsakenness—all of these are sure and infallible expressions of his life. They are not chance experiences, not accidents, not fates but substantial conditions of his life. He lives them in their entire fullness. His death is not the sinking of his life into nothing but a perfect expression of his being alive, a part, an aspect, a possibility, a living out of his life.

And you also will live. His life, which moves between life and death, leads down beyond death into hell, and then returns to the world and leads up to the Father: that is the life of the Lord that they see. But beyond this personal path of his life that they can somehow see, survey and follow, whose direction they can give and whose segments they can describe, there stands his life in the Father, which he lives from primal beginnings and which the Son puts into the Eucharist for mankind. Believers see him because they themselves will live. The Eucharist is his divine form of life on earth and at the same time his form of life that has been made accessible to men, in which he lives and in which we likewise live. For himself he sees a direct continuity between his temporal life and the Eucharist, which in reality is beyond time. He lives perpetually, whether he is in the world in the shape we acknowledge as the human life form, or whether he abides in the Eucharist, of which we know in faith that it is his assumed and yet eternal form of life. But he also sees a continuity between his life and our life. Both flow into each other, and a real separation is no longer thinkable. When he establishes this community between his and our life in the Eucharist, he not only gives us a share in his divine life, but also in the mysteries of his temporal life. Every aspect of his life—Cross, descent, Resurrection or Ascension—becomes definitive for our life. Which mystery will apply to us lies wholly in his judgment. There is no rule prescribing which of the Lord's mysteries will be the sign of a Christian life. Thus, for example, little Thérèse remains fixed at the very beginning of the Passion, while other destinies roll through the whole suffering. The Lord can communicate his life in totally different ways: to one he mediates it very suddenly, without transition, as if from heaven; to others gradually, through their seeking;

to one on the occasion of a very particular experience; to another in a meditation or a Holy Communion. Perhaps such a person has communicated for years, but this time he receives the Lord in the mode of a sharing in his divine life. But he can also give his life in the Eucharist differently every day, so that each day's work is defined and colored by the particular character of the Communion that one has received. Or perhaps he gives a person only a participation in his first thirty years of life, in which nothing conspicuous, nothing extraordinary happens.

In the Eucharist too there is the space of time in which one sees the Lord, and the space of time in which one does not see him. For the person whose faith is not really alive, the time in which one does not see him, is that during which he is hidden in the Tabernacle. He becomes visible in the host during Mass, at Holy Communion and in Exposition. In the Tabernacle he is not visible, and the visibility of the host is replaced by faith alone. But those who truly believe will see him even then. They should be so permeated by their faith that they see him only within their faith, whether or not the visible form of his presence is to be seen. For the visibility of the host in the Exposition and its invisibility in the Tabernacle, this alternation in the Eucharist's conditions, is a mystery within faith itself, showing that most of the Lord always remains hidden. The host is shown in Exposition, but it is shown in the sign of not-being-shown. What is shown is the hiddenness. The hidden and the shown host reciprocally contain each other: each of the two mysteries embraces the other and reveals it as well: the Hidden is the Shown, and the Shown is the Hidden. Therefore, too, neither is to be ranked above the other or set up as the only admissible or desirable one in the Church. For precisely this alternation shows the impenetrability of the whole mystery: on neither of the two conditions can a system of the Eucharist be constructed. In one church there can be Exposition, in another not; both are correct, and each presupposes the other. This possible simultaneity of the two conditions is disturbing, for it shows how much the mystery of the hiddenness and openness of the Eucharist always transcends us. It will not satisfy our urge for total understanding.

But whether shown or not shown, both forms flow into the common mystery of his life and our life. The Lord creates in our life a place for his life, which is hidden as well as apparent; he causes our life too to become both veiled and visible. Thus he also places our life in a rhythm of contemplation and action, and in the Eucharist he shows how both conditions, grasped at their roots, encourage and penetrate each other. For not only hiddenness is contemplation, and not only exposition is action. The Eucharist is at work also in the Tabernacle; there is also vision in Exposition. Contemplation and action are, so to speak, different isotopes of a single and transcending reality of the life of the Lord and our life in him, which can appear under different aspects. Thus too there is no division between action and contemplation, no equipoise to be established between them.

Exposition of the host may not be preferred to the host's hiddenness. It may not become a religious sensation. It is not an exhibition. Prayer before the exposed Most Holy Sacrament is not better or more effective than that before the hidden Lord. Certainly, when the host is shown, it is done so that people may look at it; it is not the sign for the faithful to look away or at the floor at that moment. *You will see me,* says the Lord. Therefore one should really look at him. To look away here would be just as wrong as if, out of humility, one were not to listen when he speaks to us.

14:20. *On that day you will know that I am in my Father, and you are in me and I am in you.*

The day on which they will know this is the day on which they will see the Lord again, will meet him again on this earth. It is the day of the Resurrection and the day on which they will receive him in the Eucharist. It is a precise day, for it is a precise meeting; only the date is undetermined, because it includes every meeting. This day is the day of each individual meeting with the Lord as well as the sum of all meetings with him.

You will know that I am in my Father. On that day they will see him come, just as he is with them now. But then they will see something about him which they do not see about him now: namely, that he is in the Father. They will suddenly perceive that he is not alone at all, but lives in the Father. They will know this through the Holy Spirit, who binds the two, but also through faith in the Son, who has told them this again and again and proven to them by this return that he is in the Father. For he has redeemed his promise, given to the Father as well as to them:

to come to them when he will be in the Father. He let the promised truth become a seen truth, and by satisfying *one* truth (that of his return), he satisfied every truth—including the truth that he is in the Father. His dwelling in the Father is continual, not an accidental one that may begin and end at any time, not an interrupted one; this indwelling lasts beyond his temporal life and is grounded in all eternity. It overcomes every mutual limitation between Father and Son: it is no longer possible to distinguish between them in such a way that one could choose between them, could decide for one or the other. One can only choose the Father in the Son or the Son in the Father. This being of the Son in the Father sums up all the statements of the relationship between them that had never been grasped until now, but this does not mean that the relationship has suddenly become comprehensible. It means that we are finally overwhelmed by this truth: the Son is in the Father. In human terms, of course, we know that the child was once in its father, that it bears the inheritance of this father and that its growth and maturing are not unrelated to the father. But this relationship is a very pale reflection of the relationship between the Lord and his Father. In his mission and his Incarnation, and not only in his return to God but above all in his loneliness and forsakenness, the Lord is continually in the Father. During his life as a man, and equally in the Eucharist, he is as he is in heaven in all eternity. This being-in-the-Father is not a restriction, not a limitation of his independence; rather, it is a necessity grounded in mutual love. This necessity is so urgent that even in the moment of separation on the Cross, when the world can only see the forsaken man, the Son's divinity is laid up with the Father.

You will know that *you are in me.* This too we will know on that day: we are in him. We, sinners, are in him, the pure one. And the more profound this realization becomes, the more it seizes possession of us, the greater the mystery becomes. For when we begin to suspect that he is in us, we learn to see that we ourselves are nothing, and that he is everything. And yet his Everything would not be complete if we were not in him. We are in him, comprehended in his person, and so he is our possessor doing with us as he sees fit. And because we are in him, he takes us with him everywhere that he is. We do not fall out of him; he envelops us wholly with his presence. The fact that he is in us (as he says later) is almost easier for us to grasp than this. In the Eucharist we can realize this even in the reception of the host. Further, we know that we have received a teaching from the Lord, and that this teaching lives in us; we know that even a partial and conditional assent from our side assures us of the whole extravagance of his love. Finally, we know that he has laid something in us that will no longer allow us to let him die in us. He wants to be alive in us. All this we know, and it seems to us easier to grasp. And yet all this is only possible because we are in him. He can only be alive in us if we are alive in him. The first does not work without the second, and the apparently comprehensible does not work without the incomprehensible. But both, the comprehensible and the incomprehensible, are a mystery of *his* life, his unitary being; both mysteries mutually include each other and are so much a part of his essence that one cannot separate one from the other without destroying the whole. If one were to accept one and reject the other, the whole would immediately cease to be alive.

And I am in you. In the Eucharist we have an idea of how he is in us, and in his teaching, too, we see how he dwells in us. But how he is in us in his teaching: that, again, is difficult to comprehend. And yet, even if we *fight* against his love, we are still always fighting against his *love*. It is in us; we simply do not want to accept it, but seek to blockade ourselves against it with all possible means. We never want really to understand what it means that he is in us. It would completely overpower us, and it would be the end of our self-glorification. We are always trying to make suggestions to the Lord, make treaties with him; we offer him many things, great sums and gifts, our goodwill, our entire possession in the form of an inventory. But all this is irrelevant and completely obsolete when once he lives in us. He is beyond all that. He knows mankind and its requirements; he can use them if he will, but he can just as well do without them. Ultimately, he can transform them, grant them different possibilities and capabilities. He lives in us as the Lord who governs the household. And because he really lives in us, he also demonstrates his vital power: he can do battle against our setting boundaries, he can overcome them and raze them to the ground piece by piece. He fights against us, and that struggle only comes to an end when he gives us, the vanquished, over to the Father. He must continually be killing us to make us living in God, until we have grasped that it is not we who bring him to God, but he us. What we accomplish by way of mortifications (even if they were the harshest possible) is nothing compared with what he daily and hourly has to kill in us in order to be able even to breathe in us. We always want to claim all the air for ourselves; we only want to let the Son live in us in such a way that he would not need any room, except perhaps a tiny cell. But he needs all our room in order to live; he must fight for it, do battle with us for the whole floor space of our soul. And when we are finally obliged to admit that he now really lives in us, it is not because of our asceticism, but because of the effect of his unwearying battle against our denial and resistance.

LAW AND LOVE

14:21. *Whoever has my commandments and keeps them, he it is who loves me. But whoever loves me will be loved by my Father, and I too will love him and reveal myself to him.*

Having and keeping the commandments are not the same thing, although the two flow into each other. Whoever has the commandments really knows them, and he knows them in such a way that he is gripped by them, and in such a way that there is no other possibility but to keep them. Or, rather, to have the will to keep them and to make the attempt to keep them. For to have the commandments does not mean just to know them theoretically as a possibility that does not touch us personally. The Lord's commandments, above all other commandments, come from love and radiate love. To have them means to have love; to know them means to know love. They are not dead matter, comparable to any human ordinances. Even when one studies with one's reason—assuming a bona fide will really to understand them, to think them through completely—they already radiate a blessing of love. They draw us toward love, into love. It is not possible in the long run to handle them as a simple scientific object without being seized by them oneself. Just as with any special study a passion, a love develops in the long run, the study of the Lord's commandments envelops us, in the long run, with the grace shining from them. No one can say he has studied Christian teaching and it has left him cold. Or if so, he would have closed himself in his studies to the content of the commandments; he would deliberately have resisted them. This resistance is the only thing that can prevent us from seizing the commandments of the Lord and being seized by them. Instead of opening ourselves to the subject as it is, we would have projected our own doubts into it, and so we would have gotten a distorted picture that would naturally lack the power of communication. It would be possible to demonstrate this to a disappointed person, and for him to grasp the commandments as a result of this explanation: this would happen if he allowed grace free movement within him.

In the keeping of the commandments we are all deficient. We keep them to some extent, perhaps, and then refuse to go further. Or we select the commandments that seem keepable. But the person who really has the commandments and tries to keep them will find that his keeping of them will get easier. The keeping of the commandments means above all the keeping of the chief commandment of love. And this love can never be wholly extinguished if someone tries to keep the commandments. Even if he fails, he still has a remnant of love in him, for he is striving after something he does not yet possess, that is, love; he is on his way toward it and has within himself the possibility of a new attempt. On the other hand, anyone who lets himself grow cold in love is further from God, even if he tries outwardly to keep the commandments, than the one who is always falling, but falling within love, in his striving after love.

Whoever has and keeps the Lord's commandment, that is, whoever loves his neighbor, loves the Lord. He may be aware of this connection, or he may entirely overlook it. Perhaps the Lord is a stranger to him; perhaps he really does not know about him. And if he truly loves others, he loves the Lord, and the Lord draws him to himself. Anyone who does good works, not out of some egotism, but out of genuine love for his neighbor, is very near the Lord. He is already within the Lord's love. He would perhaps be very surprised if someone were to show him the connection of his love to Christ, for he did not even know Christ. And yet it is so. It is so because the Lord considers his own mission more important than his person. What he desires is the Kingdom of the Father, the fulfilment of the Father's will. That mankind should love him and, strive toward him as a person is not the most important thing to him. Rather, he wants to bring all the love of the world home to the Father, and to be able to do that he must inflame men to mutual love. If he succeeds in this, he feels loved himself. He takes it as love that is meant for him. For whatever brings mankind nearer to the Father is done for love of him, the Son. Even when someone originally has taken up a task or a work out of love for the Lord, but then becomes so pressured by the activity of the work that he hardly has time anymore to think of the Lord, the Lord will still perceive and accept this work as love shown to him.

But whoever loves me will be loved by my Father. From love for him the

Lord goes over at once to the Father's love for mankind. Only afterward will he speak of his own reciprocal love. He is not the most important thing to himself, nor is his love; rather, he brought the commandment of love into the world and proclaimed it solely for love of the Father. For him everything is accomplished when the Father loves mankind; mankind's love for him, the Son, is only a means of facilitating this love of the Father's. In everything he sees only the Father. The Father, on the other hand, sees the Son in each person who loves and loves him for the Son's sake. The Son, again, is so happy that the Father loves this person that he loves him too. *He loves him,* because the Father loves him. *And therefore he will make himself known to him.* Known, above all, on the Cross. This knowledge of the Cross attests that he bears the Cross for mankind out of love for the Father. He does it out of love, because the Father loves mankind. At first the Cross appeared as a part of his mission: through it he was to bring the love of the world home to the Father. Then he began to fulfill his mission. He came into the world, got to know mankind, gave them his commandment of love and himself fulfilled the commandment of love, paying allegiance to it as a member of the human race to whom it applied. For he felt himself to be such and implemented his commandment on the Cross. And now there is something new: he will love mankind *because* the Father loves them. He reverses the whole mission. He is no longer the one who offers up his great love to the Father; he is no longer the one who loves men so much to teach them to learn to love one another: he is now the one who is compelled by the Father's love for mankind. He experiences the Father's love for mankind as something quite new, as if it were not his own love, but the love wholly belonging to the Father. In this lies the Son's greatest self-expropriation: he not only regards all of his own as the possession of the Father, but he receives his own from the Father's hand as new as if it had never been his. And in this love he will make himself known to the person who loves him, by showing him that he loves him in the Father, unto death on the Cross. In this knowledge there is no room for any doubt or reluctance; this knowledge, communicated by the Lord, is also his perfect love poured out for us. This revelation of the Lord's love through knowledge is the Holy Spirit, in such a way that the Spirit becomes the mediator of love. He binds Father and Son to the human person and chains the human person so closely to God that he has no room for deliberation; all distance between him and God is abolished and everything transforms itself into devotion and passes over into humility. Every human "grasp" is surpassed in this knowledge. We are overcome, knowing once and for all that we cannot compete with the love of God.

14:22. *Judas, not Iscariot, spoke to him: Lord, how can it be that you will reveal yourself to us and not to the world?*

Judas is astounded that the Lord is revealing himself only to the small circle of disciples, instead of to the whole world. He himself has a great plan: he wants to see the gospel immediately spread over the entire world. He thinks that they, the disciples, would have recognized the Lord in any case and that the Lord has already done enough in this regard. He thinks they have now grasped what was to be understood about him. Now that the mystery of the Cross has raised itself up, he believes he has known the Lord. What he knows suffices him for the present. He and the others have known and loved the Lord in the framework of what is possible, appropriate and fitting. What was to be achieved with them seems to him to have been achieved. Now the Lord should no longer delay with them; he should not hesitate any longer but should communicate himself to the world as well. What Judas has performed as a disciple of the Lord has very narrow confines. But he does not see them. He imagines that the boundary has been reached. But not because his own boundary is no more expandable, but because the gospel of the Lord is no greater than he supposed. That this gospel is infinitely greater than any individual's ability to comprehend—including his—is something he has not grasped at all. Nor has he understood that in comprehending the Lord's gospel he is unconditionally bound to work in the name of this gospel, or that the revelation of the Lord to the world is the task of the disciples themselves. For this involves love of neighbor, and the Lord wants to work on mankind through our love of neighbor. The working is his, but he lays the apostolate in our hands. Judas, on the other hand, imagines the Lord's relationship to the disciples as a sort of bond of friendship, a "circle of disciples" or something similar, as something that carries no further obligation. What he does not see is that through this relationship something infinite has arisen; a worldwide task has opened up before him that is in no way exhausted in the hours of being together with the Lord.

Thus he underestimates the Lord's gospel. And yet he does not underestimate the Lord himself. For he accepts it as given that the Lord can and also should reveal himself to the whole world through some miracle. He thinks this would be easy for the Lord. There is nothing wrong about that in itself. But that is not the Lord's way; it does not correspond to his nature. The Lord never seeks the easy way for himself. His way is different: it is the way of suffering, of renunciation and sacrifice, the way of overcoming. It is a painful way, and at the same time an insignificant, a *little* way. Not the great and impressive way of which Judas dreams. And the way of the disciples must also be shaped like the way of the Lord. They must allow themselves to be startled and exploded out of their snug barriers and boundaries, and must learn that sacrifices give love its worth. If everything went as Judas wished, the whole thing would be a fireworks display. It would fascinate, but it could not redeem. It could not last. Only struggle, sacrifice and renunciation give the Christian way the stamp of love. Great as the content of the preceding verse was, and great as the content of the one following will be, here everything appears slow, clumsy and laborious, for the radiance of the "before" and "after" is here compressed into the narrow pass of the insignificant, the small, of suffering, of sacrifice. The greatness of the Lord's love is in no way the greatness of the revelation Judas expects.

14:23. *Jesus answered him and said: If someone loves me, he will keep my word, and my Father will love him, and we will come to him and make our dwelling with him.*

The Lord's answer to Judas' question, as before to Philip's, is not just adequate but overwhelming. He does not let the infinity of his answer become limited by the limitedness of the question. In the exuberance of the answer, the questioner is to be so overwhelmed that he realizes that what he has grasped is only one point within a whole world.

If someone loves me, he will keep my word. To keep the Lord's word means above all to let his word work in oneself. For his word is not something limited that one could allot to a certain place. Rather, it is something growing that the Lord imparts, and that must unfold in the individual in such a way that it explodes his personal boundaries. It will so alter the nature of the person that it becomes a function of the Lord's nature, and the Lord becomes more and more the formative principle for his ego. But this happens when the recipient loves. For in love we give the word the room that it needs to take its dwelling with us and expand ever further, and in this expansion of the Lord's love in us our love also expands and becomes capable of offering the Lord more and more room in us. Thus love for the Lord and the keeping of his word are identical. For the word of the Lord does not grow, as Judas thinks, anywhere in the world; rather, it grows in the souls of those who receive it in love and as love.

And my Father will love him. The Father will love this person because the Father loves the Son, and because he recognizes the Son in this growing word of the Son in the human person. This is yet another side and possibility of the Father's love. He loves the human person because this person preserves in himself the word of the Son, and this word of the Son is also his own word. For the Son is the Word of the Father. The word that grows in souls is the Word that was in the beginning and was with God. But the human person ought to be nothing other than a vessel for this growing Word. He should be like a corridor from God to God: the Father brings forth the Word of the Son, the Son plants this Word of the Father in souls and from them it returns to God.

And we will come to him and make our dwelling with him. Father and Son will come to the human person, in whom—it is already assumed—the Son lives. The Son will not stay alone in him, but will take the Father with him, because he has fulfilled his mission in this person, because he has made him alive to the Father and because he loves him himself. They will not only *come,* but also *make their dwelling with him.* They do not simply make their dwelling in all people, but in this individual who loves God and his neighbor. This person who is already a lover now becomes the dwelling place of God. God comes to him, not as he came in the stable at Bethlehem, into a foreign land, but he comes to him as to his home. This human being with whom God dwells is the saint. There is no automatic similarity between him and the sinner who is receiving grace for the first time. For whoever loves, already possesses grace. And the coming and the dwelling only take place because of this present grace and love. It is something much more special when the Father and Son come to a soul and set up their dwelling in it, in order to work and to radiate from it as from a temple. This word supplements the Lord's response to Judas' question why he does not reveal himself to the world. This revelation does take place, but it takes place through those in whom the Son dwells with the Father.

To take up their dwelling means to stay. This is not a fleeting visit. This indwelling is such that God becomes the possessor of the occupied dwelling. He becomes so more and more, the more the former owner of the dwelling is turned out, until finally God reigns all alone in his dwelling. The earthly laws that regulate human life are somehow made relative through this; they can even, according to the need of the Lord of the dwelling, be altered, reshaped and suspended by him. Thus, what would be fatal for another human person can be entirely harmless for this particular one: it can actually be an occasion for life. The laws of sleep, of nourishment, of recreation, of work, of all things and conditions that make up daily life, lie from now on in the hand of the Lord, who uses them as he will.

In this way has God resolved to reveal himself to the world. He does not want to convert the world suddenly with a striking miracle. Rather, he wants to conquer individual people, and out of these prepare an abode for others. He wants to distribute his light, to shine out from new centers into the darkness of the world. The only condition made when God wants to take up his dwelling in someone is love. It is also the only common characteristic of those whom God so distinguishes. They can belong to all states of life, all classes, all levels of education, and therefore the Lord can let his light flow out from them into every region of humanity.

14:24. *Whoever does not love me, does not keep my word. And the word which you have heard is not mine, but the word of him who sent me, of the Father.*

Whoever does not love the Lord either hates or is indifferent. The Lord does not at first differentiate between the two. He sees only what they have in common: that they do not love and do not keep his word. He knows, then, only two classes of people: those who love and those who do not, those who keep his word and those who do not. Whether the latter fail to keep it out of spite or out of ignorance is not at issue initially. For the Lord, the primary mark of recognition of mankind is whether they keep or do not keep his words. Those who *hate*, who resist him, who do not want to make any room for him, must have knowledge of his commandments; otherwise they could not hate. Their hate stands in a conscious opposition to his love. They know what they are rejecting. The Lord loves them: he knows what he is losing in them, what they perpetually owe him, namely, the keeping of his commandments. There are different levels among those who do not keep his commandments and resist them. There are those who are always talking about the fact that they do not acknowledge him and want to know nothing of him; and there are those who continually protest how much they love him and who yet despise or hate him in their hearts, because in spite of all outward keeping of the commandments they have no love and therefore do not keep them. Among these, again, are such who know the commandments especially well and know how to interpret them, perhaps even make their living by this interpretation, and yet are not capable of keeping them, that is, of loving. Either they love themselves, or they make themselves a substitute for the love they ought to have for God and for mankind. This substitute, again, can take all possible forms: it can consist in extreme industriousness, in Christian action, in scholarship, in any activity. Such people are ready for anything—but not for love. Perhaps they stir the admiration of the whole community, and the Lord alone knows that they do not love.

In addition to the haters there are the *indifferent*, who do not keep the word of the Lord because they do not know it, have not heard it. It is these who are entrusted to us. Perhaps they have heard something of the words and commandments of the Lord, but it has not penetrated them to the heart and so they have remained untouched by it—but they have not closed themselves to it. The Lord still has access to them, and, through his grace, so have we. We know that the Lord has a claim to them, and that part of the task that he sets those who love him lies in caring for these indifferent ones—a task that calls for ever-greater love.

Thus it might appear as if humanity were divided into two classes: into those who love and those who do not, those who keep the word of the Lord and those who do not. But although the Lord in his discourses speaks again and again of those who love him and those who do not love him, he never separates mankind, but fundamentally is always talking about everyone. Here he speaks of all mankind as those who do not keep the commandment and who, therefore, because they do not keep the commandment, do not love him. When the disciples hear this word of the Lord: *Whoever does not love me, does not keep my commandments,* each of them must be terrified in his innermost heart. For they probably thought they loved him. But now the Lord sets up a criterion for this love, namely, the keeping of the commandments. None of them are up to this standard of measurement. None, then, can count himself among the lovers. None can answer the Lord's question as to whether he really loves him. Here we see the infinite difference between the Lord's commandment and all other commandments, whether human ones or those of the Old Testament. In the Lord's commandment there is an intensification, an Evermore, and thus an unbridgeable, eternal discrepancy. Of its very essence there is no possible coincidence between the demand of God as God, and its fulfilment through the human person as human. It is in this chasm that grace lives, and without this chasm it would no longer be grace. This essential trait of the Lord's commandment was not fabricated by later writers; it is clearly evident in the Lord's word.

Through the Lord's grace man loves the Lord, but he still sins. When he sins, he demonstrates that he does not have love. And there will never come a time when he will not need to confess that he sins. If he were to say that he was not a sinner, he would be a liar and the truth would not be in him. He sins because he remains infinitely behind the demands of love, which is not an optional, relative or postponable demand, but an urgent, absolute and immediate one. He should love God with all his soul and all his powers, and not only merely lukewarmly and halfheartedly and incipiently. Thus even as a sinner he should strive with his whole soul and all his powers to sin less and to love more—that is, to make progress in love. But if he is called to make progress, he cannot be completely denied knowledge and an evaluation of this progress. So he will compare his present condition with his former one; he may ask whether or not he has progressed in love. But how can he judge? He cannot possibly regard himself as better and more perfect—to do so would be pharisaical. All he can do is ascertain again and again that he has in no way corresponded to the demand of love as it was really presented: that his attempts at love, compared with what love means in the eyes of the Lord, were so poor, so meager, so lukewarm that they do not even come into consideration. So he does not love; he does not keep the commandment of love. He not only keeps pace badly, he cannot keep pace *at all* with the intensification that dwells in this commandment. What should he do, then? He stands between the demand for conscious and ascertainable progress and the fact that he cannot evaluate this progress. And yet he must unite the two. On the one hand he must stop trying to assess and calculate love itself, for love only lives by the movement of eternal increase. On the other hand, if he were completely to abandon all consideration of where he stands and live only in the invisibility of love, he would fall into a kind of enthusiastic, spineless overemotionalism. His love would have lost the sobriety of truth. This would also render any confession impossible. For in confession we should not confess our sin simply as the formless fog of failure, in general, but concretely and precisely as what it is: as our personal, actual and individual sin. The sinner must see it, then, and somehow judge and weigh it. But he cannot and should not consider it apart from the Lord's love. His only wish should be to see his own sin, like his own love, as included in the love of the Lord. His desire should be to open himself toward this love and into it. To this love he entrusts both his sin and his love. His reckoning must culminate in his perception that the Lord's love is always greater—greater than his sin, as well as greater than his love. Therefore he can certainly lay an account before God and his representative, the priest, but the assessment of gain and loss is something he must leave entirely to the Lord. This rendering of account is man's necessary preparation for the reception of absolution. For this can only build on the truth. In confession grace as grace must become visible, that is, the transition from justice to mercy must become clear. This occurs in the transition from the account of the sinner to the unaccountability of grace. The penitent goes through this account with the confessor in a momentary relationship created for this alone, which is then abolished again, along with the examined account, at the absolution. The whole account has no other goal than its abolition in absolution, than the cancellation of sin, which consists in nothing other than reckoning with God and bestowing grace, which again is nothing but the revelation of God's unaccountable love for us. In presenting his account the penitent may indeed ascertain that he has committed certain visible sins less often or not at all. He may even remark on this in confession. At a certain point, perhaps, progress is to be noted. But in doing this he will have to keep two things before him. First of all, that his total account is wholly relative, because he has no comprehensive view of love and can therefore in no way assess the overall importance his deficiency in love has before God. Secondly, therefore, that his progress is only a progress of grace in him. In gratitude he can know that grace has preserved him from more sins than formerly, although of himself he would have been capable of all the previous sins, indeed of any sins at all. So he cannot say that he has done better than before, but only that the Lord's love has proved stronger than his resistance to it.

When the Lord says: *Whoever does not love me, does not keep my word,* he says it so that everyone who hears this word will feel that it applies to him. For this word too is addressed to everyone, and anyone who failed to apply it to himself would certainly know nothing of love. It is a word that is spoken out of love, and its purpose is to awaken love. It is a word that shines as light in the darkness. In the light of this word the darkness should know itself as such and thus become illumined. It is a word of judgment, but of a judgment that issues out of love. Out of love for man it demands and effects that man know and judge his own darkness. It is a word that demands confession and brings it about. In this word everyone stands naked before the Lord and his gaze of love. When the Lord asks whether man has kept his word, no one can step forward and say that he has. Ultimately, in this word the Lord tells each person that he does not love him. He says it in order to awaken his love. Only he who sees this—namely, that he does not love—is capable of keeping the word of the Lord, of which *this* word is a part, and of loving him. Christian love lives in this movement. It is as if someone were washing a dirty cloth in a washhouse. He knows that the cloth is full of spots; he washes it as well as he can, using all his strength. But the washhouse is dark and his human powers are limited. Then he brings the cloth to the Lord, but the very moment he unfolds it before the Lord's eyes he discovers that it is still full of stains and blemishes. In the pure light of the Lord these spots really stand out. But while man wants to wither away for shame, seeing he is powerless to cleanse himself, suddenly all the spots disappear through the grace of the Lord. Thus too the account that the person renders in confession is always rendered finally in the light of the Lord. Therefore he can never be tempted to compare his cloth with other cloths, with the sins of others or with his own earlier sins. It is as it is this moment, dirty; it will become clean only by the Lord's grace.

And the word which you have heard is not mine, but the word of him who sent me. This word of which the Lord speaks and which his disciples have heard is just as much the commandment of his love as the word that he has just spoken, namely, that they do not keep his word and so do not love him. These two words are one single word. This latter word shows the whole seriousness of righteousness. It shows that, judged according to righteousness, no one satisfies love. But this word is spoken out of love. The righteousness it manifests is hidden behind love, so that anyone who hears the word "righteousness" from the Lord always hears the word love at the same time.

But it is a word of love because it is not his own word, but the word of him who sent him. It is a word of mission that the Father issued out of love and the Son received out of love. Thus love steps forth. The fact that the Father does not utter it himself but lets it be proclaimed through the Son makes it a word of love. Certainly it is a word that contains a commandment. But the commandments that God issues are not to be understood other than as coming from the Father, that is, they are decisions of the Trinity itself, and thus exhibit the qualities of the Father, Son and Holy Spirit. They are commandments that always stem from God's life and express and contain it. Man cannot be oppressed and discouraged by the commandments, but on the contrary only enlivened and supported by them. The commandment of love is not issued so that mankind will realize that it cannot love. For the commandment of love is itself living; it contains what it demands and communicates it. It is the Holy Spirit who is behind the commandment's creativity. It is he who covers and makes bearable the infinite discrepancy that appeared in the light of righteousness. He is Consoler, Advocate, Helper, but he helps in a living way: he gives us the knowledge that in the Lord's commandment we can lay hold of the Lord's life, and in it the life of the Father. At the moment in which we are about to give up everything and die, he lifts us into this life. The Father is the origin of this whole movement of life. But he is, as it were, the hidden guarantor: he has placed his entire vitality in the Son and gives us the Holy Spirit so that we may find it in the Son. Because he gives everything that is his to the Son, surrenders all judgment and all love to him, he is the origin of this word of the Lord. And for that very reason the Son does not want to be anything other than the Father's word, because the Father in turn wants to be nowhere else than in the word of the Son. The Father has instructed him as the official authority through whom access to the Father is possible, and the Son wants to be nothing other than this access to the Father. It is as if there were an agreement between the two that each will be concealed and found in the other, so that everything may happen as gently and as homogeneously as possible, so that in everything the unity of love may be more to the fore than the distinguishing of the Persons and so that the absoluteness of the commandment of love may shine over and beyond everything.

14:25. *This I have said to you, while I still remain with you.*

The Lord emphasizes what is apparently self-evident; that he has spoken these words to the disciples as someone present, so that later his words will carry the value of what is sealed and decided; so that mankind will really know that the Lord was here and really said all this. Neither his existence nor his word is an illusion or a construction, but a simple fact. It happened; it was an event. It was an uttering within an abiding. In the short time that he was a man, knowing the exigencies of being human, he brought to us what God gave him for mankind and what he, the man, brought from himself as God. Both should grow together: as God he knows what he says, as a man he knows mankind's need and as God-Man he knows how this need is to be supported through his word.

While dwelling among them he spoke to them in the terms of their daily life. Subsequently, it will not be possible to point back to his time as an extraordinary, unique period. It is part of his humanity and his dwelling with them that he says things that are everyday, small and insignificant, yet that point to from where he comes and where he is going: the Father. Mankind will come to know and use and understand this when he no longer lingers in the midst of their daily life, but has already returned home to the Father. Then his word will come alive in them.

THE SECOND PROMISE OF THE CONSOLER

14:26. *But the Consoler, the Holy Spirit, whom the Father will send in my name, will teach you everything and remind you of everything I have said to you.* Previously the Holy Spirit was the Spirit of truth. Now he is the Consoler again. Between truth and consolation there exists a unity: truth is in consolation, and consolation in truth. Men do not need a consolation that consoles them away from and beyond the truth, but one that consoles them into the truth. The Lord prepares his disciples for this consolation. They are to know of this coming consolation of the Spirit and should not be overtaken by it if it is something unknown, surprising, alien and thus alienating. They must know that the promised Spirit, whom the Father will send in the Son's name, lives in unity with him and the Father, and that he is an essential part of the ever-greater God. They should know that he is not simply action but also contemplation, not something complete and finished in himself but something permanently open, something through which one can grow.

They have seen the Lord grow in their midst. In their minds and hearts they possess a history of the Lord. They have seen something apparently small unfold before their eyes, and they sense that this unfolding signifies an opening into the Infinite, into mysteries beyond imagination. And what they have experienced gives them a starting point for this infinite expansion, an ascertainable basis. Consequently they can follow. But when the Holy Spirit overtakes them, they will not have this human foundation; they will not know where the blow comes from when it suddenly pierces them. That is why the Lord must provide the necessary basis in his discourses on the Spirit. But he does not explain to them merely the fact of the Spirit's coming. Lest they conceive of the Spirit as an enthusiastic phenomenon of rapture, or as something that is too great for them and therefore has nothing to do with them, or as something for which, in maturity, one cannot open oneself because the spiritual life is already all too firmly set, the Lord explains the Holy Spirit to them as the *Consoler*. This name shows how very much he has to do with them.

For they will soon be forsaken, and they will not be able to cope with this forsakenness. They will desperately need consolation, and the temptation will be great to seek it elsewhere than in the Spirit. Without the Lord's preparation the Spirit would have been so foreign to them that they would have sought this consolation everywhere else before they sought it here.

Finally, he promises them that *the Father* will send the Spirit. He builds a bridge between the Spirit and the Father, and, because the Father sends him *in his name,* between the Spirit and himself as well. So he acquaints them intimately with the Spirit, and thus removes what is all too sudden, crude and explosive from the manifestation of the Spirit. He introduces him as something lovable that, while it will certainly transcend them, comes from the Father, about whose love he has already told them so much, and that is sent *in his name,* whose love they know anyway. They know that everything the Lord does and sends can only be good. Thus he prepares them for the operation of the Spirit.

He will teach you everything. After the Lord has introduced the Spirit, he opens the Spirit's truth to them. It is almost like when a departing teacher introduces a new teacher to his pupils. He prepares the pupils for what is new; he creates a transition. Thus the Lord describes the Spirit somehow in a human manner, and he wakens in them a trust in his teaching. He recommends the Spirit as teacher. If the Spirit were introduced to them as a stranger with a new teaching, the disciples, who have accustomed themselves to the Lord's teachings, would enter his school with distrust. But now he will always be the one whom the Lord recommended, and the grace of the Lord will accompany his course of teaching.

The Lord also is a consoler; he too is a teacher, for he too possesses all the qualities of the Spirit. But now, before the Passion, he hands over these qualities to the Holy Spirit: he lays them aside like garments and gives them over to him for safekeeping. Although both the Lord and the Spirit possess these qualities, they now exchange them. For on the Cross the Lord is no longer to be anything but pure self-surrender in suffering. Everything about him that can be interpreted and described otherwise, he now sets aside; he strips himself of his qualities and deposits them with the Holy Spirit.

He will remind you of everything that I said to you. The bond between the Lord and the Spirit is drawn even closer. The teachings of the Spirit will not differ from what the Lord has taught. On the contrary, they will express nothing other than this teaching; they will only call to mind what has already been said but not heeded. The Lord has analyzed the Spirit into his individual qualities, but now he brings together his own teaching in the Spirit once more. The whole teaching will be *one* teaching, the teaching of Christianity that the Spirit will inspire, and this teaching will be perfect unity.

THE PEACE OF CHRIST

14:27. *Peace I leave you. My peace I give you. Not as the world gives it do I give it to you. Let not your heart be troubled or be afraid.*
He leaves them peace. That sounds as if they already had it, as if he only had to leave it with them. They really have it, for they have chosen it, and the choice of peace is peace. The Lord called them and they have come, in peace, to peace. They met the Lord and they followed him for the sake of peace. They are actually living in a peace. But this peace also contains everything human that still accompanies them, and above all it holds in itself everything that draws them out of their humanity, that disturbs them, that clearly demonstrates to them that the way they are going is not the way they chose. This insecurity, this disturbance, this certainty that they are on uncertain ground: all this stems not from them but from the Lord. It stems from the Lord's love, and therefore from his peace, that peace that is unique to him and that allowed them, through his grace, to choose him and his way. It is actually *his* peace, a peace that works in them in such a way that they no longer know anything of peace. And this peace he leaves to them. He does so now, that is, as soon as they have chosen him and become his disciples, and even more in the hour in which he prepares to leave them. He leaves them this strange, this almost uncanny peace the moment he promises them the consolation of the Holy Spirit and his instruction in all things. In a mysterious way this peace is related to the coming of the Holy Spirit, although he describes it as his personal gift. For he continues:
My peace I give you. Between these two kinds of peace—that he leaves them and that he calls his and gives as his—lies the whole destiny of the Christian person: a destiny that comes from peace and goes to peace, is animated by peace, strives after peace in the Lord, wishes nothing with greater longing than to breathe in peace, to live in it, and yet can never, even approximately, be a destiny of peace. The disciples will know everything except peace. They will be witnesses of the Lord's suffering. They will—each in his own way—suffer with him; on Easter Day they

will feel joy and receive the Lord's final instruction. Then when the Lord has gone to heaven they will feel forsaken, only to be consoled again through the Spirit. They will face a boundless mission, be consumed in it, experience the little joys and little sufferings of their own existence as well and yet have the feeling of being part of a destiny that embraces them and exceeds their grasp. They will taste satisfactions and disappointments, be hurled to heights and depths of the Spirit; but something will be totally missing, namely, that peace for which they strive so passionately. They will be placed in the middle between the peace that the Lord leaves them and his peace that he gives to them. But in the middle, between the two, there is only one possibility: to live without peace. And when the Lord issues this immense promise, the promise of double peace, he warns them at the same time by saying:

Not as the world gives it do I give it to you. Even here, even in his gift of peace, he will transcend their expectation and thus will have to disappoint it. They will experience his peace and receive it as their own. That is his unbreakable promise. And what they experience will really be peace. But they will not recognize it as peace. Their human senses will not be sufficient to grasp this peace. Their spirit will undergo the most profound disturbance in receiving this peace. For this peace of the Lord will consist in having every boundary taken from them. Up until now they thought that peace meant a guarantee within protected boundaries. When they thought about peace, they thought in terms of a peace treaty. But it is precisely the boundary that is made insecure. It is precisely the treaty that is abolished. They are delivered up to the boundless, where all security is taken from them. Earlier they believed they possessed peace; therefore, they do not know that peace possesses them now. The Lord warns them that this peace has nothing in common with the limited peace of the world. We always want a peace as this world gives it: a peace that keeps us safe from attacks, behind whose walls we can lie down to rest. But the Lord's peace is the opposite of this peace of the world; it makes everything insecure. It is dangerous because it cannot be wholly grasped. No one knows into what adventure the Lord's peace may lead him. We seek peace out of fear of war. But nothing is fundamentally more insecure than a worldly peace treaty. For it gives the enemy time to make his preparations in secret. One has never to be more alert and suspicious than during the world's peace. But the Lord has no fear, nor has he any fear of fear. He knows that everything rests in the Father's peace, and that even the worst that can happen to him and to those who are his is a gift of the Father's peace. Therefore he removes all secure boundaries in order to let the boundless sea flood into the land of mankind. Let the swells of this sea go ever so high, let everything appear as chaos and disorder, in truth it is the peace of eternity that is so deep that mankind cannot grasp or savor it at all. Because the Lord knows this, and because he takes it on himself to give them this peace, he adds:

Let not your heart be troubled or be afraid. He has warned us about his peace, for it will not be the peace that we know. But the disturbance he has stirred up in us is met by his call for calm and peace. We should be at peace with this peace. No human, petty confusion should seize us when he surrenders us to what exceeds our grasp. We must know that it is the peace of the Lord, and that we may receive it as a gift from his hand. His call for peace also contains a promise: he will help us to bear his peace. He does not ask if we want his peace. He simply gives it, leaves it behind. One cannot refuse a gift of the Lord. There is no choice, either for him or for us. Not for us, because we have already chosen the Lord and must let ourselves be initiated by him into the ever-greater world of God. Not for him, for he cannot and may not conform to man's standards. His peace is beyond our comprehension in that it does not adapt to us. The Lord did not come to shrink God to the human measure, but to expand mankind to the measure of God. But it remains an expansion into peace. The way of the disciples will eventually end in suffering and anguish. But they should remember that their whole path as apostles, which ends in this darkness, is the peace of the Lord, and that this peace was promised, together with Holy Spirit. This terrible peace is the most beautiful, however, for it is the peace of the Lord. And even if it possesses none of the expected qualities, it possesses the most beautiful of all qualities, which is enough to make it the most lovable—namely, it is the peace of the Lord. It is the unity of himself and the Holy Spirit, which the Lord has previously analyzed and then reassembled. The Lord, like the Spirit, is richer and more mighty than any concept. Sometimes he is peace, sometimes fire, sometimes truth, sometimes life, sometimes the most objective and sometimes the most subjective. But all this—and infinitely more—is always just one more aspect of his unity, of his infinite being. And when any one of these aspects is communicated—and none of them, fundamentally, remains uncommunicated—it is each time only a participation in his unity. He gives us everything under the most various names and modes in order to take us into himself and thus present us to the Father. As his Mother held him on her lap to show him to the world, he holds us on his lap to show us to the Father. Therein lies peace. The peace of the Lord is not something that could come to an end between him and us, nothing finite or closed. Rather, this peace is something open and expanding; it can bring forth fruits, but it is itself only a seed of the eternal life between the Son and the Father.

14:28. *You have heard that I have said: I am going and I will come to you. If you loved me, you would rejoice that I am going to the Father, for the Father is greater than I.*

The Lord has just told them that he is going away and will come back to them. He tells them this in almost the same words in which he told them earlier that he came forth from the Father and will return to the Father. As the departure from the Father always implied the return to the Father, so now his departure from them implies his return to them. Each time the Lord goes away, there is the promise of his return. For he is always going forth and always returning, and therefore he is fulfilment and promise at the same time. Thus he manifests a side of his nature that is hard for us to comprehend, that we can never totally understand: that his own fulfilment is always in the process of fulfilling itself. This change of direction is part of his truth, which we can never grasp. Beforehand he went forth from the Father in order to return via the world to the Father; now he goes from the world to the Father in order to return from the Father to the world. He takes the opposite direction. But the second movement is like a smaller ellipse enclosed within the greater one. For the return to us is also implicit in his mission, which comes from the Father and goes to him. And yet the great movement is also included in the smaller one, because in the Lord things are not limited and fenced off against each other in terms of smaller and greater. The two movements, taken individually, are very clear images that somehow exclude one another. But in the Lord they exist not only side by side, but united. This is a unity we cannot understand. For it is a divine way that has nothing in common with the single-track roads of mankind. It can only be comprehended if we let him plant in us the demand that we comprehend more than we can comprehend. This divine movement contains something else that we could not understand about his peace: that everything divine knows no standing still; that eternal life is eternal peace only because it is eternal movement; that where God is concerned we never possess but only acquire more; that, having the mind of the Lord, we should always be journeying because he himself is journeying: from the Father to the Father, from us to us. We suddenly realize that it will no longer do to divide this one way into a twofold one, for that would destroy its infinite vitality. Rather, both ways are a single way. Our divisions and distinctions are arbitrary; the Lord himself is involved in a process in which there are no stages. He is on a perfect way, which is no less perfect at the beginning than at the end.

If you loved me, you would rejoice that I am going to my Father. Now the Lord describes his path in one-way terms again. Earlier it seemed as if his way united two opposing directions, thus abolishing all sense of direction. Now his path again resembles a route. It leads away from us and to the Father. But the moment this route becomes visible, almost like a comprehensible stretch of the journey, it becomes clear that it really implies an incredible imposition, demand and intensification. In the beginning our comprehension seems able to keep up: we can understand that someone is now taking leave of us, that he is going away, and we can sense and share the experience of this departure. Somehow this mystery unveils itself. But then suddenly everything bursts the bounds of our comprehension: the human person Jesus is taking his leave of us. But how is he going away, and where is he going? Here the immense mystery begins. He, a man, goes as God to God. It becomes clear that the life he lived among us is only a tiny fraction of his life in God and with God. Nor is this departure a mystery that we could somehow let be. Rather, it affects each individual very personally. For the Lord is not simply departing from this world; he is also taking leave of each individual, and in this leave-taking he takes the sin of each individual with him and expiates it in a mysterious fashion on his way to the Father, to place it in his judgment of love. Everything he accomplishes along this way is mysterious, and we will understand it in truth only when he no longer goes forth from us to return to the Father, but when we are there with him, with the Father. This idea of returning with him, of being together with him in the Father in a new mode of being in which we are no longer the creatures we were and knew on earth, but have become what he expects us to be, what he sees in us, implants in us, causes to be in us—this idea is so mysterious, so transcendent, so alien, so unattainable that we would not mind letting it lie and leaving it alone. It does not occur to us to seek our essential joy in this mysterious direction. And yet the Lord wants to initiate us into this very mystery of what we are and are to be, not only in his eyes but in our own innermost essence. He wants to educate us to be the sort of people who develop in him to such an extent that he can take us to the Father and present us to him.

Earlier he showed his double way: from the Father to the Father, from us to us. Now his path runs from us to the Father. Thus he gives his path a new core, a new focal point: ourselves, the point of departure for his path. We assume a new, important place along his way. Not because he made this path for us, but because we have become a part of the fulfilment of the path he took for us. The moment we discover that his way to the Father is not a way he walks alone as Son, but rather a way on which he mysteriously takes us with him and in which it is inconceivable that any one of us is not included, he places us under an immense obligation. This path is concerned with us ourselves, with the ultimate, decisive element of our being. In our eyes there is something so extravagant about this obligation that we immediately grasp that we cannot simply let ourselves be carried along without participating: what is at stake is something else, something much more. But we are not able to grasp this "much more"; we know where it begins—in our meeting with the Lord—and where it ends—in resting in the Father, together with the Lord. We also know that it is the Lord who accomplishes this path, this transition, for he says clearly *he* is going to the Father. But we know equally well that we must travel with him in a mysterious, indeterminable fashion, and that we have been presented with such an unequivocal summons to this way that in the end it makes no difference if we say yes to it or not: we simply *must* go. It is as if the Lord were to point to an infinitely high mountain and announce that he is going up, and we are all going with him. He does not ask who feels like going and who does not, who hopes to be able to make it to the top and who despairs of ever reaching it. He tells us only one thing: that he will give us no peace until everyone is up there, the good mountain climbers as well as the lame and the sick who are not capable of taking three steps; those who are ready to start out at once as well as those who from the start would not even consider such an imposition. All see themselves drawn into an apparently insane adventure through the Lord's apparent recklessness and frivolity, pointed toward a height that no sensible person would have dared to think about, a height at which he normally would not even be able to breathe. This is the exorbitant nature of the absolute demand that is made of each person.

Nor are we allowed any time to think about it. Rather, we are immediately required to *rejoice* that he is going to the Father, knowing that we will be separated from him. For the mystery that includes our going with him to the Father also implies this separation from the Lord, in which he must be left free to return to the Father. It is a real parting because he not only withdraws from us physically but also slips away from us spiritually on his way to the Father by becoming more and more incomprehensible to us. And all the same he expects us not to consider ourselves forsaken, not to be disconsolate at being deprived again of him whom we have scarcely met, but to rejoice that he is going to the Father. We should rejoice in his joy, forgetting whatever may appear strange and dangerous to ourselves and letting whatever threatens us be completely outweighed by the joy of the Lord's return to the Father. This joy is his joy; moreover, it is his joy that the Father is greater than he.

The Father is greater than I. He is greater than the Son because the Father is Father. He is greater also because he sent the Son, and will receive back the commission carried out by the Son. The Father is the exit gate and the reentry gate for the Son's entire path; indeed, he has the Son's entire path in himself, even his Passion, even his separation from the Father and his death. None of all this is excluded from the Father's infinite greatness, which becomes clear in the fact that the Father can first let the Son out, in order subsequently to let him in again. With us, the letting in would come first; it would be the condition for any letting out. That is a sign of our limitedness, whereas the reverse is a sign of the unlimitedness of the Father. And finally, in his glory and in his righteousness, the Father has somehow become, as it were, more glorious and greater through the Son's love: through his love the Son contributes to the Father's being greater than he. For the love of the Son causes the love of the Father to grow. For his fatherly love is so great, indeed, greater than everything, that he can accept even the sacrifice that the Son offers him; thus the Son's love is received, preserved and included within the love of the Father. Thus profound depths of truth lie in this word of the Son: *The Father is greater than I.* No human person says this or could say it, nor is it a word of the Father, who would not say it; rather it is a word that only the Son's love and humility can utter.

14:29. *And now I have said this to you before it happens, so that when it happens, you will believe it.*

The Lord is now referring more to his earthly return than to his return home to the Father. For he wishes them to believe when what he has related occurs. But at their return home to the Father they will believe anyway. Therefore the Lord speaks of what they will experience on earth as his disciples. He knows how limited a place their faith takes up, how unsteady each one of them still is, though in the most various ways; he also knows that his earthly time is so short that he must make every effort to strengthen them in their faith. And the efforts he must now make are of an entirely human nature. Even now he could infuse strong, all-enduring faith into them by supernatural means. But he must renounce this for the sake of the perfection of his mission. He must speak as a human being to human beings and use his human powers of persuasion. Certainly the core of his prophecy is supernatural. But the way he speaks about his death and Resurrection addresses their human understanding, and he makes use of no means incomprehensible to this understanding. He addresses their understanding in order to strengthen their faith, simultaneously telling them of this intention. He wants their memory to grasp the whole, so that later they can make use of what he told them in advance. He wants them to be able to appear as witnesses before those who will come afterward. But he does not leave the *interpretation* of what they are experiencing to them. He does not want them to color that in which they have participated with their subjective feelings, with the admixture of their subjective experience. Rather, he wants them to recount what he is going to experience just as he tells it to them; he wants their recounting to be purely at the service of his mission. He came from the Father in order to redeem mankind; the work of redemption will culminate on the Cross; they will be witnesses of this culmination. And they are to pass on what they have gone through with him as simply and clearly as he himself told them. For if they were to tell it as they might interpret it, they might frighten more than attract and conceal more than they reveal, because subjectively his act of Redemption is incomprehensible to them. They are not to relate their understanding or their nonunderstanding but are to remain simply witnesses. Of course, as witnesses do, they experience different things in different ways, and also give different names to the same thing, and thus what they say has a personal quality. But between what they experience and what they recount there should be that center that the Lord himself sets as a foundation in his own words. This word of the Lord must remain the central point of their interpretation. In explaining to them, he holds firmly to a very few data, and these data must not begin to change and adapt to the color of personal experience. Just as they are to be strengthened in their personal faith through this word of the Lord, so it should impart an objectivity to their witness.

14:30. *I will no longer speak much with you, for the prince of this world is coming, and he has nothing to do with me.*

There is little time left for the Lord to remain among the disciples. The time for speaking is coming to an end, and the time is approaching for pure deed, the deed of the way of the Cross, of suffering and death. This deed is so much a mystery between him and the Father that during this time he will scarcely say anything to mankind. They will watch him as he pursues his path, and he will let them accompany him in their fashion. But what he will say will be spoken more to the Father, even to the Father who is no longer felt and no longer present, than to mankind. During the Passion, mankind should learn more of silence and endurance than of speech.

For the prince of this world is coming. The work of the devil will unfold at the same time as his work. And yet: *He has nothing to do with me.* The devil's work does not touch, inwardly, the work of redemption. The two works occur in parallel: the highest work between Father and Son is accomplished while the devil's highest work is also accomplished. But they are only externally simultaneous: internally they have no point of contact. For the devil has no power over the Lord. The two will come incredibly close to each other. For without the devil the Lord would not be in the world, and the higher the Lord's working and suffering rises, the more obstinate and aggressive the devil's work becomes. And yet this is not to say that his work thus becomes more effective. Rather, adaptation is one of the devil's basic traits. If man is lukewarm, the devil is also lukewarm; but if man begins to warm to God, then the devil awakes as well and begins to interest himself in this person. The lukewarm person is nearer the devil than the awakened one. Therefore, the devil need not stir himself over the lukewarm. He has time to wait, and he is sure of his possession. If the good awakes in a human person, the activity of the evil one also awakes: there must be a battle, and a decision must be made. But the greater activity of the evil one around the Cross is already a sign that his power is failing. The devil knows that something is slipping away from him, and he can no longer hold it. The devil is most effective where people do not believe in him, among the lukewarm and the sated. Anyone who does not believe in God does not believe in the devil, and thus there is no need for a fight. The devil's power lies in adaptation, in compromise. The power of the Lord, on the other hand, lies in the opposite of adaptation, in the unconditional. True, the Lord has a variety of ways of introducing himself into a soul and gradually expanding in it. He can begin with certain natural inclinations, in order to saturate them gradually with his Spirit. Yet in all this there is never any compromise. From the outset, he wants everything. The devil adapts, and therefore he can find no way of attacking. He cannot get a foothold in the Lord. The Lord is the one and indivisible Son of God. In order to gain ground in a soul, the devil must find it ready for adaptation somewhere. But the Lord is ready only for the will of the Father.

Therefore the night of forsakenness on the Cross has nothing in common with the work of the devil. It is something much deeper, and at the same time something that takes place purely within the mystery of Father and Son. The hour of the devil's darkness is prior to the hour of the Father and Son's darkness. The first is not the cause of the second, for the second rests completely on God's pure decision of love. Sin is not the cause of the mercy and the grace of God.

Yet the Lord fights a genuine battle against the prince of this world. And he fights this battle as a man, with his human powers. Were he to fight as God, it would be no battle at all. But he fights as a human being, to show what our human power is capable of when it is pure and when it has a share in his power. It is true that when we fight he bestows on us his divine power. But in his own fight he veils his Divinity, in order not to humiliate us and cause us to despair of our own power. If the Lord did not fight as a human being, we would not be encouraged to fight ourselves but would rather wait until he, in our place, had finished with the devil. But because the Lord gives us a share in all his mysteries, he wants us to fight together with him, in order to attain to the glory of the Father with him as well.

14:31. *Rather, so that the world may perceive that I love the Father; and as the Father has commanded me, so I carry it out. Arise, let us go hence.*

The prince of this world is coming, so that the world may perceive. Twice in the same sentence he speaks of the world. The first world has the devil as its prince, and the second world is to perceive that the Son loves the Father. And yet it is one and the same world. Through its prince it should perceive the love of God. It is given a worldly, sinful chance to know that the Son is good, that he is God. This opportunity does not stem from God; it stems from the world, from the enemy of God. But although it lies in the devil, it is permitted by God, so that the world may perceive, through an extreme of evil, what the good is. Even this opportunity should lead it to know and understand the Lord.

The Lord sees what is to come under the sign of his love for the Father. But this love now takes the form of carrying out an order. Until now, whenever it was a question of the relationship between the Father and the Son, one saw above all the unity of their will in love. The plan of salvation was discussed and agreed between them both. Now, on the other hand, an order is carried out, and in this carrying out one can only see the Son's obedience. His self-determination and his freedom withdraw completely behind this obedience. This does not mean that his attitude has changed, that he was not obedient up until now or does not suffer the coming suffering voluntarily. Rather it means that by simply obeying he seizes the opportunity of doing nothing but suffer. He does not want his suffering to be interrupted by making decisions of his own. Now the resolve he made in the Father, namely, to show the Father his whole love, no longer lies in his hands but entirely in the hands of the Father. During the Passion he does not even want to remember this resolve and his own consent. Such a recollection would be a distraction from perfect suffering. For in order to grasp it, he would somehow have to measure his suffering. But he wants to be nothing more than the sufferer commissioned by the First Person. His whole power, everything he possesses, is now immersed in the suffering to the uttermost. If he could be aware during his suffering that he himself had wanted it and decided on it, some of the suffering would be spared him. He could cling to his own resolve in consolation. But things must go so far that he no longer seems to know whether he has part in the plan of Redemption, that he is no longer anything but obedience in love, and that as a result he suffers perfectly. A suffering that could see its own resolve would still have a point of view, a standpoint. But here the Son must hang, completely naked, in the pure resolve of the Father.

Arise, let us go hence. What is coming is not to be put off any longer. It is the Son's great departure into night and separation. And as he himself presses on toward this night, he also presses his disciples toward it. He challenges them to go with him, just as they are, without preparation. Any preparation would only delay obedience. When the Son sets forth, there are no excuses. He takes them all with him, just as they are, understanding nothing. He takes them with him intending to complete them and round them off. He takes them with him as they are, but with the intention of taking them as they should be. He will bear the difference. He takes them with him where he is going: to the Cross. He takes them into the Passion in the only way they can endure it, namely, *not at all.* He takes the reluctant ones with him as if they were willing. He takes them with him as yea-sayers in order to present them as such to the Father, although at bottom they are nay-sayers. He takes them with him as perfect Christians, although they are lukewarm doubters. He takes them, his disciples, with him as the first ones he has to redeem. He has bestowed an extreme measure of grace on them, and in spite of this he still has to transform them from start to finish into redeemed people. He has given them everything: baptism and Communion, teaching and miracles and his constant intimacy. And yet the whole work of redemption must take place in them.

He is urged forth: *let us go hence,* into the urgency, the execution of the Father's command. He goes, but he does not go alone. He goes to the Cross, which none other than he could bear, and he must bear it all alone. But as he goes he gives himself in such a way that he takes the others with him to the Cross although he will bear it all alone. He takes them with him so that they will stand next to the place from which the fountain of grace flows forth. He will suffer, but he appoints them to be the recipients of grace.

THE VINE

15:1. *I am the true vine, and my Father is the vinedresser.*

In the parable that the Lord now tells, he characterizes himself and the Father by their tasks. He himself is the vine, living and growing, which bears fruit and delights mankind with its fruit. But he is not the vine alone or of himself, but in the Father's cultivation. The Father cares for his vine, he gives it what it needs in order to thrive, and this care is long lasting, continual and uninterrupted. Thus it may perhaps seem that the Father's task is a very arduous one and the Son's, on the other hand, very simple: all he has to do is let himself be cultivated by the Father so that he can thrive and delight mankind as well as the Father with his fruit. But in order to thrive, the vine will have to endure much; he will not only be dependent on the cultivation and care with which the Father surrounds him, but also on what lies in himself, on his own power and his inner potential for developing and equally on the external influences over which neither he nor the Father apparently has any power: on mankind.

The vine, then, embodies not the Son in himself, but the Son as the point of connection and exchange between God and the world. He belongs to the Father because he is the Son of God, but he stands in the world and thus becomes the prototype of all *true* relation to God. Everything that is to thrive and bear fruit in the world must suffer being cultivated by God the Gardener. But it must also actively receive what it passively endures, and incorporate it into its own potential. But in the end both the passive side and the active side of the vine stem from God, and as God has given their possibilities, he also gives the realization of both, and in the end he takes the fruit as his, although it belongs to both vine and vinedresser. In no case does he leave the vine to its own powers after he has pruned it. For even if the Son is now in the world and the Father in heaven, all the Son's powers, the passive ones as well as the active, still stem perpetually from the Father.

15:2. *Every branch in me which brings no fruit he removes, and every one which brings fruit he prunes, so that it may bring more fruit.*

At first the differentiation of the roles of Father and Son in the work of Incarnation and redemption emerges very clearly. The Father is active; he determines the mission, assesses the fruit and does what is necessary in order to cultivate it. The Son is passive at first. He undertakes the Father's mission and gives himself up to the Father, in a full, let-it-be-done surrender, accepting everything the Father finds necessary. Thus the Incarnation reveals the individual spheres that each Divine Person possesses despite the unity of their being and working.

The service the Son performs for the Father in the work of Redemption requires that he be not spared. The Father may not spare the Son, nor may the Son let himself be spared by the Father. The ineluctable nature of this service will culminate on the Cross, and it is no accident that the Son chooses precisely the moment when the Passion begins in its pure passivity in order to proclaim this parable. Here he gives his spirit over to the Father once more before the Passion, before the unavoidable begins to unfold, as the vine holds itself out to the vinedresser. The latter knows what is good for the vine and what is not. Once more the Son places himself at the full disposal of the Father, in a dependency that knows one single law, that of its derivation: that as much as possible be accomplished now, and that love be harvested as richly and perfectly as possible. So the Lord sketches his own, passive way, which he walks not for himself but for God and mankind: for mankind, insofar as they will really receive the fruit; for God, so that the Father may be shown how completely the Son surrenders himself into his hands.

The Son is ready to accept everything from the Father's hands. This "everything" he describes more closely: the Father *cuts away every branch which bears no fruit, and those which bear fruit he prunes, so that they may bear more fruit.* In this the Father acts according to his discretion: he determines what is to be regarded as fruit. He cuts away what he perceives as insufficient. One can ask how there can be anything unfruitful in the Son. It is possible because the Son, in bringing forth fruit, sees himself in a unity together with mankind. The vine's insufficiency stems from the branches with which it forms a fruit-bearing unity. As soon as the Son appears in the world, it is no longer possible for mankind, his branches, to lead an independent life. For the Son appears as *life;* we are already the branches. When he views his life, then, he immediately sees his unity of life with us. Only on the basis of this unity is the redemption possible. If it were an isolated deed of the Lord, its effect could never extend to us. Nor is it the case that we only receive our life from him after the deed of redemption. No: by living with us he redeems us, and, redeeming, he lives in us. Therefore we are his branches even during the redemption itself, and must participate in the life of the redemption and the redemption to life. This participation is from the very beginning: ever since there were branches at all, they were branches on the vine. But branches and vine are a unity because the Father, the Gardener, cultivates them, he whose greatest care is that the vine thrive in the unity of stem and branches. And because this thriving in unity is of the utmost importance, the vine willingly submits to the cultivation of the Father who planted it and tends it.

The branch, then, is humanity, which is in the Son of God. It is in him because he has a claim on it. This humanity in him can bear fruit or not. Those who bear no fruit and yet are in him are first and foremost those who have met him, on whom he had a claim from the start because they were given over to him through baptism and through the fact that they are in his Church. Or also, in a broader sense, they are those whom the Father has given him and who hear about the Son outside the Church and could meet him. If these do not bear fruit, then it is because they do not want to. There are the most varied possibilities for such a refusal. A person may know what fruit would be expected of him—for example, a commission from God, or simply love—and he may not want to bear his fruit. This would be the most serious case. By not bearing the fruit that might lie in him, he deprives others of their fruit as well. But it may also happen that he does not recognize as such the fruit he senses within himself, but only knows that he ought to produce a fruit unknown to him, for a task of which he is unconscious. Further, it is possible for someone not to know of a fruit at all but only of a call that is heard, some cooperation that is called for, some answer that is required; perhaps with only a hunch that if I, the human being, were to call, God might perhaps answer me; with a kind of obscure intimation that in both cases there might be a fruit concealed between question and answer. Finally, there is the most frequent case: the person knows the fruit required of him, but he makes himself only conditionally, only partially available. He wants to be used only for a particular kind of fruit. He limits God's fruit in his own soul, as in unchristian marriages when the number of children is decided on arbitrarily. He wants to be able to survey the whole and refuses to make himself wholly available. The ego wants to rule; its will is to be done. The fruit of such a branch is a dead fruit. For the Lord will not adapt to the measures of the human person. It is as if God himself intervenes here and cuts this fruit away from the stem of Christ. For God knows only one single measure for the Son, and that is unconditional. He wants us to belong to him unreservedly. As long as we apply measuring rods and seriously want to survey the whole, he cuts us away, although we are in the Lord, although we are branches that could bear fruit. The leaven of death that God discovers in us requires that we be chopped off. What happens next is not something we can go into at the moment; the point here is that God tolerates no dead branches on the vine of his Son.

The ones who bear fruit, on the other hand, are those who surrender themselves, who are willing, who abandon themselves to the call of grace. The first ones, those who refused, also possessed grace. But the two sorts of grace are different: one is accepted grace and the other is not. Those who accept it can also make mistakes, but they sin within grace, and the others sin outside. Those who sin within grace are like little children getting into mischief: what they have done is silly and deserves punishment, or else it has the humor and radiance of childlikeness. But there is also mischief—and this would be sin outside of grace—which is only malicious and unchildlike.

There comes a moment in the life of every human person in which the offer of God's grace and the person's decision form a kind of balance. This balance can look different in each person; the proportion between the grace offered and the nature of the individual can be a changing one. But the balance is there, and this is the moment of decision whether the grace will be accepted or not, whether the person is willing to bear fruit or not. At this moment the person must throw himself unresisting on to the scales to make them sink. If he does not do so, his life remains dry and fruitless. He may subsequently be an exemplary person, perform a great many good works, perhaps live a virginal life and seek to avoid every sin and every fault, but he will lack one thing: the fruitfulness that stems only from grace accepted. This fruitfulness can be wholly hidden, perhaps concealed in a modest Christian household that is not striking outwardly, but inwardly it will always be full of graces and love's radiations.

Those who bear fruit are purified by the Father. They belong to the Son and remain in him; they are the beloved of the Lord, and he showers them with his love—but the Father purifies them. The Son lets them grow in his grace and develop, he keeps them in the closest proximity to him, he pours his love through them, he lives with them in a bond that could not possibly be closer, because the life of the vine and that of the branch is one single life—but it is the Father who prunes them. It is strange that the pruning occurs through the Father. But the Son regards his branches so much as his own, he lets them participate so much in his personal life, that he sees them, as it were, from *within*. But the pruning must happen from without. It is a kind of test, and stems from the Father. When a beloved person dies, Christians say it was God's will to call him to himself. They see the origin of this test with the Father, not with the Son. The Son is the one whom they expect to console them in this loss and to reconcile them with the will of the Father. Thus it is with all purification, and it is good and right. For the bond between vine and branch is established; it needs no further testing. The testing can only come from without. It can be severe; it is in order to test how strong the established unity is, how much it can take. Thus the martyrs are tested. Their faith during martyrdom is not greater than before, but it proves itself outwardly; others and the Church can see how strong it was. But the Father never purifies in such a way that a person who desires to believe and to love is so overburdened that his initial faith, his incipient love, is shattered. There is always a relationship between a person's mission and his trial: the trial is always aimed at purifying and strengthening his mission. Anyone who does not pass the test only shows that he did not really believe and love. Those most tried are the saints, not for their own sake, but for the Son's sake. For the outward purification by the Father is visible; it is noticed by others. The good grapes are praised, but they do not glorify the branch but rather the vine. Thus this purification of the saints by the Father has the Son's glorification as its goal. In purifying, the Father takes precisely those that are already bearing fruit, *so that they may bear more fruit.* He purifies them by freeing them not only of dirt but of everything superfluous; by cutting them back, perhaps even to their very substance, to the very pith of the branch. He may even prune away what the branch saw as most essential to it, what it regarded as indispensable in the service of God. But when the Father prunes, he never does so without the Son's consent. Everything takes place within the agreement between Father and Son. The Father never purifies *against* the Son, although it is he and not the Son who purifies. The Son permits it, so that the Father also shares in this way in the whole work of redemption, and will afterward recognize the Son's brothers as his own children when the Son returns with them, his cleansed branches, to the Father.

15:3. *You are already clean, by virtue of the word which I have spoken to you.*
This word of the Son is almost dangerous, for it could tempt the disciples to be presumptuous. But he knows that this word can do them no harm, that at the most they will grow in humility through it. And he also knows that they need a powerful encouragement just now. The coming Cross that he will have to bear will mean an immense burden for them. They are not up to this burden; they could only be up to it if they were in him as his branches. But this interior being-in-him is still hidden from them. All that they know or perceive, up until now, is that they are together with him in God. They are simple people, and they have lived together with him as a human being; how could they imagine, while he is still side by side with them, that they are living in him! This idea is much more difficult for them than for later Christians, who know the Lord only in faith and in the Spirit. Therefore the disciples need his encouragement twice as much. He says to them, then, that they are clean. Of course, they have not yet had to endure any of the more difficult trials. They have been exposed to many surprises, they have witnessed the miracles and earlier they left their families and their possessions. But that does not mean that they are clean. Rather, it is because they have done all this at the Lord's word and command. They have left everything to take up an unknown destiny, not out of curiosity or the urge for adventure, but by *virtue of his word.* It is primarily this word they obeyed that has purified them. Such cleansing results when a person surrenders

himself for whatever the Lord requires of him, even when he does not understand it. It lies in this inner attitude, which stems from the grace of the word, not in the great external upheavals and trials.

The disciples can know that they are clean because they have deeply perceived their own inadequacy, and also because in the hard time that is coming they will need to know that the Lord has found them clean and counts on them, counts on them in the clear knowledge of their sinfulness and imperfection. Despite this he has seen that they have left everything at his word in order to follow him. They have accepted the word that he spoke to them, accepted it in a sense that they themselves did not fully understand but that they were still ready to accept, and they did so in such a way that they put themselves increasingly in the service of a message that increasingly transcends them. This message was not just any message, but the word the Lord proclaimed. Thus they are cleansed by the Father through the word of the Son.

15:4. *Remain in me, and I remain in you. As the branch cannot bear fruit of itself if it does not remain in the vine, nor can you, if you do not remain in me.*

The Lord requires the disciples to remain in him as they are in him now: in this same readiness, in this surrender, knowing that they belong to each other. But he too will remain in them as hitherto, that is, entirely, without ever forsaking them. The essential character of this being in one another is the "remaining". This must be unshakable. Much will happen that could shake the disciples. Yet they should "remain". And they should remain in a Christian way: their remaining should know no rest and no stagnation, but rather should be alive, growing and developing. At the same time they should remember that they are purified by the Father, that their remaining in the Lord is thus also a remaining in the Father and that in future no separation is possible any longer between that in them that is the Father's and that in them that is the Son's.

In order to emphasize this, the Lord adds: *As the branch cannot bear fruit of itself if it does not remain in the vine, nor can you, if you do not remain in me.* It is he who helps them to bring forth fruit, and he also knows that, despite their humanness and their deficiencies, they regard this fruit as the meaning and the center of their life. He knows that their assent to him is confirmed and strengthened through their assent to his work.

They will have to continue the work, with their full inner consent, even when he is no longer there. They have grasped that that is a part of their assent. But the work will remain the work of the Lord, even when he has forsaken them. He promises them that. They will be able to bear fruit because he will remain in them. The bond will be maintained even when he no longer dwells visibly among them. Thus he hands them over to the future, a future without his sensible presence. He gives them over to the work of the Church, which is a Church of human beings, a visible, material Church, and thus a Church of preaching, of works of charity and of the most diverse human undertakings. But this entire visible and material substance of the future Church can and must be rooted in the invisible substance and in the Spirit of the Lord. Only in the Lord is the Church alive, just as, on the other hand, the Lord needs the Church, the members and branches, in order to move and grow in them as in his organs. But the branches only grow and bear fruit by virtue of the sap of the stem. If the works of the Church were to happen without the Lord, they would be dead branches. They are alive insofar as the Lord's Spirit lives in them.

15:5. *I am the vine; you are the branches. Whoever remains in me and I in him, he brings much fruit, for without me you can do nothing.*

Once more the Lord sums up what has been said: he, the vine, is life, and they, the branches, are those who share in his life. But the life is undivided between them. They do share it, but what they share is undivided. And the life of the vine outlasts that of the branches, but it is still the same life. Between the two there is a living exchange, so much so that no one can say that there is more life in the vine than in the branch. For both together form one single life.

Whoever remains in me and I in him, brings much fruit, for without me you can do nothing. Life in the Lord, then, is the only precondition for bearing fruit—indeed, much fruit. The individual branch cannot assess the quantity of fruit; it is the Father who possesses the overview. But all the branch's fruit, however much it may be, stems from the Lord. Every activity outside his would be sterile, and all work apart from him would be a waste of effort. This applies to the disciples and to everyone who, in following them, will bear fruit. It applies, in fact, to everyone who wants to perform any work. Their work will not ripen into fruit if the Spirit of the Lord does not inspire their action. This applies whatever kind of work it is: it can appear to be a work of Christ, a work of the Church, a Christian work. Or right from the outset it can bear the stamp of what is unchristian, indeed the denial of what is Christian, whether through ignorance, being untouched by it or a conscious rejection. In themselves all these works are only attempts at works, the beginnings of works. They are not works in the Lord's sense. In themselves they are as if born dying. The life that they manifest is only an apparent life; in reality it is death. They disintegrate in the activity of those who perform them, even if they have borne a visible blossom: they are like mayflies and soap bubbles, or perhaps they do not even develop as far as the blossom. Regarded from outside, they may have the appearance of a work, but one will see their emptiness on examining their effects. This applies, for example, to many spiritual works in which people immerse themselves because of some attraction, because they seemed to promise greatness. But if one attempts to live on the basis of their lives, they do not fulfill what they promise; they disappoint and prove to be hollow. For they do not live from the Spirit of the Lord. Or there are social works that are aiming at some worldly good, but one that is not inwardly a Christian good. These works also are condemned to become torpid and cold. They can perhaps give an appearance of life, but they can never beget real life. For the value of a work rests in its truth, but there is only *one* truth, which is contained in the Spirit of the Lord. Every action is only activism, every deed is only a substitute for a Christian deed, every work is not a building up but vanity or even destruction, if it is not undertaken in the power of the Lord. In the eyes of the Lord, no other work is valid but his own, no deed but his own, that is, no work and no deed that does not lead to the Father. For him everything that is not really fruitful is sterile, and only that is fruitful that serves his glorification in the Father. This fruitfulness does not stem from mankind but from the Son through the Father.

15:6. *If someone does not remain in me, he will be thrown out like a branch and dry up; the branches will be collected and thrown into the fire, and they will burn.*
    The entire parable is recapitulated once again, but now in an intensifying,

almost threatening way. At issue here are those who were once in the Lord, who have tasted his life and who have turned away. Among them are all the unfaithful ones who have broken with the Lord, and above all those who stood before the Lord in a privileged position: priests, religious, lay people with a special mission. They have turned away; they are thrown out and dry up. Examining them closely one can see how they bear the marks of their turning away, how they are already exposed to the process of drying out. The Lord distinguishes them carefully from those who have not attained knowledge and acceptance of his word, those who are seeking and perhaps discouraged. He is speaking of those who have turned away, who are visibly drying out: unable to remain alive, to regain living intercourse with the Lord, to belong to a living human community or to work fruitfully even among those closest to them. If they can actually look inside themselves, they will recognize that, indeed, they are not the same as before: what is living and positive in them is being suffocated through resentment, or at least through resignation. The feeling and consciousness of having turned away colors everything they are and do. The tasks they still undertake, the reflections they still make, the friendships they still form, will all be undertaken and evaluated from this point of view. Everything bears the stamp of apostasy.

The one who has turned away *is thrown out:* first invisibly by God, and then perhaps visibly as well, by the Church. He himself does not take his excommunication very seriously; he thinks of it as a temporary measure that could be reversed at any time. But for the Church it signifies a decisive break. The excommunicate has no more access to the springs of life, the sacraments. His turning away is absolutely and utterly incompatible with the life of the Church. This barring of the way to life, even if it only lasts until he is penitent, still has the character of finality for as long as it lasts. He who has turned away knows in his innermost heart that if he should ever turn back, it will never be as the person he is now. Now, turned away from the Lord, he sees nothing but weakness in his Catholic period of life, and he does not want to be the person he was. The only thing he can say of himself—for no one can guarantee his future—is this: if he should ever fall back into his former beliefs, it would only be because of some new weakness. In order to turn back as a true believer, he would have to be a different person from what he now is.

But it can happen that he is only cast out by God, without the Church separating outwardly from him. The Church, as a visible and human institution, cannot force access to someone's conscience. The sacraments she administers far surpass, in their effects, what she can observe of them. In them she fastens a bond between souls and God, but the inner life of this bond remains unknown to her to a great extent. In this sphere God may have rejected the person, while in the spheres accessible to the Church everything may seem in order. Outwardly, a Christian may participate in everything the Church requires of him, perhaps until his death, but inwardly he has failed in the essential question that God put to him; he has dried up and died at the secret point in his soul that is crucial for a living relationship with God. He may look like a blooming and even a fruit-bearing branch on the vine, but in truth his whole life is a pretense. And he himself knows it. He may not see everything pertaining to his condition, but he knows the decisive thing, namely, that at a very particular point, at some time in his life or more than once, he said no to God. Not a No that could be obliterated immediately through penitence and confession, but a No that keeps him aloof from the desire for conversion and decides the meaning and direction of his whole existence. He has withdrawn that level in himself that is important to God. It is the very level at which he might have become fruitful for the Church. It is that wholly personal gift of himself that would have unsealed a fountain of life in the community. The Church cannot determine whence her deficiencies come; she cannot inspect the origins of Christian life in her. It is God who implants the living seeds in her. But the nay-sayer knows that, through his fault, the vine was unable to bear a particular branch foreseen by God.

They are collected. The one who collects them is the spirit of alienation. There is a league of those alienated. They bear the common mark of not wanting to belong to Christ. Their loneliness does not agree with them, but even less endurable are those who belong to the Lord and do not know this loneliness. Therefore they band together. They think that they gather themselves together, but in reality they are themselves gathered. It is the spirit of alienation, which refuses to bear and refuses to say yes, that gathers them. They all live from the same resentment. What they do together, once they have found each other, is this: *they burn.* They burn because they cannot live, because life is suffocated in them. It is not a burning of life but of death. It is a passion that consumes them, not a purifying but rather a suffocating fire, which seizes on everything in them that was still untouched and unclaimed by the spirit of alienation and uses it as fuel for the fire. As a Christian who believes is seized by a fire and consigns everything that does not belong to the Lord to the conflagration, so these others are seized by an opposing fire that consumes everything that still outwardly bears the appearance of belonging to the Lord. Because these people once belonged to the Lord, they can no longer live for themselves even after falling away. They would like to, but they no longer succeed at it. They would like to be able to refer to their own life, but they no longer have one. They want to be people who can deduce their law of life from their own "nature" and publicly proclaim that Christianity kills nature. But this is exactly what they can no longer do. They cannot escape the curse that has fallen on them.

There are also those who occupy themselves with reform plans within the Church; they are incensed at abuses in the Church. Much of their indignation is understandable and justified, and with a certain idealism they want to help to build a better Church. Their ideas are not to be dismissed out of hand. But they gradually withdraw to the margin of Christian life, so that in private and off to one side, they can plan new things. They slip out of the middle of the Church toward the periphery, and finally they leave. From this moment on all their good intentions and arguments are doomed to death; everything that, within the Church, could have served for building up, is condemned, outside, to an unavoidable drying and withering. Every defection from the Church is accompanied by this curse. The fire of alienation overtakes the defector, and he is consumed.

15:7. *If you remain in me, and my words remain in you, you may ask for what you will, and it will be given you.*

Anyone who remains in the Lord in spite of all the reasons against it that are put forward, in spite of his realizing that much in the Church could be different and better than it is, is like a child of God who knows that it is a grace to be allowed to remain. It would be presumption to want to measure and understand everything oneself. Anyone who remains in the knowledge that the Lord will always be the ever-greater, more mysterious One, desiring only to live from his grace and his love, is granted a new grace beyond all previous graces: he can ask for whatever he wants with the certainty of receiving it. It is strange, again, that the Lord says this openly to his disciples. He does not say it to them as an attraction, as an incentive; they are not to remain with him in order to receive one grace more. He says it to them, as it were, entirely impersonally, to show how limitless his grace is. Nor does he promise it only to his disciples; he promises this grace, so much to be desired, to all who remain with him, without distinction. He speaks of this alone; his word is a part of his teaching, a part of his promise as Redeemer. He means the disciples to know of this grace, not so much so that they may return to it in times of trial but because it is a message that is to be transmitted through them to everyone and is destined more for others than for themselves. The word is less an incentive to make use of this grace for themselves than an affirmation of the Lord's love and of the boundlessness of his imparting of grace. Fundamentally, it is never uttered in such a way that one might be tempted to use it for oneself, but rather so that it can be repeated to someone else as proof of the Lord's grace, less in order to hold him firmly in faith than to enable him to tell others and to see it fulfilled in them. Anyone who referred it to himself would never in fact achieve it: everyone should regard it as a grace given to others.

The granting of this grace depends on remaining in the Lord. Anyone who resolves, despite all objections, to remain in the Lord and in the Church, will be rewarded for his assent on a much higher plane than he could have expected. His reward is the unheard-of gift of being allowed to ask for whatever he will. In addition, the Lord gives him the grace of being able to be so selfless in his asking that the personal side is turned off, as it were, so that he can enter all the more effectively into the Lord's asking. He is enabled to look away from himself, from the confines of his little existence; he is enabled to insert himself into the limitless expanses of the Lord's existence in his Church. The petition that is thus granted us is a Christian petition, not a personal one. It is a petition that is made in Christ and thus cannot be other than the petition of Christ: "Thy will be done." For that is the content of his petition, and under this sign every Christian prayer takes place. This petition has not only a Christian framework, but also a Christian content, and therefore a Christian fulfilment. This petition, along with the petitioner, is ready for anything that may seem good to the Lord; it flows into the Lord's petition to the Father. In the end, the Christian petition has no other content than this: to be allowed to be at the center of the petition of the Lord himself. It wants to strip away any private character that is not assimilated to the Lord's prayer, in order to live completely within the Son's prayer to the Father.

This petition can become concrete only if it is made within grace, that is, in the context of a particular mission and task. God also grants mankind this grace of being allowed to ask for concrete things, but always within mission. This definition is not a limitation or restriction of our freedom, but ministers to the extension of God's glory in the world. For the Christian petition itself always involves a person's making himself wholly available to God and God's task. This surrender includes both the Christian's adjustment to God's will and God's hearing of the petition. True Christian petition, which may ask for something particular and may keep on knocking until it is answered, can only take place within the will of the Father. While it is God's will to let himself be determined in his will by mankind, this "being determined" is also God's will and may not be subordinated to human egoism or to his egotistical wishes for others. Every petition God grants, he grants in mutual love, which also makes demands of the petitioner and gives him a share of responsibility; for when God gives fulfilment he also gives the person something to bear—which is again a mystery leading to new fruitfulness.

15:8. *In this is my Father glorified, that you bear much fruit and become my disciples.*

The goal of the Incarnation is the glorification of the Father. The entire redemption of humanity and its being led back to heaven also serves, in the end, to glorify the Father. That men should become disciples of Christ and bear much fruit would have no sense if it did not glorify the Father. But as the living bond between Father and Son already constitutes glorification, so too the living bond between God and mankind is already his glorification. For the Son's commission to glorify the Father coincides with his commission to bring mankind to the

Father. He can not fulfill it in any other way than by bringing us to bear fruit. Thus our fruit becomes a part of his commission and hence a part of the Father's glorification. But he who causes this fruit to ripen in us is the Son and, in the Son, the Father; thus God glorifies himself in our fruit.

The bearing of fruit is not something the disciples accomplish on their own; it is itself a fruit of the petition granted through the Lord's grace. His grace contains the promise of much fruit. But this fruit is characteristically Christian. It cannot be monitored by the individual. He cannot assess this fruitfulness; he does not know where it begins and even less where it ends. He does not even know where the middle of the fruit lies. And yet he is supposed to bear much fruit. But it is no part of this command that he should also grasp and feel the fruit. It is one of those commands familiar to the Christian—he does not know precisely how. Certainly he knows what fruit is and what it means to bear fruit in the Lord. But what is withheld from him, because it is hidden in the essence of this fruit, is his part in it. The Lord's fruit is always catholic, that is, universal. It is the fruit of the Church, that is, it is a community fruit. No one can mark off, with regard to fruit in the Church, what is his fruit and what is the fruit of others. Ultimately it is always the community that bears fruit. No individual, humanly considered, is indispensable, even if he is irreplaceable from the Lord's point of view. In human terms, others could accomplish our work just as well and better, because they possess the same or better prerequisites, abilities and experiences. From the Lord's point of view, on the other hand, each individual is irreplaceable, because each one is required for the fullness of God's glory. But this fullness itself is catholic and ecclesial, and in its unity and simplicity transcends all personal boundaries.

The fruit is the glorification of the Father, because it is manifested within the grace of the Son's mission and is therefore the fulfilment of the Father's will. This is so much the case that the Son's mission to glorify the Father would not be fulfilled and perfect without this fruit. But no fruit deserves the name unless it is a fruit of love and belongs unconditionally to the Son's mission of love.

In this is the Father glorified, that you become my disciples. By virtue of the fruit, the disciples become what they already are by virtue of the Lord's love: his disciples. For this is what being a disciple means: to have placed life and love, everything one possesses, at the Son's disposal, including those things that are only indirectly at one's disposal, that is, only through the Son. The disciple is inserted into the work of the Son together with him, interwoven in the latter's love for the Father and for the sake of this love; thus, ultimately, he is at the Father's disposal in his love for the Son. In this the Father is glorified.

FRIENDSHIP AND SERVICE

15:9. *As the Father has loved me, so have I loved you. Remain in my love.*
The Father has loved the Son in an undivided and unlimited love, in true love. He has loved him as his nearest neighbor, to whom he entrusts everything, whom he always accompanies, of whom he expects everything in an expectation that is boundless. For he expects everything that the Son can give him, namely, perfect love. But this love, though expected, is never a calculated one; it is encompassed in the Father's love, yet we cannot say that it is a part of his love. This expectation can never disappoint, nor can it ever be disappointed.

With this love with which the Father loves the Son, the Son loves his disciples. He loves them just as undividedly and unlimitedly, and in his love too there is no possibility of disappointment. We, indeed, must admit to ourselves that we disappoint the Lord, because we fail again and again; but his love overlooks this, because even where we disappoint him it continually opens up new springs of grace. We disappoint him, always giving only partial responses to his perfect word of love. But he does not let himself become in any way discouraged by this, for his love for us is the love with which the Father loved him. And because the love between Father and Son is an eternal question and an eternal answer, both eternally fulfilled and fulfilling, and because it is precisely this eternal love that the Son brings to us, he also expects a fulfilling response from us. Coming from the Father, he is prepared for nothing other than this continual exchange. Although he knows that we are sinners, although he sees our faults exactly, he does not let our rejection interfere with the attitude of his love; he is so ready to take on himself everything that is lacking and to cover everything faulty with his grace that he can say in truth: *As the Father has loved me, so have I loved you,* with a love that never feels disappointed and that, although it demands more of us than we give, never draws back rejected. All love woos, even love that is perfectly fulfilled, and this courtship does not grow weary in the Lord. He does not turn away from the sinner in disappointment. He behaves as if his wooing were accepted, even when it is rejected by us. Even on the Cross he will not cease to love us and woo us, because it is given to him to suffer; to be overtaxed; to be isolated and to feel forsaken; to feel no more love, given or returned, neither the eternal love of the Father nor the hesitant love of the disciples, nor that of his Mother and John: but he cannot stop loving, any more than the Father can stop loving his Son.

Remain in my love. The disciples must know that he always loves them. They themselves are not yet capable of acting as those who are truly beloved, showing the lover that they know they are always loved, even if they are not able to give full reciprocal love. They are not yet capable of letting themselves be loved. Their sinfulness stands in their way, and they feel all too unworthy of this love. And yet the Lord does not want to see them discouraged. They are to remain in his love, and know that despite their poverty he loves them as the Father has loved him. He does not even speak of service given and rendered or of their faults and sins; he does not compare or make a reckoning. He only shows them the profusion of his love. He does not even want to see how they respond to this love. All they need to know is that they are loved by him above and beyond everything. But that is precisely what they cannot yet grasp. They still do not feel like loved ones. Fundamentally, they do not know what is happening to them; they only feel overpowered and astonished by an attitude of the Lord that is incomprehensible to them. But the proofs of his love continue to rain down on them, and all the Lord requires of them is that they do not draw back from this torrent. Anyone who is loved only has to let himself be covered by love; gifts he did not expect are given him, and he may not reject them because they are given in love. So also the disciples should let themselves be recipients, living only from the gift of his love and surrendering themselves in gratitude to his grace.

15:10. *If you keep my commandments, you will remain in my love, just as I have kept my Father's commandments and remain in his love.*

If the disciples keep the Lord's commandments, the consciousness of his love will not leave them, not even subjectively. Objectively, of course, the Lord knows that in many cases they will fail and will not keep his commandments. But he wants to make the keeping easier for them by promising them that if they keep his commandments, they will remain in his love. Nothing will be able to separate them from knowledge of his love. He does not speak of what would become of his love if they did not keep his commandments, nor does he tell them that he will always love them, even then, in spite of everything. Rather, he promises them his tangible love; and in order to encourage them, to smooth and explain the path of his love, which he knows better than all is not always an easy one, he adds: *Just as I have kept my Father's commandments and remain in his love.* He tells the disciples this as consolation, but he also says it to himself, as a final consolation before the Cross, so to speak. When he takes up the Cross and suffers all that is imposed on him, he does so at the Father's bidding and thus fulfills his commandments and remains *in his love.* He does it in order to offer mankind, and thus the Father too, opportunities of a richer developing of love. He does so out of love and in love, and therefore he knows that even in the coming forsakenness, when he will be deprived of light, he remains in the Father's love. By speaking in this way of his utterly secure remaining in the love of the Father, he wants to inspire the disciples to remain in his love, which is the same as the Father's. He wants to give them ultimate security. Whatever may happen outwardly, whatever darkness may raise its head, if they only remain within his commandments they are certain of his overwhelming love, just as certain as he remains in the love of the Father.

15:11. *This I have said to you that my joy may be in you, and your joy may be perfectly fulfilled.*

For the first time the Lord speaks of his joy. He does so in the face of the Cross. He talks about it as something self-evident. The joy that is in him, his joy, is part of him; it accompanies him and has always been in him, but in a special way, perhaps, since the decision to be parted from the Father in order to demonstrate to the Father his perfect love. Since undertaking this task he never felt it burdensome, oppressing him with its heaviness, but rather the pure expression of his joy. He rejoices at being allowed to serve God and mankind, and he serves them in joy. All his thoughts are thoughts of love for God and for mankind, and thus thoughts of joy. For he knows that every joy is an expression of love, nor can it be anything else. Loving is a delight: the truer the love is, the more joyful it is in all its suffering. But everything that confines, brings vexation and calculates is against both love and joy.

The Lord wants his love to remain in them as joy. He wants their love to be only and always a love in him and in God. Every love they feel, including love for their fellowman, ought always to be held and contained within his love: only thus can it become true joy. Every love, even the earthly and physical, can be true joy if it does not selfishly close itself, but opens toward God. If a lover knows that his love is unflolding toward eternity, it cannot be disturbed by time; he leaves his love to God, so that God may take care of it as he finds good and may fashion it as he will. Then he knows that his love is kept safe in God, whether it be the love between mother and child, between siblings or friends, between man and woman or the love of neighbor pure and simple. Each of these kinds of love, if it has both its root and blossom in God, can become a perfect joy. The death of the beloved may bring it to an earthly end, but true joy is not cut off by this, for the lover knows that the beloved has gone to God and rejoices in the Lord. Thus the one remaining behind rejoices in the joy of the beloved. His joy is no longer his own, but the joy of the one whom he loves. Or when the lover does not understand many things about the person he loves and would have acted differently from him, it cannot annoy him, because he knows that the beloved's deeds are entrusted to God, and he no longer needs to judge them. If he really loves, he no longer needs to judge the beloved. Even if the beloved sins, he only needs to judge this sin as far as the necessity of love requires. Everything else he will cover with the mantle of love. It will not be an ethical "sense of responsibility" toward his friend that presses him to confront him with his sin, but only love. Even if it becomes necessary to speak of guilt, in order to create the required clarity between them, this personal point of view can never be the final one. In the end one has to allow one's fellowman to keep his mystery with God—in love, which is greater than judging and explaining. The beloved can be unbelieving; he can also lack love—but these things do not suspend the obligation to love him, and they only involve a limited restriction of joy. If God is the source of the lover's life, the latter will find his joy in the attempt to lead the beloved to God, to let God and his joy become clear to him. Only if he saw that he was not able to bring the other to faith would he have to renounce this person, for the sake of the Lord's joy. For this perfect joy, which is promised by the Lord, could not be maintained if such a person resisted love to the end. Love of the Lord and joy in the Lord are of such primary importance that where they are concerned everything else, even a person's endeavors on behalf of someone, must give way. But if God wants the lover to suffer on behalf of a sinner—perhaps extremely—he will tell him himself. He will then be granted permission to suffer in the joy of the Lord. It is God who distributes joy and suffering to Christians; they must not let the measure of their joy be prescribed by human beings.

Every joy that is in the Lord is given to us. But no joy that contains any opposition to the Lord will be countenanced. Just as a person who lives in love and in faith in the Lord cannot share the joys of unbelief, so he cannot receive love from an unbeliever, a love that is outside God. For there is ultimately no fellowship between a believer and an unbeliever, because their love does not even spring from the same root, and the love of the unbeliever cannot be integrated into the joy of the Lord.

Everything we do for one another in love must be done in the joy of the Lord, for the joy of the Lord and in order to let this joy become fruitful. Every fruit that the Lord expects of us, in whatever work it may be, is a fruit of our joy in his joy. This joy will be *perfectly fulfilled* only when it is presented to the Lord and receives its blessing from him. A joy that only remained in itself, in which one rejoiced alone, would be imperfect, unfulfilled. It becomes perfect if we may offer it to the Lord, and if he accepts it into his love.

The Lord wants us to live in his joy. He also wants us, of course, to go through suffering and tribulation. But the basic direction of our Christianity points toward joy. Christians should be like balls that can be squeezed and pressed but always resume their round shape. The basic condition that always reestablishes itself must be joy: in marriage; in friendship; in intercourse with people; in the Church; everywhere the Christian lives in joy, without wantonness and without envy; in the joy that allows the joy of others to exist; in Christian joy.

15:12. *This is my commandment, that you love one another as I have loved you.*
Again the Lord comes back to his commandment, to this chief com-

mandment that he always expresses in the same fashion: as he has loved us, so should we love one another. Through what we have heard and seen of him, through what he has told us about his love's origin, nature and path, we should learn to love our neighbor as he loves us. In fact, we should learn to love him for love's sake. The Lord loves us, in the end, for the sake of the Father; because we are creatures of the Father and because he finds and recognizes the Father's love in us. And we should see the Lord's brothers and beloved ones in our neighbors and love them because he has loved them. But one cannot be loved by the Lord without receiving a grace from him that, even if it is hidden, is still so real that it cannot completely elude the eyes of a fellow Christian. A person may be unknown to us, but if we know that the Lord loves him and we ourselves claim to love the Lord, this person cannot remain a matter of indifference to us: we will seek the Lord's love in him. We will regard him with the Lord's eyes and look for that in him which the Lord loves and has placed in him through his love. Through this love of the Lord we will move toward him, not through what attracts us at the natural level.

Love should be neither calculating nor calculated, and in any case it should not find its measure and limit in ourselves. We should neither be able nor want to assess what we are offering in our love. It should be more than the gift of something we can spare, what we think we are able to give. For:

15:13. *No one has a greater love than he who gives up his soul for his brothers.*
The giving of one's own life is fundamentally the only unlimited, and thus the only true, gift. One can give one's property, or a member of one's body, or a child, or some other thing, but all this will still be a limited gift: one could give even more. But giving one's life is different. To give one's life means to give everything one has. And not simply the sum of one's countable years of life, one's observable capabilities and potential—for that too, totaled up, would result in a finite sum. To give one's life means also to surrender the transcending of earthly boundaries in the direction of the infinite and hence to surrender the infinite itself, which surrounds our boundaries at all points. Giving everything, we also surrender the unknown Infinite into which we are pouring our lives. Indeed, fundamentally we surrender certainty about our own salvation:

for who knows how we will be received in the beyond, after such a sacrifice of our own life! The person who squanders himself so extravagantly might have been able to obtain a greater certainty of his own salvation through a longer life; but out of love he has renounced this. And finally, the gift of life is infinite if it is a Christian gift, for it flows into eternal life itself and already has a share in the infinity of eternal life, because it is love.

The Lord utters this word before giving up his life for those who are his. It is a divine word, pointing to the work of redemption that he accomplishes in his mission from the Father. He utters it before presenting the perfect sacrifice: perfect, not only because he took on human life solely with this sacrifice in view—and this sacrifice will be the Pure One's expiation of our sins—but furthermore because in it he has chosen the most excruciating mortal agony, and because his agony will be matched by the most complete loneliness, a loneliness inaccessible to both man and God. It is in this final forsakenness—which even now, although as yet untasted, he desires and accepts in all its immensity, which is not even slightly lessened, not for a moment, by the thought of its end, nor made easier through anything that might be the new beginning of a hope—it is in this forsakenness that he will give his life. He gives up everything: his bodily life, his spiritual and his divine and eternal life, his love for the Father, even the Father himself; nothing of all this is left in his final forsakenness. He tells his disciples this in order to show them what he intends to take on himself for them, and also to encourage them not to shrink back from anguish and forsakenness for the sake of human love.

He gives his life for his brothers: this surrendering of his self contains the mystery of substitution. We should, as he did, give our life for our brothers. This substitution can take the most various forms. For example, someone can discover that a child unknown to him has lost its parents and is left alone and helpless; and he can decide, out of compassion for this child and in gratitude to the Lord, to love it and take it as his own. He knows that the Lord loves this child because it is a poor, forsaken creature, and he takes over this love on the part of the Lord and bestows it on the child. It is not the child's natural advantages that are the basis for his love, but rather the love of the Lord. He offers himself to represent his love to this child. In this case the substitution is still something chosen. But man can go further and offer himself for any other substitution, for tasks that God gives him one after another, tasks that are entirely new to him and that God alone has in view. The one offering himself may be shown what he is being used for, or it may remain for the most part concealed from him. This one's offer can intensify and become the offer of his whole life for his brothers, letting God control his life and also his death according to his good pleasure—above all, letting God control his inner mortification, in every form pleasing to God. God can also take from him precisely the spiritual goods he loves and that are his own by nature. Perhaps he is very cheerful by nature, and God gives him hardship and forsakenness; perhaps he is spiritually pampered, and God takes from him all refined intercourse, for example, by sending him as a missionary to peoples among whom he cannot develop his spiritual gifts at all. With a view to an offer of this kind, God obliges the person who has certain preferences to do things he does not like: he accepts such a person's sacrifice of giving his life in substitution for his brothers. God does not take away the bitter taste of this sacrifice; indeed, he lets the person savor it fully. He can even take away all insight into the rationale of the sacrifice; then everything appears completely inexplicable, and there no longer seems to be the slightest connection between the required deed and the intended gift. All of these are forms and possibilities of giving one's life for one's brothers. There is far less call to give one's physical life, for its surrender involves only one brief and unique deed. Rather, it is a matter of psychic and spiritual life, and all forms of the person's vitality. Our part, of course, is only to offer our life for our brothers; God alone decides the time and the manner of the sacrifice. And he will almost always demand of us what we do not expect, and we will not know why he requires *that* of us. For substitution always has the hidden quality that characterizes every complete sacrifice.

15:14. *You are my friends, if you do what I command you.*

Anyone who has friends, of whatever kind, accepts them fully: he is ready to share everything he possesses with them. The Lord will regard us as friends like this if we fulfill the one condition: to do what he commands us. Given this condition he is ready to wipe out all separating differences and to regard us as if we were his equals. With the eyes of his purity he will see us as pure, and he, the Son of God, will regard us as children of God. All distances created by our sins, all the differences that exist among ourselves, are taken away. He will see in us only his friends, friends for whom he makes the sacrifice of his life. Even in the act of making the sacrifice he will see us as his friends, for whom he gladly and willingly does even difficult things, even what he previously described as the deed of greatest love. In return he demands of us nothing but obedience, the keeping of his commandments.

The commandment is clear: it is the commandment of love. He was continually giving new explanations, and from all sides, of what it meant. But he did not differentiate individual commandments. The content always remains love. This is the Lord's chief concern. Yet at particular moments he also gave it very concrete expression, and enjoined precise and definite things on the disciples. In obedience to these individual instructions they fulfill the commandment of his love. But for the sake of visibility and concreteness, the Lord, who will no longer dwell visibly among mankind, has instituted his visible Church to represent him. This Church is closely connected with him who issued the Commandments of love; it has a share in his authority. At the same time it forms the close bond of those who believe and love that is visibly expressed in ecclesial obedience to the hierarchy, summed up in its representative the Pope. The chief will of the Lord remains his will for love, and all the ramifications of obedience in the Church have no other purpose than to lead the members of the Church to this love. But because there are many ways of realizing this will to love, and because if each member wanted to interpret it as seemed fit to him the greatest differences of opinion would arise and no one would perceive the unity of the Lord's will anymore, the loving obedience of Christians had to be given this visible ecclesial form. The power of the Church would also be splintered if each person tried to do the Lord's will in isolation, for any cooperation in the Church would be made impossible. Where unity is to reign, there must be order, and therefore, for the attainment of this order, there must be obedience. Every order that comprises different offices requires obedience. In the Church, therefore, each person in his own way is bound to obedience: one person is bound only to obey the most general commandments that the Church presents to him as the commandments of God, another to particularized forms of the chief commandment as well. Some things are permitted to the one and forbidden to the other, according to the mission and task of the individual members. It is mission that differentiates obedience and stamps it in its uniqueness. It is also mission that makes the final decision between religious life and life in the world and hence the two fundamental forms of ecclesiastical obedience. Each Christian must at some time ask himself what state he is called to, and each ought to place himself at God's disposal for the one as well as for the other, deciding according to God's choice. For out of this first obedience to God arises the concrete form of his life and obedience in the Church.

Obedience would die at once if one were ever to forget that it stems from the Lord and returns to him through these two human beings who both command and obey. Obedience is not an invention of the Church; it is commanded and lived out by the Lord himself, so convincingly that everyone can understand that obedience is not a dead letter, but life's salt. If the Lord had not become obedient unto death on the Cross, the obedience of Christians would of course make no sense. But because the Lord walked this way, Christian life makes no sense without this obedience.

Obedience, finally, is nothing other than the bond and the unity of faith, love and hope. None of the three would be alive, either in the cloister or in the world, if they were not held together and bound by obedience. Faith, love and hope are themselves obedience, because they stem from the Father and the Son has adopted and chosen them in the obedience of his mission; they form its content, which he has lived out in obedience. It is obedience that keeps the three alive—indeed, it is their life. Just as in a marriage the life of love between man and wife would become exhausted if nothing nourished it but the mere I and thou, love for God in the Church, too, would soon die without the forward-looking bond of obedience. It keeps everything fresh. Therefore it has a special relationship to the Holy Spirit: as he eternally animates and renews the life between Father and Son, obedience does so with faith, love and hope.

Finally, obedience is based wholly in love, for the prototype of all obedience is the relationship between Father and Son. Everything the

Father commands is love, even if it is harsh; everything in which the Son obeys is love, even if he no longer grasps the command's meaning in the night of suffering. Obedience is the expression of love, its strongest expression perhaps, but love is always its measure and the all-encompassing reality. The Son's loving obedience to the Father is thus the measure of all human commanding and obeying; only in love may we command and obey. It can happen from time to time that commands are no longer made in love, but obedience takes place in love; the one who obeys will not be lost. Even if there is a hiatus in the context of obedience at a particular spot—whether commands are no longer given vitally in the Lord, or obedience is no longer rendered vitally in the Lord—no *permanent* harm can occur because the great interrelation of obedience in the Church is a work of the Lord, and he guarantees its invulnerability.

15:15. *I no longer call you servants, for the servant does not know what his Lord is doing. But I call you friends, because everything I have heard from my Father I have made known to you.*

The servant does not monitor the activity of his lord. The disciples, on the other hand, are aware of the meaning and the greatness of Christ's mission. They know that it is infinite and aims at total Redemption. They also know that a certain task has been allotted to them within this mission. The strange thing is that they thus actually receive a real overview of the Lord's mission. They know exactly where it begins and where it ends, and within the mission itself nothing is withheld from them. When a master commands his servant to do some task, the servant certainly can know, in many cases, what the master needs his work for. But in others he cannot even guess the connection. At most he knows that what he is doing must have a meaning, because his master is not in the habit of assigning meaningless tasks. Perhaps the servant does his work without reflecting on its purpose. But he will surely have no joy in such unreflected work. He will lack the feeling of taking part in building something active. He is bound to get the impression that any other person could do what he is doing just as well. He no longer feels what he does to be a personal commission. Christ does not want to have this kind of servant, and so he makes his servants friends. The Lord lets each individual work as appears right to him, but he also gives him the sense of personal participation and involvement. Certainly, in serving and obeying there is a distribution of labor that comes solely from the Lord, but the Lord never robs his friends of the satisfaction of a personal, coresponsible achievement. Every commission he gives is personal. Perhaps someone else could fulfill it better. But the Lord has given it to that individual, whom he calls friend, and the service performed is a service of friendship that he wanted to entrust to no other.

However, the disciples become friends because the Lord has made known to them everything he has heard from his Father. There are mysteries between Father and Son, mysteries of divine life, and there are also mysteries of Christian life between us and God. But there are no mysteries, no darknesses within the mission of the Son and our mission. Where life remains mysterious, the mission is clear: it is always manifest, the Lord's mission as well as our own. For ours is based entirely within his, and is therefore just as evident as his. Action is never mystery, even if contemplation always remains mysterious. The mystery accompanies the mission, but it is not itself the mission. The mystery is the trinitarian life in God, but the Persons involved are clearly distinguished from one another. Thus, too, the Son's mission in the world is plain. And it is only our sins, at most, that hinder us from accepting, and thus understanding, the very simple clarity of our mission. This mission is always much simpler than we thought; only because we close ourselves to it does it seem complicated. The action we are to take is clear, even though in the background there are always elements of life that are mysterious. Thus the dogma of the Church too is very clear, even though there are always infinite depths of love in the background, depths that cannot be plumbed. The Cross, for example, is fully clear; nothing about it is confused, but who can penetrate and assess it in all its depth and mystery?

Thus too the Son's word to the disciples is very clear: they know everything that pertains to his mission and to themselves. The Lord has withheld nothing from them. But in making everything known to them, he has also made known to them the mystery of the Father, the mystery of the divine life that no human person will ever fully grasp.

15:16. *You have not chosen me, but I have chosen you, and have instituted you, so that you may go forth and bear fruit and your fruit may remain, so that the Father may grant you everything which you ask for in my name.*

Long ago, when the Lord decided to come, he chose us, all of us, in order to redeem us. He took up a work of Redemption that was not designed for individuals only, that knew no separation and limitation, that was meant for all. Then he appeared in the world and met individual people. These people followed him in a particular way by leaving everything in order to go with him. Because they did this, they were somehow convinced that they had chosen him. But they were mistaken in two ways: in the first place, even before they knew him, he had included them in his work of redemption; but secondly, he called each of them individually and they followed at his call, even if they did not happen to hear it with bodily ears. Both elements apply to every vocation. The Lord always calls first, and when we condescend to hear him, our following is always merely a response. But often we are so taken up with ourselves and our importance that we do not even think that the Lord has anything to say to us. And yet it is he who chooses us for Christian life. He can call us specially to the priestly or religious life, but if we do not perceive this call within a certain time, we know that he has made the choice of the lay state for us, and we are to enter into this choice by means of an explicit act.

The Lord's call and choice are always grace. Even when it seems to us that our contribution is important and indispensable, only what the Lord does in us and for us is truly indispensable. Even our activity, perhaps in days of recollection and retreat, is only the preparation for interior silence, in order to hear his call in it. Should we decide, without the Lord's grace, to choose his way, we would not even know what this way is. It would be a path chosen, thought up, laid out and decorated by ourselves; we could pretend that it was the way of the Lord. It might perhaps be a very extraordinary way, an extremely imaginative way, and thus we might think it was a way of the Lord. But the Lord's way is essentially not one we have chosen. For the Lord's way is the Father's mission and commission. His way is the glorification of the Father, and our way is his glorification. Someone might have the idea of remaining virginal, to live a life of penance and to found some work in the Church. But all this would only serve his own glorification if it were not based on a call from the Lord.

The Lord has not only chosen, but *instituted* them. The choice is followed by institution in one of the Christian states of life. The Lord goes with us as we step from the choice to the beginning of the mission. He not only calls; he also institutes. What is not instituted through him is not instituted at all. If a Catholic has never listened to the Lord and then happens to marry a Catholic woman, and, because it seems appropriate, receives the sacrament of marriage, he has not consciously let himself be instituted by the Lord into his state of life, but has taken it on himself. He will not receive assurance that he is on the way of the Lord. If this marriage turns out unhappily and there is no way out, he must know that a part of his misfortune lies in the fact that he did not listen to the Lord in the beginning. In former times people considered much more carefully whether a child was destined for the world or for the cloister, but because this first, fundamental consideration is so often lacking today, many modern marriages are built on shaky ground and present a picture of devastation. And institution by the Lord is a once-for-all act. We can pass by the time for the decisive questions to the Lord, or rather, the time for listening to his call. Much, of course, can later be retrieved and set right, but other things cannot. There are things for which it is simply too late. Of course the person concerned will still have access to the Lord's grace, which is greater than his hardness of heart. But his situation in life may be outwardly beyond help; then the only possibility left is to bear what is unavoidable with the Lord's grace, for the Lord gives the person who has willfully chosen his life the grace to live according to his will even here. But it is a grace of penance for a life of penance. This grace can be so powerful that one can even have the Lord's joy in bearing the painful expiation of one's former deafness.

The disciples are chosen and instituted *so that they may go forth and bear fruit,* that is, so that they develop in the sense of their chosen state in life, stride toward it vigorously and bring forth fruit corresponding to their state. This fruit is very manifold. But whether it is a fruit of the body or of the spirit, it is at all events the Lord's fruit.

The fruit of the body is twofold: the fruit of the child and the fruit of penance. Parents beget children, who represent the fruit of their marriage. This fruit will ripen in them; in the beginning they cherish and tend it, but it does not belong to them but to God. It must be returned to God.

Thus it becomes a seed again, as every fruit is of itself fruitful in God. This applies in the physical realm, but it applies no less in the spiritual, sacramental realm, since the child of a Christian marriage is the fruit of the sacrament, and is fruitful in this sense too. Fruitfulness begins in the physical-sexual realm, ascending the spiritual in Christian love; but the sexual starting point and sensual desire are also blessed by the Lord. He does not leave them on the outside, but allows them to be fruitful in him.

Over against the physical fruit in marriage stands the physical fruit of abstention in celibacy. Here too the body becomes fruitful for the spirit, although with a reversed charge, so to speak. In one state desire is fruitful for the Lord, while in the other state penance and mortification are fruitful for him, for this is a genuine, not simply a metaphorical fruit of the body, bringing spiritual fruit. In marriage and in celibacy, then, the body is fruitful. Therefore the body does not remain unfruitful even in a childless marriage: it has placed itself in the service of the Lord, and he will show it other possibilities for bearing fruit. In the Lord there is no sterility. What would be sterile, on the other hand, would be a marriage outside the Lord and a penance that was not placed at the Lord's disposal. But in the Lord children are raised in order to be given to God and to the Church, and the exercises of penance too are put at the disposal of God and the Church, so that they bear their fruit in the community. The two ways of bearing fruit are different; in a certain sense they exclude one another. In the choice of a state in life one must be clearly aware that one is forfeiting one of the two ways of bearing fruit, but not both. The fruit of the body, then, will also be determined by the choice.

The spiritual fruit is one that at first ripens and develops in us, but then immediately grows beyond us and makes itself independent. It opens us and makes us live away from ourselves and toward God. As fruits are, it is something particular and rounded off, because its main purpose lies in being distributed and given away. It is impossible to perfect oneself for oneself or to be converted simply for oneself, to surrender to the Lord for one's own sake. To become a Christian means continually becoming something that is to ripen for others. One can desire to better oneself in order to give joy to the Lord, but never for the sake of one's own happiness. The observer of our efforts is the Lord, never the ego. We even love ourselves for God's sake, and this is ultimately, therefore, an expression of our love for God. Perfecting oneself solely for one's own sake would simply be exchanging one sin for another, one form of egoism for another. But sin is never a fruit, for a fruit is always something that one can give to others. If one renounces a sin for love of the Lord, one does not offer him the emptiness created by the avoidance of sin but rather the fullness that has arisen through his grace at this vacant spot. And this giving never occurs wholly privately between the soul and the Lord; he accepts the fruit only under the condition that he may use it at once, with our consent, for his work, and thus for others. As far as the effect is concerned, then, it is all the same whether we give our fruit to the Lord or to our neighbor. It is like marriage: when husband and wife give themselves to each other, it is in view of a further fruitfulness that has the child as its goal. Out of my self-giving will come your child. That is how it always is: when a person opens and gives himself to another, he gives the other the opportunity of a further self-gift. He facilitates an ongoing movement of self-giving. The form of this self-giving is not quite the same with men and women. When the woman gives herself to the man she is completely focused on him, while the man who gives himself to the woman is somehow focused on something further in this very self-giving. But he draws this further self-gift out of the woman's self-giving, and thus, through the man, her self-giving is opened up and used for further ends. In the same way every spiritual self-giving contains genuine fruitfulness. A human being's self-gift to another contributes to that person's store of life. It enables him to develop; he can draw courage from it and make his life more joyous and lissome. The higher this love is, the more he can do so. If the love with which he is loved is a really Christian love, then he knows that in the lover he has a treasury of prayer, someone who represents him before God. Thus love for the Lord and love for neighbor grow in step. When someone who loves another surrenders his prayer to the Lord, the Lord uses it for the work of the one he loves, even if the lover did not expressly request it. In harvesting our fruit, the Lord always takes account of what we love with Christian love. He does not ignore the personal circle of the person praying. And correspondingly, what a person gives to another, the latter gives as a Christian to the Lord, if he receives it in love, whether through his prayer or through action. And if he understood nothing of Christian love, he would have to be gradually educated and opened, through the love that has come to him, for a love that gives. His egoism would be gradually broken through; love would cause a surrender to God to mature within him, because every love has the need to expand the beloved so that the Lord can rejoice in him. When someone loves the Lord, his joy is only perfect when it goes to God; as long as the beloved Thou does not open himself to God, joy cannot be perfect. Love is like a child who immediately wants to show its mother all the beautiful things it finds or receives. So it was with Mary: she communicated all her joy to the Son. That is why she brings all mankind to him.

From the beloved Thou, the fruit expands to the community and finally to all Christendom. There must be no stopping at the Thou; for the Lord never devoted himself only to an individual, but always, through him, to a community; from those nearest him his love expanded in ever-widening circles, because his gospel was ultimately destined for all. So he tries to get us to use our self-giving and our fruit as he did, never wanting to restrict it to a limited circle, but to give it away freely so that it may serve as many as possible, as he would wish. Because our spiritual fruit always stems from the Lord, he is also entitled to ask us to leave its distribution entirely to him. This is how it should be even in the active orders, which let their fruit ripen and make it available within a particular framework—because there is a high probability that the one bearing fruit is being used for an activity matching his abilities—and yet always make it available beyond that framework as well. It is different in the contemplative order: here the one bearing fruit is by no means so employed, for contemplation is always anonymous in its effect, and its fruit is watched over by the Lord, entirely according to his discretion. The neighbor to whom this fruit is directed is no longer concretely visible. The contemplative can and may pray for individual intentions too, but the essence and core of his contemplation must be placed wholly and blindly at the Lord's disposal.

So that the Father may grant you everything you ask him for in my name. The Lord receives all these sorts of fruit on his Father's behalf. God's response to this variety of fruit is equally various. There is only one restriction: the request must occur within the fruit bearing. For what we ask of God in the Lord's name must correspond to the fruit we offer the

Lord—naturally not in the sense that in one's fruit bearing one should somehow keep step with one's petition, offering God the appropriate price so that he will hear our petition. But it is equally impossible simply to ask without concerning oneself with the fruit, and particularly with the fruit appropriate to *this* petition. Rather, one must be prepared to pay a certain price that God may set for this request. Man's wish must lie within God's wish; man must want to correspond to the will of God. True fruit is always a real emptying out, a real desire to give oneself, to give even those things we would rather keep, which it is painful or unpleasant for us to give. The fruit that we offer must be presented without condition or reserve. If we are fully open to God he will fully grant our petition. In man's offering to God there is many a restriction that hinders the fruitfulness of his fruit. When husband and wife give themselves to each other and are thinking of something completely different at the time, they cannot truly grow together in love. It is also thus in the love between man and God. Much in the prayers and penance of Christians is egocentric, petty, not focused on God; all this hinders their fruitfulness.

Petition to God must be made in the name of the Son. To ask in the name of the Son means to ask with his agreement. What a person desires and what is in the Son's heart then form a unity. But when do we know exactly what the Son wants and wishes? Only in the rarest cases will we be able to describe it. So there is only one way: to insert oneself into his will, to ask for what the Father wishes, even if we do not know in detail what it is. This is the great grace that is given to us: that we, in the Son's place, may request of the Father what the Son desires. The Son has obtained everything he wanted from the Father: the entire redemption of the world. But for this he paid him the full price of redemption. He brought back to the Father the whole, undivided fruit of the world, receiving from him in turn the whole undivided grace of being allowed to bring forth fruit in the world. Neither the Son's fruit nor the Father's permission is restricted or hindered by anything. And into this infinite reciprocity of love the Lord places our fruit as well as our petition. Our petitions are restricted; our fruit is scarcely apparent. But in connecting ourselves with his fruit, we may also dare to connect ourselves to his petition. And the Father will regard us as those who are a part of his

Son's fruit; he will see us as the redeemed brothers of the Son and grant us what he grants his Son.

15:17. *This I command you: Love one another!*

Again and again the Lord intensifies his commandment. But each time it is in a new context and with a different emphasis. This time it is love in connection with fruit bearing and the fulfilment of prayer. The Lord wants us to be able to ask the Father in his place. But at the same time he knows that this wish can only be fulfilled if we love one another. We must love one another in such a way that we can all bear fruit in the Lord, bear fruit ourselves through love and, even more, produce fruit for the Lord in others through the effect of our love, turn people to him so that he can shine on them and cause them to ripen in his light. The entire love of mankind for one another develops in the light of the Lord, in the realm of the Lord, in the will of the Lord. It is *his* commandment. Through their love runs the love of the Lord, both through the lovers and the beloved: one single stream of the love that is his binds both, and as final fruit there remains only love itself, who is the Lord. Nothing goal oriented adheres to it anymore; all utility is submerged in the Lord's love, which is its own goal. But the Lord is love only because he loves the Father in the Holy Spirit. It is the Father who makes possible and receives the infinity of the Son's love, and the Holy Spirit gives us the fire of this living love, which, without him, would only confront us as a commandment.

THE WORLD'S HATE (I)

15:18. *If the world hates you, know that it hated me before you.*
It is not unconditionally said that the world hates the disciples, only that the world hates the Lord, and that if it hates the disciples it hated the Lord first and will meet him in this hate. What the world hates about him, and what it will find hateful in his disciples, is one thing above all: his Spirit. It hates this Spirit because it has nothing in common with it, does not recognize itself in this Spirit and cannot make use of him for the enhancement of its own spirit. This hate of the world for the Lord is a primal hate: it already hated him even before he came to the world, before he appeared visibly, before the world could confront him in words and deeds. It hates him as expectation and promise, long before he is there. It knows that his coming will challenge it and that this challenge will call for something it is not willing to give, namely, the surrender of its own standpoint so that he may transform it, according to the will of the Father and in a sense that is beyond its grasp, but whose direction is clearly indicated by God in his promise. The world, having more or less admitted the Father's position, being more or less prepared to accept his law and not openly to resist it, believes it has gone as far as it could. To let itself be led beyond this into something new—something that will always remain new—that is beyond its ken. By accepting the law—and even in actually infringing it!—it feels it has come halfway, since it designates and acknowledges sin against the law to be just that and hence stresses the positive side of law. What more can the lawgiver want! But what the Lord brings will not let itself be fit into any particular law, or into any elucidation of a particular law. It must be lived and experienced, and to this end it must be accepted over and over again. It must be transformed in the person from a word into a life, into something that accompanies and guides him at every step and that soon bodes to become more important than the person's own ego. It can never be monitored because it is never concluded. A person may know the point in his life when it began, the direction of the path that has been taken, but beyond

that it loses itself somehow in concepts such as faith, love and hope, which while they all signify something concrete, as soon as they are accepted by someone, reveal their innermost essence in an ever-intensifying and forward-pointing movement, and thus are not exactly the same today as they were yesterday. The power that indwells them is life itself, the life of the Lord, which transcends the life of the individual and to a certain degree depersonalizes it, in order to reform it into the life of a Christian personality in which Christ is more important than the person. Personality traits certainly remain in their uniqueness, but they have to subordinate themselves to the character that the Lord in his freedom stamps on the person.

The world will not accept this. It wants to be and remain what it is, and not be reformed in this dangerous, unpredictable fashion. Therefore it hates the Lord from afar, even before it knows him. And when he appears, it sees from his talk and from the life of his disciples—even though this is still very imperfect—that it was right to hate him. Its negative expectations have been proved correct. The new actually possesses an explosive power, whose greatness can only be guessed at but not yet properly measured, in the disciples. Because the power is beginning to take effect in the disciples, the world must extend its hatred to them.

The world hates the disciples because they are nearest to the Lord. He tells them this in order to console them. He knows that the hate is not easy to bear, but if the disciples grasp that they are hated for his sake and that he endured the hate before them, they may see an encouragement in this and try to show themselves not unworthy of this hate—not only by bearing it patiently out of love for the Lord, but also by feeling an obligation, now that they bear the mark of Christians in the world—a mark that they cannot see clearly at first and whose significance they can in no way estimate—to live up to it faithfully.

15:19. *If you were of the world, then the world would have loved you as its own. But because you are not of the world, but rather I have chosen you from the world, therefore the world hates you.*

The world loves only what is its own, what it knows and grasps. And that is because the world has no countenance, because it is faceless. One can never say that the world has a character, a personal stamp. It is rather a sum of individuals who somehow adapt and assimilate to one another by abandoning whatever distinguishes them more sharply from one another in order to achieve a sort of impersonal and colorless mean. The world as the Lord describes it is the world of the average—both inside and outside the Church. Everything above average is rejected, and what is below average disappears in the crowd. In this mediocrity there is no longer any direction, for that would signify life and movement. There is only adherence to what has proved durable, what has so little contour and so little character that it is not conspicuous. One can imagine a world that would consist wholly of clearly defined personalities, good and bad, each of whom had the right to assert himself somehow, to embody his fundamental essence, to live out what he has acknowledged as right. But such a world would only be possible if each person were filled with respect for his neighbor and his uniqueness, and thus was inspired and convinced that this neighbor—neither understood nor understandable, because he is different—should not be despised and persecuted because of being different. It would only work if each of these world citizens came to the conviction that even things he does not understand can have a right to existence. But such a world does not exist, because the only thing that can elicit and maintain respect is love. Loveless as the world is, however, it will not tolerate otherness. It wants to check and understand, and so can only put up with what can be checked. And since it must look after its own preservation, it must take its refuge in laws that support what it regards as the norm. Being of the world, then, means adapting oneself, avoiding everything that stands out, not only in the bad sense, but almost more in the good sense. For what stands out in the bad sense, especially striking misdeeds, is something the world understands somewhat better than its opposite, striking goodness, because its attitude here is formed by the individual, who in his inmost heart knows of the possibilities of evil through its instincts and inclinations but does not possess the love that would be necessary to conquer them. On the basis of his own negativity, the individual can understand the other person with regard to sin but has no means of understanding him with regard to love. Anyone who tries to depart from sin, through his will to be good and to live in love, will be treated with particular suspicion by the world. It can only doubt that the good that is seen in him really has its source in the Good itself. It does not know this source; it has no understanding for it. And what the world does not know, it denies and persecutes.

Not being of the world, in the Lord's sense, means having broken with mediocrity all along the line, taking the risk of living in his love and for his love. It means letting oneself be newly formed by his new teaching, preparing oneself and holding oneself out for his living reformation. Because his disciples attempt this, they are no longer of the world. But they attempt it because the Lord *has chosen* them out of the midst of the world. Being chosen by the Lord means that it is no longer possible to live in the world. This must die in order to make room for the new life given by the Lord, which is the life of Christians; moreover, it is a life that is continually becoming. Here there is no more lingering behind barriers of one's own making, but only growth beyond them toward boundaries set by the Lord. He knows them and also gives us a certain knowledge of them by pointing out the direction, but we can never see them and say that we have reached them. This growth involves giving up all ties with the world in order to obtain the freedom of life in the Lord. It is the surrender of the sheltered life that is protected by small and detailed laws, protected by the society of the nonextraordinary, of sufficiency, of satiety and contentment within a staked-out reserve in order to exchange it all for devotion to the Ever-Greater, which comes as a perpetually new gift from the Lord. That is why the world hates the disciples. Its hate springs equally from its inability to understand and its lack of desire to understand. Its suspicion begins at the very point where it can no longer comprehend. And just where the world's mistrust sets in, love sets in for the disciples. True, they comprehend the transformation as little as the world does, but for them this noncomprehension is a fundamental cause for trust and for greater love. So from the same point both hate and love diverge.

15:20. *Think of the word which I said to you: The servant is not greater than his Lord. If they persecuted me, they will also persecute you, and if they have kept my word, they will also keep yours.*

The servant is not greater than his lord. The servant, as servant, is there to receive and carry out the commissions of his lord. If the servant and the master are somehow insignificant, none of the latter's commissions will be significant or extraordinary. Servants who carry out such commissions can change masters without difficulty, being at the service now of this one, now of that one. Their mediocrity will always be able to adapt and effect the change without having to refashion itself inwardly or manifest it outwardly. They change masters and commissions as one changes clothes. For the servants of Christ, however, the moment they are enlisted by him and receive his first commission by attempting to utter their first assent, they receive the stamp of the Lord. This makes them incapable of ever obeying another master. Their Christian mission is and remains a clearly recognizable, visible mission, and even if they wanted to they could not do away with this quality. Their growth continues within their mission, but however much they may grow, they can never outgrow their mission. The mission always remains greater than they, for it is the Lord who has sent them, and he who sends is greater than he who is sent; the lord is greater than his servant, because the one sent must always serve the sender. Certainly the servant should enter thoroughly into his mission and assimilate it as his own, but all the time he should remain conscious that he himself is not the mission but perpetually receives it from the Lord and is never identical with it. He is to adapt himself to his mission, whereas the Lord will never adapt. He must continually examine himself to see whether he is still living at the center of his mission. To stray from this center would be to forget that the servant must never be greater than the Lord. In any case such a thing is impossible, for one is the servant and the other is the Lord.

If they have persecuted me, they will also persecute you. The Lord's destiny is inseparable from that of the disciples. None of the disciples can live as he had before meeting the Lord. He can only live as the Lord has determined. But there is no single instance of Christian life given by the Lord that is not foreshadowed or hinted at in the Lord's life. In his earthly life the Lord unites all Christian destinies, however varied these may be when compared with one another. He unites them, cementing them together and causing them to indwell one another. Any scene of his life's work or his Passion presents a whole series of Christian possibilities arising for his disciples, possibilities that are contained in him and made available by him. The relation is always unique, but develops in its uniqueness into the multiplicity of paths of discipleship. The Lord lives out certain possibilities with all clarity, almost without missing a single detail; other features of Christian life are only as if hinted at in the life of the Lord, without his seeming to linger over them; but these situations too, on closer consideration, are exhaustive, for they present nothing but Christian possibilities for discipleship. Again and again Christian life is seen to fit into the Lord's framework. This is what he means when he says: *If they persecuted me, they will also persecute you.* Not only is persecution common to both, but also the manner of the persecution remains identical. The way the disciples are persecuted and endure persecution will be like the Lord's. One can only be persecuted as a Christian while in motion, that is, on the way from and going to the Father. This is not to say that the way to the Father is necessarily a way of persecution, but certainly one encounters the spirit of Christian persecution only along this path. No endurance of persecution would be Christian if it were not at the same time a movement toward the Father. Therefore Christian character can be recognized especially clearly in persecution. Its stamp, certainly, is always the same, both in a peaceful and in a persecuted life. The fundamental mark of this life is that it is a journey. But in suffering it emerges more unequivocally. Of course the Christian can suffer in loneliness, often not knowing what good his persecution is doing. And yet, even though he may be enduring extreme agonies and feels completely forsaken, he still knows with his whole being that he is enduring it for the Son in the name of the Father. Even if his whole capacity for suffering is filled up and he tastes it to the uttermost degree, he does not keep it for himself but offers it to the Son so that the Father may freely dispose of it. He, the persecuted sufferer, journeying to the Father, receives this suffering as if it were absolutely, exclusively and for always destined for this human being, this person, this ego. Yet despite this he knows that he is only a channel, that in him the Lord is affected more than he is himself, and that just as the Son takes up the disciple's suffering in order to pass it on to the Father, the disciple also takes it up in order to give it to the Son and, through the Son, to offer it to the Father. His taking up and passing on the suffering involve a whole transformation of the essence and meaning of persecution, and this transformation is the key to his human role as a persecuted person. The grace of Christian endurance essentially alters persecution and makes something greater out of it than is contained in the degree of physical or natural pain imposed. And this applies both when the Christian is persecuted clearly and plainly on account of his Christianity and when he finds himself in an unintelligible persecution whose purpose he cannot penetrate. In both cases the mystery of substitution is operating. The person persecuted is often not persecuted for his own sake at all, but perhaps for the sake of those entrusted to him, or on account of Christianity in general, or because of the Lord. In persecution, then, he receives the blow that was not primarily intended for him at all, shielding with his person both the Lord and the Church. He passes on his love to them by placing himself before them as a shield and being struck in their stead. But for that very reason he is never affected as the blow itself was intended. If it is the Christian *spirit* that receives the blow, as such it can never be really affected. And insofar as it is affected, it transforms the blow into something different than was intended. It is like what happened on the Cross. Mankind meant to deal with the Lord in such a way that he would be finished with forever, but in doing so they set the whole redemption event in motion. So it is with the persecuted Christian.

If they have kept my word, they will also keep yours. Just as previously the same people persecuted the Lord as persecute the disciples, so now the same ones kept the word of the Lord as keep the disciples' word. They will see the unity between what the Lord proclaimed and what his disciples proclaim. They will see this unity so clearly that at certain moments it will not matter to them whether they receive the word of the Lord from him or from his disciples. They will recognize it as the same word, which stems from God. The word itself does not change, whether the Lord speaks it or the disciples say it. It is proclaimed differently, of course, but if it is proclaimed in the faith of the Lord, the power of its effect is the same. For when the Lord gives his disciples the commission to proclaim his truth, he gives them at the same time, in faith, his own power. The word they speak in his name possesses the power of his own word. No differences can be discovered between them, because the truth, his unique truth, forms the content of both the Lord's word and the word of his disciples. The Lord also knows very well that when he no longer dwells in this world he will impart the same living faith to his disciples, no less than now while he is still among them. He knows that the truth he has received from the Father admits of no alteration. It is eternally the same. Therefore those who are receptive to his word will also be receptive to the word of his disciples. In both the content of the word and the receptivity to it there lies a constant power that goes out from him, but he radiates it as the Son of the Father, that is, equally during the time of his earthly journey and subsequently.

A kind of bronze immutability and rigidity, established forever, show themselves here in the power of the word. It is not something the word receives later, as a result of its distance from the living source of the Lord in the Church. It possesses this untouchable majesty even in the very beginnings of Christianity. It is and remains something absolute and unretractable, the word of the Son of God. His chief commandment, love one another! is unshakable. It is a commandment, not carte blanche for a "free life-style". It cannot be relativized; it will not be a falsely understood *"ama et fac quod vis"*. The word of the Lord is the one word, and the power of its uniqueness is so great that it is able to include everything in it. This power of unity radiates from the Lord and binds him to his disciples, binds them to him and his word in all essential questions. Every later development in the Church has its measure and its center precisely where the Lord's center is. Entirely new aspects may appear, and the future can continually reveal new ones, but in all its development, expansion and interpretation Christian truth will never be able to shift by a hairsbreadth from the Lord's center. This centering of truth in the Lord is the touchstone for the genuineness of every development in the Church. The word of the Lord is alive, and for that very reason the word of the Lord, once uttered, remains unantiquated, fresh and new throughout all times, the established word of the Lord, spoken at one time and for all time. Everything that comes after is to refer back to it.

If they have kept my word, says the Lord. If mankind accepts his word as a living word that cannot remain inert and dead in them but is to grow to such an extent that their center is fused with the center of the word and the word becomes their main concern, then they will also seek to understand the disciples' word in such a way that it begins to grow in them as in the disciples themselves, until they, like the disciples, are able to pass it on. Anyone who is a disciple of the Lord does not let the word

203

die in him, passing it on as a dead word. He lets it develop his Christian life in him, which is the life of the word, both in receiving it and in passing it on. Then the word will go out from him as something alive, to continue to exercise its living influence in love. In its living influence in love it finally reveals its true nature: it is the real truth of the Lord.

15:21. *But they will do all this to you for my name's sake, because they do not know him who sent me.*

Again the Lord returns to the idea of persecution. Men will persecute the disciples less for their own sake than for the sake of the one who stands behind them, the Lord. And all this is because the persecutors do not know the Father. The Lord sees Father, Son and the persecuted one inseparably linked together, forming a kind of succession. By virtue of this succession the martyrs become saints. They stand just behind the Son: they are, so to speak, lifted out of the rank of mankind by being persecuted on a level that is no longer their own but that of the unrecognized Lord. The persecutors themselves know this. For it is clear to them that they persecute people in order to hit at the Lord, and behind the Lord at the God whom they will not accept. They see as negative what the Lord does positively in allowing people to be persecuted in his place. The Lord knows that his name is hateful to them, the name of the Messiah sent by God not only to fulfill the promise but also to make mankind's relationship to God become a living and loving one. But someone who does not love cannot endure being loved—therefore he must persecute. The persecutors sense something of the love that glows in the persecuted ones, and they sense the Lord's love even more strongly. But the more they sense the presence of love, the more incomprehensible and detestable they find it. They scent the Infinite in it, exploding the limits of the world, and that is precisely at what they want to strike. Therefore their very persecution itself, while it outwardly remains in human limits, is necessarily involved in the transcendence that characterizes Christianity. Persecution opens so wide because it coincides with the angle of man's opening to the word of God, which itself corresponds to the angle of the Lord's opening toward the world. Thus the blow and the receiving of the blow are not without a secret connection. The blow administered to the persecuted conceals a power that gives them a greater longing for the love of the Lord. The blow that strikes is actually several times heavier than what was intended for them personally by the persecutors. This has the effect of letting them be more consumed in the love of the Lord, and this greater love reflects back on to the persecutors. This is the Christian justification for martyrdom; it also explains why people sometimes take martyrdom on themselves and why nonbelievers cannot understand why they do not avoid it. In this prophecy the Lord shows that he knows all this and consents to it.

Christians are persecuted, in the end, because mankind does not know the Father. As Jews they do not know him because they want to hold him captive in their law, and thus will not trust to the liberating power of his living life. They encompass him using his law, not wanting to let themselves be encompassed. The appearance of the Lord has caused their relationship with the Father to shut down, so to speak, because they have closed themselves at the very moment when God wanted to open them up in his word. Therefore they are no longer receptive to the word of love, and since they do not want to love, they can only persecute love.

15:22. *If I had not come and spoken to them, they would have no sin. But now they have no excuse for the sin.*

What they believed and how they lived was unimpeachable until the moment of the Lord's appearance. Therefore, it looks as if the Lord were responsible for their sin. They were the righteous and have now become sinners. Their sin, then, can only lie in their righteousness itself, insofar as they were unwilling to surrender it for love. Formerly, they could take their righteousness as a measure of God's working among them, and, with their righteousness, they almost held God in their hands. Their righteousness had a definite value; it was a virtue that had substance and vital power. But as soon as the Lord appeared, what was alive in their righteousness turned into a dead thing that was the seed of sin. They were righteous, but not redeemed; their sin began precisely at the point where their righteousness refused to serve and make room for the work of redemption. They could not take the step that involved leaving their righteousness and clinging to the mercy of God. They could not drop their measuring sticks and give themselves in faith. They did not want to abandon their own activity in order to make room for the Lord's passivity, and thus make room for a new activity in the name of the Lord. Love alone could have made this step possible for them, that love that knows only love and leaves righteousness behind in order to entrust itself, unprotected and naked, to the love of the Lord.

This transition was certainly not an easy one. They lived within the finite law, preoccupied with their virtue and with becoming perfect according to the law. There was nothing culpable about this. They were like pupils who devote themselves entirely to the solution of their assignment. And now the teacher suddenly presents them with something completely new, where the old rules that they have diligently and laboriously learned are no longer valid, where none of their school learning is applicable anymore. They are transplanted out of school into the midst of life. The transition is so abrupt that it seems like a complete break. And yet school existed for no other purpose than to educate them for life. The material they have gone through—the law and the prophecies—was nothing other than a preparation, a practice for life. So after all, they are responsible if they cannot accomplish this transition from school to life. They have not used their schooltime to mature for life; in keeping the law they did not always keep the promise before their eyes or leave room in their soul for what might be totally different demands on the part of the living God. All God's pupils must make room for this. The Christian in the New Covenant, too, must leave space in his Christian daily life for extraordinary commands of God: today or tomorrow God can approach him because he needs a saint or a martyr or something else, something hidden and apparently insignificant that must be complied with without question and realized. This destiny can come to anyone, and no one may evade God's sudden commands by referring to his wonted Christian daily life. And this applies not only in youth, at the time of choosing a state in life, but up until the hour of death. That is why the Jews are guilty: they have been operating only for themselves and their own perfection, instead of doing it as training for the will of God. Their law is something they have managed, and therefore they also want to manage God and love.

But now they have no excuse for their sin. For in the face of the Lord all their guilt comes to light. They want neither to see it nor to repent of it, because even now they are still convinced of their righteousness. The less they want to concede their sin, the more it grows, not outwardly but certainly inwardly. They do not commit any special, outward misdeeds, but inwardly their sin grows monstrous, because they refuse to accept that they are sinners. They move further and further from their righteousness the more they insist on it and deny knowledge of their sin. Their attitude is the opposite of confession, in which alone excuse, that is, exculpation, is possible. Instead of opening themselves to God, they turn in on themselves in their righteousness, and thus turn away from mercy. The only way to exculpate sin is to repent of it. Only in repentance can one perceive sin. But since they do not want to see it, they cannot repent of it. That, and only that, is why they are inexcusable. If they could be convinced of their guilt, their sin could also be taken away and they could be excused, exculpated.

The harshness of this word of the Lord lies in the fact that it requires the Jews, for whom the law is the norm, to mature beyond it. Thus a pupil is required simultaneously to be absorbed in his tasks, look up to his teacher with respect and yet be "learning for life", over and beyond the entire present situation. Or even, put more sharply, a young girl who grows up entirely sheltered by her parents and knows nothing of married life is expected, when she marries, to be equal to all the obligations of a spouse. The transition is so abrupt, so unexpected, so incomprehensible that many pupils and many girls are at a loss in the face of it, and yet they have no right to evade life or marriage. Thus the Jews were also "sheltered" by the law, and the transition is hard for them. The demands seem too much. But with love it is possible. And it is only because they do not want to love that they do not succeed in making the transition. That is the only reason why they have no excuse. If they risked the leap into love, all would be forgiven them.

15:23. *Whoever hates me, also hates my Father.*

From now on it is not possible to love only the Father or only the Son; similarly it is impossible to hate the Son without referring this hatred, through him, to the Father. Hatred knows no limit, and every living hatred affects the Father through the Son, and the Son through the Father. And even if someone expressly wanted to hate only one of them, neither the Father nor the Son would allow such a restriction. They are one in love, and they will not be separated even in being hated. When someone claims to know the Father or not to know him, there is no third possibility beside love and hate. At most there might be a third possibility for those who have not yet come into any contact with Christian truth. They might be waiting in a condition of indifference. For all those, however, who have heard something of the word of God, there remains only the choice between love and hate. The decision is always urgent and is made and accepted as a whole. There is no such thing as a step-by-step decision, nor is it admitted. A mixture of hate and love is not tolerated in God. Mankind, to be sure, keeps trying to produce such combinations, but God will not have them. He will not stop shaking and goading until something total comes into being, until he who is lukewarm has decided to be either cold or hot. Hatred is at least alive: it is open to conversion. The hater must admit that he hates, but the moment he admits it, the gap becomes evident: it is the negative of love. Hating, he admits that he is not indifferent, that he cannot get anywhere with love. He lays himself bare by this admission. Hatred implies declaration of war, challenging God to a duel, and so God himself cannot remain indifferent. Lukewarmness is the temperate state in which we seek to pacify ourselves, but in which God will not be pacified. He wants a Yes or a No. Hatred, on the other hand, is the agitated, inflated state that burns and consumes itself until it collapses because it can no longer endure inner emptiness. From the outset hatred involves an admission that reveals its true nature and includes the beginning of a turning away from hatred.

15:24. *If I had not done among them the works which no other has done, they would have no sin; but now they have seen and have hated both me and my Father.*

Earlier the Lord said: If I had not come and had not spoken to them. Now he says: *If I had not accomplished among them the works.* Thus he relates their sin to their failure to acknowledge his unique deeds. He has worked miracles among them that identify him without question as the Son of the Father, miracles that can only be interpreted in terms of the love that binds the Father to him and moves him do such deeds for the glorification of the beloved Father; miracles that leave questions open for which there is only one answer: love; miracles that themselves become a question: From where does this love stem? For it is as if these miracles of the Lord everywhere point toward love, always posing one single question and looking for a single answer: love. They are miracles where love is the sole theme; miracles that, in themselves, are ultimately only love, whose substance itself is love, and that call forth the cry for love in all who hear, see or are affected by them. Each person who meets with these miracles is bound to wish to cease to be, in order to make room for this incomprehensible love. The new thing the Lord brings begins as miracle, and this miracle casts its radiance back on all that has been. The light of the miracle reveals what was lacking in earlier times. Everything questionable finds its answer in miracle, and everywhere the answer is—love. Everything that was incipient or tentative in humanity suddenly comes together as fullness. It is as if a child had been playing the piano with one finger, and now the maestro suddenly sits down and strikes full chords. Up until now mankind certainly had a concept of God, but God was far away and one thought of him with a shudder. Then the miracle takes place: he is among us, and he loves! Everything we had not even dared to suspect is a reality more real than we could guess. And everything impure and in bondage in us is suddenly pure and free in the Lord, because he does the works *which no other has done,* the works of pure love. And while doing these works, he requires only one thing: to be lovingly acknowledged. If a person will not do this, the sum of sin will become too great for love in that person to become free. He remains bound to himself; he takes himself as a standard of measurement and applies his own measure to love, obstructing love at all points and resisting every liberating increase of love within him. If we take ourselves as the standard of measurement, everything that does not originate with us is unreal and must be rejected. Because the fullness does not lie within us, we believe ourselves incapable of bearing it. And because we do not want what lies outside ourselves, we make what we want, and thus what we do not want, into our law. That is hatred of Father and Son. Whoever really hates, hates them both because he sees the connection between them. He does not see it in love, however, but because of what the Son says of the Father, claiming him as his Father. But since the one who fails to love rejects the Son, whose commandment he finds past enduring, he must also reject the Father to whom it is intended to lead. His hatred of the Father follows directly out of his hatred of the Son. Perhaps he was quite happy with the Father before, but now, through the Son, he is shown in a different light; man does not wish to accept the Son and is alienated from the Father. Although he does not acknowledge the Son as God, he cannot avoid perceiving the inner connection between Father and Son, and he is forced to reject the Father as well. Up until now he was like a girl preparing for marriage who has only a vague liking for her bridegroom. She works on her trousseau, keeps a kind of fidelity to her future spouse and somehow fulfills his wishes. When she utters her consent she is thinking more of herself than of him. But suddenly he approaches her with an unexpected demand against which she rebels in indignation. Now she hates the man, hates everything to do with him—their entire married life, all his relatives. She lives to hurt him; she associates, perhaps only out of spite, with other men. Her rejection extends itself to everything connected with her spouse. But this only shows that she was seeking herself from the very beginning. She never knew a true devotion to her husband, to marriage, to the household, to the children. Previously this egoism was simply masked as love. It reveals its true nature at the moment when love is faced with a serious demand. But from now on the hate and disdain will never be so lukewarm as the supposed love was: they will be intense and burning. Thus people hate the Father in the Lord: he is hated as his law of life, the world that surrounds and defines him, which he brings with him and to which he would like to introduce others.

15:25. *But the word in their law must be fulfilled: They hate me without reason.*
They hate the Lord so that the prophecy may be fulfilled. Such a promise always contains a positive and a negative aspect: a work of grace and its possible rejection through our sin, light and darkness, love and hate. And those who reject hate the Lord *without reason*. A reason for hate could only be found if the person of the Lord could be separated from his work of redemption, if his demand did not completely coincide with his mission. But because they coincide perfectly and his mission is love, they hate him without reason. The love he brings with him from his Father in order to redeem them coincides with the love he offers

them. And his coming is the pure fulfilment of his Father's will, so that the love he shows the Father by coming into the world is not different from the love he showers on them by making them his brothers. Both are the pure expression of his being in the Father. If they too wanted to be in the Father (as the Jews claim to be in the Father), they could respond in no other way than by unconditionally letting themselves be inserted into his love and surrendering to it unconditionally. There would be no room for hatred from either a divine or a human standpoint. If, in spite of this, people still hate, they do so without reason.

THE THIRD PROMISE OF THE CONSOLER

15:26. *When the Consoler comes, whom I will send you from the Father, the Spirit of truth who proceeds from the Father, he too will bear witness to me.*

The Spirit of truth proceeds from the Father, and although he proceeds from the Father in order to be sent into the world, the Father does not send him so much as does the Son. And the Son sends the *Spirit of truth* not only as Spirit of truth, but also as *Consoler*. The mission and task of the Holy Spirit, then, can be manifold—manifold in its simplicity. Father and Son grasp this sending as a simple one, but to us, whose minds are limited, it has to be made clear bit by bit. Consideration is given to our inability to grasp the totality and fullness of this mission, and so the Holy Spirit is introduced to us, as it were, in parts—but in parts with fluid boundaries, in concepts that represent, so to speak, the nodal points of his unity, between which lie transitional zones. And it is precisely these zones that we cannot grasp, because our sinful earthly condition denies a unified vision and an increasing understanding.

The Son says five things about the Holy Spirit: he himself will send him, as the Consoler, who proceeds from the Father. He is the Spirit of truth, and he bears witness to the Son. He differentiates the sending, the proceeding, consolation, truth and witness, and yet asserts the synthesis. The Spirit who goes out from the Father is sent by the Son, our brother, and none other will be the Consoler but the Spirit of truth who begets the Son.

The disciples will understand the Spirit best as the Consoler. They have been continually strengthened and consoled by the Lord's presence. As long as the Lord remained among them, no serious anxiety could arise in them. As soon as there were signs of anything of the kind, the Lord stood there as Helper and Consoler, and without this consolation their inconstant faith would have been completely unable to stand firm. But the Lord knows that later, when he will be taken away from them, they will only grasp the continuing nearness of his love with great difficulty. They will urgently need a Consoler, and therefore he sends them the Spirit. He might also have called him the Spirit of love. But he does not do so, because earthbound men are scarcely able to bring love and Spirit into a living, experiential unity. Spirit and consolation are easier for them to connect, because Spirit is, so to speak, less concrete and bound to the human than love, and therefore also less directly related to God (for they grasp the Lord's being God best through his being human). In order to comprehend the full divinity of the Spirit, they will need the outpouring of the Spirit itself; now the Lord wants only to establish an initial approach between the Spirit and them.

But the Spirit will be Consoler only as the Spirit of truth. Here the Lord forever excludes the possibility of Christians having any consolation outside of truth. The Lord gives truth an absolute sense. Never, and in no connection, can it be circumvented or left to one side. In this absolute sense of truth all Christian qualities can find their homeland, their bedrock; they can never come to stand outside the truth. The faith of each individual is personally shaped and the Lord leaves him this special hue. He also leaves each person the freedom to love as he will and as he can, or to let his faith be strengthened by this or that. But everything is based in the one truth that is unshakable. That is what is *dogmatic* about Catholicism: the immovability of the nucleus of faith. The Lord passes from the subjectivity of personal consolation to the objectivity of divine truth, whose nucleus is dogma, firmly grounded, which no subjectivity can shake. Only within this fixed form is there the consolation of the living life of love.

Now this Spirit of truth that proceeds from the Father is sent by the Son in order to bear witness to him. Thus the Spirit is drawn into the Son's course from the Father to the Father: he goes out from the Father via the Son and back to the Father again. More precisely: sent by the Son, issued by the Father, the Spirit goes to mankind by bearing witness to the Son, consolingly strengthens the faith of mankind through this witness and thus leads mankind back to the Father in faith.

Seldom, until now, has the unity of the Trinity been so clear and vivid as in this word of the Lord. Each Person is distinctly there with his particular function or mission, which, however, he can only carry out in unity with both of the other Persons. The Son sends the Spirit; but in order to send him, the Spirit must go, must proceed from the Father; and the Father must let him go out from him. But in order to let the Spirit go forth from him, the Father must accept the Spirit's sending by the Son and presuppose his desire to be sent. Ultimately, the Spirit too is bound both to him who lets him go forth and to him who sends him. The unity between them is a perfect one, then, and one senses that it is a unity of love. At their center the sending, the letting go and the being-sent contain a mystery of love.

Hearing this, the disciples see in the Lord love above all else, and await the Spirit's consolation that the Father will give them in the Spirit of truth. Each Person in God appears in the disciples' expectation with his special hue. And yet, after the Son's return to God, all three form such a unity—a unity that will not unfold in any new Incarnation for all eternity—that henceforth all the qualities of the Persons are, as it were, interchangeable. The Son is just as much truth and consolation as love, the Father just as much love and consolation as truth and the Spirit just as much truth and love as consolation. The properties of the Persons do not, however, become blurred, but they become so rich that each believer can meet each Person personally and according to his inclination. There is even less possibility of them being confused since, after the Son's return into the perfect unity of God, this unity does not close in on itself but immediately results in a new procession to the world: the sending of the Holy Spirit. This sending does not take place like the Son's sending, where one of the divine Persons "separated" from the others, veiling his Godhood and leaving it behind with the Father, and dwelt on earth. Now, after fulfilling the Son's mission, the Spirit himself proceeds, but without divesting himself of his heavenly glory. Only after the Second Person returns does the Third Person truly emerge into the world. And he does so as a Person (and not merely as an attribute of God), since the Spirit personally obeys the Son's sending, on the one hand, and on the other hand, shows himself to be distinct from the Person of the Father from whom he goes forth.

It is no longer the same situation as at the baptism by the Jordan. There it was the Father who sent down the Spirit on the Son. The whole process of sending remained within the relationship between the Persons, even though, because of the Son's human nature, it was made outwardly and sensibly evident. It illustrated the unity of the Trinity in the sacrament of baptism, and thus our faith was directly centered in the core of the Trinity. Now, on the other hand, the Trinity opens itself when the Son sends the Spirit to mankind, not pointing away from itself into the world but pointing to the unity of the Trinity and thus to the Father. So the Spirit comes in order to complete the Son's work and love in the world, and thus lead everything back into the unity of the Father.

In the realm of the sacraments, confirmation corresponds to this new sending and administering of the Spirit. Here the Consoler Spirit appears as the perfecter and multiplier of love. The love mankind needs in order to fulfill the Lord's commandment is contained in the gift of confirmation, which is also, and inseparably, a duty. In confirmation the faithful receive their mission, both in terms of strength from God and a sense of direction for their lives. In this mission of theirs the Spirit is the Consoler. They receive the consolation of the Spirit in the form of the mission he imparts, that is, it is more for others than for themselves. When, the moment he speaks of consolation, the Lord introduces them to the movement of the Holy Spirit—proceeding from the Father, sent by the Son—and describes this movement as the Spirit of truth, he shows them, in a supermundane sense that they are to translate into earthly life, of what the consolation and truth of Christian existence consists: apostolic mission. This mission is the fullness of life, hovering between the most subjective realm of consolation and the most objective realm of truth. This Spirit of truth and of consolation, who proceeds, is sent and bears witness—this Spirit the disciples are to receive, and in this Spirit they are to live.

15:27. *You also will bear witness, because you are with me from the beginning.*

Once again we can see the line from the Trinity via the mission of confirmation to the apostolate, and the disciples are inserted into this line because they were with the Lord from the beginning. Just as the Spirit, with his mission, was present from the very beginning, at Mary's conception and at Christ's baptism, the disciples were also present from the beginning. Their mission has no other source than the mission of the Spirit; it has its roots in the same trinitarian event. And just as there is no break in this multifaceted sending of the Spirit within the Trinity, neither is there any hiatus in the mission of those who were with the

Lord and to whom the Lord was sent. Both beginning and end are characterized by richness and fullness beyond comprehension.

The sending of the Spirit is always like the result of a whole bundle of movements: from the Father to the Son, from the Son to the Father, from the Son to the world, from the Son via the world to the Father, from the Son via the Father to the world. All this is totally beyond our grasp. And now the Spirit is both Consoler and truth, at the same time bearing witness to the Son and completing his work by enabling the disciples also to bear witness. This is no less baffling and staggering. And yet it is one and the same Spirit, no vague synthesis but a clear-cut Person, with a precise direction—One who blows where he will. Everything works together toward a result of the Spirit, which is in no way a simple, quantifiable total, the final, round sum of some complicated given, the simple and clearly observable river emerging from the net of tributaries, but the superabundance of a vast and limitless movement. Only in this unity does everything become really rich and full and personal. Nowhere is there a standstill, nowhere a having arrived; everywhere there is movement. Indeed, thus the Spirit is recognized, in this movement that cannot be pinned down. Mankind's mission is to participate in this Spirit: it should be the spirit of this Spirit. Their mission too will be the result of infinite directions, beginnings and sources, and what appear to be the most disparate elements in their life will be welded together into a single clear direction, but they will not see this unity as something they have manufactured. But again it will be no vague, syncretistic unity, but a sharp, clear unity full of character: it will be the unity of their mission, the revelation—through their life—of the Son returning to the Father in the Spirit. Everything is drawn into the movement of these last two verses: Trinity, mission, truth, dogma, consolation and the most vital Christian life, the growth character of faith, the Church and finally the mystery of transubstantiation itself. For the latter is based in the determination never to call a halt, to continue letting oneself be transformed, insofar as even the Trinity, within all its permanence, reveals itself as constant motion, forever flowing in eternal life, the endless spiral, the ever-new explosive power of what might appear to be an end and a fulfilment. But the fuse that causes everything to explode is the Holy Spirit. Wherever he goes, he sets things in motion. And although it is a result, it is always the most incalculable result: the Spirit always starts where no one expects him and thus, himself peaceful, he brings everything into a state of unrest. A sermon is effective hardly ever through the preacher's design, and Christian education is hardly ever effective in the things the educator sees as being especially well done. The Spirit keeps his secrets, and his grace is not transparent to us. It may become visible, but not exhaustively so. The Spirit's emphasis is always different from ours, and this is because he works in us just as personally as does the grace of the Lord. But because he works personally, because he does not treat one person the same as another, because each of his testimonies is unique, all of us who believe are bound to give our testimony. Every witness we give is not only a passing on of the words of the Lord, but is effected in us through the Trinity and has a share in the uniqueness and personal nature of the divine Spirit. No one may withdraw from this giving of witness; otherwise a particular note and color would be missing in the prism of the Spirit. The working in the Lord is never a countable sum, but many-hued, qualitative harmony.

THE WORLD'S HATE (II)

16:1. *This I have said to you so that you take no offense.*
The Lord has said all this to the disciples so that in the moment of fulfilment they will remember that everything that occurs really is fulfilment, something that the Lord knew and spoke of in advance, that was in no way a surprise to him. He wants to educate them toward this perception. For they will have to bear witness, just as he and the Father in him bear witness. Thus he has initiated them into his truth and has shown them that this truth will not be able to have its effect in the future without drawing nourishment from their very substance. Without their cooperation, the Lord's mission cannot be perfectly fulfilled. Their mission is a part of the Lord's mission. Therefore, the moment a clear divine commission is being fulfilled, they may no longer have any questions; they are not to show any uncertainty, even if they are persecuted. On the contrary: persecution is to strengthen them in the knowledge that they are on the right path. In it they are to recognize the Lord's promise and thus his nearness. He is already rehearsing them for this hour. He wants the time of expectation to be properly used, so that the time of fulfilment, when it arrives, may be fully perceived. Now, through his instruction, he is placing tiny parts of the whole into their hands for them to look after, so that in the moment of urgency they will realize how much these parts are complementary building blocks of something that is still to come. For the Lord knows their human unreliability. If they came to the hour of mission without preparation, they would not only lose all poise themselves, but probably create confusion among others as well and endanger the Lord's work. In their confusion they would run a great danger of falling back into their sin and perhaps conclusively denying the Lord, failing to recognize him in that hour. Therefore the Lord does everything to prevent them ultimately falling, not only because he needs them for his task, but even more because he loves them.

16:2. *They will shut you out of the synagogues, and indeed the hour is coming when he who kills you will believe he is doing God a pious service.*

Although the disciples have long been part of the New Covenant, they have not yet detached themselves externally from the Old. In their own eyes they are a continuation of the Old Covenant; they have drawn no dividing line. Nor, at their conversion to the Lord, were they required to give up the past forms at once. They were left with a broad foundation of the Old on which to erect the expanding New. For of itself the Old Covenant as God made it was good; through it, people could have accepted the promised Messiah with his love, letting themselves be purified and deepened by him. But pharasaism made this transition impossible through its defensive attitude. Despite this, the Lord did not require his disciples to leave their religious community. Rather, he leaves them there until they are thrown out. The break is not made by them but by the members of the community that resists the Lord. By leaving the disciples in the synagogue, he forces those who do not want to follow him to confront him and his teaching. They are forced to make resolutions and throw the disciples out. They will not be able to say that some fell away from their community and are no longer their concern; they will have to plan the excommunication actively. And they will have to take cognizance of the fact that something new is indeed there, something that the adherents of the New see as the legitimate continuation and expansion of the Old and that therefore did not oblige them to leave the Old of themselves. There is something profoundly Catholic in this attitude of the disciples: the Church never brings about the break itself. The Church is not a sect that arises through separation from an earlier community. The guilt of the schism falls on those who push the disciples out.

If they were to leave voluntarily now, the disciples would also have the consciousness of founding something, a feeling of having accomplished something positive through this leaving. Instead they are to endure the shame of being thrown out. Right at the beginnings of Christianity they are to learn to take this disgrace of the Lord on themselves; being in retreat, and not even a fighting retreat but a dishonorable defeat, being thrown out into the street. But they will not only throw them out and heap this disgrace on them: *The hour is coming when he who kills you will believe he is doing God a pious service.* For the ones thrown out will be outlaws in the eyes of those remaining behind and of the world. But this

God to whom those remaining do their pious service no longer has anything in common with God the Father of the Lord. It is a God that they themselves have pieced together from remnants of the Old Covenant, from obsolete laws that they are still trying to make into a totality, and in the process they replace grace and love with their own discretion and self-righteousness. Their opinion that they are doing God a pious service will alienate them more and more from the possibility of being Christians. Through sheer fear and incomprehension the persecuted ones will be driven to a courage that is no longer their own but the strength of the Lord in them. The persecutors, on the other hand, encouraged by their success, acquire a personal courage that consists of disdain for the hesitant, weak and desperate actions of the persecuted. The ease of their cheap victory will make them feel like masters of the world. Their courage grows in proportion to each new defeat of their enemies. Their religion is no longer anything but the expression of their self-mastery and personal superiority. Everything it contained that really came from God and referred to God is carefully removed. It is a kind of religion of the dance, in which nothing matters but the enjoyment of one's own movement. Every truly religious factor is replaced by a worldly one. But this danger, that is, that of being nothing more than a dead husk and man's self-adoration, threatens every religion; even in the Church it can go so far that inwardly all the religious life of a Christian is choked, throttled and hollowed out by a complete lack of surrender, and the empty life is stuffed with distorted or arbitrary laws.

16:3. *And this they do because they have recognized neither the Father nor me.*

They do not know the Father, although their religion is allegedly the religion of the Father. And because they have not recognized the Father, they have also remained closed to the Son. Everything they do against Christianity arises from this lack of knowledge of Father and Son. If they had known the Father rather than themselves, they might perhaps have had difficulty accepting the Son immediately, but they would still have heard his demand, recognized its validity and at least confronted it. In prayer to God—perhaps at first to the Father alone—they might have found a way of access to the Son. Out of their relationship to God they would have been able to draw knowledge of his Son. They would have come to the Son in very different ways, but all their paths would have led to him. For there exists no contradiction between Father and Son, and they would have recognized the same direction, the same divine love in both. They could have compared the Father's religion and the Son's with each other, and they would have discovered an identical content in the two religions, if they were not capable of believing in the Son at once and primarily out of love for God.

Everything that they will do against Christianity will be the logical consequence of their nonrecognition of the Father. It will be shown in deeds of egoism and, within this egoism, an ever more deeply entrenched defensiveness. Everything they have picked out of religion is secondary: they are things that were useful but not essential to religion and that now remain dead husks. They will not even retain the righteousness of the Old Covenant, but only their own righteousness, and they will no longer hear the voice of God, but only their own voice. And the administrative decisions they once made will finally lose all ecclesiastical character, for they will not be made in the grace of prayer but in consideration of their short-term advantage.

16:4. *But I have told you this so that when your hour comes you will remember that I told you of it. I have not told you from the beginning, though, because I was with you.*

Again he indicates that he is telling them all this so that they will remember when the time comes. But now he adds further predictions. Affliction is in store for them. They will be thrown out by the community of which they feel a part. It is important for the disciples to remember, when the time comes for them to be thrown out and to die, that what is taking place is the fulfilment of a prophecy. It is also important so that when the hour comes they will not be tempted into fleeing. Humanly considered, there was a way of escape prior to almost every martyrdom. But the disciples should not avail of this possibility at any price, preferring the greater, Christian service. For when they are pushed out into the unknown or are led to their death, they should not imagine their life to be more important than their testimony; rather they should understand that the persecution suffered in the name of the Lord, indeed death itself, is the service and the living witness required of them.

Its fashioning, both inner and outer, is now withdrawn from them, so that they may be wholly in the Lord's hand. They should trust that the Lord himself will attend to the effect and fruitfulness and expansion of their witness. They should understand that their action is now replaced by the Passion, which through the Lord's grace will result in intensified action in his name.

The Lord's earlier exhortation to remember his words was meant personally, so that they personally should not fall. The Lord instructed them for their personal experience, their personal service in his love. Now, however, the commission is expanded. What he says to them now is not designed to prevent them falling, but rather to help them remember when the time comes that they are in his service. The extent of their personal power and faith is not at issue here. But they should not look for excuses. They should live only by and for their mission. Here the Lord shows them great trust; he treats them in truth as his brothers, whose lives spring from his love and his service. He tells them this for himself, in the interests of his own work. He no longer asks if they want to or not; rather he assures them that they will *have* to remain then— for him. The door will be closed behind them. They will perform absolute obedience. In the suffering for which the Lord prepares them, wanting or not wanting is no longer an issue: everything is as it must be.

I have not told you this from the beginning, though, because I was with you. He was with them, and during this time he personally looked after their destiny. Nothing could happen to them as long as he was there. For he was the first one to go this way. As long as he had not suffered his Passion, the passion of the disciples could not begin, for every Christian passion is imitation. The Lord suffered the whole Passion completely; he did it first, all alone. All others will suffer with him imitatively at best, tentatively at most. He has produced suffering's entire substance, and out of this substance, which belongs to him, much can be formed by way of imitation and discipleship. He has seen the disciples grow and has slowly educated them, and so far they have understood nothing of suffering because their instruction had not reached that point. For first they had to *see* his own suffering. Only as a result of this suffering, with the great expansion of horizons it entails, will they be able to understand, for up until now (the Lord does not say this aloud) their faith would have been much too weak to cope with this promise. With his word, then, he draws them into something that was beyond their horizon until now, and they have no idea where he is leading them. But he does not overburden them, for he is ready to bear everything he requires of them; indeed, he bears it before them and only lets them help him bear it. Nor could he have explained it to them in some universal teaching, for the particular destiny between him and each individual always remains out of sight. It is not governed by any universal law, for everything is different and new each moment. His burning demand, the way he draws us, his love in us are always different and always more than one can say in words. One can witness a martyrdom from outside, phase by phase; one can admire the calmness and patience of the martyr; and yet one will never know what is going on from moment to moment between him and God. Everything essential can find itself in perpetual change and be differently apportioned each time. Now, perhaps, the Lord can bear the whole and leave very little of the burden to the individual; conversely, he can expect of him an extreme measure of suffering, which may seem past bearing. He can tangibly strengthen the sufferer, or he can give him a share in his own being forsaken by the Father. He can leave him with faith, love and hope, or he can withdraw them experientially from him. Thus it is always between God and the soul. Nothing can be universally established and expressed in temporal laws. Everything remains personal, unique life. Every confession, for example, is an unrepeatable encounter between the penitent sinner and the Lord. The father confessor, commissioned by the Lord, speaks the words of the Lord, but he does not know what the Lord uniquely effects through his official words. The same words can achieve a different effect a thousand times, not only because the penitent is in a different disposition, but because the Lord in his freedom acts differently each time. Although the father confessor shares in this mystery of intimacy between the sinner and the Lord, although he sees the sin and himself speaks the words of the Lord, all the same he stands to one side of the mystery and the ever-different relationships. All this, this whole world of personal love, is something the Lord did not reveal as long as he remained visibly among the disciples. They will become acquainted with it when he has become invisible.

In announcing all this to them, he also speaks of his departure. But he is at pains to help them understand his going as a continuation of his remaining. He gives them words of farewell, a legacy, but this legacy is not like a human testament, for it is the opposite of a conclusion. Rather, his words contain a promise that will be recalled when he will once more be close to them. This recollection is not "piety". What is done in that hour will not be done "in pious remembrance of the dead" Lord. It is recollection out of life and for life, and in the decisive hour the disciples are to know that the living Lord *is here*. It is the opposite of emotion: it is strength, obligation, responsibility.

THE SENDING OF THE HOLY SPIRIT

16:5. *But now I am going to him who sent me, and none of you asks me: Where are you going?*

He is going away. He has been speaking of it for a long time, in fact even when his mission first came into view, for he continually spoke about his way from the Father to the Father. Thus he was always journeying. This time he says it in order to educate his disciples to be able to pursue his path. He does not bid farewell as if it were an end, but almost as if he is accompanying them. He shows them that a new section of his path has begun, and he is taking them with him. But he does so in quite a different sense than before, by leaving with them most profound mysteries that they will steward for a time and that will find their final fulfilment in him, when they bring them back to him. This deepest mystery of the Christian life that he has given them has shape and outline in his own eyes. For them, however, it remains formless, although binding. He gives it to them, yet in such a way that, returning to the Father, he retains it. For them it remains an open question; the answer lies with the Lord. Thus when he goes away they will be lonely, because they do not understand themselves. Without the Lord, the disciple no longer knows who he is. The Lord who is going away, who is about to walk the way of loneliness himself, shows them that their loneliness is inseparable from his own, and that his loneliness, in which he and they are involved, solitary and individual, is moving toward the Father. For this loneliness to become perfect, it must be deprived of sight, and so the Lord does not even speak of the joy of reunion with the Father; he does not speak of any union or any end of loneliness. In his parting words he lets his perfect loneliness sound through, as it were. He hints at something that goes mysteriously into the open, in the direction of the Father, but is so great, so absolute, so final, that at the moment it does not need and cannot endure the prospect of unification with the Father, because along the way the isolation is to be thoroughly savored, without the admixture of anything that might be relief. And yet he says he is going to the Father. He marks out the goal in a purely objective fashion, but the closer he comes to it, the more it becomes entirely invisible and withdrawn from him.

And none of you asks me. They cannot ask him where he is going, for they have not grasped from where he comes. But the Lord speaks the whence and the whither simultaneously: he is going to the Father *who sent him.* This path is his essence and his life. For the disciples, on the other hand, his present departure is only a single event. They are not close enough to him to understand that this departure was already included in his coming. They thought there would be an intermediate state between coming and going, a time of rest during which the Lord would be with them. They have not yet grasped that to be a Christian means never to stand still, that that middle ground they dream of would be the death that the Lord wants to keep away from them.

The Christian life is movement. The working day of the Christian is movement in action and work. But it is not restless action, but rather a work that has its pauses, its times of rest. This rest is prayer, contemplation, vision in the Father. But it is designed to serve the movement of action, to enliven it. Thus at the beginning and at the end of the Christian week there is Sunday, the day of the Father. As the Lord comes from the Father and goes to him, so the Christian goes through the busy week from Sunday to Sunday. Sunday must be a day in the Father, a day of rest and of contemplation; for just as the body needs its relaxation, so does the spirit, in God. This rhythm of going out from and returning to God, this movement from rest toward rest, is the pulse of Christian life. In this temporal life the true Sunday of eternity is not attainable; the temporal Sunday is only its reflected image and approximation. It can be abused by letting one's rest be disturbed by the unrest of work, and even more by not seeking relaxation where it lies—in God—and thus distancing oneself from God even further on Sunday than during the rest of the week. Our day of rest is only a metaphor of the day of the Father. But is has something in common with the eternal Sunday, namely, that every rest in God is a transition to new movement.

Where are you going? The Lord stands before his disciples as a human being, as one of them, communicating with them, someone whom they see and hear. And yet he is a very different person than his appearance might suggest. He is God among them, among men. They are ready to serve him somehow; to acknowledge that he is more than they are, other than they are; that he stems from God and is going to God. But they are not yet touched and affected to the innermost by the fact that he is God. They do not know that they have been taken possession of by him. And now he sets about taking on yet another form on his way to the Father, a form that is much closer and more subject to inspection than the human form: the form of bread. A human person, free and spiritual, is never wholly comprehensible, but bread is impersonal, insignificant, almost contemptible, fully at the service of man. The Lord now enters into this form of existence. But, drawing close to men, incomprehensibly, in the form of bread, he is at the same time even more withdrawn from them. He becomes anonymous, and in this hiddenness his divinity appears anew. In the humiliation of transubstantiation, he lets his divine qualities be given back to him by the priest. He lets himself become anonymous so that men may give him back his true name. He wants to become their nourishment, something they cannot monitor (as the process of nourishment itself remains mysterious), in order to address them no longer outwardly as one like them, but to possess them in such a way that he really lives in their innermost being. As Host, he wants to prepare the way from God to God for each one of them. This is where he is going: this too lies along the great path on which he is about to set out. By being fragmented in the Eucharist, he becomes the path for everyone. But this means that the individual Christian's path is also fragmented, dispersed into an infinite number of ways that can no longer be seen to be *one* way and yet are still traversable and traversed. In the Eucharist everything becomes more and more small, earthly and anonymous, in order to become so much more universal and heavenly. The Lord becomes bread so that we can receive real power over him and also concretely enter his movement toward the Father.

The disciples do not ask where he is going. They do not dare to ask this question, because they would find themselves drawn into the infinite, limitless scope of his path, which they feel is beyond them. They long for shelter and do not ask about boundless horizons. Otherwise they would find themselves going with him on his explosive path. They want a small piece, a section, a today. But as his own fragmentation becomes boundless, they are unknowingly drawn along his path. There is no finite answer to their question anyway; it has already been made obsolete through the Lord's infinite movement.

16:6. *But because I have said this to you, sorrow has filled your hearts.*

He has told them things that burst all human bounds, that are to grow in them, expand their hearts and fill them with that new reality he is creating in them. This new reality is that they are to share his fate. But they are completely caught up in the human idea of separation, and they see nothing of this new union that will be much more intimate than all previous closeness to the Lord. Where the Lord makes a beginning they can only see an end, and therefore they are sad. They see the end of their shared path in the world, the end of the sensible things they have seen and heard, and they do not grasp the fact that the Lord does not depend on the senses in order to be near them, that he only used them in order to adapt to their nature—in the spiritual realm he never "adapted" at all—and to prepare a way to the Spirit through this world of appearances that is so essential to them.

All his words awaken only one feeling in them: sorrow. At first it is a wholly human sorrow, which has its place in the limitations of their spirit: it is the mournful mood of farewell. And it is no longer the individual who feels this sorrow, but the community. At this moment they form a community of sorrow; it binds and unifies them. It is the first time that they are gripped thus by a feeling, a mood, a situation, which is somehow superpersonal because it belongs to the community as a whole. The individual is of course affected by this feeling, but only as a member of the community: it lives through, permeates and fills the community as such. True, this feeling, this mood ought, in the eyes of the Lord, to be different. The Church's mood is not what the Lord wishes in this situation. From the Lord's point of view it is a concession to our humanity. Something of this concession on the Lord's part exists in all the changing moods of the Church's year—for example, in the uncertainty of Advent and in the sorrow of Lent, in which Christians at times mix too much personal feeling and too little of the Lord's divine sorrow. In his previous words, the Lord opened up infinite vistas and tried to expand them beyond all limits; now he descends into what is humanly measurable and enters into our emotional life. Using both together he addresses them, trying to awaken them from indifference. In the alternating rhythm between the two, they are shaken out of their comfortable rest. And when the Lord refers to this feeling of those who are his, putting his finger on this spot, he claims it for himself. By saying "You are sorrowful", he puts them all in a uniform of sorrow. It is a kind of depersonalization. It is still *their* feeling, for each of them is really sorrowful, as the Lord says. And yet, at a deeper level, it is something given by *him:* fused together in this common form, this color and hue of their hearts—which is an ecclesiastical color and hue—each of them will be qualified to understand the colors and hues of human hearts and be able to carry out their mission. Each individual will retain his personality, and his way will be a personal one. The Church, even when she experiences things as a community, is never treated as a mass by the Lord. But the color of a shared ecclesial reality, which as such belongs to the Lord, flows through everything that is personal. He can require his Church as a community to accompany him in her human fashion on a certain part of his way, in sympathy and in tune with him.

But there is also a boundary between sorrow that is permitted and despair that is not. The disciples' sorrow does not obstruct ultimate joy. The Lord himself, fully aware of what lies before him, is glad to be allowed to prove his love to the Father to the end. His faith and his love are so strong that even in the harshest test, although tangibly removed from him, they will survive his sorrow. He does not retain joy by inwardly turning away from suffering but by affirming it in such full awareness and such strong love that his consent includes his entire love for the Father. It is a Yes in sorrow, laden with the most extreme burden of suffering, but beyond this it is a Yes in the glory of love, in the joy of surrender.

Despair would be sorrow, not in love, but sorrow as an end in itself and therefore without room for hope. That would not be Christian sorrow, for this is always a limited sorrow leading to unlimited love and hope. The finite is sorrow; the Infinite is love, so that there can be no room for despair. It is in this form of the Lord's sorrow that the sorrow of the disciples participates. Even though it is a small, human sorrow, by becoming a sorrow of the Church it is poured into the form of the Lord's sorrow and is thus unavoidably immersed in the deeper joy and love of the Lord.

16:7. *But I tell you in truth: It is advantageous for you that I am going away, for if I did not go away, the Consoler would not come to you. But if I go, I will send him to you.*

The Lord does not simply wipe out their sorrow. He respects it; indeed, he welcomes it. But precisely by doing so he removes its superficial hopelessness. It is good for them to grasp his departure. It is good for them to see how empty they will be without him, how much they will miss him. It is good for them even now, while he is still among them, to get used to the thought of being separated from him. This expansion of their hearts is necessary so that their faith, their love and their hope may have the proper proportions. But he goes further, comforting them with the promise of the Consoler, who could not come if he did not go away. The arrival of the Spirit is dependent on this departure; the Son must send him from the Father. And he must send him into a situation of sorrow, so that the Spirit may really find occasion to console. He could not console happy people; those who receive him must really need consoling. The Lord does not spare them sorrow, but he promises them consolation. By going away he opens up in them possibilities of suffering, but also possibilities of hope. He expands them in both directions: they are to learn to feel and experience more deeply. If their souls lacked the experience of sorrow and of consolation, they would lack a part of perfection. They would not have a Christian feeling of something that, since it is human, is part of the perfection of human nature. They would be lacking something that is indispensable not only for themselves but even more for their mission to others, and most indispensable for understanding the Lord's mission. He shows them that their service to his cause will be incompatible with inner indifference; that on the contrary he requires the very highest measure of what is most personal, what has been experienced, felt and surrendered. No true surrender claims only a part of one's capacity to love and potential for service. It calls for the whole person with all his gifts and all his possible modulations. Every human string must sound and vibrate in sympathy; every human experience must be undergone and included; everything that lies in the human person must be drawn out and realized. The Lord wants not only our simplicity, but also our multiplicity and fullness; he does not want Christians who are disappointed with the world, but those who are ready for every task. Worldly disappointments must open and refine Christians for specialized service. They do not live on their memories but turned toward the Lord and to his ever-new commissions. If a real renunciation is required of them, they do not set themselves stoically beyond pain. They know how to experience what is sorrowful with real sorrow, and they do not arrogantly rob the Holy Spirit of the opportunity of consoling them. Nor will they receive this consolation for themselves but in order to be richer in giving to their brothers. They have understood that joy and sorrow, when they are both lived in God, signify fruitfulness for the apostolate. The richer their soul is, the more personal is the service they can perform, and the greater too is their responsibility. People have very different ranges of experience. For simple souls, the Lord's going away and the coming of the Consoler will perhaps always remain beyond their grasp, and yet in their plain lives they can perform the service the Lord expects from them.

It is advantageous for the disciples that the Lord is going away, for they have been chosen to understand many things. It is good for them to have the opportunity of sharing in all the vicissitudes of the Lord's destiny. Further, there is a particular fruitfulness in this personal experience with the Lord, this painful withdrawal of his presence. Were one to consider only the individual human life, one might ask which destiny is more enviable: always to have been happy or to have had sorrow and been consoled. But as soon as service to the Lord is put on the scales as what is essential in the life of the individual, the question disappears. For the one who serves, it is best to have been consoled and, therefore, also to have sorrowed. For this destiny is part of the greater service: it is more fruitful and more useful for the Church. One's own advantage, one's own perfection is not the issue here. It is not that he who was tempted more, who had a more difficult life, whose service was more exposed and vulnerable will receive a greater "reward" in heaven than one who was happy his whole life long and had no trials to face. That might perhaps apply in the case of retributive justice, but not of redeeming love. The advantage under discussion here is the advantage of service in love.

But if I go away, I will send him to you. The sending of the Holy Spirit depends on the Lord's departure. Although the Lord possesses the Spirit, the two are not present simultaneously. The Lord must go away to give a clear field for the Spirit. Here we can see that the Spirit does not come of himself but must be sent. He is the Third Person in God. His coming, then, is a new level of revelation, which cannot be opened up independent of the Son's revelation. But the Son fulfilled his mission among simple people. He did not overstep the bounds of his circumscribed, earthly commission. Now that he is going away, his mission must be expanded into the universal dimension. He has tilled the soil. He simply pointed to God and showed love. Now comes the Spirit, who formed him as a human being but who withdrew into the background as long as the Lord remained as a man on earth. He comes to proclaim the whole fullness, the otherworldly richness of the Son and his revelation. Again, the Lord, having completed his mission, commands the Spirit who formed him and lets him complete what he has begun. He sends him as a new seed to his fruit, but equally as the fruit of a sowing, in order to complete its harvest. Reversing roles, he sends him who once begot him. Once again, in a new way, we become aware of the unimaginably rich and living relations between the Persons in God, perpetually alternating between reciprocal superiority and subordination, in a continually overflowing vitality that, precisely as such, is the continuity of the Trinity. Thus the Spirit first has the Son within him as seed and sends him into the Virgin's womb; then the Son "separates" himself from the Spirit—otherwise the latter could not descend on him at baptism—and carries him within him during his public life, and then sends the Spirit out again as he returns to the Father. Thus the circle is to a certain extent complete, because in his mission the Spirit has the Son within him once more and sends him into the world in new, spiritual form. But whereas at the baptism Son and Spirit are closely and visibly together in the humanity of Christ, at the end it is as if they have flowed apart, as if they are scattered and splintered: the Son in the Eucharist, the Spirit in being poured out over the whole world. Son and Spirit appear as if seized in infinite movement that requires a constant exchange of roles, while the Father surrounds and clasps the whole movement, like the vault of heaven under which the pulsating process takes place. It is he who sets everything in motion, without himself being drawn into its circling. And yet all three Persons, precisely in this movement, are so much one, so little to be separated and parted from one another, that Christian life can only be a life within the full Trinity.

16:8. *And when he comes, he will make the world aware that there is sin and justice and judgment.*

The Lord has already spoken earlier about sin, justice and judgment. He has always shown how his mission is to be understood, how he came so that God might receive more love than insult from the world, how his, the Son's, love is greater than the sum of the world's sin and how the Father cannot resist this love and lets love reign at the judgment in place of ordinary justice. The Son, then, spoke about sin, justice and judgment in the relationship between mankind and the Father. But now comes the Holy Spirit, no longer sent by the Father as was the Son, but by the Son who has suffered, who has presented the sacrifice in proving his love to the Father and who now has brought the completed mission back to the Father. But he himself will not regard it as truly completed until he has sent the Holy Spirit, whose mission it is to establish a new equilibrium not only between mankind and God, but equally between mankind and the Lord, from the Father to the world. In order to produce this relationship, the world must first be made newly aware, both the individual Christian and the Church, of what sin, justice and judgment signify. On the basis of this new perception in the individual and the Church, a new, deepened form of cooperation and inclusion in the work of the Son is created. The new perception is no longer based above all on the personal love relationship between Father and Son, and therefore not on the personal love relationship between the Son and mankind, but on a new standpoint that signifies a kind of objectification vis-à-vis the first relationship. It lets this first relationship continue in its entirety, but it considers it almost from outside. It is the standpoint of the Spirit, who is neither the Father, nor the Son, nor simply their mutual personal love, but a third Person in God, and who therefore can best give information about the two and their relationship. As long as the standpoint is that of the love between Father and Son, all one can see is the infinity of this love in its boundless, personal animation and increase, which is overwhelming. But the Spirit is able to illuminate this infinity as if objectively, and thus he also makes possible an objective *choice* of this love. When the Lord gives us a commandment, his whole personal life and his relationship to us are involved in it: he speaks to us as the one who became man for us, who loves us humanly, who has suffered unspeakably for us; when we respond to him, we will do so perhaps on the basis of an entirely personal relationship, an entirely personal consideration. Regarded from the world's point of view it might appear as if the Lord, through the greatness of his love and his suffering, exercises a sort of personal pressure on Christians. This solely personal element vanishes as soon as the objectivity of the Holy Spirit appears to show that the love between the Father and the Son in its entire truth exists *in itself*.

The Lord counts the price of love, and so his commandment is wholly a commandment of love. But perhaps we are not accessible to his love. Love is not the word that grips and challenges us in our innermost being. Perhaps we have a better grasp of what justice is, right behavior, decency, loyalty. Perhaps the deepest thing we know is that certain things should not be done because they go against reason, against the basic rule of life. The Holy Spirit can lead on from such an insight. He can—as the Lord does not—lead us beyond sin, justice and judgment to an understanding of the love of the Lord. For the turning to the Lord he chooses not the immediate way of devotion, but that of reason, of careful consideration, of fitness, and so he slowly unveils the mind of the Lord. And yet this whole approach toward love is already accomplished within love, for it is the Lord's love that sends the Spirit, whose final duty is always to prepare mankind for love. Here too the Spirit continually shows his trinitarian function: he leads via the Son to the Father. Here too is love in God, not the personal love between Father and Son, but rather an impersonal love, become anonymous, as it were. Love lies before him and behind him: he comes from love and is going to love; his whole mission is love. But the act that serves love does not let the love become evident as personal. In this function the Spirit resembles a physician who operates on a child in order to give it back to the mother's love. His objectivity is a function of love in which love objectifies itself.

This objectification itself is love. It does not stand uninvolved beside personal love, but precisely at its inmost focal point. Therefore the Lord also calls the Spirit the Consoler. He does not want this enlightenment of the Spirit to happen outside of love. The Spirit is not a falling back into the justice and judgment of the Old Covenant, but on the contrary, a continuation of the revelation in the New Covenant. And the continuation lies in the way he draws even the justice and judgment of the Old Covenant into the love of the New, opens the closed circle of what is Christian, and establishes the living transition between the non-Christian and the Christian, a transition that he himself constitutes insofar as he binds Father and Son, the Kingdom of creation and that of Redemption, the Old Covenant and the New Covenant into a unity, and does so in love. The enlightenment and objectivity of the Spirit are at the same time the most subjectively consoling things there are, because he includes in love even what seemed to stand outside it.

16:9. *Sin, because they do not believe in me.*

First of all, the Spirit will explain the essence of sin. He will show mankind the beginning and end of sin, which lie in the fact that *they do not believe in me*. If they believed in the Lord, his pardoning grace would be primary and sin would have become secondary. Nor would they need any particular enlightenment about their sin. Out of love and in the state of grace given by the Lord they would detest their sin, turn away from it and turn to the Lord; sin would be only a memory, left to lie, because it had been dealt with by the Lord's grace. But they would be continually aware that without the grace of the Lord they would still be what they were, and they would also know that sin was the only thing preventing them then from living wholly in love. That would be their knowledge of sin. But now their faith is weak. In this weakness they think that, having received so much of the Lord's love, they have a certain right to it. They regard the Lord's act of forgiveness as something that, in his grace, he can repeat at will. They are inclined to misuse love, less through a positive will to sin again than through the readiness to excuse sins they are going to commit and to reckon in advance with the Lord's pardon. But this way of reckoning and measuring is deadly for love; it causes it to cool and shrivel. The Holy Spirit, when he comes, will show them how heinous this evaluation of sin is. With regard to sin, he will show them precisely what the Lord, in his protective way, conceals, namely, that it is a misuse of the Lord's personal love. He will not only show them the sin that they already know but will also indicate its connections, of which they had no idea until now. He will show them everything that stands as an obstacle between them and the Lord. He will show them that everything that is not compatible with the Lord's love must be called sin—not just those things that bear the label "sin". And that this form of quietism, this easy confidence about love that, basically, does not really love, is sin, too. As an objective evaluator, he will initiate them into the mysteries of personal love. He will sharpen all the senses of their soul. It is not the Lord's business to draw attention to all this. Otherwise, it could seem as if he were covertly asking us for compassion, so that we would cause him to suffer less. But that is not the mind and intention of the Lord. We should not refrain from committing sin so that he will not have to suffer. It is not this thought that should be our reward. For he does everything for love of the Father and for his honor. Therefore it is the Holy Spirit who indicates it, who makes us aware of the Lord's suffering. Because he is "uninvolved", he can show how involved the Lord is.

The way the Spirit makes us aware of sin can also be a gradual one. The Son's proclamation tends not to make stages and degrees. From the beginning he shows his whole love and, within it, the whole demand. He wants everything. But the Holy Spirit educates us toward the Lord and his total love. He prepares us for the complete self-surrender that the Lord demands immediately and almost without any transition. If the Lord is the Bridegroom of the soul, it is not his function to prepare the Bride for full self-surrender. Another must fulfill this task: the Holy Spirit undertakes it as the Friend of the Bridegroom, so to speak. We cannot surrender ourselves to him, but we can all the more entrust ourselves to his direction, which leads us to the Bridegroom.

Thus the Spirit presents sin differently than the Lord, because the Lord's love for sinners did not suffice to make them completely aware of sin. Because of their sin, sin—their lack of loving faith—must be given a different plasticity. Because they do not believe as they ought, they must take their sin far more seriously than heretofore. The Lord would like to understand their faith as total self-surrender. But they do not feel ready for this. They have, indeed, given the Lord what they possessed: their outward life. They have followed him. And yet the Lord accuses them of *not believing in him*. For they are not yet aware of to what this initial following obliges them: that it makes a bond for all eternity. Therefore they do not yet understand him, his way of life, his love, his suffering; despite all his explanations they keep setting limits to everything. They gradually extend these limits, but they do not give them up. The limitless, the unconditional is still a closed book to them. They think there will always be time for this final thing. They are waiting for something that has long been there already. They do not understand that there is nothing left to alter, because everything is already present in the Lord. The Holy Spirit will make them aware of this sin in the midst of love, this unbelief in the midst of faith.

16:10. *Justice, because I am going to the Father and you will no longer see me.*
Justice is not a concept the Lord tended to use with his disciples. What he demanded of them was never demanded in the name of justice, and still less did he offer them his love in the name of justice. Justice is a human concept, which always weighs up good and evil. Certainly it attempts to eliminate evil, to emphasize the good and distribute it fairly. But fair distribution is just what the Lord does not want. He does not want to divide, but to give everything to everyone. To give himself separately to each individual, without possibility of an equal return or recompense. He wants everything, his entire sacrifice and his entire love, to be accepted in its entirety, because his sacrifice springs from his entire self-surrender to the Father and expresses his undivided love for mankind.

This entirety is perhaps what the disciples understand least of all. Through intercourse with the Lord they have been weaned to some extent from their everyday calculations and measurements, but without consciously reflecting on it. Perhaps they were simply unable. But now that the Lord is no longer among them, they must again face the concept of justice. If they had perfect faith, this would not be necessary. But their faith is shaky. Because he is going back to the Father, they will no longer see the Lord, and will certainly no longer comprehend the fullness of his love, on the visible expressions of which they are still all too dependent. Therefore the Spirit must explain justice to them. He can begin with the justice of the Old Covenant, which in those days found its expression in the laws and teachings of the Jewish people, but which has now been reformed by the Lord and is to remain reformed, namely, assimilated to his love. Here again the Spirit will point out gradual ways of approach. Since men will not allow themselves to be seized by the fullness of love, they must take the detour through justice in order gradually to grow into love and thereby to recognize that the new justice of the Lord is no longer a mutual, finite fairness, but a proportion in which one of the parties remains infinite and incomprehensible.

For example, a person might offer himself to God with all his potentials— his goods, his talents, his friends and so forth—and in return expect a certain recompense from the Lord, for example, "wisdom" or perseverance in faith or love. He has imagined the entire thing as a sort of pact, a kind of justice between himself and God. But it may be that God will not enter into such a treaty, that instead he leaves him in unrest, dryness, darkness and anxiety. Despite this, such a person must know that although his imaginary justice was not fulfilled, a much higher justice is fulfilled between him and God in which he, who thought he was giving himself, stands before God with empty hands. Although he does not see the gift God gives in return, gifts have been bestowed on him beyond measure. In justice as God understands it, man never has the right to expect something definite of God, because all of God's gifts, both those he gives and those he demands, are indefinable and indeterminable. God desires the complete offering without conditions and clauses, and from this he takes what he needs. And for his part he gives everything—that is, precisely what lies in *his* intention. He gives this everything as he wishes, and that means precisely not as man expects it, because human expectation is always conditioned by his nature, his sin, his limitedness. But the human person's expectation ought to be to expect nothing definite. If he really loves God, he expects everything of him, even though he sees nothing. But if he does not offer everything to God, and thus does not fully believe, then it is as if he had given nothing. For what is expected of him is nothing other than total consent, total readiness to everything that God decrees. All of this would have been self-evident from the start if man had grasped the Lord's love. Since he did not do so, the Holy Spirit must educate him through the levels of justice to grasp the full justice of God, which is wholly enclosed in love.

He does this by bursting each level of limited justice to reveal a higher one, and by showing that in the upward path the steps hewn by justice simply become invisible in the one path of love.

If a person is already within Christianity, he can be led to the Lord by the shortest route. He only needs to be brought to confession, where he will be showered with the Lord's mercy. But no one can grasp this if he is still outside the Church. Such a one must be led gradually, with many objective proofs of justice, nearer to God. As long as he stands outside, he will always see confession as a matter of justice: a balance of sin and grace, of confession and absolution. But confession is not that at all: it is such a measureless grace that sin and the confession of it are totally lost in it. It is the Spirit who, through proofs and arguments of justice, gradually leads to the standpoint of justice itself being overstepped, and the love of the Lord being made plain in its immeasurability.

This whole explanation of justice will be necessary because the Lord *is going to the Father.* He will leave the disciples behind in a certain confusion. Many among them will perceive that they have missed out on something essential, but in the weakness of their love they will not find the courage to seek what has been lost. For them everything is made harder by the Lord's disappearance. His relationship to them, however, remains identical; his living love for them is no further from them than before. But in order to give them a visible expression for this love, to pull them out of their timidity and confusion, he will send them the consolation of the Spirit, who will make them aware of the final meaning of all justice, of the Lord's love.

16:11. *Judgment, because the prince of this world is judged.*

The prince of this world ought to be Christ. But now it is the devil. He is judged by the death of the Lord. And the Holy Spirit will make mankind aware of judgment because the prince of this world is judged. He is judged from the moment the Lord appears in the world. He carries his death sentence in his hand, and he only has a short time left. During this time he can still act. For the Lord does not want to conquer without a fight; he wants to give the devil opportunity to show his power, so that in this fight he may be overcome by the greater power of God.

Therefore the Lord let the devil tempt him. He did not need to do so, for it was determined from the beginning that he would win. But he did it all the same, in order to increase the sum of love that he wanted to bring back to his Father and to become acquainted, as a human being, with the temptations to which his human brothers are exposed. He wanted not only to know them at a distance and from hearsay, but to feel real, gnawing temptation. His love was not to be merely symbolic, nor was his temptation to be so. He does not take it on out of curiosity or delight in battle, but solely out of love, in order to prove his love more manifestly to the Father and to mankind. He did not talk much about the devil. Still less did he talk about his temptation or display it as a deed of his love. He let this especial proof of love be hidden in the whole treasure of his love. He bore the temptation as quietly and hiddenly as possible because he did not want to submit any bill of love to God and mankind, or lay any further obligation on his disciples through this new deed of love. Once again, it is the work of the Holy Spirit to point to this battle of the Lord with the prince of this world and to proclaim the judgment over the latter. He is judged by the Lord's all-conquering love. This judgment is proclaimed by the Holy Spirit because the disciples have not yet grasped and accepted the Lord's love in its fullness. They are still at a stage in which, in order to measure this love, they must compare the prince of this world, the devil, with Christ, its future Prince. It is necessary for them to see the dominion pass from one to the other. The Lord has already accomplished it in his love, but they need to be continually entering into it in their own experience. As long as their love is not yet perfect, the devil retains a certain power over them in temptation. But if their love has become perfect, they stand with the victorious Lord, and the power of the devil in them dies to make room for the power of the Lord. Again, in the Lord's discretion he does not speak of all this, leaving it to the Holy Spirit to explain things and adapt it to mankind's understanding.

All three concepts—sin, justice and judgment—belong together. Men can have a certain understanding of these concepts even outside of love, on the basis of their feeling of community, their common sense, their social attitude. In this purely human sphere the Spirit comes on them in order to lead them from there to love. He creates the transition between what is purely human, even sin, and the Kingdom of the Lord.

In all this the Spirit seems like a function, almost neutral; despite this he is love, a love that adopts no human shape. He remains the pure radiance of God's love. And in this very neutrality of service he proves to be pure love. As the Son willed to be sent in order to be pure love, the Spirit lets himself be sent out of love in order to be pure service. Humanly speaking, he has taken up a thankless task here, for men love the Lord, whom they can see in their own form, who suffered for them and went to the extremity of love. They can love him with all their senses. They scarcely know the Spirit as a Person. There is little to help them discover that he is lovable. His invisible role, which renounces all apparent form and all visible testimonies of love, expresses the innermost love of the Holy Spirit. Through his love we love God, without thinking about the fact that it is not we who love, but his love in us. All qualities that are attributed to him, all metaphors applied to him, seem feeble to us compared to the radiant qualities of the Son's love. But the manifest wonders of the Son's love are brought to light through the hidden love of the Holy Spirit, and it is in this that his love consists.

16:12. *I still have much to say to you, but you cannot bear it yet.*

The Lord still has much to say about his life from all eternity in the Father, about the meaning of his arrival in the world, about his coming suffering and his return to the Trinity. And he would have just as much to say about what is happening to him now and in the coming suffering, as a human being and as Son of the Father, whose mission becomes increasingly pressing and all-embracing. Things that go far beyond the mere outward events that will be visible—the capture, the trials, the scourging, the Crucifixion—things that are wholly in the sphere of the Father, in those mysteries of God of which the disciples as yet suspect nothing.

In this moment he has a perfect overview of his work. He sees precisely what he has accomplished so far. He can assess its eternal significance, and no less does he survey everything that is coming. In this overview of past and future he sees the entire actuality of his mission. As a human person, he would like to speak with his disciples about this mission and about what went before in order to prepare them for what is coming, not only so that they can draw the greatest possible profit from it but also to help him in the fulfilment of his mission. As a human being, he would like to initiate them more deeply into God's plans for the sake of their fellowship in love. But he must renounce this help. They have not come far enough to be able to understand his mission. They are not even capable of bearing their own mission, how much less his! But they must at least know this: everything he has said up to now with regard to his Sonship is only by way of preparation. He has only granted them glimpses, such as they could take in. These glimpses may indeed seem like broad vistas to them, yet to him they were merely preliminary glances.

The "more" he would like to tell them includes all the mysteries. The mystery of his separation from the Father, of his birth, his youth, his work, the institution of the sacraments, his Passion and his Redemption. These are all mysteries that they know in faint outlines, but that become more vast and gaping each time they are approached. Moreover, up to now he has always spoken in general terms. What he said to one person applied equally to the others. He often singled out one of them in conversation, but he was always thinking of everyone. But what he would want to say now would be a revelation designed for each individual, only suitable for general consumption after it had been addressed to and grasped by this individual. In this sense one person might be ripe for one truth and another person for a different one. But he does not want to make this differentiation in the utterances of his earthly life. It is something he will begin on the Cross and continue in heaven.

In all the Lord's personal words to individuals, in all that might be called personal encouragement and private revelation, there is always a double aspect: there is something that one can communicate and should pass on, and something that remains personal and incommunicable. It so concerns the mystery between the Lord and the individual that it is not translatable into the language of universality. Every private revelation has these two sides: one turned toward the Church and meant for wide circulation and another that is communicable only indirectly, through the transformed life of the one who receives it, and that as word remains a mystery between God and the soul. Not that this second, indeterminable side is purely private, outside the mission. Rather, it continues working just as strongly as the revealed word and the commission to preach: it is the very being of the faith of the one addressed by the Lord, a being that remains inexpressible because it is the Lord's grace and yet is what is actually effective. In the Church and the environment, however, it is only the person who already believes who will be touched by this reality, or at least the person who has himself already been touched by the Lord's grace. Another would see things only from the outside. He would see perhaps an "enthusiastic", an "awakened", a "religious" person, but never one touched by the word of God. While the believer himself can already have been touched by God, he still needs encounters with others who have been touched, in order to be touched anew and to realize the contact with God that he has received. The Lord can say nothing of all this now, because he has not yet spoken personally in this fashion with any individual.

16:13. *When he comes, the Spirit of truth, he will initiate you into all truth, for he will not speak out of himself but will speak that which he hears, and he will proclaim to you what is to come.*

The Spirit of truth will initiate the disciples into all truth. He will explain to them everything that the Lord does not now express. For he will not, like the Lord in his conversations until now, be depending on ground that has been prepared. He will proclaim the truth objectively and objectify it. He will not have to appeal to the disciples' already existent love, but will be able to present the truth completely independently of personal dispositions and to substantiate it objectively. Yet he will initiate them *into all truth,* that is, into the truth that lies in the effect of the Lord's words, the truth of participation in the Lord's destiny, beginning with participation in his outward path as the disciples have shared it up to participation in his Cross. The latter begins for them where the Cross rises before their eyes and ends where the Lord gives his Spirit back into his Father's hands. But the Spirit will transform this entire truth of the Cross and participation in it from an outwardly visible fact into an inner truth. He will expand the Cross from a simple historical event into a basic fact of Christianity. He will help Christians understand that the Lord's suffering is and remains fruitful, that it is used and distributed in every individual life and suffering and that every Christian life stands under the sign of the Cross and is led by the Cross to the Lord. This objective truth that the Spirit will mediate will have the basic Christian characteristic, namely, it will be limitless. It will not let itself be contained in any tidy formula or final concept; rather, every truth will open in ever-wider vistas onto greater truths. And yet there will be nothing arbitrary about this truth from the very beginning. Its limitlessness will not be the free rambling of religious fantasy. The framework of the truth will be God's objective truth. When a person loves another, he makes an effort to enter into everything that the beloved values and holds dear in order to love it with him. A great deal of common ground will result from this, and yet there will always remain personal barriers and secrets between the two. It would also be thus between us and the Lord, if the Holy Spirit did not initiate us into all truth. He expands us for everything that the Lord loves and values; he creates for us, so to speak, an overview of the Lord's whole love; he causes it to appear to us in an objective light. We are given insight into the connections between his love for the Father, for the world, for his Mother, for the Cross, for the poor and so forth. The whole Kingdom of love is spread out before us.

He will not speak out of himself. Rather he will speak from the Father and the Son. The same character will be proper to his speech as to his being when he formed the Son in the Mother at the Father's commission: it will have the character of a mediation. In and from the same character that he possessed at the Son's begetting in Mary, he will now present the relationship between Mother and Son. His representation will exhibit the color of him who alone was present at the begetting of the Son. Then too he was the Holy Spirit, and so the begetting was accomplished in the Spirit. And yet the Holy Spirit is at the origin of the Son's body in the womb of the Mother. It is he who places this origin in her. He is thus also present at the origin of the most intimate mysteries between Mother and Son. He was witness of how the Son chose his Mother and of how Mary was ready to receive her Son. And he, the Holy Spirit, brought the two together. He caused their mutual readiness to become reality in the relationship of Mother and Son. From the beginning, then, he was the deepest and most inner share in their mystery, not only as pure Spirit but also precisely in the physical relation of Mother and Child. He was hidden in the deepest fold of this physical-spiritual relationship and therefore followed it all through the lives of both. But on earth the Son scarcely spoke of his relationship to his Mother—even less, almost, than of his mysterious intimacy with the Father. It was not a subject about which the Lord could speak in the public squares, in talking to the people. He kept this intimacy between himself and his Mother to himself, for it would have been unthinkable that the Son could have made the mysteries of his Virgin Mother the subject of public proclamation. There is even a purely human mystery between each son and his mother—that he lived in her and was born of her and nourished by her—a mystery that the son does not betray. This silence is the expression of the reverence that every son has for his mother. But infinitely deeper than the mystery of human sonship is the mystery of the Son of God in relation to his Virgin Mother. It is an impenetrable mystery that in its movement always contains new sides: the Virgin becomes Mother by becoming the Bride of the Spirit, and from Motherhood she grows into being the Bride of her Son and the Mother of his brothers. And her mystery always contains the entire mystery of a Christian state of life: of bridehood, of motherhood, of virginity. All this is infinitely mysterious not only in the sense of human, private intimacy but, beyond this, of a personal uniqueness kept safe in God. The Son, as Son, cannot speak of all this. And yet since his revelation there no longer exists any purely private mystery. For love's sake everything he possesses by way of inner wealth must be revealed and surrendered. Everything the Lord has, even if it is his mystery, is to belong to everyone in the future. It will be the Holy Spirit's task to reveal this fullness. And precisely these personal mysteries of his intimacy are among the things that the Lord does not want to mention at present because his disciples could not bear it. Inwardly, they would understand nothing about the mystery of his Mother, because they know nothing yet of renunciation, self-denial, asceticism. But that is the access to an understanding of his Mother.

From all the Christian states of life the Holy Spirit makes ways of access to Mary. To the unmarried virgin she is presented as the perfectly pure one, to the bride as the one who has given herself in chastity and to the married woman as the ideal image of the Mother. Every state of life looks up to her and projects itself, so to speak, into the ideal. But it is those who are virginal, the priests and religious, who have the most immediate access to an understanding of the Mother because of their celibacy. This renunciation opens in them a receptivity for the essence of the Mother, for the true mystery of her fruitfulness. The Holy Spirit proclaims all this. He, more than the Son, will be the founder and promoter of Mariology in the Church.

He will speak what he hears, and he will proclaim to you what is to come. What he has to say does not stem primarily from the time of the Son's earthly life. Rather, it draws its essence from where the truth was laid up in the Trinity from the beginning and now unfolds on earth. From there the Spirit will testify to the world about what is to come and thus give new nourishment to faith. He will not do this like the Son, who spoke in his own name, as it were, on earth like an official herald, but rather he will speak directly from the source: from the womb of the Trinity. But when he proclaims what is to come, it will be less a matter of individual future events than of the future quality of truth itself. He will proclaim his message in such a way that it appears imminent, something that is coming about in the Spirit. He will prophesy the development of the Church, the community, and on that basis the development of individuals, not, however, in the historical dates and details that human curiosity so likes to hear, but in such a way that in the proclamation the essential requirements of the Christian life become clear. For example, to those who are able to hear his prophecy, he will show what could be made of a community, a nation, a people, if they would open themselves to the grace of God, or conversely, what punishments lie in store if they close themselves to grace. Everything in the Church that is dogmatic and regulated is equally the subject of his prophecy: in the Church he will be not so much the visible love as the firm structure, her objectivity over time, the formed framework within which her life develops. Although all this seems to be rigid and of the present, and in no way living and of the future, it is precisely here that the Spirit prophesies. For everything living takes its starting point here, time and again. Every newly perceived truth appears in the Church as a deduction from what has already been perceived. It is the Spirit who makes new branches and blossoms sprout again and again from the stem of dogma. He gives the believers insight into all laws that are necessary for the existence of the Church at a particular time, in order to lead to God the people who are living in that time. He gives the interpretation of the gospel appropriate to the time. He mediates at all times between the firm structure of what perdures and the varying requirements of the present. It is in this that his prophecy will consist. He will also objectify love by bestowing on it a character that orders it in the framework of Church life. Through his working, Christians will recognize clearly-contoured laws within love; through these laws and their observance they will be given a support that will testify to them that they are operating within love. Until now, everything in the words and deeds of the Lord was a challenge to pure love. Only through the Spirit does it become clear how one can actualize love in the individual case. This will not mean an impoverishment of love, but on the contrary its enrichment. For now it will also be possible to make plain to others, through clear laws, which ways lead to love and how one can persevere in it. It is as if the Lord had given his people a piece of land with the order to cultivate it. But the Spirit clears, makes paths, plants, prunes, sows and harvests.

16:14. *He will glorify me, for he will take what is mine and proclaim it to you.*
The Spirit will glorify the Lord, but he will not do even this of himself, but by using what is the Lord's. He will not glorify the Lord from without, but will take what distinguishes the Lord, in order to erect his glorification on that. He will take the love of the Lord that is, with equal directness, his love and the Father's love for him. For the three Persons never possess their qualities for themselves in a closed way, but always catholically, in common; which is not to say that they are confused. They belong to all the Three together, in such abundance that much remains left over that can be squandered on what is outside the Trinity, and squandered in such a way that in the squandering itself no more boundaries can be seen. When we consider this love objectively, it is possible to distinguish up to a certain point between the love of the Father, the love of the Son and the love of the Holy Spirit. But when we receive this love as a gift, if we sense it in a living way, we cannot say how great is our share of the Father's love, or the Son's or the Holy Spirit's. Love, given to the world, no longer allows us to distinguish the Persons. But when the Holy Spirit glorifies the Son, he is drawing on the Son's love. He shows the world the Son's love, with all its distinguishing characteristics. He shows it the way the Son possesses it, but also the way the Holy Spirit senses it and even more the way it is offered to mankind.

He needs this love drawn from the Son in order to glorify the Son. There is a mysterious basis for this. Through this the Holy Spirit wants to move us, for our part, to glorify the Son in the same way. We too are to learn to glorify him through what is his and not what is ours. We too ought to take from what is his; indeed, we should know that everything that glorifies the Son is really his. We should become aware that if we feel the stirrings of a love in us that we believe glorifies the Son, this stirring stems from the Son. The Spirit wants to uncover the grace of the Son living in us, which comes from the Son and returns to him. If the Spirit were to use his own love for the Son for his glorification, we would find it less appealing. It would be as if a human being were praising another human being. At most we would see the love of the one giving the praise, and this would perhaps leave us cold or indifferent. The Holy Spirit, on the other hand, is able to uncover the amiability of the one he praises, opening a direct approach to the Son's love so that we cannot resist glorifying him. The Son's glorification through the Holy Spirit is in the end a limitless one, for it occurs within the Trinity. And thus he also opens the way back to the Father—for the Son is the glorification of the Father—and thus sketches, in the splendor of the Son, the living Trinity itself in the glorification of their love.

16:15. *Everything that the Father has, is mine; therefore I said: He will take of what is mine and proclaim it to you.*

Nothing the Father and Son possess belongs only to one and not to the other. Thus it is with what they *possess*. In what they *are* there are essential differences, insofar as one is the Father and the other is the Son. These differences are rooted in their essences and are ineradicable. But in terms of what they possess, they both possess Fatherhood and Sonship. This mystery becomes more clear to us with the Son than with the Father. The Son also possesses the Fatherhood. In relation to mankind he possesses the qualities of the Son and the Father at the same time. He calls himself Son of Man and yet is the Father of the faithful, whom he also calls his little children. At the moment of separation he possesses paternal qualities even in relation to the Father; as Son he separates from him, but he takes his entire mission from the Father with him and tends it, not as a subordinated Son but as autonomous collaborator and finally as the bearer of responsibility who, because he has taken on a commission, somehow even becomes the "superior" (*Vorgesetzter*) of him who gave him superior authority (*der ihn sich vorgesetzt hat*). He must accomplish the Father's commission on earth completely for the Father, because he alone and not the Father has become man. Insofar as the Father did not become man, the Son, as it were, must represent and steward the Father's fatherliness with doubled responsibility and conscientiousness. This being so, the Father takes on the role of the Son: he leaves the Son perfect freedom; he does not interfere; he does not supervise the Son's work as one supervises the work of a minor. He lets him act as one who has full responsibility; he does not set himself up as judge over the Son's work of Redemption. He knows how enormous the task is that the Son has undertaken, and that if it is to reach true completion, he *must* accomplish it precisely without the Father, in separation from him. In knowing this and stepping back before the Son's autonomy, he sets the Son above himself. Thus, for his part, he adopts the filial qualities of the Son.

But since everything that is the Father's also belongs to the Son, it is also the property of the Holy Spirit. The Spirit takes what is the Son's in order to glorify him, but precisely that which he takes from the Son stems from the Father. It is common property. In order to glorify the Son, he takes the Son's love. This love, which has a particular characteristic of the Son, stems from the Father, for it was from him that the Son received love, just as the Father perpetually receives love from the Son. The Son's love continually receives its vitality, and also its characteristic of having to be mediated, from the Father. It is this characteristic that makes the Son's love perceptible to us as love. It is never a fixed quality, however, but rather only a movement, a direction, a pointer: namely, from the Father to the Father. This quality of love is eternal and without boundaries. If one were to try to seize and pin this love down to a particular point, it would already be dead. One must be drawn oneself into its eternal movement to grasp something of its essence. But if one believed one had grasped it, one would not have grasped love but at the most a concept. This love of the Son is somehow the opposite of erotic love, which finds its peace and relaxation in the act and must recuperate in order to be capable of new love. The Son's love—and, through it, all Christian love—needs no recuperation; it is eternal movement and increase.

Every act of Christian love, as such, calls forth a More; it multiplies; it surpasses itself; it knows neither rest nor slackening. Christian love has this character because the Son's love has the Father's in it. If the Son were alone, his love and his glorification would be simply filial. But because this love goes beyond itself to the Father, the love that the Spirit takes from the Son in order to glorify him and reveal him to the world is infinite in its movement. It is so because the Son's love itself possesses paternal qualities, as the love of the Father includes filial ones. Each mirrors the other. If an actor has never experienced real love as a person, it will not be possible for him to play a lover's role perfectly. And if he has not experienced what sorrow and despair are, his tragic roles will not be credible. The love and the suffering he has experienced are mirrored in him. Some other person has left behind tracks in his essence; they come from outside and are therefore "other", and yet they have still awakened what is most unique and profound in his own soul, things that would never have come to light without this encounter. Thus the Father caused what is filial in the Son to blossom precisely through awakening what is paternal in him, and the converse holds for the Son in the Father. Both become what they are by eliciting it from the other.

This infinite mutual increase of the love between Father and Son includes every sort and every possibility of loving. All love in this world that points from mankind into infinity is a simile and reflection of this love. It happens that a person loves another absolutely, but the other does not respond to this love and rejects it. Or he does not reject it; he responds to it with his feelings, but because he is already committed to someone else he cannot respond to it in surrender. Or he is free, and mutual love finds its fulfilment. Each of these forms in love has a side that is not contained in the other forms and can illuminate the love between Father and Son. In happy, requited love we can discern the eternal finding-each-other of Father and Son. But every happy love remains finite on earth; marriage closes a circle that in God remains eternally open. Thus the remaining open of unrequited love is also a simile for God. But this particular remaining open is not compatible, in the world, with a true finding, and this is once again a consequence of finitude and does not correspond to love in God. Unrequited love, seen in a purely human way, is deadly and futile; but in Christianity even it can be a simile for divine love insofar as, through grace, in the love on the Cross between Father and Son, in the love that for love's sake is no longer felt or perceived, it is opened into the infinity of the divine love.

The divine love is so open in itself that is is eternal increase; its essence is the Evermore of love between Father and Son. This constant bursting forth within infinity belongs to the essence of God himself. For God's beginning knows no beginning: he precedes all his own beginnings, and therefore, too, he continually overfulfills himself. This form of increase is therefore very different from the increase of Christian love for God, because the human being, in his finitude and in the course of his temporal life, experiences an expansion of love that he did not previously possess. This temporal growth of human love is only a distant reflection of the eternal increase of love between Father and Son.

This love is eternally fruitful. It is so because the Holy Spirit is the principle of its life. Therefore the Spirit, the principle of living fruitfulness, formed the Son in Mary. The Lord, for his part, appeared as the proclaimer of a new law of love, and thus as the fruitfulness of the Father. Now the Spirit comes after him and proclaims what is the Lord's, concluding, so to speak, this fruitfulness. He completes it, and in such a way that he shows its inner infinity. When spouses love each other, the highest measure of their physical fruitfulness lies in the begetting of a child. Even here, comparing the fruit with the number of sperm cells, human fruitfulness is greatly limited. But the child emerges out of their love, and when it becomes independent it is no longer subject to the laws of parental love. Perhaps it dies, and thus further limits the parents' earthly fruitfulness, or rather merely shows the inner boundaries of all natural love. The love of God, on the other hand, is of an infinite fruitfulness. Everything sown in it becomes not only fulfilled but overfilled, and yet it does not run out of itself or out of love or lose its own splendor through the fruit. This fruitfulness of God lies in the Holy Spirit, in whom the Godhead at the same time expands and is brought to completion in infinity. But mankind also receives a share in this divine fruitfulness through the redemption; man is elevated beyond limited natural fruitfulness into that of the soul endowed with grace, which is important insofar as it participates in the immortality of ever-greater love.

PARTING AND MEETING AGAIN

16:16. *Yet a little while and you will not see me, and again a little while and you will see me, for I am going to the Father.*
The Lord is speaking of his death. He will die, and his own will see him no longer. He does not say that he will forsake them; he does not say that this not seeing signifies a separation; he speaks of his death as if it were simply his becoming invisible to them. And he does not expand on the theme. A normal human being who knew that his death was imminent and what kind of death it would be would have other things to speak of than his coming invisibility. But the Lord indicates it because his invisibility will be of such importance for everything that follows: it is as the invisible One that he will guide his people, let them share in his invisibility and indeed will annihilate the borders between visibility and invisibility. The disciples and all who associated with him saw him and knew him as one sees and knows one human being among others. That was their privilege in their time. After this he will no longer be seen on earth. And yet he immediately continues:
And again a little while and you will see me. His invisibility will be of short duration because he is going to the Father, because his dying is a dying toward the Father, a very different dying from that of other people. It is a death that, seen from an earthly point of view, lasts only a few days, serves only to return him to the Father after he has tasted total separation in human death and in the descent into hell. Then he will be seen again. But this new vision will be totally different from the one that the disciples had been privileged to see until now. When they see him again after the Resurrection, they will know clearly that he is no mere human being. In their eyes he will possess a new quality, no longer separable from faith. Faith and vision will form a unity from now on, even for those who knew the Lord before the Cross. From now on he will only be visible to believers, including those believers who have not seen him in earthly form. They will be able to see him from now on in his true corporeality, which will no longer be separable from faith. Thus

Paul, and many after him, will see him at Damascus. But even those who do not see him in such a vision will not be poorer thereby (although that vision is a grace), because their faith contains a certainty that participates in the vision.

The Lord himself says why he will be seen again after his death: *For I am going to the Father.* This gift of rising from death and becoming visible to the believing disciples comes from the Father. It includes the Lord's potential to appear in a form that is always new, down through the centuries. The Father himself, who is always at work and who loves us, has always been invisible. But he gives the Son the possibility of being visible, out of gratitude for the love that the Son demonstrated to him in coming into the world, and in order to open up to him new means and scope of wooing mankind. Because, in the visibility of his earthly life, the Son has proved to him that the world loved him more than despised him, the Father gives him this surplus, this additional grace, of being able to become visible whenever he will, even after his return to heaven. The Son's ability to be visible addresses not only men's eyes, but their entire physical-spiritual nature: he can appear to all their senses and imaginative powers. Thus the person meditating in faith can imagine the Lord as he was in this or that scene on earth, how he looked, what he said, how he acted. This is not a mere offspring of the natural imagination, but an imagination of faith, of the Christian imaginative power, and as such an expansion and expression of the gift of visibility that the Lord receives from the Father. Different as the pictures of individual prayers may be, and however little these imaginative pictures may correspond materially with the situation as it was then, they can all be valid at a deeper level insofar as, in them, the Lord appears in faith and for faith. God gives us this room for imagination so that we may be closer to the Lord with our senses also. We cannot imagine God because he never became visible, yet through the Father's grace and the Son's return to the Father we can imagine, in faith, the Son and his entire nature and life.

16:17. *Then some of his disciples said to each other: What is it that he is saying to us: A little while and you will not see me, and again a little while and you will see me? and: Because I am going to the Father?*

The disciples do not understand the word of the Lord. They know that he calls God his Father. But they do not grasp why his return to the Father should necessitate his invisibility for a little while. Their views of the Lord are still wide apart. Either he is a human being who dies and thereby becomes invisible, or he is a Divine Person who possesses eternal life and can return to the Father without having to die. They cannot understand the unity of his God-Manhood; they do not even want to understand. This unity—which they, however, see as something twofold—makes them uneasy; they have no idea in what direction the union lies. But they do notice that the crux of the entire question lies in the Lord's word: *Because I am going to the Father.* But they can find no human explanation for this, or any explanation within their faith. And the obscurity that lies in these words oppresses them. They feel yet again that they have fallen into an adventure that they can no longer control. They see before them only partial solutions that cannot be unified into a synthesis. But their unease does not cause them to open themselves further to faith; rather, they are pressing for a simplification at the level of thought. So far they have not grasped that what is transcendent in this mystery should be a spur to greater faith. On the contrary, it closes them off. What they would like is a clarity, an overview, which would remove the need for a greater surrender. They approach the question like some school task that they are to solve together. They do not see that the solution of all tasks that the Lord sets always consists simply in an increased faith and trust.

16:18. *So they said: What is it that he says: A little while? We do not understand what he is talking about.*

They suspect, to be sure, that more must be implied in the Lord's words than this either/or of being human or being God. But they want an unequivocal answer. And this little while that is left them for seeing the Lord seems dubious to them. The Lord is threatened on all sides; his life is in danger. But because they have a human trust in him, they do not give up hope of having him among them always. They regard themselves as his companions and cannot imagine that this companionship should come to an end through the very One who summoned them in the first place. They do not know what he is talking about because they cannot believe in the Cross or in his meeting his end, and still less in a resurrection from the dead.

16:19. *Jesus knew that they wanted to ask him, and he said to them: You are enquiring among yourselves about the fact that I said: A little while and you will no longer see me, and again a little while and you will see me.*

The Lord knows that they are uneasy and would like to question him. He knows it without hearing their words, because he knows the state of their faith exactly. Although he always tried to give them a faith that would grow stronger, they are always held back by what is human, and their faith continually requires proofs. And much of what he has just said to them was not apt to expand their faith—at the present time. It served as a landmark and a foundation for later times, for themselves and even more for those who will follow after in the Church. For the disciples, the Resurrection will suffice: then they will believe. For those who will follow, more will be needed. Correspondence between the prophecies and their fulfilment will be needed, each mirroring the other. That will be one more proof of faith for them, replacing the direct sight of the Risen One or complementing faith in him. It will also satisfy their minds. The Lord does not desire an unformed faith; he wants a knowing and perceiving faith. Questions are to be left open, the solution of which can prove fascinating, fulfilling and satisfying to later, educated spirits. There should not only be the fisherman's faith in the Church, but also a theological faith. There should be nourishment and satiety for the whole spectrum of human intelligence. Therefore the Lord affirms the existence of the disciples' question. Their question will live on in the Church. And the better and more satisfactorily it is answered, the more new questions it will raise. In the interplaying unity of question and answer lies the truly Christian and inchoative element of all study of faith and theology. The apostles are like pupils whom the teacher has given a task. They believe they have grasped precisely what it is about: only when they have been left alone do they suddenly realize how little they have understood of the whole affair. Completely new aspects and problems crop up. And so they begin to question each other, just as those who come later will question themselves about faith. Such questioning is quite in order; thus they admit before one another their ignorance and the narrowness of their understanding, and as long as they are questioning each other about the Lord and trying, in unity, to find his truth, they are on the path on which the answer can meet them. The Lord will be in the midst of these questioners, and he will give them the answer himself.

In referring to the "little while" and his reappearance, the Lord also anticipates something of the mystery of the Mass. What lies on the altar first of all is the host, bread, a substance that one can humanly comprehend as one can imagine a normal human person, but after transubstantiation the Lord is there in its place, the Lord whom one can no longer comprehend. So the disciples' faith, through the "little while" of the Lord's disappearance, advances from a faith in the simply present earthly Messiah to faith in the God who is once more visible and yet ungraspable. And just as the apostles will see him again, but as the One who lives mysteriously in the Father, so too future communicants should see not only his corporeality, but the ever-greater reality of his Godhead; indeed they should see this more and more.

16:20. *Truly, truly I say to you: You will weep and mourn, but the world will rejoice. You will sorrow, but your sorrow will turn to joy.*

The disciples will weep and mourn during the "little while" of his invisibility, during the Passion. It will be a hard test for them—not only because they will see the Lord whom they love suffering, not only because he will die, but because they will be separated from him and menacing doubt will rise up in them. In this bitter time they will no longer understand the purpose of the Lord's life, or of their own surrender. Up to the last they will hope for some rescue from the Cross. They will hope that at some point, when the measure of suffering is full, the Lord will break off his suffering in order to bring about the happy end. So little will they understand of his Cross.

Thus the Lord's suffering comes unexpectedly for them. If Christ is God—so the *disciples* thought—he is above suffering. If suffering were to touch him in any way, it would be only so that the Lord could triumph over it perfectly. This victory would be a heroic one, and his power would be so great that he would not even be brushed by the anguish of suffering. The Lord would stand so high above suffering that it could not even come near him. Or the Lord would have turned away from suffering. He might have let it approach him and then averted it by some sudden movement. And now they are to see something totally different. They are to see how the Lord suffers truly and earnestly as a human being. He is exposed to real torment, and in the end he dies an agonizing death. They do not know how to reconcile this with the idea of the Son's glory. The Lord's Passion is so great that a *com-passion* awakens and takes shape in their hearts. They suffer with him, on the one hand because they see how great his pain is, and on the other hand because a feeling of deepest dismay overwhelms them. They suffer from acute noncomprehension of the Cross. This compassion that they feel for the Lord also includes a fear for themselves: they feel, although obscurely, that this dark, incomprehensible side is part of all that glory in which they had part, and thus that in following the Lord they risk falling into a similar darkness. If the Lord who was their Master must endure so much, then it is by no means impossible that they too, the disciples, the followers, will have to share a similar fate. What horrify them as much as the physical agonies are the unmistakable signs of the Lord's deepest spiritual suffering. They hear how he feels forsaken by the Father, and they see that he is in an inner darkness, which they find unfathomable and uncanny, but which most certainly outstrips their own capacity for suffering. They are suddenly placed before a mystery that is horrifying rather than one with which they can somehow empathize. The Son is hanging there in a condition that proclaims the very opposite of what he always said about himself: that he was one with the Father, that he was inseparable from the Father. He had said that he came from the Father and was going to the Father and that his whole course was in the Father. And now this frightful end in agony and total forsakenness! The disciples feel as if they are infected by this darkness, although they know that what they are going through in no way matches his experience. Their suffering is certainly connected to his in a hidden way, but the questions it raises are of a much coarser, more primitive nature. The Lord's darkness is pure forsakenness by God. Their darkness is their being forsaken by his strength and friendship—and this once again raises the problem of their love for him. They have loved him, having been challenged by him and responding with ready trust. And now that he is dying thus before their eyes, they are losing him as friend and master, and more: they are losing him as what he claimed to be, the living connection between them and God. This calls into question their entire faith, their hope and indeed their life itself. They doubt their friendship with him and their faith in him, because in the face of the darkness enveloping him they can do nothing other than doubt his faith in God and God's fidelity to him. In the beginning they suffer with him to a certain degree, but the further the Lord's suffering advances, the less they understand and the less they come with him. Hopeless, they fall behind; they do not suffer in union with him anymore, and ever louder the question arises whether everything was not a mistake, whether they have not simply been betrayed. He schooled them in faith, love and hope to a trust beyond everything. This entire structure is now falling apart completely. The teaching of the Lord directly contradicts what is happening to him; he did not keep what he promised, so perhaps he is not who he claimed to be. And the whole fiasco is conclusively sealed by his death. Up until the last minute they could hope for the miracle. But it did not come. Thus their faith and their hope have died as well. This is how the disciples suffer.

Next to the Cross stand John and Mary. The other disciples would not have endured standing under the Cross. And yet it is John and Mary who bear the least, because they love most; it is their love that lets them bear the unbearable. *John* believes, loves and suffers without being forsaken. He possesses a very special grace of suffering in the Lord's night while turned to what is coming, with his gaze fixed on the redemption. He is like one who is undergoing an operation and can keep in mind how beneficial it will be. For John, the Cross is a proof of the Lord's love. He also knows that it is the Lord who gives him the power thus to endure the Cross. In this special grace, while the Lord is forsaken, it is given to him to suspect and see how much of what is happening is essential to the Lord's living love for mankind and for the awakening of mankind's love for one another. Thus, to a certain extent, John suffers in an opposite way to the Lord: he suffers with new hope, with new insight, and even in the midst of suffering he reaps the fruits of the Lord's suffering. Father and Son are robbed of that which otherwise binds them; he, on the other hand, sees the unity between suffering and love. This unity is something wholly new and inexpressible to him: he is given, as it were, the solution to a problem that he had not yet even recognized.

Mary is living through her most difficult hour: she sees the terrible suffering of the Son, whom she loves above everything, and she is drawn into his darkness much more than John. The sea of suffering has become so endless that she no longer grasps anything. She cannot even understand her own consent. Her whole destiny is as if in darkness. In love and purity she placed her whole existence at God's disposal for the Son's becoming, and beyond this for his growth, his work, all his thought and endeavor. And now it is not only as if everything she did was for nothing, but the life of her Son also seems devoid of meaning. Her whole sacrifice seems scorned, and she no longer knows why she has carried this mystery with her all her life long. But her own suffering is only like a painful frame around the real bitterness, namely that everything that her Son undertook, and that she accompanied with her whole love, has completely failed. Although she always knew that this hour would come, she never tried to taste it in advance. And now that she does taste it everything that was faith and hope disappears. She shares her Son's suffering in such a way that she has part in his forsakenness. Only she also knows that she is to continue living, and she does not understand on what possible source such a life could draw. The Son was not the entire content of her faith. She also had a faith in the Father and in the Holy Spirit, but now that the Son is dying in pain it is as if she is forsaken by her whole faith. She believed in God before she believed in the Son, but the Son's death has apparently torn away her faith in God as well. And with this the whole commission of her Motherhood appears to be dashed. She lives in the Son's darkness, as the Son lives in the darkness of the Father. Everything in her was self-giving, but now that she sees that everything was in vain, she actually has no one else to whom she can give herself. And her Motherhood, which was not only physical but also spiritual, no longer has an object, because she sees the Son's body and spirit doomed to destruction. John's love survives this catastrophe; as a chosen apostle he has a more than merely personal love for the divine Friend and Master; his love lives from the Lord's supernatural love for mankind, which he also imparted to him. Mary, on the other hand, loves the Son most fundamentally as Mother. Her whole person is turned to the Child, and as he was conceived in her and born from her, he now dies in her, and she dies with him.

The *Father* loves his Son. He sees what the Son is suffering. He has known from the start that this hour would arrive, but now he experiences it in its entire substance. He cannot reveal himself to the Son, because in so doing he would lessen his trust in the Son. He must allow the Son's love this final demonstration, this uttermost test of capacity, of complete separation from him. This is how the Father cosuffers the Cross. In God's renunciation of showing himself lies the source of Christian suffering. For in this renunciation lay the Father's uttermost love. If suffering was connected only to the Son and not to the Father, if the Father remained uninvolved in suffering, then there would be no possibility of a Christian suffering, and the Christian would have to prevent as much suffering as lay in his power. But in Christian life, according to the Father's example, room must always be made for the neighbor's right to suffer—however beloved the neighbor may be. It is wrong to wish, out of love, to spare him every suffering. Certainly there is a fruitful mystery of loving substitution, in which human persons can take suffering from one another. But this does not exhaust the mysteries of love. It can be proof of a greater love to grant the other his wish to suffer. If the Father intervened in the Son's life, he would thus limit the Son's love. His compassion would testify to a mistrust of the Son's love; he would have measured this love and decided that it could not extend into limitlessness in suffering. He would have considered that it was enough—not for himself, but for the Son. By letting the Son go on to the ultimate, the Father shows himself willed to acknowledge the entire limitlessness of the Son's love and to accept it from him as perfectly unfolded.

In this course of love unto the very end, *chaos* ensues everywhere. Before the suffering there were many attempts to make a single, connected work. Many who met the Lord had thought about a conversion; many had felt their way to the truth and circled about it from a distance or nearby. But nowhere was the final word spoken. The speakers did not utter it themselves, nor did God let it be spoken in himself. All these beginnings are now interrupted. All these paths suddenly come to an end. All are now at a point where their earlier beginnings appear to them folly, and every perseverance along this way strikes them as senseless. Doubts toss them back and forth; their spirit is confused. The Cross does not afford them any strengthening of their initial faith, nor does it lead them to a full No. The Yes that they once spoke, which they had tried to speak, is simply lost to them. They spoke it then as something that remained open for the coming weeks, months and years, looking toward a fulfilment that was still pending. This openness has now transformed itself into dizzying formlessness, in which everything is confusing and changeable: faith and superstition, reality and appearance, guilt incurred and guilt borne. Faith is taken away from them so that they might attempt of themselves to remain open. But it is precisely this attempt that the human person cannot make. He can perhaps strengthen those entrusted to him in their openness. But he cannot decide for himself on something conclusive and limited while at the same time saying that he remains open for further things. For if his remaining open were a consequence of his own decision, everything could invade him through this gate: good and bad in confusion. One can remain open for God only in a once-for-all total assent, not in a tentative, limited, cautious Yes. Such a Yes leads into chaos. The simple nay-sayers are not chaotically confused. They are the ones of whom the Lord says that they rejoice. The ones who are chaotically confused are all those who are lukewarm, who have tried a mixture of Yes and No. They have already given a part of their person, but not the whole, and so now everything in them is divided, at odds. They are pulled back and forth between night and day. That is their night. It is completely different from the night of the Lord, which is a total, unequivocal night. He is not in chaos, but in the orderliness of annihilation. But the chaos extends so far that even those more distant and most distant—those who have observed Christianity with a certain uninvolved sense of goodwill—feel themselves touched by it. They too can no longer withdraw; they too, through this initial goodwill that they have shown, are drawn into the chaos of the Cross. But because they have known no love, their inner poverty now comes to light. This poverty only exposes them, and they have no more opportunity to cover themselves. None of them wanted to know that the Lord is really serious. And now that there is nothing more to veil, now that everything yawns open in terrible nakedness, they stand there sheepish, stupid and vexed. They have been crossed in their plans and their whole being is shaken, giving their existence the unendurable quality of directionlessness. They had hoped to be able to make an arrangement with the Lord, and they assured him that they would view his cause with goodwill. They never let themselves get out of hand. They thought the Lord owed them more detailed instructions and before that they were not obligated to anything. This is how they calculated and hoped, and even made a vague promise: if everything went well, they would engage themselves further. And now the Lord is dying, and they see that he did not even wait for them, that he has left them alone, that he is doing it without them, and that from the very start everything was much more binding than they had thought. Precisely where they tested and measured in order to stand secure, the ground has sunk. He "did this to" them, dying without asking them, without arranging for the succession, without taking care of their concerns. Now they are the deluded ones—deluded by their sin. They had played with fire. Wherever they look, they stare into a vacant hole. All the threads that attached them to the Lord are torn away. The Lord has pulled out a stone somewhere, and their whole structure has collapsed. And the ruin is much mightier than was the construction. What they do not suspect is that they are being helped precisely through this. And that is the form of their participation in the Cross.

But the world will rejoice. Those people rejoice who want to know nothing of the Lord. They rejoice because it is now proven that they were right all along, that there was nothing supernatural about the whole affair, that the entire proposal in this form was impossible, that the whole "renewal" that was attempted here—and they had always warned people about this—necessarily had to flow back into the "old". Now it is shown how right they were. They feel confirmed in their own attitude; they are glad to have known everything all along, and they can now devote themselves with so much more pleasure to their turning away and their pharisaism. They do not think of the Lord's end with pleasure merely on their own behalf, but rejoice that those who were unsure and even let themselves be converted will now come back to their party. So happy are they about this increase, that they decide to be generous and not make the repentant ones pay for it. They have forgiven them, and this forgiveness will further enlarge their own glorification. Now they feel strong enough to construct their God themselves. The God in whom they previously believed was already to a great extent a product of their own wishes and their imagination, but the new God that they will now come up with will really be entirely their own work.

You will sorrow, but your sorrow will turn to joy. The sorrow of all those who stand around the Cross, nearby or at a distance, who are gripped in any fashion by the sorrow of the Lord, is a fruitful sorrow. Therefore its fruit will become visible, and it will turn to joy. It was purifying sorrow, which revealed the limits of the human person, his insufficiency and sin, and glaringly showed up the ideal that he wanted to attain. Above all it made clear the grace of the Lord, the greatness of his love and his intentions. What is one's own and what is his are clearly juxtaposed; the way is perhaps still opaque, but the striving toward the Lord has been awakened. That is the fruitfulness of sorrow. For in this striving lies the turning away from oneself and the turning toward the Lord. Levels and sections of the way are not visible; only one thing is unmistakable: the Lord's love is greater than my betrayal. And thus the sorrow for one's own ego can turn into a joy in the Lord. This joy can take on many forms. It can suppress everything else from the start and fill up the whole soul. But it can also develop very slowly in hope. It can be overpowering or soft and imperceptible.

The Lord foretells the disciples of the fruitfulness of their sorrow. He knows, then, that his death signifies a new life for them, not only in the objective sense that they will be redeemed, but in such a way that each of them in his fashion will also feel this joy. They will really rejoice. This joy will not remain veiled behind their sorrow, nor will an equilibrium arise between sorrow and joy; rather, sorrow itself will turn to joy, and that alone will remain. This joy will be the joy of the Lord, a joy that he administers and that remains in him, a joy that they will possess but that will never be without him. He makes it arise; he makes it develop; he makes it sweep away everything else. It always remains his own sole work. It is *his* joy, which returns to the Father. This joy really goes the way that he goes: the earthly way along which it takes into itself the sorrow of mankind, but that flows into the same place he does: into the Father.

16:21. *When a woman gives birth, she is in distress because her hour is come. But when she has borne the child, she thinks no more about the distress, for joy that a human being has been born into the world.*

The Lord compares the disciples' sorrow before and during his suffering with the sorrow of a woman in labor. Labor is such a distress for a woman that in her affliction she forgets its meaning. She forgets that only through the labor pains will the way become free in her for the child. She lives wholly in the present pain. She has lost her overview of the process. Only what she feels at the moment—distress and loneliness—is real for her. During labor she no longer feels the life of the growing child that has accompanied her for months. At the time when her dearest wishes are about to be realized, all her hope in their realization is as if vanished. And when her pains are at their worst, the child is born. One can scarcely speak of a transformation of pain into joy, because this moment of birth is almost more an abrupt alteration than a development. It is really birth: in the moment that the child appears, joy appears too, and all distress is totally forgotten. The joy is so perfect and so basic that it suffers nothing else beside it. The content of the joy is the child born into the world: it is joy as participation in life, as the joint cause of a new life in this world. The joy lives because life has been given to a new living being. The woman rejoices that she has a child, but no less that this child was born of her and is a sign of her fruitfulness. And she does not stop at this joy: she senses that this joy will grow above and beyond the child. If the woman is not Christian, she rejoices in her family, in her continuation of the line, in the thought of her children's future children. If she is Christian, she rejoices in the eternal life that is passed on here, in the grace that will spread in the world through the sacrament of baptism. She rejoices that she has given God a child, and she knows that the true fruitfulness of love lies in this self-giving to God. She has physically given birth, and in this fruitfulness has received a metaphor of the fruitfulness of all love; out of this she may learn to give herself to God more deeply in the Spirit, because this self-giving means real birth.

Thus Mary awaited a Child whom she had conceived by the Holy Spirit. She too awaited him more in fear than in joy. She had spoken her assent from a full heart, but knowing that it would mean the utmost demands. She will accept an unknown into herself out of obedience. But this unknown, whom she loves and for whom she gives up her whole life, will grow in such a way that the joy of her consent will soon be forgotten in the difficult things that are coming—that will look like impossibilities. At the beginning of her assent there was a very clear relation between herself and the response, but the more the response grows in her, the more the relation is displaced. She herself grows along with it, to be sure, but her comprehension does not. God's action in her gradually outweighs her own action to such an extent that it becomes more and more impossible to match it. But then the Child is suddenly there, and there too is the great joy, the joy of Motherhood, of fulfilment of the commission, of fulfilment of God's will. Her prayer is rapturously fulfilled. These two feelings—having a child that comes from God and yet is her own—form a single joy in her. It is a lasting joy that no one can take away from her. It belongs to her, with the Son, throughout all time. And yet, as soon as the Child is there her second expectation begins, the expectation of the Son's life, of the fulfilment of his mission in the Father, of his suffering and death. She accompanies his whole life almost as she had accompanied his growth in her womb: so closely bound, she shares everything with him, as a mother can share the life of her child. She lives his whole earthly destiny with him. And yet the mystery of pregnancy lives on in her even now: she can now influence the event even less, if that is possible, than at the time she was expecting the Child. "It" grows on in her. It grows in such a way that the entire mission of the Son and her own mission grow together into a developing unity. She knows about the coming event, but she comprehends it less than ever. Her whole existence during the Son's earthly mission is one extended pregnancy, which moves toward her bitter hour; the Cross will be her hour of birth, and on the next day she will hold the Child in her arms. And once again all these wonders proceed out of the infinite distance between the greatness of God's question and the humility of her maidenly response. Her paschal joy when the Son rises is in no way opposed to that of Christmas, but on the contrary is its completion: she now participates perfectly in the work of the Son. Her first joy went directly to the Child, while God, to whom she had spoken her assent, remained, as it were, in the background. It was a joy that was related to expectation in pregnancy, even though Mary's joy lay from the start in obedience (and not in infatuation). Her second joy fulfills itself when she goes together with the Son to God. Although she is full of grace from the beginning, she still grows in a true sense, through the life of the Son, toward her own fulfilment. Her perfection is not a rigid one, but a living, self-fulfilling perfection. This joy is a privilege of the Mother of the Lord, for whereas every other human person is born turned away from God and turns to him only in the bestowal of grace, in order to then begin growing in grace, her perfection, which was present from all time, is privileged to fulfill itself in the Resurrection of the Son. We hear of Mary for the first time in the scene of the Annunciation, when she speaks her assent to the angel and to God. But this assent reflects back on her whole youth up to the first moment of her *conception*. When she steps forth in the assent, through which God's design is fulfilled, it becomes clear that she could never have been other than sinless from the beginning, immaculately conceived. So completely was she enclosed in God from the very beginning that no other destiny could have been reserved for her than that of her assent. That is what is hard and inexorable in her fate. And yet it is also the softest and most surrendering element, because she may share as no other in the Son's destiny. Not least because her Son will also be a virgin. A mother has a much different share in the life of a virginal child than in that of a child who marries. Through marriage some of the intimacy of the man, which was reserved until now to his relationship to his mother, is transferred to his spouse. Therefore a mother also always takes a special part in the destiny of a son who is a priest. And Mary's Son is celibate because the Mother was celibate, just as the Mother was a virgin because the Son's way will be a virginal one. Together they form the first virgin couple. Later, priests and religious will renounce marriage because the Lord was celibate. And nuns will renounce it because Mary was a virgin. But priests will also share in Mary's celibacy, and the nun will be virgin for the sake of the Lord's celibacy. Thus in the Church the celibacy of man and woman enhance one another in pairs, as it were: because the priest is celibate, the nun can be so, and vice versa. Far from alienating themselves through virginity, they rather enhance each other as a couple that corresponds to the first virgin couple, Christ and his Mother. Celibacy, therefore, gives a certain access to the Lord and his Mother that the man who is convinced of his creative power and experiences his potency does not have. When he approaches God, he comes with himself, with the whole weight of his personality; he comes to declare himself, to have his say. The celibate, through the freedom that he has, is also free to enter *wordlessly* into the relationship of Mother and Son. He is perhaps no less a sinner than the other. And he may not boast of the fact of his celibacy, which is not an advantage in and of itself but only for the Lord's sake. But certainly virginity is the basis for a direct relationship to Mother and Son and for something like an opening to God.

This special opening of the one who is chaste in virginity must somehow be made evident and clear in confession. If a person who is not celibate comes to confession, one does not need to stop long over his sins; one can quickly pass on to absolution. But when he who is chaste in virginity opens his conscience in confession, it must be uncovered to the bottom of his soul—to the point where it becomes evident whether his virginity is perhaps only accidental or one of spiritual sterility, or whether it is real opening to God and this openness is perhaps based on a call of God to the priesthood or the religious life. For in such virginity lies a kind of surplus of grace, which on the one hand is based on the fullness of grace of the Mother's Immaculate Conception, and on the other hand is related to the surplus of grace in the Son's sacrament of confession: through the readiness of the soul and its expansion through absolution into God's Evermore. All three forms of opening are related, and together they form a single mystery of opening to God. This opening, again, is always a mystery of fruitfulness: if the way to God's call is revealed by the priest to the virginal person who lays his soul bare, and he in his assent corresponds to this call, he does not attach grace to himself but on the contrary lets is become available to others as well: just as the Mother, through her assent, helped to mediate grace to all. Anyone who says no at this point must accuse himself of having put a hindrance in the way of grace which is to be spent on others. Of course, no one may feel injured and still less make excuses for himself, if he sees that another person has failed to correspond to the call of grace.

Up until the moment that one is called, one must bear the sorrow of waiting: a waiting of which one is perhaps scarcely as yet aware. The boy, for example, who is called to the priesthood and is not yet following this call, carries within him a seed of the Holy Spirit; he is pregnant with it, and the birth occurs in the moment in which he gives it his consent. In this moment he also experiences the joy of birth, and all earlier distress disappears. It is the joy of being useful and of being allowed to serve. In this service lies the meaning of his life, just as the meaning of the pregnant woman lies in the bearing of the child. The assent to service is fruitful again in the second pregnancy, which follows him and urges him to new birth: to fruitfulness for others. For each person who, as a virgin, places his life at the Lord's disposal, brings other Christians into the world. And one cannot say that this virgin fruitfulness is based on sacrifice, renunciation and abstention, and God gives it another fruitfulness by way of consolation or compensation. The Christian fruitfulness of the Church is not erected on something negative and somehow somber. It rests above all on something fulfilled, on the assent to God, on radiant readiness for his service, on the openness, together with the Mother, to the Spirit and to the Son. Just as the grace of confession does not rest above all on the negative fact that a person has mastered himself in order to disclose himself or to break with his sin but rather on his becoming free for God, so too the priestly and religious vocation is not primarily sacrifice and deprivation, but joyous readiness for God. Out of the formless background of sin, the clear form of new grace stands out in confession. And out of the formless background of one's previous life, which was characterized by expectation in sorrow, the clear form of divine calling stands out.

In confession the sinner who has made his confession in perfect contrition is pure even before the absolution. The moment between confession and absolution is lived in purity. The one confessing is open and awaits God's response. It is a span of time that actually belongs not to the human person, but to God. In this moment the priest has a special power to impart the call of God to the penitent. His word is the word of the Lord, which is spoken to that in the penitent that is the Lord's. Here the priest is able to say things that he could not say in normal everyday life, because they would be too great and too direct to be accepted. But here they are accepted. It is a moment of purity that in the end reaches back to the purity of the Mother in the Immaculate Conception. Every pure effect is based on a condition of purity. The Mother herself, in order to give birth in purity, had to live by the grace of purity that was founded and deposited in her Immaculate Conception. A priestly vocation must be based on an earlier purity in the boy's life, and finally on the purity of the Mother. And somehow it must also be based on a moment of full openness to God, a pure confession and a pure response by the priest.

Thus Christian joy arises as the second purity out of a first purity; it proceeds out of a distress like a fruit out of the seed. In the end, everything is distress: waiting, sorrow, the trials and sufferings of this whole earthly life. And out of this totality, the meaning of which is purification, expansion toward a second purity, there arises the new, other life: *heaven*. Thus Purgatory is distress too: it is an expanding purification toward the second, conclusive purity and joy. We cannot penetrate the condition of purification: it is always mysterious and beyond our grasp. Certainly joy is basically no less mysterious than suffering; but in joy we are so fulfilled that its opacities do not occur to us or attract us. We are, after all, fulfilled. Finally, the transition from purification into purity is also a mystery: as the child was not there until birth and now suddenly *is* there, joy too is suddenly there, come forth out of distress, released from it, as when a shell or peel bursts and releases the fruit. It emerges out of sorrow as something definitive that cannot be revoked, just as the child who has been born cannot return into the mother. Both are definitive, like everything God does. When a suffering is over, really finished before God, it never returns again, just as a child is only born once. If other sufferings come later, they signify new pregnancy for new birth. The woman no longer remembers the sufferings of the labor pains; she forgets them with almost incomprehensible speed. Perhaps she is still aware that she suffered for a long time and that she cried out in pain, but she knows it as a fact that no longer belongs to her, that has nothing more to do with her, that is wholly submerged in joy. She has forgotten the intensity of the pains because they are dissolved in the joy, which lets nothing else vie with it. Thus the Christian sufferer, in the joy that follows, can no longer imagine what his suffering was, nor can he describe it any longer. Once the fire of Purgatory is over, it is also quenched; there is no recollection of it in heaven. Purgatory is a condition of loneliness, in which the soul is occupied with itself and with God's relation to it. But as soon as the soul is in heaven, there immediately arises a living bond with all other souls, whether these are in heaven or on earth or in Purgatory. This bond is part of the fruit of joy. On earth a perfect union between human persons is not possible. One always remains separate, even in the most intimate union attainable; a latent loneliness always remains through the distinctness of bodies, through ignorance of the ultimate mysteries of the other's soul, through the condition of sin. Every love remains imperfect here; it never becomes total immediacy. Only by way of God, that is, by way of faith, is a lasting, genuine bond possible. In heaven, on the other hand, true union is there as the fruit of Purgatory.

Every purification is also an expansion. It affects not only the precise points at which a person has sinned. It purifies the whole, even those parts of the soul that have not sinned; it purifies the soul in both its vices and its virtues. These too must be led and expanded beyond personal circumstances into circumstances that have their purity from God. Thus men will be able to understand each other in heaven even in ways in which they did not understand one another on earth. They will even be able, through a negative knowledge of sin, as it were, to understand and love those sinners on earth whose sins they themselves never committed, and who used to leave them completely indifferent. The knowledge one has in heaven about sins on earth is no longer a personal one based on experience; seeing a person sin, we shall not remember that we also committed or did not commit the same sin. We shall no longer measure sin by our own measure, but with God's standard of measurement. This is not to say that sin on earth is a matter of indifference to the saints in heaven. It remains painful to them also, not because of their personal inclination or disinclination, but solely on the basis of love in God. They retain the egos, personalities, characters, missions and thus too the particular tasks they had on earth. Thus a saint who was once a prostitute on earth can, from heaven, particularly assist fallen women on earth. Doubtless she will do so. But she will not do so with reference to her own life or in recollection of it, but solely on the basis of a mission from God connected with her own life. Everything is transferred out of the sphere of sin into the sphere of grace, which upholds and develops the entire uniqueness of personal character. Everything that was nature and grace remains, including our little preferences; only sin is purged away. Preference and personal inclination play their part in the bond that the saints in heaven have with people on earth. There are laws of preference and also—in the midst of heavenly joy—the possibility of a certain limitation and intensification. Everything in the essence and character of the person that stems from God remains; only that that the sinner added from time to time—that is, evil—disappears again. Thus life in heaven is something personal and living, with heightened joy even in the midst of perfect joy. Heaven, the fruit of earthly distress, is a living fruit: it sprouts, it is pure movement in God, whereas distress on earth also involved being imprisoned and bound. Now I am as God conceived of me in the beginning: no longer in the narrow womb of this time, but born to a free life in eternity.

16:22. *You too are sorrowful now: But I will see you again and your heart will rejoice, and no one will take your joy from you.*

The apostles' sorrow consists above all in the fact that now they comprehend nothing of what is going on with them and around them. They are drawn into an event that is uncanny and threatening, so dark that they are not even able to evaluate the present. They are almost like blind people who have been put on a street and commanded to walk, and yet they do not know in which direction they are to go. All the same, the disciples are on a path to which they once assented, in full freedom, a path that they once desired and even now, in their sorrow, still desire. Their sorrow is not the kind that would make them curse their past life. They have strayed into a fog, and although the sun will disperse it at some point, at the moment they are not capable of doing anything but standing still and waiting. Because they are men, they have a very pronounced feeling of sorrow in this passivity and inability to act. The Lord does not leave them to this sorrow; he discusses it with them and transforms it from something lacking consolation into something hopeful. At the same time, he shows them that there are moments in life where one must leave all the guidance to him, in darkness. That is why he chose the example of the woman in childbirth earlier. He knows very well how difficult it is for the disciples no longer to be able to direct and determine things, not even to be able to feel as guidance that guidance to which they have surrendered themselves. They wanted to be blind in order to be led—but now that they are blind, they no longer feel the guiding hand and believe they are walking astray.

The consolation that the Lord has to offer them lies in his words: *I will see you again.* He does not show them his guidance of them in the dark; he does not speak of the redemption, or of the suffering he has overcome, or of his return to the Father. He only speaks of the fact that they will see him again. He places, so to speak, all the joy on his side and thus shows what perfect love is. When a human person loves another in imperfect love, he rejoices to see his beloved again. But if he loves him with perfect love, he knows that the beloved's joy at seeing him is greater than his own joy; therefore he rejoices more at the joy of the beloved than at his own. The Lord treats his disciples as if they had perfect love, as he describes the joy of meeting again entirely from his side. Thus he also makes them understand that in the commission that they were ready to fulfill, he is taking over not only the guidance but also the distribution of graces and joys. Their reward for going his dark way with him will be that they will be allowed to share in *his* joy of meeting again.

Otherwise he would always have spoken in a way that responded to their needs. But now he is promising the fulfilment of his own need, as if this were the highest thing that he could promise. He treats those who are in this darkness not as sinners to be redeemed, but as his redeemed brothers, who are already so thoroughly redeemed that nothing gives them greater joy than the joy of their Master and Friend. He is taking them seriously as Christians.

Your heart will rejoice, and no one will take your joy from you. When they really feed and live from his joy, nothing more will be able to attack them and darken their joy. From the moment of seeing him again, they will draw their entire life substance from him. Their life will lie in the immediacy between him and them; nothing human will be capable of insinuating itself and upsetting it. Certainly, even though they live wholly in the life of the Lord, they will not be alienated from the joy and suffering of this earthly life. They will not be turned away from this existence. On the contrary: their worldly reality will intensify, it will receive its fullness from their reality in the Lord. It will not receive simply a kind of opening toward above, but will be expanded and rounded off in all directions. This new totality is the prerequisite of their future work in the Lord. He lets them participate in his vision of the world, of mankind and of things. He communicates his perspectives to them. And he does this in joy. As his joy becomes their joy, his vision of the world also becomes their vision. He has taken from them the arrogance of self-determination, self-knowledge, self-choosing; all that has disappeared, really and earnestly disappeared, in darkness, in sorrow, in the impossibility of stewarding what is one's own any longer. Now they are fully opened for him, their obedience to him no longer ceases and from now on they can really act as commissioned by him. They have learned true humility, in which they no longer depend on themselves. The darkness of sorrow through which they had to go was like a novitiate—an abbreviated one, for the Lord has only a little time left—and the result is a gift beyond the wildest imagining: the gift of being allowed to live in his joy. This gift includes the fact that it will last, that no one can rob them of their joy anymore, that they thus can no longer sin in such a way that would separate them from him and his joy. In the future they will be allowed to live within the Lord's purity. They will not feel set apart in this purity; in it, they will be more open to the world as well. Their ability to understand others, to feel, suffer and rejoice with them, will in no way be impaired by this life in the Lord. They simply receive the grace of humility and contrition, the grace to overcome everything personal. And on this basis they grow into the fully Christian life. It is the classic way of the Lord, along which he educates his co-workers. Before they went through this school of humility, they were his co-workers only very conditionally; they remained bound to his earthly being, his earthly place and time. Now they have become free and can move in all directions, in him, without suffering harm; they can accomplish his work, wherever he may be.

PRAYER IN THE NAME OF THE SON

16:23. *And on that day you will ask me nothing more. Truly, truly I say to you: If you will ask something of the Father, he will give it to you in my name.*

When they finally live in his joy, there will be no more questions. They themselves will be so transparent that he too will have become transparent for them. He will not have changed; he will be the same as he always was. But they, released from their sin and their dullness, will be capable of seeing him as he is. Up until now he is a human being to them; perhaps a more-than-human being, a human being with divine potential, one who surpasses them and to whom they gladly minister, but still one like them, a fellow human being. If they want to comprehend more of his mystery, they must start each time from his earthly being. They must start from what they can understand because it is like they are. But when they live in joy they will no longer see him as *they* are, but as *he* is: as God. They will understand that his Incarnation was only a deed of grace and the love of God, and that the Son chose this way because it was the best way of showing his perfect love to the Father and to mankind. He gives joy to the Father by taking on the form of One created by him in order to show him that the human being, as he had conceived of him, the human being without sin, was something perfect. And to mankind he shows that what they are is something that *could be* sinless and perfect. But he does not stop at this demonstration, but at once leads mankind beyond it, by letting them know, when they are living in his joy, that he is God. This is something they could not possibly see with their sinful eyes. Only when they have become capable of seeing as he expects them to—only then, through his grace—will their eyes be opened for God.

Then they will have nothing more to ask. For they will encounter his answer everywhere. Through the Lord's grace they will be permitted to ask and to wait for an answer. Until now they themselves were always the question, because they were still bound to sin: he was, and he mediated the answer as the Redeemer. From now on he draws them into his essence and thus into the answer. From now on other people will ask, and they will be able to answer in the name of the Lord; for now they live in the sphere of those who see, in the world of the Lord who, in the Father, is He-who-sees.

Truly, truly I say to you, if you will ask anything of the Father, he will give it to you in my name. Thus the Father will redeem his obligation to the Son. He will not look at the worth of the petitioner when it is a matter of fulfilling the petition. Rather, he will simply grant the requests of those for whom the Lord has said that he has become transparent. And the Father will grant the gift each time in the name of the Son. Those who receive it will know that what they receive from the Father is a gift of grace from the Son. Thus it lies rooted in the agreement between Father and Son that they reached before the Son separated from the Father. For just as, in the Incarnation, the Son refrained from proclaiming himself in order to bring the Father to mankind, in order to become transparent, letting the Father shine through him, now too he refrains from distributing the gifts to them himself in order to point only to the Father in everything. The Son could grant the requests himself, but he does not want to do that; those who have received a share in his joy, who have become a part of his answer, should share his joy in the Father and always remember that he himself is the Father's Word. He wants to be so transparent for them that they sense the Father through him and are grateful to the Father for every grace received. He does not want the Father to feel somehow surpassed by his act of Redemption. He wants the Father to have the joy of giving gifts to his creatures, of heaping them with answers and with joys. Just as the Son at the Incarnation felt obligated in both directions, he now desires that the Father and mankind remain in a vitally growing relationship. He gives the Father the people who are on his own path, and he gives the people the Father, as he experiences and possesses him.

But all of this is a gift of the Holy Spirit. It is he who makes this unity possible. He, who is scarcely visible here, who seems to be pushed to one side, is in truth the living connection between the Father and mankind, because he is on the one hand the living connection between Father and Son, and on the other hand the living connection between the Son and mankind. Everywhere he is the one who mediates, enables, unifies. The Lord promises: *You will ask me nothing more.* For they will perceive him clearly. But this perception is the effect of the Holy Spirit. Through the Son's Incarnation a clarity has arisen between the Son and humanity that makes every question superfluous. Men will continue to question the Father, on the other hand, because the Father remains veiled in the mystery of his invisibility and only becomes evident to them in the fullness of gifts that he gives in the name of the Son. They do not see the Father himself; it is not as if they could deduce and work out his essence bit by bit, on the basis of his gift. His mystery remains undivided. His image is not to be limited and determined by his gifts. The Son is accessible to them, insofar as he has become a human being. The Father never walked this path of Incarnation. And yet the revelation of the Father in enduring mystery is also a work of the Holy Spirit.

For the clearest revelation of the Father consists in that he allowed his divine Son to descend and become a Son of Man. And, allowing this descent, he simultaneously provides—in order to make it possible—for the Mother, who is a pure human being, to be elevated into the mystery of God, promoted to the dignity of being Mother of the divine Son. It is the Father who allows and effects both at once, the double movement of ascent and descent. Therefore he himself remains above, and invisible; what we see of him is the Son's descent and the ascent of the Mother. Just as the Son truly descends below his level, the Mother is truly drawn up above her level. And just as the Son experiences in his descent what humanity is, the Mother in her elevation experiences what God is. She is far from being a counterpart of the Son, equalizing him, so to speak, for the Mother participates by grace in what the Son is by nature. And yet she is the Mother of the divine Son and stands thus, as the lowly handmaid, beside the heavenly Father. Ranging between the Son's deepest humiliation and the Mother's highest elevation, the essence of the Father is most radiantly revealed.

The petitions that we direct to the Father are prayer. Prayer also lives from the same movement: from below upward and from above downward. It describes the trajectory of the praying person's desires, contemplation and adoration, and the trajectory of what the Father grants: the request, the contemplation and the adoration. But the entire prayer, whether it is going from man to God or from God to man, if it is real prayer, is always an act of love that never has its final source in the human person (not even when he thinks he is praying) but always in the love between Father and Son. This is the source of every prayer. This source is so living, so many-sided, it flows so eternally, that, whatever form and fashion prayer may take, it signifies life in love. Even a prayer that is only a helpless stammer, perhaps never getting beyond such a stammer, would receive the same richness from this source, the same extravagance, as every other prayer.

16:24. *Until now you have asked for nothing in my name. Ask, and you will receive, so that your joy may be perfect.*

So far they have asked in their own name, because they have not considered the relation between Father and Son as a living relation belonging to them. They have set certain limits to their faith and have therefore regarded themselves as standing outside the relation between Father and Son. But there is one thing they are beginning to understand: what the Son brings to them is more than they expected. It is "more" not merely once and for all, but increasingly and progressively "more". They have been able to contemplate the Son from continually new human standpoints, and each of these has given them a new vision of his relationship to the Father. Each of these views has opened up new and greater things, incomprehensible depths. From all points they have been lured into the mystery, into the mystery of the infinite love of the Son for the Father, and the Father's love for the Son. But they have not yet discovered that they themselves stand in the midst of this relationship of love. They have to some extent grasped that the Son brings them his grace in the name of the Father, and they are also prepared to accept this. But how should they grasp that they themselves make up a part of his relationship to the Father? That they are at the focal point of love? And that what is immediately expected of them is an equally immediate expectation on their part? But in order to be able to ask the Father in the Son's name, the Christian must believe properly. He may not make his request out of personal considerations, but he must know that the Father looks for his request in precisely this form and not otherwise. Indeed, he must know that even his desire, his wish, his longing to express this request is rooted in his faith and thus has its origin in the depth of the relationship between the Father and the Son. In order to be a living

Christian petition and not a mere word, it must have matured in living faith. But through their sorrow the disciples have attained to that maturity that anchored their faith in the true starting point of Christian existence: in the love between Father and Son.

Thus they can now ask and receive. Until now their reception was wholly dependent on their desire. Their capacity for reception corresponded to their longing. Now their expectation itself has matured and changed. Now they really belong to the Lord; his thoughts fill them. They will ask God not only for earthly goods, but for the fulfilment of the Lord's will. They ask this of the Father because the Son wishes it so. Every Christian desire stems in the end from the Father, but it becomes evident through the Holy Spirit. All Christian wishes together, therefore, are one with the will of God. Christians are heard by the Father if he encounters the Son's will in their will or sees their will expressed in the will of the Son. But the will of the Son is one with the Father's will. And although this agreement exists, it is not as if all wills are simply traced back to the will of the Father, as if basically nothing happens when one asks the Father for something. On the contrary: more happens, always, than the petitioner can expect. If the thing that he expected on the basis of his particular will and prayer does not happen, something else, something better and richer, will happen in its place. One cannot say that the Father determines everything alone and each individual will must adjust itself to his, that all prayer has only the purpose of bringing mankind into conformity with the will of God. Rather, it is equally true that the Father too, in his supreme and ultimate will, wishes to be determined by the Son and, in the Son, by mankind. This riddle can only be solved if one contemplates it in love; as a merely rational calculation it cannot work. The power of prayer over God is, in the Son, a power of love over the Father. In this power God gives mankind a share in grace. It is an act of the Father's love that he allows us to influence him in love, and it is an act of the Son's love that he allows us to use his name and title in prayer to influence the Father. Thus we may enter from both sides into the mystery of the Father's and Son's mutual determination of wills, since the two determine each other in love to one and the same decision. For the unity of God's will consists in nothing other than in the Father and Son determining one another, in the unity of the Holy Spirit. We are drawn into this unity, and this drawing in is accomplished through a sacrifice. This happens first of all through a sacrifice on the Lord's part, who takes it on himself to attract us and make us serviceable to the Father. But this also includes, hiddenly, the sacrifice of the one who is attracted and who, through sacrifice, grows into the unity of love of God's will. All the Lord's love always rests on his love of the Father, and this love, which becomes visible in the Incarnation, includes sacrifice. Sacrifice, prayer and love form a unity that becomes more and more binding and demands more and more love. And so God also gives more and more love. But he gives it in such a way that he, for his part, expects more love, love that must have the mark of the Son—that is, sacrificial love. Therefore every petition is also a sacrifice. It includes in itself a real renunciation: a renunciation of the one's own, in order to leave everything to the will of God. Even if a person were to thank God for the love of another, he would have to turn away from human love in this act, in order to turn toward God in love. It is this sacrifice, this being sacrificed, of the human person that obliges God in love to fulfill the person's will in the Son. Every love of a human person that includes real devotion and real sacrifice influences God to reveal and give himself.

So that your joy may be perfect. It is perfect because this joy that they feel is no longer only theirs, but above all God's joy. And all joy that comes from God extinguishes that in the human person that is against God, namely, sin, and transfigures and elevates the person's creaturely nature. What comes from man is always human even in sacrifice, prayer and love and is therefore not capable of perfect devotion. It does not get beyond initial movements that are imperfect, fall back on themselves and remain unfulfillable. So it is with human joy, too. Every human joy has its spatial, temporal, personal limits. If a person wanted to experience boundless joy outside the love of God and outside faith, he would be trying to explode his limits in an intoxication devoid of consciousness. But the whole attempt would end in a wretched illusion and disillusion. But anyone who rejoices as a Christian does not first have to make himself forget himself, for he has already forgotten himself. He does not need abandon his own reality; he already has a share in the reality of the Lord. He does not have to move away from the standpoint of his ego in order to devote himself to joy somewhere else, for his own ego is no longer regarded and does not demand to be regarded, because the "other", what is Christian and divine, so outweighs it that it dissolves in it as if weightless. And yet this does not mean that the Christian has any less a share in the joys of this earthly creation. He can celebrate and rejoice in his fellowmen without an outsider being able to see the connection between this joy and the perfect joy of the Lord. And yet this earthly joy is permeated and preserved by the joy of God. The Christian is not depersonalized, but his whole life, joy and sorrow, occurs within the Lord, and thus everything is stamped with the sign of his perfection: both sorrow and joy. Everything in his life is personal converse with God. When two human persons fully trust one another, they can demand what they will of each other, even things that the other does not understand at first. The one will grant everything the other asks for because he trusts that everything is taking place in love. Thus anyone who is in a relationship of trust with God can ask of God whatever he will. God will give it to him, because he trusts him and entrusts himself to him, because he knows that he, for his part, can ask anything he wishes of this person. In this relationship there is perfect joy, which is a joy in God. Perfect joy is the unity of faith, love and hope. This joy causes the whole promise of the gospel and the life of Christ to enter fulfilment. It is almost like word of reply to the initial word: *In the beginning was the Word.* Just as this latter was an overall view, the word of perfect joy is also an overall view of everything that the Lord brought by his coming: a final survey before his suffering. Here faith, love and hope fulfill each other, just as faith in God and hope in God fulfill themselves in love for God, which is the last and the greatest.

16:25. *This I have said to you in parables. The hour is coming when I will no longer speak to you in parables, but will tell you openly about the Father.*

In his words up to now the Lord has taken pains to speak in such a way that the disciples could understand him. He adopted the words, the concepts, the images of their world of perception. Therefore they did not look for any parable in his words, but assumed that he wanted to say exactly what they understood from his words. Despite this, the Lord regards this whole instruction as a parable. He delivered only a very few parables in John's Gospel. If in spite of this he uses the word "parable" for what he is saying, then it is because he was speaking of heavenly things in earthly garb, and thus, so to speak, interchanged the emphasis: what comes from heaven, what is eternal truth, he has presented to mankind in a form that seems to be reality for them, whereas for him it is only a parable. Now, by characterizing all his speech as a parable, he opens a door into the Infinite; he demands of his disciples nothing less than that they become capable of grasping in a heavenly way, together with him, the things that are heavenly. Thus he shows them that everything they thought they understood was only a parable for a truth lying far beyond it. They have a certain readiness to understand him as he is, but they are not capable of it. They limit him again and again through the measure that they apply to him and their relationship to him. But now he characterizes it all as parable: even their relationship to him, their concept of him, their attempt at following him. It is just as parablelike as the words that he has spoken to them until now. They must know that they are always just at the beginning of the movement, and so they are to be educated to faith. In every word that he speaks they should sense, hidden within it, an infinity of experience, interpretations and expansions. And if each of the hearers understands to a certain extent and then fails, then these limits do not lie in the word of the Lord, or in the faith that he gives, but in the sinfulness that remains even in the redeemed. No human person, not even the loving disciple, will ever grasp what the Lord is saying to him in truth. After a few steps he will come up against the mystery, the Ever-Greater, which lies hidden in the greatest he can comprehend.

And yet the Lord does not stop at the parable: *The hour is coming when I will no longer speak to you in parables.* The Lord loves this word, *"the hour is coming"*, because his teaching does not attain any conclusion on earth, but always points to what is coming, to what is greater, to new developments and surprises. Nothing that he explains and gives them is concluded. As long as we are on this side of the grave, the hour is always coming. That is at once comforting and disturbing. We are thrown into this greater dimension, which we cannot grasp, and yet we are also kept safe in it. One cannot tell the exact hour at which any psychic or spiritual event took place. No one knows when he began to believe and how faith has grown in him. And no matter how abrupt an experience of conversion may be, perhaps it is only the manifestation of something that has long been there. There is only one thing that the believer knows with certitude: that the hour of his faith *is coming*. So it is with the lover. He does not love solely from his love's beginning. He always loves toward the love that is coming. For him the hour of love is always coming. Everything in us is always only a seed.

In the coming hour the Lord will *speak openly of the Father*. He will do so in heaven, when the hour is finally come. But he will do so even now, in this world: in that part of us that no longer belongs to ourselves, that is no longer our personal understanding and will, that part of us that no longer concerns us, because it belongs entirely to him, lies in him, is deposited with him. In each person who believes, loves and hopes, there is this place in which he speaks openly of the Father. The believer may become conscious of this spot, perhaps when the Lord speaks to him in a meditation or in the words of a sermon, in which he can touch the listener quite differently than can human eloquence. For the earthly person, of course, while he is here below, the hour remains an hour that is coming. But the believer and lover lives, even here, in the beyond with the Lord, where the hour has come. For the limited person of this world, the word of the Lord appears to be the truth already, but it is truth primarily because the believer can perceive that it is only a parable. This capacity in him is an indication that he is already able to grasp something of otherworldly truth. But at the same time it signals the end of any overview, any calculation. We must be continually reversing both the sense of the Lord's words and our own entire being in order to get from the parable to the truth; we must shift the emphasis and transfer the standard of measurement out of ourselves and out of the world into heaven, surrendering the meaning to God. We would like to enclose every earthly perception in ourselves in order to possess it and to make further use of it. Just as one can plot a circle through any three points in space, we would like always to draw a closed circle through the points of our perception. We would like to have mastered the truth. The Lord, on the other hand, always wants to open everything. He makes our insights open into his truth. He makes human love open into his ever-greater divine love, without our knowing how he does it and to what end.

In this openness he will *speak of the Father*. He has been speaking of the

Father for a long time, but always in such a way that we could approximately comprehend it. Openly he talked more about himself, because he has a side that we can understand, the human side. But his divine side remained almost closed to us, and particularly the Father, to whom the Son's heavenly countenance is turned. We see this entire heavenly world between him and the Father only in a parable, because everything is shown only in the colors and forms that are comprehensible to us. Without such signs and images we understand nothing. And yet the Lord will now speak openly of the Father. He will do so on the *Cross,* at the moment when he is most separated from the Father. In his forsakenness he, the human being forsaken by the Father, will speak of the Father. Now he is still speaking as one who represents and interprets the Father for us, through a veil, as it were, so that we can understand. Now he still has his twofold being, his Janus face: what his heavenly countenance contemplates, his earthly countenance proclaims. On the Cross he will no longer represent or translate anything. He will be only one thing: the man forsaken by the Father. It is as such that he will speak. He beholds the Father only in the form of not seeing, although he is suffering entirely in the Father's hands. He has achieved the full degradation and humiliation of the Incarnation; he is no longer anything but a naked, forsaken human being. He has deposited his divine Sonhood so completely with the Father that it is as if, as a human person, he has lost it. For him, who has two natures, *to speak openly of the Father* can have two meanings: to speak as a human person speaks of his Father whom he has lost and is seeking, and to speak as the Son of God speaks in heaven when he openly contemplates and openly proclaims the Father. The latter he will do in heaven; the former he does on the Cross. The Lord's death on the Cross is almost the reverse of a human death. Whereas the human being is before God in total truth at birth and death, naked, helpless and unfeigned, the Lord comes out of the eternity of the Father, bringing his entire vision with him. Not until death does he attain the full poverty of being nothing but human, which a human person already has at birth. His death, fundamentally, is his birth. Here too he first lives through the experience of total forsakenness, in which he as a human person speaks openly of the Father. He does so at the moment when he no longer has the Father protectingly in the background. Up until now the Father had—so to speak—covered all the Son's expenses in this world. He was like a companion on a journey who pays for everything. That was the self-evident assumption in which the Lord spoke of the Father and lived in him. This assumption falls away at the Cross. Therefore the full openness, the simple truth about the Father becomes visible, as seen by the forsaken human being. The full distance of forsakenness leaves his whole gaze free to behold the divine distance of the Father, just as the exalted Lord in heaven will be able to utter the simple truth about the Father. The admixture in the truth, which was always present up to now, is done away with; now there is no more translation of heavenly into earthly truth, no adaptation between above and below, no parable, since the Lord has gone, on both sides, into the final openness and the final truth, into the final humanity and the final Divinity.

But while the Son, as a crucified human being, is seeking the Father, his openness toward the Father is yet surpassed by the openness of the Father himself, through his silence in which he accepts the Son's sacrifice. By veiling himself completely, the Father makes himself completely manifest. This openness will never be surpassed by anything else. He lets the Son's life on earth end in complete suffering, and that is the most eloquent thing the Son can say about the Father, because in his night he is nothing anymore but the mute word of the Father himself, that is, the acceptance of sacrifice in silence. It is the fulfilment of the agreement between Father and Son, which they made in love, and therefore it is the revelation of the innermost Being of God. It is the ultimate that mankind can sense of God's greatness.

16:26. *On that day you will ask in my name, and I do not tell you that I myself will ask the Father for you.*

That day of which the Lord speaks is first of all the day of the Cross. Many petitions will be made to the Father in the Son's name, and the Son will not support them. He will not support any petition that is self-seeking and hides itself behind the Son's cloak. He will not support the petitions of those sinners who have turned away from God, who still remember the possibility of prayer but use it, outside faith and love, like a magical formula. He will not support the petition of the disciple who stands nearby during the suffering and asks the Father in the Son's name to shorten the horrors of the Passion. He will not do so because he wants to bear the suffering perfectly. Nor will he support the petition of the other disciples, which will refer more to the impersonal aspects of the situation, the victory of Christianity and the good cause and the continuation of the work that has been begun. Nor, apparently, will he hear the requests of the disciples who are at a distance, because he has now laid everything, including his work, into the Father's hands.

In this the Lord's state on the Cross is like that of those in Purgatory: both are passion, passivity, a pure endurance. The Lord suffers this "purgatory" on earth for all those who, without him, would have deserved hell. Common to both sufferings is the state of being unable to act. And in both states it is impossible to gain an overall view of sin. In Purgatory the soul is thrown into a suffering of which it understands nothing at first, since it is only gradually *through* this suffering that it learns the weight of its own sin and thus is cleansed. The Lord on the Cross suffers for all unknown sins: in his suffering he does not see these sins; he only carries them. The soul only receives the total view at the end of its suffering, as the Lord receives it on Holy Saturday on his journey through hell, when the Father shows to him conquered sin. But even here there is no petition yet, but only the vision of what is.

Once we are in heaven, too, the Lord will no longer ask on our behalf, because then he will no longer need to mediate. Then we will be his brothers completely; he will no longer stand between us and the Father. We will have immediate access to the Father and will receive everything we ask of him in the name of the Son. In this the Son has not become superfluous or withdrawn behind us. Rather, it is a mystery of love between Father and Son: the Son no longer wants to insert himself in such a way that the Father cannot also immediately grant the petition of his brothers. The Son does not want to take this joy from the Father. He no longer needs to answer for the granting of our petitions, because the granting is already implicit and is already fulfilled in the fact that we are asking in the Son's name, in heaven.

The two forms of not asking stand in perfect opposition: on the Cross it is a stage of being totally shut off from the Father, and in heaven it is the state of being totally open to and at one with the Father. But this uttermost span from perfectly passive suffering to perfect glorification is the entire span of the Son, his wholly personal, inimitable way. And because it is *his* way alone, he opens it to everyone and gives everyone a share in it, in the transition from forsakenness to heaven. It is the way of the Son's return to the Father, via perfect surrender in the night of suffering to perfect surrender in the light of glorification.

16:27. *For the Father himself loves you, because you have loved me and have believed that I went out from God.*

The Father loves men, then, because they have loved the Son. This love of the Father's is no longer simply his love for the human being of creation, the being created by him; it is the Father's love for the Son that he carries over, just as it is, to mankind. Certainly God has loved man from the start as his creature, his work, and it was his love that determined God to keep him as his child under the discipline of his Fatherhood. Thus it was until the Son separated from the Father. From then on the Father's love changes, for now he loves mankind because he loves the Son who has become a man. It is a very different love from the first, a love without the strictness of righteousness, an almost uncritical love, just as we find it between father and son. It is there that the Father's new love arises, and thither also it flows. No longer is it a work to be furthered in the sense of an education and growth for his creatures. What is dear to the Father's heart from now on is the development of creation toward the Son. And when people love the Son it moves him; it creates for them a far different access to his heart than they had earlier. He loves these people so much, not only because they *have loved* the Son, but also because they *have believed that he went out from God.* In this having gone out lies the source of the Son's amazing love for the Father; therefore mankind, through this faith and through participating precisely in this mystery, has been inundated with love. They *are* in this primal love because they have believed in it; and since they live in this love, the Father can do no other but love them with the same love. It is almost like love's blindness, in which the Father no longer even wants to see mankind as sinners but as the brothers of his Son, participating, in faith and love, in his eternal life. This love of the Father is not actually the redemption. For in the latter the loveless sinner first stands opposite the God of love. But here the man who loves the Son

stands before the love of the Father and is loved by virtue of this
love.

16:28. *I went out from the Father and came into the world. I am leaving the
world once again and returning to the Father.*

The Lord compares his way from the Father to the world and his
return from the world to the Father. He stands, as it were, at a turning
point of his existence. He surveys both ways in their perfect clarity. He
sees that the two ways together are his way. His life is cast in both
directions: from the Father to the world and from the world to the
Father. By going out from the Father and coming into the world, he
separated himself from the Father. Even his life on earth up to this point,
in which he continually enjoyed the vision of the Father, was a life of
separation from the Father. But because he also lives in the other movement,
that of leaving the world and coming to the Father, he can also, in the
mode of separation, unite himself with the Father again and again. Thus
he has a twofold knowledge: he has the knowledge of a perfect human
being, who can see everything in purity and clarity and is not troubled
by any sin. And at the same time he is able to see and judge the world and
mankind as God, in unity with the Father. This is something he is always
able to do, not only when contemplating and praying but in the midst of
the crowd, in his most active work. With this twofold being and twofold
vision he is the Mediator: he mediates himself; he is his own Mediator. He
is so because his humanity is a completely transparent instrument for his
divinity. This mediation is also the prerequisite for all the *miracles* he works.
He works these miracles as God, not as a human being, and yet his humanity
has a share in all his miracles: he works them through his humanity,
insofar as it is the fully transparent, pliable medium of his divinity.

The first Christian miracle was the assent of the Mother, which was
the prelude to the miracle of the Incarnation. But Mary was not God but
a human being. In this very first Christian miracle God shows why he
always makes use of a believer for such a thing. In speaking her assent,
the Mother possessed no vision of God. She drew the strength for this
miracle (for which an eternal strength is needed) from faith, which
knows that its prerequisite is pure readiness. In this moment the Mother
believed that God could use her just as she was. He could work through

her without her being a hindrance. If God wanted to work through another person, the latter's sin would hinder him. Such a person would let some part of the miracle through, but part of its effect would be made impossible by his unbelief and his resistance to God. For God's entire work to be possible, the person would have to be completely permeable. He would have to be nothing more than the shell of the miracle mystery. Mary possessed perfect readiness, and therefore she could mediate the first Christian miracle. Being allowed to do so was a reward for her pure faith, but equally it was an act of the Father's love for the Son, to whom he wanted to make a gift of this perfect Mother. She who stood at the origin of the Christian miracle is given to the Son; she will also be present at all Christian miracles. And just as she was present, physically or in spirit, at all the Son's miracles, so all later miracles in the Church will never be worked without the Mother. No one who has worked miracles in the Church has undervalued Mary's assistance. Thus the Father adorns the Mother, so that she may be worthy of him, but also to give the Son joy, and finally to put continually before the Christian's eyes the highest possibility of readiness in faith.

But the final source and original precondition of all miracles lies in the perfect love between Father and Son, which also includes the decision of the Incarnation. This love is the eternal miracle from which all worldly miracles continually spring. First there is the miracle of the Mother, who as a human instrument is drawn into the love of God. Then come all the miracles of the Son, which well up one after another out of this inner-most point of love, and finally all miracles in the Church. During his whole earthly life the Son abides within this original source, even when he feels separated from the Father. Where the separation becomes greatest, in the night of the Cross, he still stands in the innermost center of love. There, more than ever, he is pure readiness for the will of the Father. In this night he works no miracle, for even he feels that the source of love has dried up. And yet all miracles will arise out of this night of no miracles, which contains the highest love and brings everything human, small and sinful into the source of love, in order to make even rebellious human nature pliant for the miracle. Out of the night of the Cross radiates the light of all miracles, great and small, revealed and hidden, in the future Church.

The Son comes from the source of the Father and enters the world. He comes pure, and he lives purely in this world. And he leaves it pure but laden with all the sins of the world, which he takes with him on his return to the Father. But he does not take them back to the Father as he encountered them—as our sins, our property—but as sin for which he has sacrificed himself, as expiated sin, as the infinite measure of our sins on which he has squandered the still more infinite measure of his love.

Until the Cross, then, he has a knowledge of sin, which on one hand he owes to his Godhead, and which on the other hand he possesses as the pure human being who does not know sin inwardly. Thus at the beginning, there is a contradiction between his knowledge of sin and sin itself as it really is. This contradiction is resolved on the Cross, where the Redeemer becomes inwardly acquainted with sin and really makes it his own. On the Cross he no longer distinguishes between himself and sin; he no longer seeks the culprit. Laden with this experience of sin, he returns to the Father. Therefore, he returns home richer than he left. On the Cross he endures sin as if it were directed against him personally, and it is directed against him, because it is directed against God. He receives it with his body as he suffers physically, and he feels it completely with his soul, because in the separation from God he no longer has the capacity to let it be absorbed in his love for the Father. He no longer has any way out; he can no longer alter anything. Just as his body is nailed down, so too all movement is taken from his soul. He only needs to hold out in order to have the experience of sin. Neither his whole divine knowledge nor his whole divine love sufficed to let him anticipate this experience, which can only be gained in suffering itself. For in knowledge one does not know what it means no longer to know. And in love one cannot guess what it means no longer to love. Previously he thought his love was great enough to love even more. But ultimately this "loving more" led to him being called on to "love no longer". That could not be experienced in advance. He could not imagine what the rebound of our sin on him would be when he was in God's night. This is an experience he takes back with him to the Father. Along with it, he takes back everything there is in the world, even the darkest things. Even these are now in him, so that there can no longer be an ultimate hindrance to love. He returns from the world to the Father with the whole sum of creation.

He not only takes back his own love to the Father; at the same time he restores his joy in his creation.

16:29. *Then his disciples said: See, now you speak openly and tell no more parables.*

Again the disciples have not understood the Lord. On the Cross and in heaven the Lord will speak openly and without parables. But the hour that he has promised is not yet come. Through each of their remarks, the disciples betray the fact that they do not adequately comprehend the Lord's words, that they are always hearing them from a different standpoint than that from which they are uttered. They have understood that he comes from the Father and is going to the Father: that he has, then, an eternal Being. But they imagine this eternity as an eternally continued existence in this world. They do not grasp the enormity of his words. They have indeed grasped the fact that they never really comprehend him, but they imagine this incomprehensibility as something merely fortuitous that one day will be resolved into a formula and a concept. That is why the *now* is so important for them. They snatch at it as if it were booty; they believe that in some *now* they can pin him down, at least partially. And yet earlier the Lord described his whole being as the opposite of anything fixed: as the twofold movement from the Father to the world and from the world to the Father. He is a pure movement of love because everything in him aims at and returns to the center, his love for the Father, which is so alive that it mocks any attempt to pin it down. The disciples think that because he is describing a way, he is no longer speaking in parables. They imagine this way as a straight, evident path. But although they are mistaken, and although they have again reached a point that is completely incomprehensible to them, they have nonetheless been expanded, for they are able to say, and say with faith:

16:30. *Now we know that you know everything and do not need someone to ask you. We believe that you came from God.*

When one person says to another "You know everything", what he means is primarily "You know everything that I know or could know, and you know it perhaps in a more perfect way than I." He is not saying "You know even what I cannot conceive of, what no human person can know." Even though the disciples concede that the Lord knows everything, this "everything" has a twofold limitation on their lips. There is the limitation that the disciples' own knowledge places on it, and that implied by what they think they have grasped in the Lord's words until now. They believe that he is no longer speaking in parables because they have finally grasped something of his knowledge. But they are still measuring everything by themselves, by their limited understanding; they find his knowledge so unprecedented because they themselves were able to see that it surpassed them. For them, his being above and beyond them corresponds to their inadequacy. They do not yet comprehend the true infinity of his knowledge—for it is an infinity that they simply could not assess using their measuring stick (which is that of their own failure). Every truth, and every word, has a limited meaning that opens itself to the unlimited meaning of God. For the present they see only the finite side of the Lord's word, not the infinity of divine truth.

You do not need someone to ask you. One poses questions in order to receive information or to reveal the ignorance of the person asked and make him aware of his deficiencies. The Lord requires no questions. How much they themselves need to ask questions is something that the disciples overlook. They see only that the Lord cannot be embarrassed by their questions or those of a learned man, and that no question is able to uncover a lack of knowledge in him. They attend to him with a touching acknowledgment of his knowledge. But they have no awareness of their own inadequacy. They are prepared to glorify their Master, but they do not wish the glorified One to put his finger on their deficiencies. They place a distance between themselves and the Lord. They do what many Christians do: as soon as they begin to believe, they accord the Lord a certain place. And by acknowledging the Lord, they justify themselves. They do not notice that their faith is scarcely at its beginning. It is good enough for them as it is, and they regard it as sufficient to acknowledge the Lord in his greatness. They put the basis of their faith in themselves and do not want to be disturbed in doing so. Therefore they seek to mollify the Lord at once by adding: *We believe that you came from God.* Again they are seeking in themselves reasons for believing in the Lord. They think they have found a key to God in themselves, because they have come across something through which they cannot fully see. They are like a schoolboy who understands three or four words of Arabic and nods his head whenever he sees an Arabic book: he knows about that. Basically they have no clear idea of what they understand by his coming from God.

CONSOLATION IN SUFFERING

16:31. *Jesus answered them: You believe now.*
The Lord acknowledges their faith. Of the value and the size of their faith he does not speak now. But he points out its boundaries by adding the *now.* It is not only an inwardly small faith, but also a faith of short duration. It is precisely this brevity that he underlines, because it is a sensitive issue. But in what is coming they will be able to remember that he himself saw this fleeting character of their faith. He does not tell them that the only faith that has duration stems from him. He lets everything be. He allows what is small and brief to have its place and span. He sees what is coming, and it is to this great thing that he turns his attention.

16:32. *Behold, the hour is coming, and it is already come, that each of you will be scattered to his own place, and you will leave me alone. And I am not alone, because the Father is with me.*
He says that this hour that is coming is already here. It is already here because what will happen in it has already begun: the scattering of the disciples. Although they still surround him they have nonetheless scattered from him, because their faith is not yet great enough to remain with him and accompany him continually. If their faith were a growing faith, this hour of scattering would not be approaching, for the scattering to which he now refers is not corporeal or spatial but spiritual.

They are scattered to their own places, each in his own direction. There are as many directions as there are disciples. They all have one thing in common: they have known hours of true devotion, but have never been so penetrated by the love of the Lord that they could even begin to have the courage and the will to remain by him really and continually. For remaining with him would have meant sharing his loneliness, standing by him even at that moment when he apparently is no longer standing by them.

You will leave me alone. The Lord would like to ask them not to leave him alone; he would like them to accompany his faith by their faith, his

293

darkened love by their love. This word of the Lord is no longer the mere perception of a fact, but an accusation on the part of a love that has spent itself prodigally and yet has found no corresponding reciprocal love. He does not stop at this accusation, but continues:

And I am not alone, because the Father is with me. He says clearly, now, when he is not yet in darkness, that it is impossible for him to be alone. Let all mankind turn against him: he is not alone, because the Father is with him. He says this looking ahead to the Cross, and he knows very well that there he will be forsaken. He will no longer feel the Father's love or—to make the suffering complete—the love of those who are his own. The Mother and John will be there, but he does not speak of them now; he passes over them, because they are already the loving believers whose faith is formed as he expects of them. He does not direct the accusation *you will leave me alone* at them, but at those who aver their faith to him and who yet possess only a narrow, personal faith that has its roots in themselves. It is interspersed with human fancies, human insurances and earthly hopes; it is not a surrender of the soul to him, but something on which the soul props itself and rests. All that will break apart in the face of the Cross, and therefore they will leave him alone.

But the Father will be with him. Even when he will not longer feel him, he will be there. He tells himself this one last time. He also explains it to the others: you will think I am forsaken. I myself will cry out: "My God, why have you forsaken me?" And yet I will not be alone. And the louder I cry out that the Father has forsaken me, the stronger will be the proof for you that the Father is with me. For then I will have completely kept the promise I made him. This was the promise of the Son that he gave the Father, namely, to suffer to the uttermost. And the Father proves his faithfulness by letting the Son suffer not halfway but perfectly. Thus the Cross will be the perfect proof of his love. The Son is happy because he knows that the Father will not shelter him, will not handle him as one whose capacity for suffering is not to be trusted. He will let him go to the furthest extreme, to the point below which there is nothing, and thus the Son will bring home to him all the love that is possible in the world.

16:33. *This I have said to you so that in me you may have peace. In the world you will have tribulation; but have trust, I have overcome the world.*

All these things, which are fundamentally full of sorrow, he has said to them so that they might have peace in him. By predicting everything he has taken the bitterness from what is coming for them. Even though the disciples will now forsake him, they will not need to grieve or to stare only at their sin and inadequacy. For the Lord knows everything. Rather, they will find peace in the Lord. In him they will receive insight into their own insufficiency, and in the face of his death they will have to come to terms with the fact that the Lord is dying for their sins, that the Redemption has been accomplished in them. As a result, something peaceful is laid in their souls: trust. The Lord's words might have incited them to accompany the Lord in spite of everything, to become heroes. But on the Cross there is no heroism. There is only the Lord, suffering in total loneliness. The role of the disciples in this is already outlined: they will participate in this loneliness by letting it become total. They are drawn into the mystery of the Cross, not to help carry it, not to give the Lord any ease but only to fill up the measure of his loneliness. And since they hear from the mouth of the Lord himself the role that they will play, that is, the inadequacy of those who have been touched but not penetrated by faith, they know what share they will have in the whole event.

That is their situation. It is perplexing. But it is a Christian situation. It is Christian in that the disciples are there to increase the Lord's forsakenness to the uttermost. It is Christian in the measure in which they thus learn the humility of knowing who they are, and what their faith, their goodwill, their love and hope are worth. Peace is inserted into this humility. For now they finally comprehend that they must put everything out of their hands in order to place everything in the hands of the Lord who—in his dying words, "Into your hands, Father, I commend my spirit"—will place their spirit as well as his into God's hands. It is this surrender that they will have to learn. They will have to learn that it will not do to let the Lord's sacrifice be enough; that it will not do to let the Lord hang alone on the Cross. That it will not do simply to let the Redemption happen to them passively. And yet they will do all these things, although they ought not. And everything they do will be *wrong* until the moment they are redeemed through the Lord's loneliness; it will be *right* from the moment that they are redeemed. Then their sin will be absorbed as humility into their new life of faith. The Lord does not tell them all this to calm them down and straighten everything that is crooked, but so that when all the confusion is past, they will remember his words and have peace in him. He tells them this also that he may appear as the one who knew everything in advance, even their betrayal and his complete forsakenness, and in order that every possible future sin may be anticipated and included in the sacrifice of the Cross. It will be a consolation for them that he knew and pardoned in advance even their future sin, which they did not want to admit and which they would commit nonetheless. And perhaps, by virtue of the Lord's foreknowledge, they may at some time really attain love. For the Lord also predicted their love. Then they will recognize it and love him for it.

In the world you will have tribulation. What they will receive from the Cross in the world will seem to be distress. All of them, each in his own way, will be *pressed* into following Christ. Every possible discipleship of the Lord on the way of the Cross is included and anticipated in his suffering. *But have trust, I have overcome the world.* They should take courage, because all the suffering that will overcome them will have the sign of genuineness: having been known, determined and suffered in advance by the Lord. And insofar as every possible suffering is included in his suffering, he has overcome the world. He overcame it on the Cross, where he died in total loneliness as the conquered and forsaken one. But he has fulfilled his commission, and at the moment in which he dies he can take the fulfilled mission back to the Father. He does not say: I will overcome the world. For he has already overcome it. He overcame it at the moment in which, pointing to the Cross, he separated himself from the Father.

PRAYER TO THE FATHER

PRAYER TO THE FATHER

17:1. *These words Jesus spoke. Then he lifted his eyes to heaven and said: Father, the hour has come. Glorify your Son, so that your Son may glorify you.* After the Lord in his farewell discourses has told the disciples the profoundest things he was able to reveal to them so far, he turns to the Father. He raises his eyes to heaven, as if to see him better. And yet he always possesses the vision of the Father, wherever he may turn his eyes. If he nonetheless solemnly raises his eyes to the Father, he does so in order to show the disciples that he, even as God-Man, regarded the Father as standing above him. This attitude also implies a certain turning away. He leaves the world and the disciples beneath him in order to be entirely free for prayer and for the Father, and so he teaches us that we too should leave everything that surrounds and occupies us in the world behind us in prayer. We should learn detachment. If we went to God with our everyday thoughts, we would never become really free for a true conversation with him; all the unrest of our cares and occupations would penetrate into God's stillness and prevent us from hearing and receiving completely without distraction. In conversation with God there must be moments when he finds us just as he expects us to be: simple readiness, simply his children. And though it is not easy to stand thus before God, totally stripped of everything of one's own, it nevertheless remains the prerequisite for our receiving his most beautiful gifts. It is not as though God had no interest in our earthly concerns, but we ought to have even more interest in his. In the course of the conversation, God will perhaps let us mention our cares and preoccupations too, but with a reverse charge, as it were. We turn from him, with his blessing, back to our daily life and continue to regard it with his eyes. But to do this we must first of all be able to be available for him. If we really are, he gives us the grace to preserve so much inner freedom, even in the midst of our everyday life, that we are his children always and in everything. The Lord too turns his gaze away from the world at first, in order later, in the Father, to draw the whole world into his prayer.

Father. The Lord fills this name with its whole significance: the whole being of the Father; but also his filial love, his obedience, his self-renewing mission, his whole being as Son. From the beginning of the prayer he places himself in the wholly naked, pure relation of Father and Son. He goes as far back as he can, to that source of love that arose at his departure from the Father, to the center of love where it revealed itself most purely, that is, in the decision of the Incarnation. That is where he locates himself. He is nothing but Son. All that is only earthly and worldly is switched off; everything is put back into its origin—not in the trinitarian origin in eternity, but in the origin where he becomes visible to us as the Son, in the origin of his mission of redemption. He locates himself in this most concrete origin, on which everything depends and which is his separation from the Father, and only from this vantage point do we see further, as it were, and understand that the difference between Father and Son has existed from all eternity.

The hour is here. As long as he spoke to human beings, his hour was always still coming. It was an hour in process of becoming. But now there is a coincidence of the eternal hour, the resolution between Father and Son, with the fixed hour within worldly time. The two hours have now coincided. The Lord does not repeat what has happened until now, how everything has developed until this moment; he merely asserts that the hour is come, and he affirms this hour. He does not outline or adorn it. All he says is "You are the Father" and "The hour has come". Two images stand at the beginning of his prayer: the image of Father and Son, and the image of commission and accomplishment. Nothing further. No security and no insurance, no emotional exaltation, no rapture. Nothing but this simple expression of manly obedience, the almost military report: the hour has come. As when two men who have promised something shake hands in silence in the hour of its execution, knowing what it means, without having to express the contents of their agreement again in words.

Glorify your son, that the Son may glorify you. This means, above all, "Let what you planned for him from all eternity be done to him; you cannot glorify him better than by letting what was resolved be perfectly accomplished in him." For there is nothing higher from the Son than this: to be permitted to do completely what the Father expects of him. When the

Father allows him to do the perfect deed, when he does not spare him anything, take anything away, or make anything easier, then he is showing the Son that he regards his love as perfect, that there is nothing to find fault with in it, that it is so perfect that it will be capable of bearing even perfect suffering. The glorification of the Son lies in the fact that he is really loved by the Father in such a way that he is allowed to bear anything. As perfect as the Son's love is its reception by the Father; he accepts it totally and without restriction. He proves this by submitting it to the harshest test. If two people love each other, and one suffers all he can for the other, then almost inevitably there comes a time when the beloved thinks that it is not enough, and that he can no longer endure seeing the lover suffer in his place. He will try to ease it as much as he can. Most definitely, as a human being, he will not allow another human being to endure total loneliness, to take an infinite suffering on himself. Perhaps the love between two human persons can even take a step or two in this direction. But it is wholly impossible for it to pursue this way to the end. Perfection is not attained. Only attempts are possible. But between Father and Son perfection has become reality. Here the Son is perfectly glorified by being perfectly abandoned by the Father. His love is accepted by the Father without any condition or restriction, for the Father is allowing him to demonstrate his love without any restriction. And the Son does not take on this glorification for himself, in order to win a glory that would find its goal in him, but only in order to become a sharer in a glory that he can at once give back to the Father: *That the Son may glorify you.*

When one person gives to another in love, the latter will keep the gift in order to leave the giver the joy of giving. He would be afraid of wounding him if he wanted to return the gift. He will only express thanks, and in this gratitude he will give the giver the joy of having given. Thus between human persons there remains this imperfection in love, that the one receiving does not want to have the gift for himself alone and yet must keep it out of love. The Son, on the other hand, can give back undivided the whole glory that he receives from the Father, without thereby wounding the Father. For the glory that he receives is the love of the Father, and this the Son returns to him in the form of his own love. It is simply an exchange of love, an ultimate sharing. The love does not stop either at the giver or at the receiver; it is the movement from one to the other, the mutual reflection of reciprocal love. In this love there is no trace of superiority in the one who gives, no trace of calculation in the one who receives, but pure humility, pure nakedness of spirit before one another, which surrenders itself completely. Thus the Son comes before the Father in his prayer, without referring to his performance until now, without a mention of his commission, his words, deeds and miracles. He comes thus stripped in order to be touched all over and entirely by the Father, by love and by suffering. He does not make the slightest reservation. He forgets everything else completely in order to stand in the exclusivity of love.

17:2. *Accordingly as you have given him power over all flesh, so that to each one you have given to him he may give eternal life.*

The Son's glorification through the Father in perfect suffering corresponds to the Father's glorification through the Son in perfect love. This latter is at the same time the work of redemption. For in accordance with the measure of love, and arising from it as its source, the Father has given the Son the power to lead all those entrusted to him to eternal life, through his solitary suffering of separation.

This power is *power over all flesh.* The Lord speaks at first only of flesh. Over against the flesh of those whom he wants to redeem he sets his own flesh, which he surrenders to suffering. Because he does not regard his own flesh, because he takes on himself every kind of agony that can come to him through the flesh, he receives power over all flesh. This power extends so far that nobody can now suffer without this suffering being open to being drawn, by the Lord's power, into his suffering. He has sacrificed his body and his life for love of the Father. He has offered this sacrifice so perfectly, that from now on he can take every human suffering into his own. There can no longer be any pain that he would not will to make a part of his own suffering. Whatever suffering a person must go through, whatever pain he may have incurred, the Lord is prepared to take it up into his sacrifice and thus let others have the benefit of it. Whether this pain came to existence in sin, and indeed is the direct consequence of sin, whether it has a completely indifferent cause or arises from a good intention, perhaps to spare another person suffering: whatever the occasion of suffering may be, the Lord wills to take what is painful into his sacrifice and lets the person who is suffering *endure* it for his glorification. He has this power over individual flesh. But he also has the power to remove suffering from flesh. Out of his own omnipotence he can ease the pains of a sufferer, perhaps by distracting him from them, by easing them for him in spirit—not by anesthetizing him spiritually, but by showing him how much greater God's love is than the suffering of the world. In this easing, the Lord, through his love, takes over the surplus suffering. This power too he has over flesh. Finally, he can also *give* sufferings on the basis of his omnipotence, sufferings that stem from him alone and do not correspond to any earthly model of sickness or accident. He himself distributes them for his own purposes, and such sufferings are not drawn into the Lord's only as an afterthought—they are within his suffering from the moment they are given. These sufferings become available on the Cross, to be granted as graces to those who desire to participate in the Cross.

But he has power not only over the suffering of the flesh, but also over its *instincts*. If a child has received baptism, it implies a seizure of power by the Lord that affects all the potentials of the child's flesh. When it begins to grow, and instincts and drives develop in him, the Lord also has power over these instincts. Thus even the child should learn to place them in the Lord's hands. The Lord makes use of the Church—the priest in confession, for example—to help the child surrender into the Lord's hands everything that may be impure in his wakening instinctual life, so that even now the Lord's grace may meet the child's flesh and flow through it, so to speak. The boy tormented by his drives and the anxious virgin must know that what is sensual in them is willed by God and has been purified by the Lord, that there is, therefore, a pure sensuality, and that even in the exercise of their awakening sensuality the Lord retains power over it. The Lord watches over both virginity and marriage. Virginity only has meaning when it is the surrender of the flesh into the Lord's power. Celibacy in the Church is like a signal for all Christians of the presence of the Lord's power over the flesh. Here it becomes visibly evident. Marriage for its part is only in proper order when the power of the Lord watches over both consummation and abstinence, and when its entire fruitfulness belongs to him. The shaping of this fruitfulness is not given to the human person but is subordinate to the Lord, because he has power over all flesh.

Even what is perverted in the instincts is not excepted from the Lord's power. Neither an inborn or acquired perversion of the instincts, nor a sinful abuse that has perhaps become a habit, removes the flesh from the power of the Lord. No perverse or devilish lusts can get so much power over the flesh of a human being that they displace the true ruler, the Lord. His power is always pure, and it is the will of his power that the flesh also be pure. This requirement of purity remains unconditional: no one can offer his spirit to the Lord and leave the flesh to his own weakness. By his power, which penetrates into everything, the Lord leaves no room open for the weakness of the flesh. He is the great, all-powerful corrective for the fallen world, in fallen flesh. In him everything that lies prostrate can lift itself up. His power is enough to break the most deep-seated habit, to make pure what is most impure. So great is this power of the Lord that no one can excuse himself; excesses are not a necessity for anyone to be able to live in health or joy. The power of the Lord over flesh is a wholly evident, almost physical power. This does not mean that the battle for purity will be easy. The Lord refers to his power while looking at the Cross. He knows, then, how near to the Cross is the problem of the instincts. He does not mask the difficulty. But we should know that he stands by us with all his power and help and thus with all his love. Love, purity and power are a unity in him. Our flesh is drawn into this unity. For it is a divine human, not a merely divine unity. The Lord too is a human person like us; he has flesh with fleshly instincts, even though these instincts are wholly absorbed in the purity of his love and his service. His final word to the disciples, "Have trust, I have overcome the world", contains the permanent victory of the Lord's spirit over the flesh. He encourages us to join in his victory. Thus too no one can tell the Lord that he needs to live out his sensuality in order to be spiritually alive. Perhaps one can imagine something of the sort outside Christianity and faith, where people believe that a person's spirit belongs to himself. Such people do not yet know that, in faith, the spirit too belongs to the Lord. And to be able to exercise his power over the flesh of a human person, the Lord needs power over his spirit. Only if he believes in the Lord's power does the human person permit him to exercise his power over the flesh.

Wherever the Lord requires renunciation, he is particularly near with his love. The harder such a renunciation is—perhaps after protracted enjoyment—the more strengthening is the offer of the Lord's love. At the very point where a person practices renunciation, he will experience the love of the Lord in a specially immediate way. For the more the Lord requires, the stronger he binds himself. And here too there can be greater joy in heaven over one repentant person than over many pure people who do not need repentance but who have also never experienced the Lord's love in a living way.

So that to each one you have given him he may give eternal life. Immediately following this discussion of the flesh the Lord speaks of the external life that he bestows. He sets the two in closest proximity. He does not pull them apart like two irreconcilable concepts. The Lord's power over all flesh extends to a power over external life. It is power over everything living in man, fleshly and spiritual, and the Lord has only accepted this power so that he can give us eternal life. We possess eternal life only through him, who has power over his own flesh: who sacrificed his flesh to the Father on the Cross, and in this sacrifice also offered him our sinful flesh along with its instincts. In this sacrifice his love outweighs the sum of our sins. And in his Cross he included not only our guilt but also all the potentialities and modes of appearance of our flesh itself. All ages from the nursling to the greybeard, all the flesh's ways of behavior, all its nuances—everything has some correspondence in him. Nothing fleshly is foreign to him; in every expression of earthly life he intervenes with his all-encompassing power.

He possesses all this power—over sickness and pain, instinct and sensuality, over all levels and ages of the flesh—only so that he can lead those who are entrusted to him to eternal life. He leads them there by taking them into his return to the Father, in that glorification in which he opens himself to the Father's love. Eternal life belongs originally to the Father, and from the very beginning the gift of the Father to the eternal Son was participation in his eternal life. Into this participation the Son leads all those whom the Father has given him, namely, all flesh. The Father, then, has given mankind to the Son, and it is over them that the Son exercises his power.

At first this handing over looks like a restriction. It could seem that the

Lord only had power over those who place their pains, instincts and age at his disposal, and that it is these people whom the Father has given over to the Son. They would give their flesh over to him because they had always been given over by the Father to the Son. But this restriction is straight away abolished, because the Lord's power extends not just over some flesh, but expressly over all flesh.

The flesh, and not only the spirit, will receive eternal life. It will rise from the dead. It is precisely the Lord's power over the flesh that meets the condition for our receiving eternal life. How this transition will occur, how our flesh and our instincts will enter into eternal life, remains beyond our ken. But it is certain that our flesh too will participate in eternal life. Everything about it will then be completely pure; everything will be absorbed in the Lord and his power, everything both personal and social. Human love will then be a communion in the Lord, in the Lord's spirit but no less in his flesh. Through his Eucharist the Lord draws us into eternal life through his flesh, even while we are still here below. It is here that he opens the doors and creates the transition. From out of eternal life he imparts his fleshly life to each host, which takes effect in the life of the communicant and leads that life into eternal life. So rich and infinite is the Lord's eternal life in the Father that he can make it overflow, through his eucharistic flesh, into every single earthly and fleshly life.

17:3. *But this is eternal life: That they recognize you, the only true God, and him whom you have sent, Jesus Christ.*

Eternal life, then, is a recognition. The Lord turns to the Father to speak this word, while he himself is still lingering in this world: he speaks from earth to heaven and thus indicates the movement of this recognition, this knowledge that contains eternal life. He does not say when the entry into eternal life will occur. And yet it is clear that the beginning of eternal life coincides with the beginning of the knowledge of God. Thus, in those who live in faith on earth, it has already begun. It is almost incomprehensible that eternal insight into God can be summarized in a couple of concepts, a couple of statements that the believer can learn in a few moments. And yet eternal life does begin in the human being, at the point where his true — that is, his believing and loving acknowledgment of God—begins, and both life and knowledge are inwardly designed for a mutual growth, a parallel, infinite increase.

God's eternal inward life is so alive that it cannot be passed on in any naturebound form, such as fleshly life. At the birth of eternal life the Holy Spirit always plays his part. He was there at the birth of the Son into the world, which, precisely because he took part in it, was an event of eternal life: a birth that led from the Father to the Father in the Holy Spirit, and therefore did not step out of eternal life at all. But because, all the same, it was a birth in our temporal world, we receive through this birth a share in eternal life. The Son possessed knowledge of the Father's eternal life even from eternity. But we would have had no access to it if he had not allowed his closed eternal life to suffer this kind of breach and opening that his earthly birth was. This mediation of eternal life into temporal life occurs on the one hand through the Holy Spirit, who effects the Incarnation, and on the other hand through the Son, who offers us eternal life in temporal human form, in words that we can understand, in a life that is like ours. Thus we gain access to a reality that would otherwise have remained completely closed to us; we receive knowledge of it.

This knowledge of God, which is eternal life and is mediated to us by the Son in the Holy Spirit, is not a mere dry communication of information but a true and immediate presentation of eternal life. Eternal life is reflected in the Son. What he reveals is not a human ideal, but divine, eternal life. But only faith enables us to grasp from within this divine aspect of the Lord. In itself, the sinlessness that is what we see first in him and before which we reverently bow, would remain only a human, perhaps a superhuman ideal, but never a revelation of eternal life. It would be an ideal; it would appear very positive to us. But it would actually offer only a negative of eternal life. With our concepts of life as we know it, both earthly and spiritual, we can in no way attain to the eternal life that the Lord reveals, no matter how we refine them. There are no slow transitions and approaches from worldly to eternal life. Only when we start with eternal life in faith, when we recognize eternal life in faith, do we gain access to this life itself, that is, to God and to the One he sent, Jesus Christ.

To emphasize this the Lord stresses: *You, the only true God.* All other gods contain no truth: they are formed by human beings and have one thing in common, that they are incapable of living. They are and remain a sort of projection of the temporal life into supertemporal dimensions. They have the outlines our wishes give them; they have perhaps qualities that we lack and that appear desirable to us; they can be excellently endowed with virtues and advantages. But there is one thing they never contain: life. For as projections of the human person they are inwardly untrue; they correspond to no worldly and no heavenly reality. They are lies. And therefore they are unfruitful. For truth and life are the same in the end. To know the *only true God* is *eternal life.*

Only he can be fruitful whose relation to God, to eternal life, is true. Of ourselves we creatures can be neither true nor living. We are not even capable of giving life to another creature; how much less, then, to a god! God alone has life, and he alone bestows it on his creatures. And he bestows it on them for them to pass it on. But to show that even then he remains the Lord of life, he does not let any isolated human person bring forth life; for that to happen a community must be established, a community that contains a mystery over which the two parents have no control, that surpasses their concepts and their known capacities and develops through them and in them without their agency. And what the parents mediate in this mystery is at first only earthly life; anything more than that is, again, an entirely new, pure gift of God. The mystery of the child's soul is hidden completely from the parents. It belongs to God alone, to whom life belongs. Thus the mystery of true fruitfulness that begets living life is not placed in any individual human being but entrusted only to a community, which always surpasses the sum of the individuals that form it. The mystery of the community itself remains in the hands of God. Every true community, that is, every community between Christians, comes from God and goes to God and is a life mystery in him. If those who belong to each other in God become aware of this community, they cannot avoid recognizing something of God and thus experiencing that in their life there is something of eternal life. In such community they discover that they do not create God as mankind creates false gods, but rather that God possesses the mystery of life and communicates it as he creates. In true community there is not only the mystery of the fruitfulness that creates new life in the form of a child, but also of that fruitfulness that brings into a unity everything that has been and thus gives the lovers true life. Of course, everyone who enters into a community believes he knows who he is. But through the community he will become different from what he was—indeed, fundamentally different. The I is transformed in the hands of the Thou, not only in the sense of mutual influence, but because, through the community, new life from God is given to and infused into the I. This newness cannot be explained only in terms of the I or only in terms of the Thou, but only in terms of the "more" that the community itself is and that signifies a participation in the eternal life of God. It is not adaptation to the will of the other or the new habits of life that transform the I, but love, and this is an influence and outpouring of God's eternal life, namely of God's love, if the lovers truly love—that is, are true Christians.

The only true God is so unique and so true that he causes all other gods to dissolve in him. A person can come to realize that he is not the measure of things, that there are a norm and an ideal above him to which he must sacrifice and devote himself. For example, he consecrates his life to love for the poor, who receive too little love in the world. Such a person might arrive at the idea of a god whose essential characteristic was to love the poor as they ought to be loved. But this ideal is just "a god"; it is not the only and true God, for it is still a finite and limited image, which lacks the fullness of eternal life. But God, who sees the efforts of this person, gives him grace and causes this "god" that the person has constructed to expand and be absorbed in the infinity of his eternal life. All the images that we form of God, which, without our knowing it, are touched by his grace, are ultimately dissolved into eternal life. God permits these beginnings in us; he allows us to start with limited human imaginings. He allows these "gods" in our soul, in order to inundate us even more thoroughly afterward when conversion comes and our imaginings must yield to his eternal life.

And him whom you have sent, Jesus Christ. In order to make the one true God recognizable to us, the Son had to show himself in human form. In the Son's Incarnation lies the origin of the explosive transition from "gods" to God. He is the bridge between finitude and infinity, and he lets us always look to God through his limited humanity: to himself who is

God and to God the Father. Through him we are drawn into eternal life without really noticing how. Through him everything that is closed opens up on all sides. Through him, the Mediator, we are finally what we ought to be: points within eternal life, no longer closed forms. So we become points and mediators opening onto the infinity of God. But as such God does not let us become submerged or carelessly overlooked, as if he did not need us; rather, he carefully sustains us within his eternal life as if we were really a part of it.

Eternal life is not a continuation of temporal life. It cannot be described if we start simply with the data of earthly life. If we take earthly life as a given datum and hold fast to this form of existence in order to explain what eternal life will be and what we shall be, experience, see and hear in heaven: if we want to interpret eternal life as an elevation and an intensification of earthly life, we are far from having felt the breath of eternal life. It is impossible to expand the boundaries of earthly life until one comes to eternal life. For this latter is the knowledge of God, which lies wholly in him, is not accessible to any creature and which he, humbling himself in Jesus Christ, reveals and communicates to us. Eternal life is not a movement by us toward God, but rather a movement by God toward us. It is not an expansion and inflation of our earthly existence, but an implosion from above that lasts until God can fill us with his eternity. Every pharisaism is excluded here. Jesus Christ, who lived out for us the perfect human life, is in no way the highest sum of what is human or the attainable perfection of a temporal life. He is eternal life itself, appearing on earth. He is the possibility of living in eternal life within time, and thus puts an end to all self-contained human ideals.

17:4. *I have glorified you on earth by finishing the work that you gave me to do.*

In the course of his whole life the Son has done nothing else but glorify the Father. His earthly life was nothing but glorification, for it was lived as a totality in love for the Father, in a love that never ceased to be the same from the moment in which the separation was decided until the moment of the Son's return to the Father. And glorification was the communicating of eternal life. For the Son represented the gift that he brought us, redemption, as the work of the Father—not as a work that could be observed within the world or even just within the Incarnation, but rather the Father's living work in which the Father perpetually reveals himself and lives. The Son says not only that he has glorified the Father on earth, but expressly that he has done so by finishing the Father's assigned work. He says this before the Cross, as if in an anticipation of its accomplishment. He acts thus because he knows that the suffering that is coming will rob him of the possibility of communication with the Father. He says to the Father now what he, as Son of God, has to say to him. For on the Cross, precisely in order exhaustively to live out his divine Sonhood, he will be only the Son of Man. He will effect the consummation but will no longer be able to utter it. So he summarizes his work now, before having lived through it. The Father must know even now that the Son clearly grasps the coming suffering, that he anticipates and affirms it even from his Incarnation and that there is no possibility of his love for the Father coming to a full stop. It is not as if he regarded his agreement with the Father as already fulfilled, but rather his growing love for the Father includes the growing suffering by way of anticipation, and he will complete the Father's work to the end: the redemption, that is, through which he wants to bring the Father a love from the world that is greater than the insult it has offered him. The completion of the work, then, lies in his human nature being stretched beyond its limits in a night of suffering in which no word with the Father will be possible any longer. Greatest strength and greatest weakness coincide in this consummation. And yet the end of the Lord's work will not be more perfect than its beginning and its continuation. We are inclined to judge everything as a preparation for the great, conclusive work, that is, perfect suffering. The Lord, on the other hand, says that the work *is* already completed, because his acceptance of the end, which occurs here expressly for the last time, is so perfect that it can no longer be revoked.

17:5. *And now glorify me, Father, with yourself, with the glory that I had with you before the being of this world.*

It is as if the Lord wanted to obliterate and pass over everything that will now follow, as if he wanted to direct the Father's attention even now on the future glorification and thus spare him separation and suffering; as if suffering should not be mentioned and the Father's gaze should be drawn to the coming glorification. *Glorify me,* thus he petitions the Father, take me up into you completely once more, so that I may be with you as I was before the world existed, only as your Son in the light of eternity, in your own light. When the Son petitions the Father thus he shows that for him the highest and best is to be with the Father as he was earlier and from all eternity. The Father should know that the fulfilment of this longing is the Son's deepest wish; that the Son is not striving away from him to something further or higher, but that for the Son the return to the First is also the Last. It is in this knowledge that the Father should endure the coming suffering. In the Son's suffering he should receive no feeling of alienation. The Son wants to savor suffering, forsakenness and night all alone, and while he does so the Father should feel in advance the joy of the Son's coming glorification with him. Here he resembles a pregnant woman who sends her husband away before the difficult part of the delivery and at the same time gives him things to do concerning the expected child. She promises him the child, and she wants him to live through the difficult time in the joy of hope. The Son knows that in the forsakenness of the Cross the Father cannot be with him tangibly. But he does not want the Father—humanly speaking—to miss him too much; rather, he should bridge the time of separation in the joy of the coming reunion. The Son also knows that he himself will no longer know of this reunion. That is one more reason for him to emphasize it again now, while he still can. It is as if his labor has already begun, but in such a way that the pains are still bearable. In the presence of the Father he acts as if he felt nothing yet. He speaks with him above and beyond suffering.

Before the being of this world everything was simply glory. This "before" is an eternal, not a temporal "before". And yet it is within this eternity that the resolution of the Incarnation once ripened, at the moment when the world existed and the sin in it surpassed the love for God, at the moment of the fall into sin. Seen in the light of the sin of all mankind, the first sin seems to have little importance. But even in the first sin, darkness triumphed over love for God; already the decision concerning the Incarnation had to be made. Until then, love in God had been completely untroubled. The Son rejoiced in the Father's creation, because it was good and because, as Son, he stands in a relation of admiring adoration to everything that the Father does. Even then he was gazing in reverence up at the Father, and although he, as Son, was as omniscient as the Father, it is as if he did not want to believe that the work of the Father could be disturbed. He did not want—humanly speaking—to look ahead to the potential future sin of the world. The glory between Father and Son was first attacked when the Son too had to understand what the sin of the world is, and could do nothing else but offer himself to the Father, to reestablish his honor in the world.

THE REVELATION OF THE NAME

17:6. I have revealed your name to the people whom you have given me out of the world. Yours they were, and you have given them to me, and they have kept your word.

The Son has *revealed* the name of the Father. He has given this name a new stamp and a new meaning in the world; he has breathed life into it. The Father has given the Son eternal life in eternity, and the Son has given to mankind the name of the Father as he is in eternity. Men knew the name of the Father already, but they knew it as something that, although it had to do with them, inwardly remained distant and strange to them. They knew the name of the Father as one knows a law or ordinance to which one is subject, as something superior in which one seeks shelter at certain critical times, from which one requests instruction and guidance in deliberately chosen moments, before which one bows the knee in respect and at a distance. But the Son has brought them a living Father, living even as a concept because he is understandable as his own Father, and still more because he is the Father of all. In himself he has united, collected and heaped up everything that the Father is, in order thus to show it to mankind, to spread it out before them, to increase their understanding of the Father. The earlier vision of the Father was like a point in heaven, something very high but unattainably distant. Now the Son places himself at the center of this distance; he takes it into himself and brings it to mankind in such a way that it becomes nearness. Every spatial and temporal distance of the Father is now overcome. Earlier it seemed to take a long time for a petition to reach God, and just as long for a response to follow. Now everything is there immediately, and the answer is given even before the question. Earlier, too, mankind's whole relationship to God seemed to be spread out over the mass of humanity, divided up by the number of human persons; only a fraction of God's grace touched the individual personally. Now, as soon as the Son appears, everything is there for everyone, and everything for each individual. There is no longer any chance in man's dealings with

God, and therefore no more calculation of chance. He has annihilated not only time and space but also number and measure, and thus really has distributed everything. Precisely by annihilating the importance of the individual, who is no longer an isolated petitioner but is rather absorbed in the community of love, he has annihilated the importance of the distinction of graces, since now everything belongs to everyone. Because the Father has come so near that only he is important now, because the name of God is from now on the name of the Father who has become living in each individual through the Son, the weight of the individual ego (which was, at base, its distance from God) disappears in the one love of the Father and of everyone for each other in the Father.

This name the Son has revealed to the people *whom you have given me out of the world*. They are those people whom God chose out of the world, the elect, who almost accidentally accompany the Lord on his earthly journey. They are not people with special gifts, chosen because of a unique providence that distinguishes them from other people and makes them something particular. They are human beings like all the others. Election is not a particular characteristic of theirs, not a quality that sets them apart from other people. When God chooses people it is almost like when someone suddenly, overcome by some great joy, decides to embrace the very first person he meets in his house. He does not know who it will be, whom he will meet, whether it will be his brother, or a servant, or a tax collector or a beggar. But it will be *that* person he will embrace. So it is with God's election. Seen from the human point of view it is entirely fortuitous whom his love encounters: nothing distinguishes the person. And yet all these people in this house already have something in common: they all have some connection with the house. But the relationships are very different. The brother will perhaps consider it right and proper that he is hugged and kissed. The acquaintance who happens to drop in for a visit may be slightly astonished, but he will not find it extraordinary. Another person, the tax collector, for example, will not understand what is happening to him. And yet they all have a relationship to the house. Thus this elective love of God affects the people who encounter it in a variety of ways, although the love is always the same. In the eyes of the world, to which the Son reveals the Father's name, they are there as if accidentally, and yet they are those whom the

Father has given to the Son, to whom the Father has already given a relationship with the Son. He has led them to the Son and given them to the Son, and because of this giving he meets them in the Son's grace. But this means that the Father gave them to the Son and the Son is giving them back to the Father by revealing the Father's name to them in a living way. Thus the choice of the elect is, as it were, an unselected choice. The chosen ones were human beings like all the others in the Father's world; they were not different in any respect from the others—and only this election by the Father, and thus also by the Son, makes them what they are: the elect.

But the people whom the Father gives to the Son are not quite the same as those whom the Son gives to the Father. For those whom the Father gives the Son have nothing distinctive about them except the Father's election. It is through election that the Father gives them to the Son. In their election they are still sinners, but by virtue of it they become aware of their sin in the light of election. They receive knowledge of God's word and thus also knowledge of the Father's love; burdened with this weight the Father gives them to the Son. The Son transforms them, makes different beings out of them, and these transformed beings he gives back to the Father: *Yours they were, and you have given them to me, and they have kept your word.* They belonged to the Father: not simply on the basis of creation, but on the basis of the Father's election. But this election is only a stage of development. Foreseen, they yet know nothing of this foresight; called, they initially do not hear this call. As yet they do not yet bear a visible stamp. This is how they belonged to the Father. They were like sheep in a flock: only the owner can tell them apart. They have no mark or brand on them for a stranger to see. The moment the Father gives them to the Son, the Son must imprint a visible sign upon them—not in order to be able to distinguish them better, for he knows his own as well as the Father knows them—but so that the Father may from now on recognize the stamp of the Son on them. For it is in this that the Father's joy in the elect consists. He does not recognize them more easily than before, but he now recognizes them as the ones given to the Son, who return with the Son's message. And the mark consists in this: that *they have kept your word.* This stamp now distinguishes them from the others. They have experienced and received an opening to

God, namely, faith. Not necessarily the outward confession of faith immediately, but first of all inner faith. They are people who have been opened, expanded. They have become a vessel, a shell, for something that is greater than their ego. They are people who can say that they no longer live, but Christ lives in them. This faith is living and effective in them, for it is impossible to preserve faith within oneself like an inert treasure of knowledge. This would certainly not be faith. What distinguishes the Christian faith from other modes of perception and enrichment of knowledge is that it is living and grows until it has become primary in a human person and the person is secondary. Then the *word* of God is truly *kept*. What a person does then is the work of faith, for it is now faith working directly in the person. Faith itself becomes a work. If it begins to operate in a person, it will be impossible to distinguish faith's work in him from his own work; he has become an instrument of faith so completely that when he speaks of himself, he is always simultaneously referring to the faith at the center of his soul. The personality is not extinguished; it is only made useful and enriched by the astounding possibility of having become free of oneself in order to live for love.

Before man believed, he was nature: flesh and blood and instincts. He did everything in order to serve his own ends. If he loved others, his love was an enhancement of his self. Whether alone or part of a couple or even in the bond of a family or performing some service to society: if the Lord and faith were lacking, everything exhibited a fundamental connection to the person's own ego, crippling the wings of love. However dramatic and intensive an earthly love may be, if it lacks faith, everything in it remains finite and limited, enveloped by the bands of nature. Only when faith is added does everything explode into an infinite meaning. Perhaps no outward alteration will be perceived in this love, perhaps it will end, in the world's eyes, in tragedy. But inwardly grace gives it a wholly different meaning. But what really frees man from himself and binds him to the Lord are the *sacraments*. They are the implacable divine discipline that, with gentle force, turns him away from himself and opens him to the Lord. Thus that inner transformation of love is given to the believer in the sacrament of marriage. Something similar happens in confession: when a non-Christian confesses his sins, perhaps to experience a certain relief or to break through his spiritual loneliness, or to participate in some way in what he considers the advantages of Christian confession, it can apparently produce a spiritual consolation in him. But even that is an illusion: his sin is not taken from him, but on the contrary falls back on him time and again. Instead of getting free of himself, he only enhances his own image of himself in his confession, and goes away with heightened loneliness. In sacramental confession, on the other hand, the acknowledgment of sin becomes simply opening to God, it remains secondary in relation to God's forgiveness, and thus the ego is really overpowered by, and taken up into, the Lord's love. And the other sacraments operate similarly.

This operation of the sacraments on us is the operation of the Lord; it consists in an opening of the entire person, in a strengthening and stirring up of the faith in him. It is not as if, after the reception of the sacraments, faith gradually sinks down again and the soul closes again, but rather faith and the sacraments continue to grow together. The operation of faith works parallel to the operation of the sacraments and also works outside of their reception. All three—the all-encompassing work of the Lord in his earthly humanity, his work in the sacraments and his work in faith—supplement each other to form a unity, and mutually assist one another.

The operation of faith in the soul is twofold: it is opening to God and passing-on of the gospel, mission to the world. But this twofold operation is a self-evident unity for the believer, just as his whole faith has the characteristic of simplicity and naturalness. It is the opposite of scruples and eccentricity. The whole direction of his life is now to look away from himself and his sin, to move toward the purity of the Lord. If someone wanted to keep looking back at himself, he would be like one who does not yet have faith. The person is standing, as it were, on a ridge; behind him lies the abyss of his antecedents, of his ego, of his sin, before him the abyss of God, of perfect grace. But he is afraid to fall into the abyss of God; that is why he so readily looks back at himself. He thinks he will not fall as far if he falls back into himself. To be able to walk on the ridge as a Christian he must always be ready to plunge into God's arms, to have only faith before his eyes. Then he belongs to those whom the Son names here when he says: *they have kept your word.* They stand where they ought to stand. They look to the Father, and expect everything from him.

17:7. *Now they have recognized that everything which you have given me comes from you.*

That the Son has everything from the Father is a truth which he has revealed to the disciples anew, time and again. But it is a long road from hearing to believing.

That a son receives life and distinctive nature from his human father, and that his attitude in life is determined by his father to a certain degree—this is something with which the disciples are familiar. In this sense they are used to seeking the father in the son. But they have never been able to imagine the Father of Christ. Actually they have always felt him to be a mystery that could not be approached or touched. Only in the Son's description of him does he draw closer in a human sense. But even here it was hard for them to see God as the Father behind the Son, through whom they thought they could see. It was a great temptation to interpret the Father as an extension, so to speak, of the Son's humanity (which they could grasp), as a sort of model or matrix of the Son. When, among mankind, a father and a son have worked in the same field, for example, as painters, one can form an idea of the father's work from the accomplishments of the son; one will be inclined to sense in the son's work a progress, a refining, a modernization of the father's style. With Christ, however, the difficulty is that *everything* that the Son has received from the Father comes from the Father himself; he sustains himself exclusively from the Father and from his substance. The Father possesses the entire perfection that the Son reveals; even the most peculiarly personal things that the Son shows about himself come from the Father. The Son is not only identical with the Father but has also received everything from him. He has disposal over everything belonging to the Father; he can reach into the Father's treasures for whatever he needs at any given moment. This possession on the part of the Son cannot be comprehended and described; it is so living and mobile that it mocks our hard-and-fast categories. It is openness to the Father, even exchange with the Father, unity of possession with the Father. Men tend to assess their property, both material and spiritual, whenever opportunity presents itself—to measure it, to define it in a sort of objectivity. However the true meaning of possession is to be seen in the way the Son has everything from the Father. Whatever people possess, insofar as they lock it up, is dead. This is true not only of their material property, but no less of their spiritual treasures. But in recognizing that the Son has everything from the Father, they ought to see that their possession too must remain a living one, which ought to open itself to the Lord just as continuously as the Son's possession opens itself to the Father. And just as the Father and the Son have everything in common and yet the possession of each remains inviolate, the possession of human beings ought to open itself to God and to mankind, without them having to be robbed of their possession.

It is believers who have this insight that the whole possession of the Son comes from the Father. They put their faith at the center of the Son's possession. A person who does not believe lives principally within himself, in his interests, his hobbies, his profession, his circle of friends. If he encounters the Lord and the demand of faith, he will either see this faith as a distant theoretical possibility that touches his previous life only externally and at most could be built into some remote corner of it, or he will recognize the real possibility of faith and comprehend that his whole life must receive a completely new center. He sees that something that was wholly alien to him until now must become what is most his own. Until this is attained, he goes through a kind of phase of self-alienation. His own life seems to him lifeless, obsolete, a thing of the past, while the new faith has not yet been built and acquired. Only when his life has again become the life of faith, when the Spirit of the Lord comes into it, does he celebrate a resurrection in the Lord. His existence has acquired a new meaning. But this new faith is implanted into the very mystery of the Son's complete dependence on the Father; it is inserted into the possession of the infinite Father, which at the same time is the infinite dispossession and expropriation of the Son. The recognition that the Son has everything from the Father and nothing from himself consists, exists and persists, in the human person, in faith's devotion to the Son. It is not a theoretical recognition, but a throwing of one's whole personal existence into this living possession of the Son. Here it becomes evident once again that any distinction between plain faith in God and faith in the Son is impossible. Christian faith stands in the middle between Father and Son, and thus at God's most intensive focal point, where his giving is most bountiful.

17:8. *For the words which you have given to me I have given to them, and they have received them and have recognized in truth that I have come forth from you, and they have believed that you sent me.*

The Son gave the Father's words to mankind just as he received them; he used words that were beyond mankind's capacity to understand them. For this was the nature of the words that God entrusted to the Son, and the Son was not allowed to diminish these words; he was not allowed to mutilate them in order to adapt them to human capabilities. He could not pass on one word and suppress another. He could not weaken any word that was too strong. He had to pass on the message exactly as he himself received it.

He had to juxtapose the word of justice to the word of love and let them be uttered together. He could not, then, allow justice to dissolve completely in love. Through his coming, indeed, love received precedence over justice. But justice could not appear to be a child's game. Nor could the Son edit the words of the Father, giving a strong word for the strong, a weak word for the weak. It is not the word that is adapted, but rather the person who is adapted to the word. Having become a human being and seen our weakness, he in his love and purity might have been tempted to use the heavenly words in a sense adapted to earth. But that was no part of his mission. For he himself was the Word of God; he embodied the living word of the Father. As the Father spoke it, so he must let it sound. Nor might he let the word come out drop by drop. Even when he proclaims one word after another, he keeps speaking unceasingly, inexorably; he never takes back a word he spoke the previous day because its effect was perhaps too strong. Wherever he discovers an opening in anyone, he takes possession of the place and will not rest until the Father's entire word has been introduced there.

The sole reason that he could allow the word to keep its entire greatness was because it was through his *life* that he undertook the mediation between heaven and earth, because, giving his love, he also gave the ability to understand. Thus he does not simply leave justice and love—he mediates it in his life's love. Thus it becomes something we can accept and understand. We would fear Purgatory if we did not see that it is a mystery of love. And so we submit to this process willingly, indeed with a longing for purification; we understand that justice must be satisfied within love. When a sinner repents of his sin and confesses it, it is finished with for this life and there is no need to return to it. But when he appears before God after death, this sin—which is certainly already pardoned—will come up once more, and he may still have to go through the fire for it. This twofold pardon seems hard to understand at first. But the first time the guilt is remitted; the second time is the as-yet-unfulfilled expiation. This purification goes to the very root of the sin. It is as if the possibility of committing this sin, that is, every form of evil concupiscence, must be burned out of the person's soul and life. But both forms of purification have their roots in the life of the Lord, in his living mediation of the Father's word. The sacraments, which were instituted in this life of his and are all a mediation and an outpouring of it, not only give the word of absolution but also, because they are life, effect the final rooting of grace in our life. They reach beyond this life into the loving operation of the final cleansing in Purgatory. Thus everywhere the Lord is the living mediation between God and us; he has one hand in the Father's hand, and holds the other out to us. He does so essentially through the sacraments, which fuse with our life wherever it is to turn to and open to God, and they work by giving us the life of Christ.

And because the sacraments are the instruments of the Lord, the Church and the hierarchy are also inserted into this work of the Son. The priest also has one hand in the hand of the Son and reaches out to mankind with the other. He too is expected to pass on the word of God undiminished, unweakened, as he receives it from the Lord. The priest as mediator is no way station but must lead immediately to the Lord, just as the Lord leads directly to the Father. That is why the priest's role is an official and impersonal one, for only thus can he be placed in the mediating movement between heaven and earth. To what extent the priest actually fills his office or can fail in it is another mystery that does not touch the primary fact: he has the authority and commission to draw everything he can reach into the movement toward God. This position should occasion no arrogance in the hierarchy, for it is an exposed and dangerous position; it is so involved in eliciting movement that it has no time to look at those who remain unmoved and make comparisons. One single thought must rule the priest: to bring as much as possible into the movement. The Son's depersonalization meant being in obedience to the Father; the priest's is to stand in obedience to the Son and to do what he commands and does. Anything else would be an instant betrayal of the mission.

God has instituted the perfect Son into his mission; the Son has instituted priests as imperfect, inadequate instruments. But there is one thing that they should and can do: place themselves in the movement of the Son and pass on without distortion the absolute word of God, which they have received absolutely and impersonally. Thus the priest must be depersonalized. He may not color the word, may not well-meaningly dilute it or mix it with words of his own. In preaching he must present at once the whole demand of God's word. He must not want to know better than the Lord. He should not construct any step-by-step paths of his own. He should always preserve God's standpoint, in love, naturally, but in the love of God and not in a falsely understood personal accommodation. It was God's accommodation to send us his Word, which spoke to us in a humanly understandable form, to each person in a way he could understand. But God's essence cannot be accommodated to the creaturely, and it is of this essence that his Word speaks to us. The priest must open each person he meets to God and plant in his heart the holy unrest that can never be avoided, because God will always be greater than the human person wishes, greater indeed than the most perfect creature can ever be. God is never the satisfying resolution of a human problem; for the self-sufficient he is always a storm and a whirlwind. God cannot be dissolved in any human life. That would not be the mediation that Christ brings. Anyone who imagined or said that everything was in perfect order between God and him would fail to know either what God is or what the human being is. God and creature never coincide in a halfway, equalizing peace.

The fact that the Lord founded a hierarchy on earth is ultimately based on the hierarchy in God himself. The Father stands at the beginning; the Son, who is identical with the Father, comes from him. And by becoming a human being and pointing out heaven from earth, he underlines once more this heavenly hierarchy. He himself is the movement pointing upward, this step from earth to heaven, because in heaven too he is the movement from himself to the Father. This heavenly hierarchy is a principle of order in God, not a valuation. Just as the Father comes before the Son, and yet there are no degrees in God, so too in the Church the priesthood comes before the lay state, without any valuation being suggested.

And they have received them. Men have received the word of the Lord in the Lord's Spirit, since they have recognized that they are thereby drawn into the infinite movement to the Father. For to recognize the word of God means to accept it; it means letting the word work as the seed that explodes everything finite: *And they have recognized in truth that I have come from you.* At the point where they are most sensitive, in the most secret part of their soul, they have grasped that their life up to now had no substance in itself, measured against this thing developing in them that is outgrowing and overtaking them on all sides. They have begun to understand that until now they have understood nothing of the truth. What constituted their life until now, what appeared to them to be truth, has begun to be nonessential. The old floor is pulled out from under them, and the new one is pure movement. They cannot rest on it. They have grasped that their future life must be mission, the movement of love, the greatest gift that God has given to mankind.

They have even grasped the twofold movement in the mission. *They have believed that you sent me.* When one human person kisses another in love he moves toward him, and after the kiss he moves away again. But this moving away is not a removal of love, but the return of the act of love into the state of love. So it is when the Father sends the Son, who touches mankind in his Incarnation. But it is just as much a part of the Son's mission to return into the Father's love. The kiss is the visible sign of love. It is not love itself, but only its revelation, its becoming visible in a sign. Love itself outlasts this brief deed, and the proof of love does not lie in the frequency of the act. The single act, once and for all, can be a completely valid proof of the durability of love. After the Son's return to him the Father is no less sacrificial, the Son no less devoted and sacrificed. But the love had to be shown and brought near at some point; at some point the sending had to occur outwardly. We would never have comprehended the love of God if the Father and the Son had not given us this sign. And so the Son had to come near to us. He did not want to become incarnate from out of the clouds, but by lowering himself in order to be conceived in the body of a virgin and born of her, to establish that entire inner contact with the human nature that he loved. This contact was not superfluous, because in love nothing that really serves love is superfluous, not even a kiss. It is never possible to restrict love to the "necessary measure". For love is welling, flowing life.

In carrying out the two movements—lowering himself to the lowest level at which we stood and at the same time always pointing up to the Father—the Son has demonstrated to us that our Christian life can and must be realized perfectly on our human level. Christianity does not lie high above us; it is not something for superhumans, but the possibility of living a life turned toward God and pointing to him in the most ordinary daily life on earth. The Son has left us everything that we are and that we ever were and will be; he left us what is lowly and needy, poverty as well as earthly love, but along with this he has opened us to his purposes. Outwardly everything in the world seems to be as it was before his coming. Inwardly everything has been turned around and is now contained in the movement toward God.

THE PRAYER FOR THE DISCIPLES

17:9. I pray for them. I do not pray for the world, but for those whom you have given me, because they are yours.

The Lord now turns to pray for those who are his own. His own are those whom the Father has given him. It is not enough for them to pray themselves. The Lord prays for them. They should pray for themselves and for others, but above all they should enter through praying into the world of prayer. They should participate in the conversation between Father and Son. This conversation is the primal prayer; in it the whole world of prayer is embodied. For the individual it is perhaps hard to know how much he should pray for himself and how much for others, how much he should think of his own salvation and how much he should lose himself for others. Were he to pray too much for others and not enough for himself, it might seem that he considered himself already justified or had no interest in his own salvation. Were he to pray too much for himself, he would be in danger of losing the Catholic spirit, which is a spirit of community. But when people know that the Lord is praying for their salvation, they also know that they are included in the world of prayer and that the Lord is thinking of them, and so they can devote themselves all the more in prayer to their fellow human beings. It is true that they should not neglect their own salvation, but they should do this more by fighting their faults than by speaking of their salvation to God in prayer and perhaps falling into a form of quietism. To avoid evil and strive for good is also a form of prayer. With the Lord's grace they should remove whatever displeases him in themselves and let him dwell in them. That suffices. For the Lord is praying for them. He enters into them where they have prepared a space for him, and since he presents himself to God in them, he also introduces them to God as those who are his own. Thus his prayer for individual Christians is a gift that he gives at the same time both to them and to God. It is a mystery of the Son's humility that he does not hesitate to enter into any individual in order to present him to the Father, although in doing so embroils himself in so much inadequacy.

I do not pray for the world. Here the world means those who have turned away. He does not pray for them, because they have no room for him, because he is not accepted by them and cannot present them to the Father from within their soul. As soon as there is an opening he can win a place for himself and present the person he has won to the Father. Certainly his commission is to redeem everyone. But he distinguishes very carefully between those turned toward him and those turned away, because his work is just developing. Those who today are turned away may turn to him tomorrow or the day after, and then belong to those who are his. He is speaking of a cross section in time. His grace is so omnipresent that it is alert continually and everywhere; it watches over each person to discern the moment when it can penetrate. In every prayer it is the Lord who is the suitor: he presses our suit with the Father but also the Father's with us. Perhaps we have resolved to turn away, but since we are living and hence changeable, since we are continually in motion, at some point we turn our weak spot toward him, which gives him the opportunity to penetrate us with his grace.

But for those whom you have given me. By praying for these, the Son completes what the Father began in them. The Father has given him people he recognizes as the gift of the Father, but whose part he takes, for whom he prays, so that the Father may recognize the Son in them. And he accomplishes his whole mission for each one by receiving each individual as the sinner for whom he was prepared to take up his whole path of life, his whole suffering. And thus, that is, redeemed, he gives him back to the Father. *I pray* on the Lord's lips means not only that he pleads with words for the salvation of the individual; it means that he commits himself totally on his behalf, includes each individual in his whole action and his whole contemplation.

When a human person wants to convert another, he has action and contemplation at his disposal. In action he can urge him, demonstrate and point out many things, introduce him to all Christian life. But in contemplation he can also pray for him, suffer and do penance for him. The Lord gives us his action—his Incarnation and his earthly life—but he also includes us in his prayerful contemplation of the Father. Thus the Church too has her action: caritative works, for example, but also preaching; and she has her contemplation: the prayer and sacrifice of individuals. Like the Lord, she distinguishes between those whom she can reach outwardly, because they come to church, and those whom she cannot reach but for whom she can offer herself inwardly. But this is a different distinction from that made by the Lord. The Church's waiting is, as it were, more *active* than the Lord's: the Lord waits until he can act. The Church, on the other hand, can undertake some preparatory activity in the meantime on behalf of those turned away: she can court them and wait for them in prayer and penance. She does so in the sure hope that they will one day belong to her. The Lord, however, *suffers* for all those who are turned away from him and continually deny him. He can only pray for them when he is in them. It belongs to the office of the Church to pray for them more than suffer for them; for too much voluntary suffering would hinder her in the action for which she has been commissioned. She cannot consume herself in suffering for everyone while a particular limited field of action is indicated to her.

Because they are yours. They are the Father's not only because the Father has given them to the Son, but even more because the Son is in them and the Father possesses nothing so much as the Son. This is explained more precisely in what follows.

17:10. *And all that is mine is yours, and what is yours is mine, and I am glorified in them.*

Everything that is the Son's is also the Father's. Therefore they belong to the Father in whom the Son lives and prays. But the reverse is also true: everything that belongs to the Father also belongs to the Son. Between the two there exists a perfect unity of possession, which always expresses itself in the unity of mission as well, since both have perfect right of disposal over one another. One of them never has to ask if the other agrees, for there is perfect understanding from all eternity. In this mutual agreement the Holy Spirit plays the role of facilitator. In him the Father and Son know that everything they possess and dispose over is one.

Even in God there are things that belong to the Persons and are peculiar to them, things that distinguish the Father who sends and the Son who is sent. These are part of the variety of their mission and task.

But even that which is the foundation of the Persons as such is common to all of them, and they know this communion in the Holy Spirit. Thus in a human household there are certain things that belong to the individual members of the family and others that all possess in common. But even what husband and wife possess personally belongs somehow to both, although under different titles: the husband disposes over all the property insofar as he is the head and has authority, and the wife insofar as she is devoted to the husband and runs the house. To the extent that love is the ultimate law between the two, authority on the one hand and the ministry of running the house on the other are dissolved in a relationship of mutual agreement. Thus in God, between the Father and the Son, there are things in common and things that are particular, but the things that are particular are common property through a fundamental agreement in the Holy Spirit. Human marriage hardly ever manifests this utmost communion, where there is no longer any reserve or secrets on either side, and where each person finds happiness in being completely transparent to and at the disposal of the other. But between Father and Son all commanding and obeying are completely submerged in love, and therefore too everything particular is also held in common, and the essence of this agreement is the Holy Spirit. It is he who causes every question and answer to disappear, as it were; it is he who absorbs them, because in his unity he embodies both and because he was present at the decision that initiated the Son's mission and Incarnation, as the assurance and guarantee of the unity of love that endured even in separation. He is not only the witness who can always testify to their unity even in separation, but also the ever-present token that, by its existence, testifies to their unity. It is as if he were brought forth by the agreement itself, just as the child of a marriage remains the perpetual guarantee and testimony of the real, consummated unity and agreement.

And I am glorified in them. The Son is glorified in everyone whom he brings to the Father. For the Son and the Father there can be no greater glorification than that the Father recognize the Son in each individual and the Son recognize in him what he is himself: the One who returns to the Father. Certainly the Son cannot recognize the Father as he is in himself in each individual Christian, but he can recognize in the Christian the most essential thing he received from the Father:

the mission, both the going forth from the Father and the return to him.

17:11. *And I am no longer in the world; and they are in the world, and I am going to you. Holy Father, keep them in your name which you have given me, that they may be one, as we are.*

From the moment that he begins to suffer, he is no longer in the world. As a sufferer he is worldless. As long as he was in the world as God and man together, in the unity of his divinity-humanity, he kept one side of his being turned to God, the other to the world. Thus he exemplified the perfect Christian that, by virtue of his mission, he had come to create. He became the prototype of what a Christian should be: a life in the midst of the world turned wholly to God in spirit. He lived out before us what he would like to see realized in us. That is how he was in the world. But now that the suffering is beginning, he says he is no longer in the world. Now he is beginning to be the man separated from the Father. He begins completely to conceal his divinity in the Father in order to suffer completely in his humanity. He is no longer the human being realizing the Christian mission of being at the same time wholly in the world and wholly in heaven. His former state was open to both sides; the state he is entering now will be wholly closed, both to God and to mankind. He will no longer be anything but an ego separated from love, and therefore from all contact, no longer accessible to love because it has sacrificed all its love to love. He will be robbed of every possibility of living and suffering together with other human beings, because that would still be love. He will even have to surrender faith in order to be naked and exposed in everything. Thus he no longer possesses God, because he has given God back to God, and he no longer possesses mankind because he has renounced faith, hope and love. He is nothing but suffering, pain, bitterness, weakness; he knows no way out. But he is never in despair, because all that he lacks is laid up in God. This is the Lord's worldlessness.

And they are in the world. They are in the new world, which the Lord has brought them through his Incarnation, in this new way of living toward heaven while in the world, in a transition from temporal into eternal life, in the vision of faith that at the same time is a vision of heaven, in a human love that is still imperfect but is moving toward the perfect love of the Father.

And I am going to you. The Son is going to the Father, but along a path that suddenly breaks off, that ceases to be a path in order to be nothing but pathlessness, surrender and suffering, and that in the midst of the most tempestuous events, will come to a standstill, as it were, under the Father's judgment presenting him as a target for sinners. The Son's whole life was a preparation for this path, but when the time comes there is only emptiness there, and he can no longer recognize anything of what he took on himself and had long prepared for. Until now he has appointed everything in him in readiness for this moment. Now he himself is the one who has been prepared and appointed to die; he is the purely passive element of the action that had formed his life. He is perfectly self-surrendered without experiencing the relief that self-surrender brings. He has been surpassed and can no longer surpass others in love. He is pulled down into the abyss, unable to guide his course, because everything of his own is in the Father's keeping. He is no longer anything but pure poverty and pure surrender. And yet he says: *I am going to you.* For the present he can still say it: on the path itself he will no longer be able to say it. He can say it in the foreknowledge that the greater part of his way will lie in this passivity of the Cross, where he will no longer walk the way but will only be dragged, where he will be so completely surrendered that one will meet, find, surprise him almost incomprehensibly along the path that no longer is a path, because it essentially goes nowhere. There he will be unavoidably encountered. He is like a person before an operation. Beforehand he has arranged everything: the doctor, the time, the payment; but now that he is lying on the table he no longer has control over himself, he is defenseless, surrendered to the knife. Thus the Lord now makes his arrangements for his return home. But soon he will be subject to others' arrangements. So great is his love for the Father that he now comprehends that he himself no longer counts for anything before the Father, but rather the surrender, the sacrifice, the pact, which is now everything and which completely overtakes and goes beyond him.

Holy Father, keep them in your name that you have given me. Earlier he merely called God his Father. Now he addresses him as Holy Father. He alters his speech; he wants to give the words he is now addressing to the

Father a particular emphasis: the accent of holiness, of the greatest earnestness. It is the solemn hour before the Cross when the Lord commends to the Father, with such great emphasis, the disciples who believe in him, because he himself on the Cross will no longer be able to keep and shelter them. He must take the Cross on himself alone, traverse suffering in loneliness; therefore he must renounce the comfort that would lie in his band of disciples. Thus he also puts his disciples along with the goods that he commends to the Father and deposits with him, as he has deposited his faith, his love and his hope with the Father. So he surrenders to the Father the dearest thing he possesses: those who, through him, believe in the Father. He gives them to the Father, asking him to keep them in his name, to bestow all his protection and all his love on them, *that they may be one* as Father and Son are one. He would like to know even now that they are in the Father's unity. He would like them to participate even now, even without feeling it, in the mystery that binds the essence of the Father with that of the Son. They are kept by the Father in such a way that he will be able to assume responsibility for them again afterward; afterward they themselves will be able to continue their way in him. But now he cannot take them with him; now they must be under safe protection. He must suffer the Cross alone, and they cannot and should not have part in his night. There is no immediate teaching for them here, and no strengthening to be experienced. Therefore he commends them to the Father. He will admit only his Mother and John to the Cross.

Thus he makes a division between those whom he loves unconditionally and who unconditionally love him, and those who have faith but cannot share his ultimate intimacy. To the first group belong those who, like John, will have a part in the Cross itself and whose presence there signifies their being drawn in; and those who, like the Mother, do not need to be drawn in because they are already in. Since her assent, the Mother is the Son's companion in everything that happens to him. She cannot be conceived as absent from any essential section of his life. It is of her essence to be where the Son is. Out of her physical motherhood there flows directly a spiritual motherhood. This is clear even from her assent, which she spoke in the Spirit and which allowed her body to become fruitful by the Spirit. She raised the Son and let him outgrow her. Thus the spiritual element of her Motherhood took precedence more and more, and when she finally appears as the Bride of Christ she is wholly devoted to her spiritual Motherhood. Others in the Church, following in the footsteps of the Mother, will walk this maternal way: brides of Christ who will renounce marriage for the sake of this motherhood. Such motherhood shows itself and testifies to itself best under the Cross, from which the Mother cannot be imagined absent.

John, on the other hand, belongs to those whom the Lord himself freely chooses and regards as fit to taste his entire mystery of suffering, in physical proximity. He cannot console the Lord through his love, and yet he is an essential part of the Son's loneliness on the Cross. This fact of the Lord's not being alone in the midst of his greatest forsakenness is a great mystery. John is not included merely so that he can later recount how it was or simply so that he might be a witness of the Lord's death. The mystery lies in the total weakness of the Son, who is all the weaker the more love there is in his vicinity. Anyone who dies alone dies in much less loneliness than if he has a loved one near him from whom he must take his leave and who is beginning to suffer his loss. Thus the Lord offers to God not only the sacrifice of his own death, but at the same time the sacrifice of the one who loves him, the friend present at the deathbed, the witness of his past life and of everything that was not attained in it. Thus John stands under the Cross, and it is the necessary consequence of their love in life that they love each other even to the point where they can no longer reach each other. Both are now out of reach, for John must ask the Father to accept the Son's sacrifice, but the Lord no longer has the strength to commend either himself or the beloved disciple to God.

These two, the Mother and the disciple, are thus drawn visibly into the sacrifice itself. The others are those who are laid up in the sacrifice. All those through whom the Lord wants to work, he inserts into the mystery of the Cross—not simply as people who are to be redeemed, like the great mass, but as disciples who believe in him and have his commission. He puts them where his faith, his love and his hope are already laid up.

He desires the Father to keep all these *in his name* as in a refuge, and also *by virtue of his name* that he gives to the Son. The Lord's word has this meaning also. The name means neither his being God nor his being Father, but something relative: the living relation between Father and

Son, the boundary that encompasses everything that is the Son's. There is almost something administrative about it: he writes his disciples down on the Father's account. There they will be best looked after, in the controlling hands of the Father, in the area of his power. He no longer separates what is the Father's from what is his: it is the name *that you gave me.* Everything is now to be taken into the Father's stewardship. Property is not divided between the father of a family and his first male descendant; rather, the father stewards the whole, in readiness for the son.

17:12. *While I was with them I kept them in your name that you have given me. I have guarded them and none of them has been lost except the son of corruption, so that the Scripture may be fulfilled.*

The Son emphasizes that, as long as he was in the world, he kept and protected the believers in the name of the Father. During his entire path it was his goal to strengthen the faith of those whom he had awakened to faith, to put himself in the background in order to let the Father come forth all the more clearly. Just as he always emphasized that what he is and what he has comes from the Father, he also held together those who repented in the name of the Father. The name of the Father was more important to him than his own name. He did not want to be glorified by them; he taught them to glorify the Father in everything. Both in seeking out and in protecting his own, then, he continually emphasized the spirit of his mission: to bring back to the Father as lovers those who had turned away from him in sin.

The Covenant in which the Son holds mankind together is the Old Covenant that the Father once made with them. It is not a second, different Covenant beside the Covenant of the Father, but the perfection and crowning of the Father's Covenant, through which he glorifies the Father's name among mankind. He does not put his name as a new name next to the Father's. But precisely through this perfect love for the Father, the Son leads the Old Covenant beyond itself and expands righteousness into love, since the Father now sees nothing but the love of the Son, which has fulfilled all righteousness and itself accomplishes the movement from the Old to the New Covenant.

In your name which you have given me. In the previous verse the Son has surrendered the believers into the Father's hand, so that he may know

334

that they are kept safe there. Now, in the same words, he says almost the opposite: he himself has protected them in the world, in the name of the Father—that is, on the Father's behalf, never forgetting how completely they belong to the Father. He has looked after, protected and counted them for the Father, as the Father's deputy. And not only in what he taught them, but also by bringing them back, opened toward himself, but always with their gaze on the Father. For he never let them cling to his human side, which he had to show them; he always led them over immediately to his divine side. He would not tolerate them to stand still until, through him, they had attained to the Father. In this he showed that he does not have a poised center, that he does not stand halfway between God and mankind. Consequently, he could not lead them *into* any center, but *out of* every center to the Ever-Greater that he as God contains, in order thus to lead them to the Father. This is his way of *protecting* them.

He received them from the Father as unbelievers, yet predestined for faith. They were part of the flock. He had to imprint his own stamp in them in order to let the Father's stamp become visible. In doing so he drew them into what he was, showing them that they could not stop at him but were to go through him to the Father. *And none of them has been lost.* He has guarded all whom he had to save and can bring them back to the Father as transformed things, as Christians. *Except for the son of corruption,* except for the one whom he cannot now give back to the Father, because he no longer belongs to the flock. He cannot present him to the Father now as one who has been saved, because Judas is still going to betray him: if he is to be saved, it can only be through the Cross itself. For Judas' deed is still before him, and the contemplated sin is worse than the sin already committed. As long as someone wants to sin, he cannot repent. Once he has committed the sin, there can be an opening for repentance and confession. Beforehand he is capable of no repentance, and therefore of no pardon and no absolution. Someone who dies at a moment when he is firmly resolved to commit a serious sin will have a harder judgment than one who has already committed it, because the deed no longer blocks the latter's way to conversion. *So that Scripture may be fulfilled.* Scripture is fulfilled now, *before* the Cross. Every passage of Scripture is not fulfilled all the time. It is up to the Lord to decide when he wants what to be fulfilled.

17:13. *But now I am coming to you; and this I say in the world, so that they may have my joy to the full within themselves.*

I am coming to you: thus the Son prays to the Father. But this coming is not simply a decision of the Son's. It is a mutual decision of Father and Son. Now that the Son is returning, the Father takes him up, draws him to himself, receives him with open arms. He even transforms him by giving him, his Son, the characteristics of someone returning, and himself adopting the marks of expectation. Not only is the Son's longing expressed in these words, but also the Father's longing to have him with him again. He shows it to the Son now, before the Cross, while the Son is still receptive and sensitive to the yearning joy of the Father, in which his thankfulness to the Son is expressed. It is not only gratitude for the completed mission, but still more the gratitude of him who will be greatly enriched through the Son's return. Certainly the Son gave the Father an extravagant gift at their parting, when he promised to bring back the redeemed world. But this gift is almost surpassed by the Son's return to the Father itself. The Father felt enriched by the Son, even by the separation, although it contained their mutual sacrifice, but he knows himself to be still more enriched through the Son's return. The Father cannot live any longer, as it were, without the Son; he can hardly wait to have the Son completely with him again, to be able once more to give himself wholly to the Son, to give him joy, to possess him wholly again. When they find each other again, they will meet in a new joy, because now the whole redeemed world will be contained in their love, and they themselves will be enriched through the sacrifice of separation and the joy of reunion. Thus the Father becomes the prototype of faith, love and hope: he has placed everything on the Son and now receives back perfect fulfilment, which comes to its final unfolding only in him, the Father. That is evident even now, although the suffering is still to come. The Father draws the Son to him through the suffering. They are almost like two lovers who have lived long in a happy marriage and now, before a long separation, consider their love and reaffirm it for the future beyond the coming separation, throwing out an anchor into the future or into eternity to secure it there. However bitter the time of loneliness may be, something remains that draws them together over and above all separation.

They retain a grasp of past and future: when they see each other again years from now, they will be different people; but in the meantime their love will also have grown and become deeper, and in this love they will rediscover each other as the Persons they always were. Thus this word of the Son to the Father contains at once both the parting and the return; both in One, in love. It expresses a perfect fulfilment of love. When human beings separate and vow love to one another, a love conquering all distance and outlasting everything, they can do so only in God; they are striving to anchor their love in God. Here it is the love of God himself that lays anchor in itself. Sacrifice, forsakenness and darkness are not only indicated and aspired to in the absoluteness of God's love but fulfilled reality; they are anchored in the mutual being of Father and Son—so much so that the communication is almost incidental, because everything is primarily lived, indeed, simply *is*, at the level of essence and being.

Now, says the Lord, he is coming to the Father. Again he sees beyond the suffering. He dates his return from today. He only wants to settle two points of this path: the "now", the beginning; and the point of arrival. The fact that the path leads through total forsakenness is something he passes over as if it were not worth mentioning.

And this I say in the world. Of himself he has just said that he is no longer in the world. He regards himself as already on the way of suffering. But he still touches his disciples with words that, for them, stem from this world and are spoken in this world, because in spite of his prophecy they still have no inkling of the suffering. They see, of course, how earnestly he prays, and they listen to him with respect, but their understanding remains far behind. They do grasp that they are referred to, that they are being specially commended to God. But what they do not see is that the abyss of suffering is opening before them at the very moment that they are being spared it.

They are spared it, for they will not experience suffering as something into which they are dragged, although it affects them intimately. To plunge into suffering requires the perfect love that goes back and forth between John and the Lord. The rest of the disciples are on a different level. They are being kept for another role, a role that always recurs in

337

the Church. John's path implies a kind of preference on the part of the Lord: he is the one whom the Lord loves. It is as if he is hidden under a veil of love that, while it does not make him invisible, certainly makes him untouchable. He is living one possibility of Christian life, but not a universally accessible one. The other disciples are only taken along a certain distance. Part of the Cross becomes visible to them; for the rest they are entrusted to the protection of the Father. One cannot say that the Lord loves the other disciples less than John, but he loves them very differently. John is like a presentiment, a sketch of the relationship between the Lord and human beings in heaven, who already share everything with him, whereas the others on earth are still encased in their crude worldly shell.

The Lord speaks these words *in the world* because they are felt by the disciples to stem totally from this world. They understand the Lord's long conversation with the Father, which clearly has to do with them as well, from the standpoint of the world. What they need to grasp in this moment is that the Lord is entrusting them to the Father. The Lord commends them to the Father, who is invisible to them but with whom he converses as if he sees him face to face. That suffices *so that they may have my joy to the full within themselves.* The joy that they receive in full here is the joy of Christian life. It is the distinctively Christian joy, because it comes from the Father and returns to him and because it describes exactly that way that the Lord has marked out. It is a joy that penetrates the disciples.

This Christian joy lives on the outskirts of the Cross, and yet it is a joy in its fullness. Essentially it follows a path, not resting in itself but permeating everything, and yet it is in fullness because it is always given in extravagant measure and consequently must be passed on by the person who receives it. It is first of all joy in the *sacrament,* which is always a source of both grace and joy. Thus baptism contains a joy of fullness. Although the child does not know it, an incredible source of joy lies in the fact that it has been freed from original sin and elevated to be a child of God. Many sacramental and Christian joys cannot be subjectively defined as joys. The gift of grace operates in the receiver even if he does not consciously feel it as such. At baptism, the friends and relatives certainly rejoice, and someday the child will rejoice at having been separated from original sin and from the unbaptized, and at possessing the God-given receptivity for new graces. Thus it is possible for sacramental and personal joy to join in such an experiential bond. But it is not necessary. For the river of joy that flows from the sacraments comes directly from the Lord, always in generous measure, overflowing. He who receives knows this in faith: he knows that in the sacrament he receives a share in the joy of the Lord, and it does not matter whether his subjective experience of it is more or less strong. Knowing this, he also knows that he is bound to pass on the joys he has received: indeed, that ultimately they are meant not for him alone but for others through him. They are to become sources of faith for others too. Thus the sacrament effects a mysterious transformation. Someone can approach a sacrament as a nominal Christian, with narrow, perhaps listless faith; but in the moment that he really receives, that is, receives in faith, his reception ceases to be a mere "obligation" and becomes a reception of joy and of joy in its fullness. Perhaps a dry, theoretical faith prompted the Christian to approach, but the sacramental reception has transformed this dessicated faith into a living, welling fullness, into something that belongs to the Lord and no longer to the man. In the anonymity of the sacraments, the Lord's personal side works itself out: the small, miserable faith that was man's and that led him to a nonliving, abstract Lord is suddenly replaced by participation in the trust of the Lord himself. This new grace depersonalizes us in a different way. Now it is *his* personal side that lives in us. Through this he makes us more than ever a member of his Church, that is, a member of the community of the faithful who is perhaps less sharply defined as a personality, but with all the more sense of responsibility.

The way the Lord hands over the disciples to the Father before his suffering belongs to the realm of his sacramental deeds, insofar as it includes confession, Eucharist and confirmation in itself, leaving them behind like a reserve. Outwardly a pause is inserted here; the Lord goes away, and what is sacramental is suspended, but in such a way that, like Christians themselves, it is laid up in God and can later be taken up again. This time of transition could be compared with the time of childhood between baptism and First Communion. In these years the child is not yet ripe for many things; there is much it does not yet comprehend and therefore cannot yet receive. But it is baptized, and consequently it lives in expectation of what is coming; it is a child of God and is free to be a child with joy, especially since it is being kept safe for later sacramental life. In a similar fashion the disciples are now being kept safe. They are not ripe for the suffering; only the later sacramental life will open their inner eyes for it. If a child were to die before receiving its First Communion, it would seem that a joy had been kept from it. But this joy is reserved for it in God: there the child will encounter it. On earth it still lacks the understanding necessary for the sacraments, namely, that a certain readiness for sacrifice is essential. The disciples are also lacking in the requisite measure of this insight. But this at least they should understand even now: that their joy goes beyond them, and that it is something that belongs to the Church and that can exist only in the mode of abundance.

Along with the sacramental, the Lord gives the *personal* joy of the Christian, who rejoices above all in the Lord's nature, receives at all points from the abundance of the Lord's joy and is privileged to draw his own small joys into this great Christian joy. His everyday joy, his joy in his family, his calling, in celebrations, in friends, in work and recreation, in action and rest: all these joys can enter into the joy of the Lord. But this joy of the Lord is always the constant precondition for true human joys. Only when an earthly enjoyment stands in the light of the Lord's joy is it more than a tedious egotistical pleasure, and only then does it really deserve the name of joy. A piece of bread, divided among beloved friends, gives more joy than a luxurious banquet consumed alone. Witty company, treating itself to all the pleasures of the intellect, remains deadly boring for the believer, whereas a good conversation with simple people who understand love gives him deep joy. For the Christian, then, in the last analysis, all joy is anchored in the Lord and passes at once into joy in the community of saints. All earthly joys can be joined to this joy; none need be excluded from this relation.

It is touching that the Lord gives his own his joy *in the world.* He wants them to possess what they possess in joy: including the world, in which they exist and which is a creation of the Father. He does not separate his own from the world in order to give them his joy. He himself announces it and gives it when he has already separated himself from the world. But he does not separate his own at the same time.

The believers who do not participate in the Cross remain in the world, kept safe by the Father in the joy of the world. But the Lord takes John into his suffering. Even now he points out, in a different fashion than with Mary and Martha, the difference between the ways of the world and the ways of departing from the world. The distinction drawn here is not that between suffering and not suffering, but the distinction, within the Christian life, between the life of the laity in the world and the life of priests and religious in the state of having died to this world. As if the Lord said: You who remain in the world can share in my perfect joy; and you, John, I will take with me, to set you apart with me in suffering; it contains my loneliness, indeed, but also the presence of my Mother. Both those who remain and those who are taken along receive something so precious that in each case the others almost seem to be at a disadvantage, but it is simply that the fullness of the mysteries is distributed differently. The ordinary faithful, along with their faith, are kept safe with God for the whole period of their life. But the chosen one, who is to walk the special and difficult way, has the joy of knowing that the others in the world have joy. In the loneliness of faith that both ways have in common there is an exchange between the two forms of life: the chosen one and those who remain live in the same faith, in the same Lord, in the same Church, and they are nourished by the same substance, which is the substance of the Lord.

17:14. *I have given them your word, and the world has hated them, because they are not of the world, as I am not of the world.*

The Lord has *given* to his own everything he has received from the Father. Thus he has also given them himself, who is the Word of the Father. He has come with all his knowledge and all his perception of God, which he possesses even as a human being, and which he never gives as his property but always as the property of the Father. When he gives himself to the world, he gives himself as the one who belongs to God. He does not give himself airs when he gives; he makes no sensation about it; he is not concerned with his own well-being. The human foibles that we all have in giving do not encumber him, because when he offers himself and gives himself away, it is not as a personality, a private existence or an autonomous ego, but only as the gift of the Father. By giving himself thus, he fulfills what he promised to the Father. When a human person gives alms, he cannot help calculating if he still has enough for himself. But if he is only giving out what he has been given to distribute, he does not need to calculate anything. It is thus that the Lord gives, as if he were simply entrusted to himself by the Father to give himself to the world.

He gives the *word,* and he gives himself: the two are one. He gives the word to mankind in such a way that they understand it, but also in such a way that they do not understand it. With their understanding they can always grasp something of his word, which becomes part of their spiritual possession. But each time there is the infinite overflow that overwhelms them, that they cannot grasp with the mere understanding. Thus his word becomes, in them, a parable of his grace, of which something is always become visible but most remains hidden and continues to work in hiddenness, perhaps to become visible later on. But both the visible and the invisible bear the mark of intimacy between Father and Son: they are always more than mankind expected.

In his pronouncement: *I have given them your word,* the Lord recalls the origin of creation, when the Father said, "Let there be . . . !" and everything came into being. In the same spirit he passes on the Father's word to humanity: this word is the origin, the beginning, that which is inchoate. In one person he has already attained much through the word, in another nothing so far; but whatever the state of success may be, in each one he has planted something that is greater than the person himself. He has placed in him the Father's word, which is faith, love and hope. Perhaps they know that they believe, or perhaps they do not know. Perhaps they are aware of their hope and see how it grows; perhaps they have no inkling of it. Perhaps they rejoice in love, and perhaps they love without knowing it. But what is ineradicable in them is the fact that they are *loved,* the beloved of the Father in the Son. And that in this being loved by the Father in the Son, they contain the entire love of the Son for the Father. But the Son gives them this love so completely in the name of the Father that he almost lets mankind forget his office as Mediator. One almost overlooks the fact that he has offered his love as a price to compensate for the sin of the world. In this extravagance of love he becomes wholly the Incarnation of the Father's love. In this pronouncement, *I have given them your word,* lies all the Lord's utmost humility and self-effacement. And it is only because the Lord loves thus that mankind can serve in his name. When a human being says "It is no longer I who live, but Christ lives in me", or when someone says "He must increase, I must decrease", it is only possible because the Lord gives himself as the One given by the Father, because out of his own gift he makes a gift from the Father. He gives himself as the Word of the Father.

And the world has hated them. Here he takes the world as it was before he came; as the world of sinners who want to know nothing of him; as the world that denied him even before he came; as the world closed and encapsulated in itself that no longer possessed an opening to God; as the world of self-sufficiency, quietism and pharisaism that does not want to move, that wants to remain where it is and as it is. It hates everything that disturbs its peace, that wants it to move. Each day is structured according to the schema of yesterday; everything new is fitted into the old. This world wants to form itself, to be its own creator. Perhaps God created it in the beginning, but that was a long time ago; the world has long since begun to create itself. It was a sort of struggle between God and the world. Because God was the first and the mightiest, he formed the world. But as soon as it was formed, it reformed God and put him where it found convenient. Now the most important thing has been achieved, a certain safety and stability, and any new upheavals must be avoided. And if the world does not regard itself as perfect, it is nonetheless full of hope that everything will develop for the better. It believes unswervingly in its own progress. It is convinced that it can handle its own existence. This world has broken off every relation to God; it is godless. Even though it still talks of God, it has silenced him. And when the Son came and brought the Father's word, the world saw no necessity to alter anything because of his arrival.

That is the world that hated the believers, and indeed has hated them from the beginning. It did so *because they are not of the world, as I am not of the world.* Between the believers and the Lord there is a unity and a bond. It is not of this world; it is not visible; it can neither be described, determined nor shaken by the world, because it lies in God. It lies so much in God that no one who shares in it could explain it to one who has turned away. It can only become visible to him who does not live in the world and receives, from the experienced unity itself, insight into its power. The difference between outward explanation and inward experience is as great as between the description of a kiss and a kiss that one receives. If one wanted to explain the Lord's grace to a stranger, he would have to be thrilled by it, want to be consumed in its service and to surrender everything of his own to it. Otherwise it would be only an unusual topic of conversation for him. But the world does not know grace, because grace is not of the world.

None of the real faithful are of the world. Some of them attain to a clear perception of the other world; others remain in this world but sense with some part of their being that there is something other than this world. The more transparent this other, divine world becomes to a person, the more he feels bound, both in action and contemplation, to live in relation to this divine world in the service of the Church.

This does not mean that anyone who wants to live completely in the Lord should break with the world in order to enter the cloister. Perhaps his task is to let his perception of the other world become visible precisely in this world. For the Lord also stands in the midst of the world to proclaim the Father there. As the Lord turns one countenance to the Father and the other to the world, so too this disciple would have to exist on a knife-edge: without leaving the world, being in the midst of the world, he must not be of the world. His mission would not consist in simply communicating to the people in this world the mysteries of the other world, but looking together at this world, in helping people to comprehend also that that is not from this world. An observer would see in this soul something like a glimmer of the divine, not so much in his words and expressions as in his unexpressed essence. For those who saw it, such a soul would embody, as it were, the existence of the divine in this world. In this soul others would become aware of the law that the Lord is the Ever-Greater. They would see through it as through a window into another world. And it would not be as if, in doing so, the soul were to surrender its most personal mystery; on the contrary, the deepest thing, the bond between it and the Lord, this mystery that belongs more to the Lord than to the soul itself, would remain hidden from the kind of sight possible in this world and would cause the souls of those watching to be so inflamed with this mystery that it would become something different and personal for each one.

This bond, which is not of the world, becomes visible in confession, in the precise moment of absolution. Here the penitent frees himself from himself and his worldliness in order to receive from the Lord the purity of another world. The moment the priest administers absolution, he embodies not only the Lord as person, whose position he represents, but the mediating essence of the Lord in his position between God and world. Just as the Lord gazes at the same time on God and the world, so the priest gazes at the same time on the one who has confessed his sin and thus testified that he wants to turn away from it in order to seek the Lord, and on the Lord whose purity and love he is to mediate to the sinner. He stands between the sinner who is to be redeemed and the perfect love of the Lord. In one and the same gaze he embraces the penitent and the Lord, and in this position he does what the Lord always did in this world: he gives the sinner to God and God to the sinner. It is like a concretization of the position, the act and the vision of the Lord. He has the whole process of redemption in his hand, as it were. This is what substitution really means for the priest: standing where the Lord stood, gazing at God and sin at the same time. The penitent, for his part, has turned away from sin; he is looking at God, not at the priest, and through the words of the priest he hears God's word. Just as the Lord always emphasized the fact that his word is not his word but the Father's, so the word of the priest is not his word but the Lord's. The penitent does not stop at the priest but goes immediately beyond to the Lord; nor does the priest stop at the sin but looks immediately at the Lord. Both penitent and priest must be wholly transparent in confession: the penitent in striving not to hide anything from God, the priest in willing to be purely an instrument that embodies God. But all this is based in the transparency of the Son's life in the Father in this world. It is like an absolute radiance of the power of God at a particular spot in the world, of God who at the same time loves his Son and the sinner who has turned away.

Someone emerging from confession is as perfect, for the space of a moment, as a Christian can be in the world. In the Lord he has become transparent for God. He ought now to extend this transparency into his everyday life. He should be able to live continually in that bond with the Lord that is not of this world. He was transparent to the priest as a penitent in confession; so he should remain transparent henceforth in love. Confession is a moment; it cannot be held fast. But faith allows confession to prolong itself, making this openness a lasting state. It is faith that makes Christians people who are open to the beyond, who should mediate their mystery of openness to others. In faith, the sacramental grace of absolution that was received in confession becomes effective in the world; for the grace received always infinitely exceeds the canceled sin: the grace becomes available and begins to flow through the liberated soul for others, for God and the Church. By virtue of this abundance, anyone who tries, in faith, to be transparent to God for other people can in truth become an occasion of their finding God. The mystery of the believer is ultimately the mystery of his bond with the Lord, who lived as a mediator between God and the world and who, from this center, draws the whole world to the Father, the Lord whom he embodies, for the world, in the miracle of unity of radiant love and transparent purity.

Purity and confession are so close to each other because the two are one in the Cross. The Cross is the great, universal and definitive confession: the confession of all sins, even unconfessed ones, the ones that are not to be confessed because no word and no expression exists for them, because mankind, because of habit and callousness, no longer sees them; above all, the sin of taking back what has once been given, whereby those who already belonged to God imperceptibly become the world's. All these sins the Lord takes on himself in his perfect purity. He identifies himself with them. They enter into him; they possess every corner of his soul and spirit. Everything in him is blocked up, choked, barricaded by sin. His eyes see only sin; his hands feel only sin; his ears hear only sin. He enters totally into sin. This is what robs him of the vision of the Father. He does not take this sin on himself as alien sin but as his own. He no longer puts any distance between himself and sin, and laden with this sin as his own he goes to the Father. But that is confession. This horror comes to an end with the Father: in absolution the darkened soul glows in the grace and mercy of God. Suddenly it bursts into light, just as the Son, at the end of his path, is suddenly glorified by the Father's glory, having overcome, by his death, the sin of the world.

17:15. I do not ask that you take them out of the world, but that you protect them from evil.

If they were taken out of the world, they could not perform their mission. Their mission begins at the birth and ends with their deaths: it is to lead a Christian life. Through struggles they are to become people who have been redeemed by the Lord. They should not be so sheltered that they know nothing about sin; on the contrary, they should look it in the eye and try, with God's grace, to overcome it. The Lord certainly knows that this can never be anything more than an attempt and that, of themselves, they would never have the power to conquer sin. But he knows equally how much of his grace and power he will give them to help them in their struggle. Again and again he foresees their stumblings and fallings, and sees it as part of his mission to keep setting them upright again, so that in the end he will be able to present them to the Father as his brothers. If he were to ask the Father to take them out of this world, he would be sitting in judgment on the Father's creation and declaring life in it to be impossible. On the contrary, however, he wants to restore the Father's whole joy in this creation, to repurchase this joy for him with his suffering. In doing so he is conscious that the best he will be able to give mankind during their lives is the grace to struggle, the grace of continually setting them on their feet. The life of the Christian is destined to be a battle, in which there can be victories and defeats. But the victories do not count, because they are attributed to the Lord's grace, and the defeats do not count either, because he reverses and makes them good. The only thing that counts is the will to fight in the spirit of the Lord. This battle begins in each individual life, and, if earnestly fought, it leads imperceptibly into greater things: into the battle for the Lord in the world.

Every Christian life has its seclusion and its opening to the world: it is contemplation and action. First of all it is prayer, petition and adoration addressed to God. And the more someone receives the Lord's grace to fight for the Lord *in his life,* the more earnestly he is obliged to fight for the Lord in his life. The first movement, in which the Lord unites the soul with himself and draws it to him, leads directly to the second movement, in which the one thus prepared is sent with a mission to his brothers. In the first movement the person owes his very life to the Lord;

in the second, an obligation immediately arises from this debt to place himself wholly at the Lord's disposal for the salvation of others. In the first movement the Lord draws him out of evil, and in the second he places him in the world as one redeemed. This existence in the world is realized in both forms of life in the Church, in the lay and the religious states. The lay Christian lives in the Lord in the outer world, in the midst of its temptations and attacks. But he stands in constant connection with the Lord, a connection he that must renew daily and that must be daily renewed by the Lord. He is not separated from his brethren in the cloister; he knows that both states bear each other's burdens and that prayer forms the bond. In the world there is an excess of tribulation of social and business entanglements; conversely, in the cloister, there is the burden of isolation. Both are overcome in the Lord and canceled out in their common root. While the more active mysteries of the Lord's life are offered for imitation more often in the world and the contemplative ones more often in the cloister, all the mysteries are nonetheless present in both ways of life, and all Christians participate in the one life of the Lord. Nor is one separated from the world in the religious state. For "to be in the world" means: to lead a life in the Lord but with its own personality, and this is "world". One brings the world into the most secluded cell, for one brings oneself; and in spite of the strictest seclusion, the fluid boundaries of the ever-present environment overflow to the outer world. Wherever we may stand as Christians, we are in the world and attempt to serve the Lord and his brothers in the world. The boundaries with the world are different in the two states of life, but they are always there. Life in the cloister is neither more valuable nor easier than life outside; the temptations are different, perhaps more difficult, for all the apparently small things acquire much more importance in the cloister. Which state a Christian is to choose is not a matter of taste or of the evaluation of his own powers; it depends solely on the choice and call of the Lord.

Christians are taken out of the world only by death. But they are always protected from evil when the Lord allows his grace to become effective in them. Furthermore, they are protected in the shared community of saints in both states, in which the contemplation of the one considers and supports the action of the other, and the action nourishes and stirs up contemplation, and all interrelations thrive in the grace of the Lord.

17:16. *They are not of the world, as I am not of the world.*

They are as little of the world as the Lord is, because they and he possess the same unity in God: the unity that is realized in them through the Son, the unity that forms the key to the community of the saints. Although they sin again and again, this unity separates them from sin, because through the indwelling of the Son and through sacramental life they participate in his life from the Father and to the Father, and also because the Son, in the once-for-all act of his suffering and Resurrection, gives them the repeatable act of turning away from their sin, the grace of confession. The Son, who was in the world, never belonged to the world, since he was always turned away from sin. Even when he took it into himself entirely, he would allow no other relation between himself and sin than this: he must totally accept it into his purity for the total purification of the world. In the Lord, Christians too are empowered to reject sin. They fall; they fall again and again. But because they are Christians and participate in the Son, they let themselves be redeemed over and over again. And every sin that someone relinquishes in the grace of the Son enables him to participate anew, and more deeply, in the mystery of the Cross. For, with his purity, the Lord takes responsibility for every life that has given itself to him. Anyone who has really surrendered himself to the Lord no longer needs to have scruples and be continually thinking about his sin and its confession or to be continually occupied with the thought of his purification: the Lord will take care of his life, so that it may really be lived in him. And the grace of confession is strong: it is strong enough to preserve the one absolved from new sin. The Lord will not allow someone who truly wants to serve him to become a scandal to the Church. He will clothe his saints with his own sanctity and will separate them more and more from sin.

17:17. *Sanctify them in truth. Your word is truth.*

To sanctify human beings means to make them like the image of the Son. To bring them, on earth at first, as close as possible to the image of the Son who sojourned on earth, but then, in heaven, to make them like the image of the Son in the sanctity of the Trinity. We make a dichotomy between sanctification in this world and sanctity in heaven. We do so because we can scarcely imagine the Lord in heaven and need sanctification on earth in order to make the essence of sanctity clear to ourselves. Thus we start with the Son's sinless earthly sojourn. We look at his countenance that is turned toward the world and find it holy; we hardly know his countenance that is turned to God, and its divine sanctity remains ineffable for us. But we may not separate his human side from the divine. The example of sanctity that the Son shows us lies in his twofold vision: he sees God and the world at the same time. One side of his essence seems accessible to us: we perceive a total lack of sin, bound with an equally complete insight into the essence of sin. This seems to us to sum up what the Lord shows the world and gathers from the world. He shows it his purity, and he gathers from it his insight into sin. But what he himself possesses as his own, what he brings with him from God, this is something for which we have no measure and no expression, although we sense it most deeply and are receptive to it: his divine essence itself, the fullness of his love, which he translates for us into the fullness of his grace. This divine fullness remains inexpressible, and yet it flashes again and again across the Lord's earthly countenance. Whereas we can contemplate his earthly essence at length, his divine essence is so blinding that we cannot look into this sea of fire. We see only one side of it: its beauty certainly attracts us, entices us and draws us in, but we cannot hold it fast because our side, which is turned to the world, is not pure enough. So our vision of eternity and heaven remains only a presentiment that the Lord gives us, and all these presentiments do not round out into a complete whole. We see only a brilliant reflection of the eternal light. It is as if a marvelous painting were hidden behind a curtain, and we were only shown a tiny corner of it at a time. What we are allowed to see enchants us; we suspect that it is infinite beauty. But we cannot connect what we have seen into a unity; we cannot get a rough idea of the picture. If we could see the Lord's totality it would be like plunging into sanctity, immersion in the Lord; we would be taken up into his infinite sanctity. For God's sanctity is something infinite. It is so much an attribute of God that no distinction is possible between him and his sanctity. It stems in its entirety from God and is always infinite in him.

A saint would be a person completely immersed in the vision of God's sanctity, and this vision would commandeer and take him over entirely. He could not gaze in a detached manner but would have to let himself be drawn into it completely. When someone has heard a glorious symphony he can perhaps give others a feeble idea of it by humming a few melodies from it, explaining the instrumentation and describing the performance. He himself possesses a vivid recollection of it, and what he relates will be only a distant echo of what he has heard. And yet what he has is only a recollection. It does not fill him completely; he can still think of other things. He does not need to hear it again day and night to let his whole life be absorbed in this music. But if he has taken a look into the sanctity of God, he no longer feels any other desire than to live in it and be immersed in it for evermore, to let himself be flooded and taken possession by it. Nor will he discuss this with just anyone, but only with those who are close to him in God. And although he knows that he will never reach the world of this divine sanctity, because there is no gradual transition between humanity and God, and because the better one comes to know the sanctity of God the more it causes the uniqueness of God's glory to shine forth, he knows nonetheless that henceforth he will occupy himself with nothing else. It is into this ocean of sanctity that the Lord wants to lead his disciples.

The Son asks the Father to sanctify through truth those who believe in him—not by using cunning, persuasion, gradual methods or partial demands, but through the truth. And he explains this truth at once: *Your word is truth.* It is through this word, then, that the Father is sanctifying them. But the word of the Father is the word that he pronounces: the Son. Both mean truth: the word and the Son. In that this twofold thing is one, he creates mediation. The Son is the truth in the form in which man can receive it. In the Son man is given the absolute and undivided essence of truth, because the Son has this double relation, looking both to God and to the world. And since he is thus the shared, communicated truth, he is for us the epitome of unity. For he is completely one with God's truth and completely one with us. Because he mediates, he brings the immediate, the whole. As mediator he is unity. He is the unity of him who brings and what is brought. If someone were to tell another that there was a loaf of bread in the next room and that he will bring him a piece as proof, the other person can believe him, and the first person can go and actually bring him a piece of bread. He could repeat this proof by bringing him more pieces. But the other person would always have the option, if he were perhaps distrustful or wanted to make sure for himself, of going into the next room himself and seeing if the bread was really there, and what size it was. The Son of God mediates to us a truth from the other world, which we do not see, which we cannot see at all. For for us there is no possibility of checking. We cannot assure ourselves that he is telling the truth in any other way than the Son's way. Whatever truth we receive we receive in faith in the Son. But the Son not only brings us the truth of God's word, he himself *is* it: he *is* what he brings and mediates to us. Thus faith is at once its own proof and its own assurance; it contains the vision of truth. And the Son mediates the truth not piecemeal but always in its totality, and just for that reason it remains incomprehensible to our finite understanding, because it is infinite.

The Son then, precisely in communicating himself, is unity. Precisely in communicating truth he is truth. For his mediation takes place in and from love; the mediation itself is love. But love is also what he mediates. Thus he is the unity of the mediated and its mediation. So outside of the love of God there is no truth, and outside of loving faith no perception of truth.

The Lord is where he is through his free decision. He stands at the division of light and darkness, surveying all light and all darkness. Therefore he can be the absolute mediator of light into darkness and darkness into light. If God is to sanctify mankind through his truth, he must let his light shine into our darkness, and thus abolish the division between light and darkness. Since the Son now stands at this spot, the light of truth can only shine into the darkness through the Son, and the human darkness can only be taken up into light by the Son.

That God's word is truth means at the same time that it is light. This word is the Son, but the Son is light, since he stands between the light of God and the darkness of the world. From our side darkness meets him, from the Father's side light, and the two come together into his light. His light that shines into our darkness and that lets the Father's light through to us, is the light that he perpetually receives from the Father and as God perpetually possesses within himself, and that finally signifies the whole expression of his love for the Father and the Father's love for him. So infinite is the Son's love for the Father, so infinite his light, that it can even be light in darkness without ceasing to be eternal light.

17:18. As you sent me into the world, so I have sent them into the world.

The Father has sent the Son into the world, with the love of the Father and equipped with his gifts, so that he might bring the world what he possesses of the Father's light—faith, love and hope—and what he has received from the Holy Spirit—the variety of his gifts. And the Son, for his part, sends those who believe in him into the world. He equips them with what he received from God and the Holy Spirit, and in addition he gives them his own love. And he asks them to undertake in their turn the mission that he undertook for the Father and to work in his name as he worked in the name of the Father. He does not divide the mission, but gives each person a share in the whole mission. He gives it to each individual, so that he may let light shine forth into the darkness. Every believer receives the complete mission from the Son, and in addition something that the Son does not have: the perfect model of the mission accomplished by the Son. The Son shaped and created his mission out of nothing and leaves this creation to those who are his as the fully accomplished original form of the mission, in which every subsequent participation has its meaning and its existence. When the teacher draws a big letter on the blackboard for the first time, and the children attempt, clumsily and shakily, to copy it, someone who had not seen the letter on the blackboard would perhaps scarcely guess, from the scrawlings in their notebooks, what the pupils had been asked to do. But the Lord, as our teacher, will recognize our attempts as such. He will regard our efforts to imitate his mission in the light of his own completed mission and measure them according to it, by regarding only the love that the failed attempt contains. He does not insist on success. Our attempt is a response to his grace, our personal response. The main thing is the serious desire to make the attempt. Someone could reject his mission inwardly and yet fulfill his apostolate outwardly; as a priest he might have the greatest success in the pulpit or the confessional. Yet God would want to know nothing of all this. Another can only stutter in the pulpit; everything seems to go against him, but he tries as best he can to fulfill his mission. God will round off everything that is lacking and will receive him in grace. The

Son, too, from a human point of view, accomplished his mission in an incredibly narrow and limited circle. Until the Cross, he scarcely had any real success to record. But that was not what the Father regarded, but rather his perfect obedience in love and in perfect suffering.

Obedience is both the most divine and the most human expression and proof of love. Love wants to obey; it wants only to do the will of the beloved and does not even want to be considered while doing so. Not because of "self-denial", "self-sanctification", "mortification" or any other ascetic training, but out of the simplest necessity of love itself. In all weakness and yet totally resolved it offers itself: Do with me as you will! This is how love is; it is ready for anything, willing to follow through anything, convenient or inconvenient. It considers only the honor and glorification of the beloved. It knows no self-regard. Nor does it think of what and how much it is giving up, or of how difficult the undertaken task is, or of what others are doing or saying. It goes its way in the strength of the love it has received. When the Lord says *Sanctify them in truth,* it is full of strength, decisiveness, manliness. It is like a ray of light in the darkness, something unique that is new each day, devotion that knows calculations, the total obedience of love. Here no one asks about the ego, least of all the one who obeys. Nor does he ask if he can or cannot. At worst he will die in the fulfilment of his mission; what does it matter?

As God sent the Son, so the Son sends his own: in obedience, entrusted with the whole mission. In these words he asks the Father to see them as those involved in the mission. The Lord knows very well that they cannot do it, that they are inadequate, that they will fail. But that is not the issue now. He wants the Father to see him and the believers in the unity of the one mission that proceeds from him, the Father. He wants him to regard the Son's own people as the Father's emissaries. And if the Father regards them thus, they will also learn to regard themselves as servants of their mission, which will sanctify them in the measure in which they place themselves at its disposal and immerse themselves in it, so that everything that is theirs may dissolve in the mission.

17:19. *And I sanctify myself for them, so that they too may be sanctified in truth.*
The Son sanctifies himself by putting himself wholly at the Father's

disposal. He knows nothing more holy than the Father, and he also knows that everything the Father possesses is intended for him, including holiness. He himself is God and is holy of himself, and yet he seeks holiness and sanctification from the Father, because he wants to mediate to the world not himself but the Father. And equally he desires God to see his work in mankind right to the very end, but a work that has been sanctified in God through the Son. He lets his sacrifice, which he takes on himself by pursuing his earthly path, recede into the background, because he wants to bring back to the Father people who are not merely Christian, but Godlike. It is like a father giving his son a private tutor: the tutor is to educate the child according to the customs of the house and the spirit of the family, and in the end he is to give him back to the father as a son who has been raised according to his father's mind. It is thus that the Lord wants to educate mankind for God. Once again he receives sanctification from the Father, although he himself is holy. He continually wants to demonstrate to the Father that he has everything from him. And that is a fundamental need of love, to receive everything that the beloved is able and wants to give. The Father wants to recognize his Son in mankind, but the Son wants the Father to recognize himself in them. Therefore he stamps them in the image of the Father—but he himself is this image, and thus the Father finds in mankind his image—that is, his Son.

As long as the Son was in the world, he was separated from the Father with one side of his being, the side that was turned to the world. But this separation was not a remoteness from the Father, for he aligned himself continually to the Father, he looked back to the Father constantly in order to stand in the exact center of his mission. He did not need to do this, because with him there was no danger of alienation. He did it out of love for the Father and in order to be an example to men, who *can* alienate themselves. And by receiving his holiness from the Father again and again, the Son mediates it to mankind as a holiness that stems from the Father. Mankind is to be sanctified not simply in the Son, but *in truth* —in the mutual love between Father and Son.

PRAYER FOR THE CHURCH

17:20. *But not for them alone do I pray, but also for those who will believe in me through their word.*

This is the first time that the Lord shows the Father not only those who are his, but also those who, through them, attain to faith in him, those who are as yet only on the way to him and still stand outside the threshold of the Church. He gives them a preferential position, basically the same position as the disciples; he presents them to the Father united with the disciples in his prayer. They will have a more difficult time than the disciples, for they reach the Lord in a more roundabout way. The disciples have recognized in him the Messiah and the perfect human being, and they have sensed, if not seen, the light that he receives from the Father. They have clearly felt that in him and behind him there lives something infinite and mysterious, which gazes at them and to which they have devoted themselves, albeit imperfectly. But those who come to faith through the disciples do not see the Lord; they only hear of him through the disciples' description, and perhaps they have only a very obscure grasp of how the latter live by the grace of the Lord. The transformation that faith has visibly accomplished in the disciples is in no way as evident as the Father's light, which the disciples saw radiating through the Lord. And the words with which the disciples describe the Lord and the new faith are inadequate. The intense glow that animates them is not unlike a purely human enthusiasm. And it can look all the more like an exaggerated enthusiasm since the disciples cannot always give a clear picture of the unity between it and their life. But the Lord does not discuss these difficulties. He takes those who stand at a distance into his prayer, just like the disciples; he lets them participate in the same supernatural life as those who lived with him on earth. Precisely because it is subjectively more difficult for them to understand, the supernatural quality of the mediation must be more strongly emphasized for them. They must be capable of seeing the faith, hope and love of the Lord even through the disciples' faulty instruction, of immediately distinguishing in an apostle what stems from God and what does not. The Lord's prayerful love is strong enough to impart this discernment to them. This love of the Lord is not a complement to and extension of the human love of his apostles and disciples. Those who seek are not to believe in and love the apostle as the first step, in order to be led beyond this, in a second step, to the Lord. They should believe in the Lord and love him as directly as do the apostles themselves. They must take the same leap of faith. And the apostle may not bind the love of the seekers to himself; he may not lead his pupils to the Lord via their love of him. He must direct all their love to the Lord. If there is some love left over for the apostle, that is a pure grace from the Lord to which the disciple has no claim. It is his task to adapt the seeker's love to the love of the Lord. It is his consolation that both he and his pupil are together in the unity of prayer; not only in the love of the Lord pure and simple but in the reality of this prayer that he now speaks to the Father. By virtue of this unity founded by the Lord, the apostle will be able to accomplish the task for which he has been sent. Whoever approaches the Church comes drawn by the prayer of the Lord. It is he who leads the seekers to the priest, who lifts them over the threshold. Thus the Lord prays specially for converts, and the particular zeal of converts has its roots in the prayer of the Lord. This zeal is a leaven that the Lord lays in his Church and that he has deliberately provided for it. Lukewarm Christians may try to make converts believe that once they have been accepted into the Church, everything is all right and they should conduct themselves quietly. But this is to conceal from them the fact that, as converts, they have been put where the fire is hottest: in the prayer of the Lord to the Father.

17:21. *That all may be one, as you, Father, in me and I in you, that they also may be in us, so that the world may believe that you have sent me.*

All believers should form a unity with one another. This unity should consist not only in faith alone, but in everything that stems from faith, is fructified through faith, is wakened to life through faith. As an example of this unity the Lord gives the unity he has with the Father. And this unity consists in the Father being in him. He has often spoken of this to his disciples. He often told them that the origin of his mission, its accomplishment and its end lie with and in the Father, that he runs his

357

entire course within the Father. Now he says more: he says that the Father is in him—not some part or reflection of the Father, but the Father pure and simple. Together with the Holy Spirit they form such a perfect unity that nothing in the essence of one is separated from the essence of the other. Everything that is peculiar to the Father or the Son is vitally one in the Holy Spirit, and vice versa. When the Son continually presents himself before the Father and seems to approach him, he is nonetheless always with him and in him, so much so that even when he takes on a visible human form, the Father always lets his word be heard through him; so much so that when the Father lets his light shine in the darkness, it is the light of the Son that reaches the darkness; so much so that when the world's attempts at love reach the Son, they also immediately reach the Father. What seems to us to be the sign of separation of Father and Son is precisely the sign of greatest unification. If the Father were not so unconditionally in the Son, the Son's earthly life would never have become possible. The separation that is perceptible to us is the highest proof of definitive unity, for if they had not been so certain of their unity, they would not have been able to go as far as the mystery of the night of the Cross without producing alienation, misunderstanding or the division of truth. In truth they are so much One that there is only one single truth: the truth of the Son in the Father and of the Father in the Son.

Not only is the Father in the Son; the Son is also in the Father. Up to and including the Cross he is not outside the Father, in spite of his human form: he does not love the Father from without but loves him in the Father. He gives the Father lasting proofs of his love's vitality by showing the Father how much the Father lives in him, to what extent he does everything in the spirit and truth of the Father. Thus the Father sees him complete his work and can continually see how much it is their common work that is accomplished in the Holy Spirit.

That they all may be in us. Now, after the Son has once again vividly described the divine unity to the Father, he presents humanity to him as something that should participate in this unity. Humanity in its multiplicity and its sin and its uttermost fragmentation is to be inserted into this ultimate unity, into a unity of essence and of love, compared to which the unity of husband and wife is as nothing. The means for realizing this miracle is the Church. Certainly, each individual human being shares directly in the unity of God, but not otherwise than by being introduced into the unity of the Church, whose unity is realized and nourished by the unity of Father and Son. Otherwise the individual, with all his human imperfection and deficiency, could not possibly enter into the highest divine unity. He would not fit in at all. With his scarcely visible attempts at faith and love, efforts and goodwill, he could have no share at all in the infinite perfection of the love of Father and Son. Rather he must go to the Church, who, as the Bride of Christ, is the image of divine unity. The Church is the unity of those whom the Lord loves. Her unity is formed much more by the unity of this love on the Lord's part than by the unity of the faith and effort of individual Christians. Thus the Church becomes a reflection of the Lord: she too has one face turned toward the world—for she consists wholly of sinners, who can be outwardly recognized as such—while the other face, which can only be recognized in faith and in the love of the Lord, is turned to God. The Lord admits no one into the unity between him and the Father without bringing him into the unity of the Church. Of course no one can rest satisfied with the mere fact of this unity of the Church; rather he must eternally strain toward unity in God. His faith, his hope and his love must desire to be complemented by the direct grace of the unity of God. But this complementing only occurs within the Church, which is, for us Christians, the perfect image of the unity of God. Knowing ourselves in the Church to be a community of sinners, we also know that we are the unity of those redeemed and beloved by God. Every individual in the community is taken seriously and very personally by the Lord; the Church never stands as a foreign body between him and the Lord. But the Lord takes him so seriously that he wishes him the best that he can give, namely, to be one with all the other lovers. The love of the Lord always touches the individual directly and not through a third party. But it reaches him in the place where love reigns: in the Church, which is his Bride and his unity in the world. The Church is the fellowship of the faith, hope and love of all individuals, for these three always tend to expand and communicate themselves. What one person loves, believes and hopes is accessible to all the others, for each has what he has in the one grace of the Lord. And precisely because everything in the Church is the Lord's property, the community is not enhanced simply as the sum of all the personal and particular qualities and talents of the members. The love of the Church is more than the exchange of personal love between her members. It is participation in the one love of the Lord. In this community, which is based entirely on the unity of the Lord's love, one's personal contribution disappears completely. No egotism or pharisaism has any place in the Church. No one can accuse another of lacking something, for whatever might be lacking in him is supplied and furnished by the others. While each contributes his part, the Lord rounds everything off; what is still human, piecemeal work he completes, because he strives for unity in everything. Things that a Christian may find scandalous in the Church are only things he himself has brought along: the human element, the ego-directed side. But the other face of the Church, which looks to God, is always striving to draw the individual ego into the community and over to God. The Lord, for his part, gives the individual everything he needs, in order to enrich the Church, his Bride. It is almost as if the Lord gives him his qualities so that the Church might recognize him as his disciple, and the Church gives him her qualities so that the Lord will recognize her as his Bride. Every Christian brings with him a small candle that is lit by the Lord, but in such a way that all the lights come together into a single great fire, the flame of his Bride. The individual light should no longer be recognizable, but in the unity of love the image of the Bride should shine forth. Anyone who joins in a torchlight procession walks along uplifted by the joy of everyone. The person watching the procession may perhaps get a better overall view of it, but he will also have a more critical eye for its defects. But those who participate are at least trying to contribute their part to make the celebration more beautiful, and they are overtaken by the joy that unites all the participants.

That the world may believe that you have sent me. That is the purpose of the Church's unity. It is not an end in itself, any more than the sanctification of the individual is an end in itself. Everything is based on the love of Father and Son, on their overflowing will to unity. This love should be at the same time a profession on the part of all those who participate in the unity of faith. This profession will be so powerful that even the world will not be able to close itself to it, and will recognize that the

Father has sent the Son and that the time of fulfilment is here. But such a profession needs the unity of the Church. If it were not so, each person concerned with the faith would grasp a part of the truth and would proclaim this partial truth. He would begin with and cling to whatever best suited him personally, whatever he understood most easily, whatever corresponded to his inclination and talents. And God's truth would be rich enough, of itself, to offer each person a particular aspect. But in this way the individual would completely lose any overall view. He would appropriate and propagate splinters of Christianity, and unity and the striving for unity would be lost. The partial truths would for their part gather adherents who, again, when they themselves became witnesses, would proclaim the partial truth they represent in the most varied hues. Thus everything would fall apart, splintering infinitely, and the further the process went on, the less it could be brought back to its original unity. Not only Christ, however, but also the life and the love of Christ are indivisible. Faith, love and hope are indivisible, as indivisible as the unity of love between Father and Son in the Holy Spirit. That is why there is the unity of the Church, which is both the necessary expression and the necessary guarantee of the unity of Christ. All knowledge of the Lord, every experience of any Christian truth, matures inevitably into the unity that is sought after by the Son in the Church and that has its paradigm in the Trinity. It is this unity that the Son requests from the Father when he prays for his disciples and for those who are to come to him through their word.

17:22. *And I have given them the glory that you gave me, that they may be one, as we are one.*

It is the glory of the Son to belong to the Father, to possess his love and live in faith in him. He lives in such a way that during his earthly life he desires to be nothing but Son, desires to live solely from the glory that he has received from the Father. He has his own glory, but he does not want to live from it, but only from that of the Father. And just as he receives it, he wants to pass it on. This glory acquires its unity through holiness; it can no longer be divided into different parts, the mission and the capabilities he has received from the Father. Every individual aspect is only a single beam of that fullness that is God's holiness. And it is this fullness of the Father's holiness that the Son brings to mankind. He does not bring it diminished and altered; he brings it just as he received it, as a totality, a fullness. Even in the Old Covenant the Father had offered his holiness to mankind. But at that time most of them preferred to live in sin. Now the Son offers the Father's holiness again, with the earnestness and urgency of love. He offers it not as something unattainable, but as the very nearest thing they can grasp. He extends it to them in human form, as a brother offers something to a brother. He offers it to them by living it out before them in such a way that it seems humanly near and attainable, no longer foreign and otherworldly, so that people almost feel that, just as they are, they could receive these gifts and allow the gifts to work in them and reach God's holiness themselves. The Son offers the faithful this holiness because it is the prerequisite for life with him in the unity of the Father. The glory of the Son, however, which is one with his holiness, is not only offered to each individual; it is also required of him. It is something he must give, although he does not even know how he is supposed to get it, although it seems unattainable because he can see the distance between the greatness of his sin and the infinity of God's glory. But just as the Lord placed himself on the edge between light and darkness, so that no light can shine into the darkness except through him, so too he places his people on the dividing line between the glory of the Father and the sin of mankind.

On this edge stands the Lord. He bridges the immeasurable difference between God and the human person. By everything that the Lord is and does, man feels himself drawn to something he cannot grasp: to God. He has no idea how this transition is effected. He approaches the Lord unsuspectingly, as it were, in the naïve expectation that the transition will be like a continuation of the human. Perhaps he imagines that before he crosses the bridge to God he will be able to put aside his sins like a bundle and then, perhaps decorated with certain virtues, cross over to God. He does not suspect that he would be torn apart by the impossibility of this transition if it were not for the Lord. In order to cross over, he must present himself to the Lord as he is and place himself at his disposal, and the Lord himself will effect the whole transition. He will expand the person to the new dimensions that are required. He will explode him. A person comes before the Lord as a liar, for example. Of himself he will make every effort not to lie anymore, yet there remains in him the disposition, the potential, even the inclination to lie. He remains a liar; of himself he cannot give himself the truth. Here the Lord intervenes and effects the leap. He does it in a way that is beyond human observation. Previously, before he encountered the Lord, it seemed to him that he could mark out the boundaries of his sin; he thought he knew when he was lying and when he was not. Since he made the Lord's acquaintance, this power of judging is taken from him; everything has become much more interior, more subtle, more hidden; everything has been taken out of the crude, material realm of command and prohibition and brought into the baffling realm of the Spirit. But something else has been given him instead: the exclusive love for the Lord. This is primarily a gift that the Lord has made him, enabling him to love him in return. And this gift of the Son is the Father's glory, which he passes on to mankind. The person who thus enters the Lord's gate is taken up into his *transparency.* He can still distinguish who is Father and who is Son. But he can no longer distinguish in man what stems from the Father and what from the Son. The givers are distinguishable, but not the gift. The receiver is simply taken into the glory that unites everything and leaves all separation behind. Formerly he was inclined to believe that he knew himself: he recognized his present faults and was aware of a whole background of sin and latent guilt in the soul. In time, the discerning glance would be able, perhaps, to penetrate into this unconscious background of the soul. He had similar thoughts about the Lord. Much about him seemed recognizable; other things remained hidden from him, and with regard to these background mysteries, he assumed that, unlike his own secrets, they were mysteries of glory and holiness. And he thought too that with time it would be possible to find out more about the Lord's divine background. But this relation between the known and the unknown ceases immediately when the person is really drawn into the glory of God. Every partial knowledge ends, for all that is required is unity and indivisibility in glory. Access to this unity is through the transparency of the Lord. If he were not transparent, he would be a barrier, something that divides. There would be a mystery "behind" him. But he is pure openness, absolute mediation. That is why he loved us before we loved him. He simply takes our love, our expectations and our efforts into his preexisting, all-embracing love. He transforms them in it according to his wish; he complements them with what is his until what is ours simply dissolves in what is his. Certainly, he remains mysterious and beyond our grasp in so doing, yet not like an opaque mystery that one cannot get behind, but rather through the very infinity and openness of his mystery itself. He draws us into his open space, and his openness becomes ours. In the end, every love longs for total devotion and unity. Among human beings this perfection of love is never totally attainable; it will always have to encounter some barrier, both in the Thou and in the I. Perfect love cannot be fashioned in the world. The Lord, however, who is transparency pure and simple, can realize it effortlessly. The grace of the Lord knows no barriers in itself, and therefore none in us. The *"ama et fac quod vis"* is not only his command to us but also our challenge to him. Every soul is like a woman in relation to him: it must and can be possessed wholly by him. Its love is pure devotion, pure surrender. And the Lord loves without adaptation or diminution of his love. If he comes, he comes with all his glory, just as he receives it from the Father. In a marriage, husband and wife still wish, after their union, to retain and control their own spheres: the man his work, the woman hers. Between the Lord and the believers there is no such going back, for the Lord brings them into the ultimate unity between Father and Son. Thus the Lord becomes the Mediator toward God: he leads us to the point where he stands and where our supposed relation to a limited human being opens into a boundless realm, opens up perspectives toward God. At this point the Lord is transparent not only as a human being but also for God. For the Father too first saw his incarnate Son as an individual, a precisely defined person. But once he has mankind in him, he becomes transparent for the Father as well: the Father sees us in him.

That they may be one, as we are one. Father and Son are one in the glory the Son received from the Father, although he already possessed it beforehand. This unity is beyond doubt and question. They do everything in unity; they need no consultation or discussion to produce a result. They know everything about each other; they behold each other continually; they are transparent for one another. It is into this unity that mankind is to enter. They live, if they are Christians, within this unity. This is their dwelling place, the best part of themselves. When a priest

leads a converted person to the Church, he does not give him a circumscribed doctrine, a few new insights, a better attitude to life, a circle of
like-minded acquaintances. Ultimately he mediates this unity to him.
Something going far beyond what he himself can comprehend and
grasp. Fundamentally he does not know how much he is giving and
mediating. He draws him into the unity in which he himself lives, but
which is so open and so transparent that he neither sees nor comprehends
it. It is the unity of Father and Son in which all live who believe, hope
and love.

17:23a. *I in them and you in me: That they may be perfectly fulfilled into unity.*
The Lord has given himself to mankind as the Father gave himself to
the Lord: perfectly and without reservation. Because the Father has
given himself to him thus, with the whole infinity of divinity and of
divine love, the Son is open to an infinite, ever-open and unshakable
love. Therefore the one he draws into his love can love him unshakably
with a love that grows eternally stronger. Human love, apart from God,
always remains finite. It yearns for ultimate unity. But when a peak has
been reached, perhaps bodily union, for instance, or something else, a
limit has been reached and the descent begins. Most definitely every
infatuation is finite and quickly reaches its limit: the ideal image of the
beloved quickly fades, and one soberly discovers his faults. It is impossible to love a human being with unshakable, infinite love, outside of
God. Love for the Lord, on the other hand, is infinite, because the Lord
gives to us of his own infinity and unshakability in love; he pours, as it
were, this love into us.

This gift of the Lord to us is the Eucharist, but no longer seen as the
simple presence of the Lord among us, but as the living process of the
mediation of love: as *Mass*. Here the Son, with the Father's love in him,
treads the whole earthly path with us and in us. The Mass is essentially
unity. The distribution of the Eucharist is only a sign of the life of the
unity, of a unity attaining to greater purity through the sacrifice. The
Mass, in this unity, is the life of Christ, accompanied by the believers, but
not in such a way that Christ and the believers would be separated from
the nonbelievers. For both, the believers and the Lord, pray together for
believers and nonbelievers. The believers are those who are already

seized by love in some way; among nonbelievers there are infinite shadings and transitions, right up to those who have shut themselves off completely. Most of them will be simply in ignorance, not yet having been touched by truth and unity. The priest is the one who is in unity with the Lord on the one hand and with the community on the other. Insofar as he stands between the two and belongs to both as a bond, he once again participates in the Lord's position, with one face turned to the world, the other to God. Wherever unity is concerned, this attitude of the Lord between the Father and the world, between heavenly and earthly vision, comes to the fore. For unity never means the equalization of all, the leveling of differences. Rather, each person always shares in the mystery of the Lord's twofold nature in order to receive a share, through him, in the love between Father and Son. True unity always contains in itself the greatest tension found in life. It is full of movement precisely because it is the point of stillness from which all movement proceeds, the ultimate origin of all life and therefore too its final goal. Thus the priest stands in unity and the faithful stand in unity, but they stand on different spots. And yet both, in the inmost center of their unity, encounter the inmost center of unity itself: that of the Son in the Father.

The unity is there before Mass begins; it is already realized in the first prayer; it is present during the entire Mass and is also there at its end. It is a unity in motion, as is the earthly life of the Son who comes from the Father in order to return to him, who even in earthly separation from the Father remains in the Father's unity until he, enriched by earthly experience, returns again into the unity of the Father. Only this unity in motion can explain, in the Church, the hierarchy that is presumed in the Mass. The priest enjoys greater honor in the Church than the layman. And yet he cannot place himself above another human being. Only in the unity of God's love can this order, this precedence be understood. Thus the Father has precedence in God, but the Son is not less God than the Father. On the other hand, the evermore of the hierarchy is an evermore of service: the higher a person stands, the more deeply he is bound to service, so that the highest is the servant of all the servants of the Lord. Every higher level of hierarchy is, in relation to the Lord, a descent into deeper service. Everything that looks from the outside like elevation looks like humiliation from within, when it happens in a Christian way. The one placed in a higher position will be humiliated thereby, because the distance between him, the sinner, and his dignity will be more conspicuous than with normal Christians. The fact that someone who reaches a higher dignity feels humiliated and humbles himself is not simply an edifying exercise of virtue, but an absolute, urgent requirement. If he were a saint—as he ought to be—he would have the vivid awareness of the infinite discrepancy between his office and his person. And what would be petty faults in another would be a real sin for him, not because of a "sensitive conscience", but because of the plain fact. Thus everyone who has a higher office must have an ever-greater love for those who stand below him. If the bishop is the highest point of the hierarchy that poor people get to see, how much more must he honor and love, in them, the image of the poor and nameless Lord!

Thus the priest and the community stand there at the beginning of Mass. They are witnesses of the Lord's earthly sojourn, for in the Mass the essential element of this earthly sojourn is represented: his coming from God and his going to God through the Cross. The *Gradual prayer* is the Church's attempt to approach the Lord, to flee from the outer sphere into the sphere of the Lord. We make this attempt in confessing our own guilt and asking the help of the Mother and the saints. The Lord himself is already present, but hidden in the tabernacle. He shows himself in both his attributes: as the one present and as the one waiting, who must be expected and sought. He is also already in the faithful, insofar as he prays for them and they pray in him; and yet he is not yet there insofar as he is not yet perfectly accepted by those not present, those who do not yet believe (and for whom he prays) or by those present. Insofar as he is not yet present, he is one with the Father; insofar as he is already present, he is one with us in the Spirit, who makes him seek us and presses us forward toward him. At the start of the Mass the faithful are like people appointed to prepare themselves for unity.

The changeable parts of the Mass remind us that, in the Lord, unity is given as the unchangeable center that included all the possibilities of life, so long as they are possibilities within his reality. The multiplicity of ways that all lead to unity is unfolded; they are deliberately allotted. Everything is not set forth each time, but in a choice that is ultimately a sign of the Lord's choice. What draws us into unity is *his* word, *his* teaching, *his* prayers as they are laid out before us in the Epistles and Gospels, not *our* seeking and *our* prayer.

The *sacrifice* is both the Son's sacrifice and ours, and both together in unity. It is a sacrifice of the Son to the Father, of the Son who desires to be sacrificed by us. That is our sacrifice. This sacrifice already includes what the Son has given and what we have received in the Epistle and the Gospel: his word, himself. The strongest expression of our assent to him, of our consent to his word, is that we declare our consent to his path from the Father back to the Father: that we give him back to the Father in sacrifice. This consent includes and accomplishes our sacrifice; we sacrifice everything in this sacrifice. The Son wants to draw us right into this unity with him, so that we sacrifice him as he sacrifices himself to the Father, all of us, each one individually but also all of us together, the anonymous multitude of the faithful. He has died for each of us, so each of us must sacrifice him to the Father. It is the Christian's most personal deed. And yet he also died for all, for the world, and so we, the faithful, sacrifice him to the Father anonymously, simply as Church. Catholicism is both the most personal thing, challenging an individual's whole person, and the most impersonal, the complete anonymity in the liturgical accomplishment of the Church's sacrifice. But neither the sacrifice of the individual nor that of the Church is a second sacrifice in addition to the sacrifice of the Lord. It is rather that the Church (and each person in her) places her sacrifice in the sacrifice of the Son, consents to the utmost to the Son's sacrifice to the Father. She lets herself be drawn into his sacrifice and, in so doing, becomes, in sacrificing, sacrificed with him. Our sacrifice is to allow the sacrifice of the Lord: to allow his word and will to fulfill themselves in us as he wishes: to make room for the whole range of potentials of Epistle and Gospel, in his unique unity. The unity is wholly his own: it is not a synthesis out of his sacrifice and our sacrifice, or of his ever-greater sacrifice and our ever-greater readiness for it, but rather the acceptance of our inadequate sacrifice (for we never know what we are actually doing when we sacrifice, or where we are going, and we always draw back) into the Son's perfect sacrifice to the Father.

The *Consecration* is the appearance of the Lord in the midst of those who are gathered in his name in order to enjoy him. This appearance is a twofold process: it eliminates everything in the host that is not of the

Lord; but it also reduces the Lord to the host. Similarly, in the believer everything that is not the Lord's is eliminated; there arises in us an emptiness that is nothing other than the space he requires, the summons to him; and he fills this space by reducing himself to our scale. Thus believers enter into the miracle that is being accomplished: they too, as it were, are transubstantiated. Preparation for the feast changes into festal fulfilment. The Lord, who makes a place for himself in the host in order to receive a place in us, also allows the Church to summon him to her. He gives us life, but in such a way that he permits us to give him eucharistic life. He does this by virtue of his unity in the Father: he let himself be sent by the Father to mankind as God's Son; now he lets himself be sent by mankind to the Father as the Son of Man—which presupposes the unity of the believers with God the Father, in the mystery of Fatherhood and of mission. Thus everything in the Mass is a mystery of unity, and exclusively of unity in love.

But the Lord does not simply transport us into God. We are not meant to get carried away. Rather, he gives us unity in terms of flesh and blood, something that we can grasp quite soberly; just as all his words were sober, just as his mission and unity in God are simple and transparent. He does not want to intensify our needs and longings into a spiritual excess; rather, he wants to be sure that they take account of our physical humanity. But he does this only when our flesh and blood have been sacrificed along with his: he demands our entire devotion, so that he can devote himself entirely to us. Behind the Mass stands the bloody Cross, and in our life and sacrifice too there must be this connection with the Cross.

And yet God has also heard our call for flesh and blood in this form. We would not be content with God alone. We wanted to see his Son, wanted to seize and touch him in flesh and blood, and God granted our wish. We were allowed to see, hear and taste the Word of Life. Not in distant recollection either, but as immediate presence. The sacrifice is not historical, but ever-present. It is an event that is always and at every time truth and reality. Again this reflects the Son's eternity: his being is primal. What he does can never be muffled into mere recollection. Always he comes to the world in flesh and blood, and always he returns in this form to the Father. He himself is always the same—one in the

369

Father—but he must bring us into this unity, and he does so by daily becoming flesh and blood throughout all ages. He streams out into the infinite, in order to lead everything to unity. But he can only lead to unity the person who already believes, that is, the one who is willing to let himself be led by the Son. To the believer he gives the grace of his presence as often as he needs him and wants to come. But he does so under the condition that he too may seek out the one who longs for him in faith, as often as he needs him and wants to come to him. If someone were to receive the Lord without believing, the Lord would not be there for him. It does not have to be a faith that sees in order to receive the Lord. It can also be a seeking, feeling faith. Such a person will also find the Lord in Communion, as a blind person feels along the walls of a room until he has found what he seeks. Indeed, the power of consecration and of apostolate stems from the power of the same Eucharist, as does the consecration of the priest who receives the grace of leading the doubters and seekers back to the Lord, and the grace of the apostolate of the fellow Christian who is commissioned to help his brother. These graces enhance the grace of Communion and form a unity with it. The one who is seeking in faith is like a color-blind person who cannot see the Lord's full range of colors. But the Church, the priest and the fellow Christian all possess the grace to help supply what is missing and lead the seeker to fullness, from partial faith into the unity of the Lord, which is the unity of faith. The Lord in the Eucharist, and the Church in her mission, lead back as one to the unity of the Son with the Father.

Communion is the perfect distribution of the Lord into all souls and every form of personal life, in order to draw everyone to himself, to lead everyone back to unity or strengthen them in unity. Each person receives something special in Communion, for the Lord in his unity is so rich that he never needs to give the same thing twice. And yet he always gives himself, and always his entire self. First of all he brings about the unity of each soul, in order to open up this unity once more to unity with the Father and unity with the Church. And this twofold unity, which is produced in each individual soul, for its part, brings about the Church's unity with God.

Conversely, the Church's unity also enters into the unity of the communicant. When the priest receives the Lord at the altar, he receives at the same time an overflowing grace that he passes on to the faithful at the distribution of Communion. What he mediates is thus part of his own treasury of grace, which he disposes of by virtue of his office and the sacrifice inherent in it. Thus, along with the grace of the Lord, the believing lay person receives something of the grace of the priestly office: he receives both an immediate and a mediated grace. If the priest is a good priest, he knows that he is to give himself to the community along with the Lord. What he gives away will be repaid to him in full measure by the Lord, but he may not calculate this repayment in advance when he gives. He ought to give himself in the same attitude as the Lord himself: definitively and without calculating ulterior motives. He should let the community feed on him and his substance. If he is a bad priest, he will simply rely on the grace of his office, without personally devoting himself to it. Even such a one will be able to mediate grace by virtue of his office, but his overflowing grace, which lies in the Lord, will slowly be depleted without being replaced, and his unity with the Lord will be endangered more and more.

No one who has communicated knows how much he has received. He has received something from the beyond and has remained in the beyond a little while. He is also to pass on the received gift as something from the beyond. Thus at the *thanksgiving* too he lacks any overall view. He will give thanks above all for what is invisible, what is stored up, of which only the slightest part becomes visible and tangible to him, the receiver. Many a person thinks he knows what a Mass is worth, but he has received infinitely more than he suspects. The most protracted thanksgiving would not suffice to really thank the Lord. The Lord's response to our attempt at thanksgiving is highly mysterious, for it is as if it resulted in a sort of new obligation on the Lord's part to let the Communion that has been received become fruitful in the Church. Something enters into the Church's treasury of grace, to be distributed immediately: from this thanksgiving those who are striving for faith receive a stronger feeling of thankfulness to God, which obliges them to enter more deeply into the unity.

Ite, Missa est: it is consummated. It is exhausted and accomplished. But this accomplishment of unity is as such the origin of mission. It implies a twofold challenge: to remain in unity, though one may go forth; and to go forth, though one is privileged to remain. You who go forth have satisfied a certain obligation. But it does not stop there. You may not take away what you have received as something finished; the consummated thing you carry home with you is laid in you as a seed. Thus the mission goes directly over into the *Last Gospel:* without a pause we go straight to the Word, which was in the beginning. It seems as if, in the Mass, we draw the Son down out of the Father's unity to us and then give him back to the Father, and as if the circle is complete, like a concluded act. But now we ourselves are thrown back into the origin and have to recognize that the beginning always remains in the beginning. Yet this origin is not formless: it also contains completion, the point of conclusion. The beginning that is proclaimed here is not the beginning of a Mass, but its fulfilment. That the Word is in the beginning is not a game, not an eternal recurrence. Through genuine fulfilments we are drawn more and more into the origin of the Lord, and we must try to grow with him into this origin.

After celebrating the Word in the beginning, we finally greet the Mother of God in the *Ave Maria* of Low Mass. In this, the *Ite Missa est* is translated into action. The Mother's assent as the human act, pure and simple, is born from the unity that is realized in the Mass and that has concluded by opening itself to the world in the Word that becomes flesh. This opening at the end was the opening both to an eternal beginning and at the same time to an earthly beginning: to the new beginning in our everyday life. If the Word was with God at the beginning, through the Mother's assent it is, on earth, a man among men. This encourages us to persevere on earth between this Mass and the next, in the knowledge that the Mother, and all the saints who were called to follow her, have persevered in unity before us. Very human weapons are put into our hands at the end, which, in their humanness, signify something entirely familiar and concrete. In High Mass this invocation of the Mother is lacking. Here the Mother is submerged, as it were, by the splendor that is unfolded, but we ought to sense her luminous presence all the better here, because as Bride she is the glory of the Bridegroom.

17:23b. *So that the world may perceive that you have sent me, and that you have loved them as you loved me.*

The entire Mass is the expression of God's living presence in the Son and the Son's in the Father, and at the same time it expresses our inclusion in this unity. It is not only a demonstration of unity, but equally a challenge and a support to unity, so that the faithful may become acquainted with perfect unity and participate in it. If they participate in it, the world will discern within this unity a mystery that it does not comprehend and that beckons to it. It will feel toward this mystery without comprehending it, but with the definite feeling that something from the world beyond is hidden here that cannot be explained in terms of this world alone. Knowledge begins with a mystery that has an expanding effect per se, but if one tries to approach it to penetrate it, one is thrown at once into a further mystery: the mystery of mission. When the unbelieving world genuinely tries to understand the mystery of believers, it will perceive that their faith has a living kernel that obliges them to follow a law that the world cannot penetrate. This obligation is derived from the mission. The world's knowledge will get as far as realizing that believers really have a mission. Of what this mission consists the world does not understand; it only comprehends that the mission exists for believers. This obligation to mission gives the nonbeliever a view of something that for the believer is grace, love in grace. For the nonbeliever it remains a baffling love, incomprehensible in its origin and essence. Believers claim that this love stems from the love between Father and Son, yet is living among them, indeed, to such a degree that they, the believers, can nourish their own life out of this love. They know and feel in faith that God loves them as he loved his own Son, and so the world perceives: *That you have sent me and that you have loved them as you loved me.*

This bringing together of all into the one unity finally implies, therefore, the bringing together of all into the perfect love of the Father. But this love of the Father, which communicates itself to the Son and through him to each person who believes, who is trying to believe or who is somehow on the way to faith, does not find its conclusive unity in the love of the Father taken for itself, but rather in the unity of the Trinity. In the end it cannot be reduced to a deed or attribute of a single divine Person; it expresses the unity of the Father and the Son and the Holy Spirit.

17:24. Father, I desire that those whom you have given me may also be together with me where I am, that they may see my glory which you have given me because you loved me before the foundation of the world.

Father, I desire, says the Son. He appears to come before the Father with a demand. He announces his own will and attempts to urge it on the Father. He does not tone it down; he does not clothe it in the humble form of a petition. Rather, he leaves it in the direct form of an authoritative wish. His own people, whom the Father has given him, are to be where he is. He tolerates no separation from them. He wants to be in the continual company of the faithful. He desires not only that they be there as long as he is living in the world; he wants them to have a share in his eternal life in the Father. With this announcement of his will he pays homage to the Father: he shows him how he values the gift that the Father has made him by entrusting mankind to him. Moreover, he now forms a unity with the beings created by his Father. Human beings are certainly sinners, and the Son has made sanctified Christians out of sinful creatures; he has rounded them out to what they now are. But he disregards this for the moment. He presents them to the Father as his perfect creatures in whom the Son has discerned the image of the Father and from whom he therefore does not wish to be separated. This announcement of his desire to be together with mankind eternally implies homage, a compliment to the Father, so to speak, on the excellence of his creation.

It is not for pleasure's sake that the Son wishes to have mankind with him, nor does he ask for them in the Father's name only in order to present the Father with them as a gift, but so that they may experience with him the glorification of the Son, which lies in the fact that the Father has loved him from all eternity, *before the foundation of the world* — a glorification that he does not see in himself, but in the Father's love, inside the eternal Father. He associates his glorification with nothing less than the Father's love for him, the eternity of the Father and finally the glorification of the Father himself. So he gives the concept of love the character of divinity, which is appropriate to it because love is eternal, primeval and without origin, because Father and Son were One in eternity, faced each other lovingly through all eternity in the unity of the Holy Spirit.

17:25. Righteous Father, the world has not known you, but I have known you, and these people have known that you have sent me.

In these words the Lord sums up everything that was resolved between him and the Father. One prerequisite of this resolve, as he previously mentioned, was their eternal life. And now he calls the Father righteous. He lays his love, and the Father's love for him, in the hands of the Father's righteousness. It is as if he were considering his mission all over again, from the beginning, when he returns it accomplished to the Father. The love of the Father, which was founded in eternity, was always given to the Son. Righteousness was designed for the Father's creation, a righteousness that would have placed every single human being before the judgment of the Father. And the Son, since he is looking back over his mission, must recognize that at the time when he parted from the Father, *the world did not know* the Father. Thus it would have had no claim to anything else but righteousness. But then came the Son's mission, and so this knowledge is immediately expanded in the spirit of the New Covenant: *but I have known you.* The Lord covers the picture of the world's nonknowing with the picture of his knowing. And to know the Father means to hold on not only to his righteousness but to his love. The better someone knows God, the better he knows love. And the Son knows the Father so well that he knows nothing other than love in him. He need not fear the Father's righteousness in the least, because no divine judgment can perceive the least thing in him to judge. Therefore he leaves judgment behind him and claims only love. He claims love all the more urgently for his people. So he speaks of them: *And these people have known that you have sent me.* Into his own knowledge of the Father, into his experience of love, he inserts those who have become his own and demands for them the same thing as for himself: only love. They have understood the act of mission as an act of love; therefore, they can claim love. The Son could not demand love for mankind if he had not placed it in them through his mission. On the one hand he has given them love through his mission, and on the other hand has given them to understand that the mission itself is love. Thus he has taught them about fruitfulness. By acknowledging that the Father sent the Son in love, mankind understands that God's love was a fruitful love, and thus this knowledge obliges them to let the love they have received grow in them as a seed and to pass it on. Understanding this, they have a claim to the Father's love.

17:26. *And I have revealed your name to them and will reveal it further, so that the love with which you have loved me may be in them, and I in them.*

The Lord has shown the Father's name to his people like a vessel with incredible contents. He has used the name of the Father before them to show them love. He has compressed everything that he knows and possesses of the Father into this name. He has passed on the Father's name to them as the most precious thing he has, as a miracle that is new every day and becomes continually greater and richer, which, as soon as one regards it as fulfilled, shows itself to be infinitely fuller. This knowledge is never complete. Every insight opens into a thousand new ones and for all eternity elicits ever-new insights and new searching. The *name* fastens this infinity together as a cord binds up a sheaf of wheat, but the sheaf itself is infinite and becomes greater and greater. But precisely when the faithful are lost in this infinity, they see that it is in this that unity consists. Infinity and unity are one. At first it is as if we looked at God's unity from without and tried to grasp it. It seems to be revealed in the name that the Son brings us, which he not only declares but also interprets and presents to us. And we seek, as it were, to reckon up the qualities of the Father: he is our Creator, Maintainer, Sustainer, the Authority over us. . . . But in this listing of attributes the image splinters into infinity. So the Son takes another path with us. He permits us to see from the inside: he moves us to his own standpoint, where he is born from the Father as eternal Son. And suddenly we see ourselves inside this infinity and understand that we ourselves stem from him, we are his children and this interior is even less exhaustible in concepts than the exterior was. This sharing in the innermost, most essential and most vital aspect in the Son's nature—that is, that he is, in love, the Son of the loving Father—this is something that needs no explanation, nor can any concept contain it because it is eternal life itself, beyond all explanation. And if we could not encompass the name of the Father from outside, we are now truly overwhelmed from inside: we stand at the center, where eternal life bursts forth, whither concept and name have directed us, where life is at its fullest and no comprehension is of any use because everything is infinite and movement and process and transcendent, surpassing reality.

And I will reveal it further. Nothing is concluded, then; everything is becoming and growing, and therefore it is Christian revelation. For Christian revelation sets a limit nowhere. Christians participate in an event that extends infinitely on all sides and in which the fullness of life always surpasses the fullness of knowledge. The Son wants to proclaim the name of the Father into infinity, not in order to lead mankind to a goal, not in order to awaken in them the feeling that something conclusive has now been achieved, but rather *so that the love with which you have loved me may be in them.* He knows, then, that he is pouring out on them the fullness of the gifts of God, that he is letting their knowledge grow out beyond the limits of what is possible in the world. But this is only so that the life that is called love may be in them, the only love that there is: the love with which the Father has loved the Son; that the whole infinity of this love, its whole strength, limitlessness and fullness may be in them. Loving, they should be loved; they should exist in a life which is only love. And so it is as if he himself has arrived at the limit of what can be said, as if he, who after all is God and has experienced this love and administers it, cannot describe it further. And thus he desires only one thing more: that his love may be in them. If up to now he has brought them the name of God like a vessel, to let them taste its contents, in the end he is no longer concerned with the vessel, but only with love. And just as one can never say how far around a flame will burn and consume if left to burn, so the love that he has brought to earth will increasingly devour everything as it grows, as long as there is a Father and a Son— namely, in eternity.

And I in them. This "I" is not the Lord whom they know, not the perfect human being whom they sense and admire, but only the living expression of the Father's love. He is the infinite God who has in himself the ever-greater God, a life that explodes everything beyond all imagining and submerges all other life in its own, because this life is the love of God.